The
Complete
Handbook
for
Freelance
Writers

THE COMPLETE HANDBOOK FOR FREELANCE WRITERS

Kay Cassill

Writer's
Digest
Books

Cincinnati, Ohio

808.02
C 345

The Complete Handbook for Freelance Writers. Copyright 1981 by Kay Cassill. Printed and bound in the United States of America. All rights reserved. No part of this book may be reproduced in any form or by any electronic or mechanical means including information storage and retrieval systems without permission in writing from the publisher, except by a reviewer who may quote brief passages in a review. Published by Writer's Digest Books, 9933 Alliance Road, Cincinnati, Ohio 45242. First edition.

Library of Congress Cataloging in Publication Data
Cassill, Kay, 1930-
    The complete handbook for freelance writers.

    Bibliography: p.
    Includes index.
    1. Authorship—Vocational guidance. I. Title.
PN151.C3   808'.02   81-254
ISBN 0-89879-044-1   AACR2

Design by Barron Krody.

Acknowledgments

For continuing support during the roller-coaster life of a freelancer as well as during the preparation of this book I want to express my deep gratitude to my entire family, especially my husband and mentor, R.V. Cassill, and my eldest son, Orin E. Cassill; to my editor, Carol Cartaino, as well as the many helpful people at Writer's Digest Books; to Carl Petrone, financial adviser extraordinaire and friend; to Janet Picone Cardin, secretary and friend, to Charles D. Taylor, Joyce Randall, Russell Gower, Donald R. German, Bob Dalton, and the many other friends and colleagues from the American Society of Journalists and Authors. Without their considerable help this book would not have been written.

We fear as mortals but desire as if we were immortal.

—La Rochefoucauld

Table
of
Contents

■■■

Chapter 3
Assessing the Markets 47

A world of possibilities. Analyze your competition. Consider major and minor outlets. Cracking a market. What kind of pay can you expect? Quick routes and slow but steady paths. Alternatives to consider. Creative thinking builds business.

Chapter 4
Space, Tools, and Equipment 71

A room of one's own. The start-up kit. Supplies. Build in overhead control and room for expansion. Office sharing and time sharing. Update when you can.

Chapter 5
Getting Yourself on Your Side 87

Staying competitive. Confidence building blocks. Conferences and colonies. The step-by-step approach. Discipline as a creative tool. Establishing priorities. Time and energy management. Situation summaries. Decision making. Procrastination problems. What's the cost of goofing off? Creative burnout. (More) Problem-solving techniques.

Chapter 6
Organizing for Profit 109

The plan. The long haul. Guide to a five-year plan. The days and weeks unfold. Organizing your ideas. Your queries. Your office. Filing and retrieving. Production planning. Basic manuscript preparation. Managing your mail. Telephone tricks. Employees. Ten time-saving tips.

Chapter 7
Research—Jackhammer of Your Trade 133

The many kinds of research. The professional approach. Systematize the search. Systematize storage and retrieval. Some research strategies. Sources of special help. The D.C. tangle. Gold mines and open doors. Interviewing. The benefits of bluffing.

Chapter 8
Packaging and Promotion
161

Graphically speaking. A star is born. Résumés and portfolios. The lecture circuit. Saturday night live? Advertising—discreet or direct? The more direct route. Basic training. The gallant giveaways.

Chapter 9
Expanding Your Territories
177

Three keys. Developing your list of prospects. Tapping the markets in progression. A new plateau. Blue-pencil blues. Revamp and retrench if necessary. Multiple submission. Spin-offs. Photography. Additional thoughts on expansion techniques.

Chapter 10
The Money Migraine
197

Fighting an occupational disease. Staying ahead of cash-flow problems. Spotting dead ends and deadbeats. Collection tactics. Augmenting your freelance income. Consulting. Teaching. Performing. Editing. Corporate freelancing. Public relations. Newsletters. Mail-order business. Other sidelines. Your hourly rate. Negotiating.

Chapter 11
The Professional Stance
223

Book contracts. Advances. Royalties. Subsidiary rights. Reading the royalty statement. Copyrights and work-for-hire.

Chapter 12
Agents, Book Packagers, and Other Helpers 241

What agents can do. Looking for an agent—the needle in the haystack? Young and hungry: is she your best bet? Agents' fees. How to keep an agent happy. When to change agents. Packagers, lawyers, specialists. Collaboration.

Preface

■■■

Every volume that finds its way into print is flavored with some joy and some heartache. This one is no exception. Yet from the moment this book was conceived, radical change was lurking in the shadows. As I was putting this manuscript together, I was constantly aware of the technological advances taking place in publishing and what they mean to the writer. These changes are fast making obsolete the ways by which most of us still get our copy into the hands of readers.

The home computer and the word processor are becoming tomorrow's necessities for many professional writers. Take a walk through a trade fair such as *Folio* magazine's annual Face to Face conference and you'll no doubt be struck by the multifarious gadgetry in the future of publishing. Memory typewriters, video magazines, web offset presses, laser photoscanners, copy mergers, and computer production are part of today's technology. VATs (voice-activated "typewriters" that may make keyboarding obsolete) are said to be but a few years from the market. When a typed manuscript can be transferred from Providence to Tokyo, then duplicated in multiple copies in a matter of minutes, or an entire issue of *Time* transmitted by telemetry so fast it can be on the newsstands in Hong Kong hours earlier than in New York, the specter of enormous change ahead becomes a reality. *Next* magazine recently reported that "three magazine people can't gather anywhere today without one of them dropping what's supposed to be the print equivalent of the atomic bomb: What's going to happen with the coming telecommunications revolution?"

This isn't the first time publishing has been confronted with profound change, of course. Forty years ago it was the introduction of mass-market paperback books. Oscar Dystel, former chairman and chief executive officer of Bantam Books, said in the eighth annual Bowker Memorial Lecture, "Since then changes in editorial thinking, . . . in the marketplace and marketing policies, . . . in the ownership of mass market companies, . . . in management leadership . . . have become commonplace. Yet managing the *process* of change rather than submitting to it remains one of the greatest challenges we all face." Dystel was speaking to an audience of publishers and editors, but his words are equally important to the writers who provide the material the publishers take to market.

Managing the process of change as much as we can, then, becomes a primary goal for the serious freelance writer. While the freelancer needn't abandon every luxury, the luxury of thinking that the profound changes in communications aren't going to really affect our business is becoming more costly every day. This book, in its attempt to define and delineate the ways freelancers can regulate their output and increase their business potential, speaks to that management. By knowing what goes on once your material leaves your premises and arrives at a publisher's, you gain vital insights into better writing and marketing techniques. By becoming acquainted with the problems editors face, you are in a position to help solve them. By seeing your freelancing as a business, you are prepared to compete in a daily more sophisticated technological arena.

Managing the process of change means accepting the challenges—and they are serious ones—before us and accepting the risks—and they are many. This book will enable you to discover and overcome the inherent risks before you venture too far out on your own. And, as there are many ways to build a freelance business, I've attempted to direct your attention to a number of preliminary and intermediate paths seldom mentioned in other books on the subject.

In each chapter I've outlined the various tricks of the trade; by no means are any of them meant to be seen as rigid rules. They should be taken as flexible guidelines to steer your business by. Add to that mix the disciplines required of any businessperson, and you're on your way to a successful freelance life.

According to the Magazine Publishers Association, some two hundred new magazine ventures will be started in 1981. Only twenty of them, however, are expected to survive the first year. The serious freelancer, confronted with such knowledge, learns to incorporate it into his or her business plan, taking advantage of the possibilities without being undercut by the disadvantages.

Other changes in the industry involve the long established but increasingly controversial policy regarding returns from bookseller to publisher, an alarming increase in nuisance libel actions, the Supreme Court's "Thor" inventory tax ruling, conglomerate take-overs, and aspects of the new Copyright Law—all these and more are parts of a publishing picture freelancers of the past did not have to heed. Today we do.

While at first glance all the looming problems might seem over-whelming for the freelancer just starting out, they are part of the challenge we undertake when we make the decision to head out on our own. By starting with a well-thought-out plan and by daily vigilance over the details that can make or break it, you'll be able to bend with the variable winds of publishing.

Introduction
The Great Freelance Escape

■■■■■■■■■■■■■■■■■■■■■■■■■■■■■■■■■■■■■■■

The best job on earth

First some credit: Sir Walter Scott is believed to have invented the term *free lance* for itinerant mercenaries who traveled with their own weapons—lances—and sold their skills to the highest bidder. These brave, independent, and adventurous souls helped shape history and contributed to the romance of which legends are made.

Freelancing still has romantic connotations, and rightly so. Few occupations offer as much flexibility in work and living styles or as many satisfying, human compensations. If you don't believe me, simply get out and around in your town and announce you're a freelance writer. You'll be surrounded by others who want to know the secret to your success. When you think about it from their point of view, you can see the fascination of the equation: freedom from the regular eight-hour day, five-day week automatically equals liberty, power, the big accomplishment! (I won't quibble at the moment about how "free" is free.) I, too, agree it's an especially happy occupation that allows one to sleep late, stay out of bad weather, knock off early on occasion, and grocery shop during non-rush hours. The merits of the freelance writer's life *are* legion. Writer Ronald Gross reminds us of some of the best of them. "Look at the advantages freelancers have. Find ways of capitalizing on them. By squeezing the maximum benefits out of the special conditions under which we work, we can be more productive, have more fun, and make more money." Ron's list of a freelancer's blessings:

1. We can generate and act on our own ideas.

2. We can use our time and energy to suit our personal style and rhythms.

3. We get continuing credit, exposure, and recognition for our work.

4. We can cut down or eliminate activities and contracts we find distasteful or unproductive.

5. We save the several hours each day most salaried people spend in travel, meetings, office socializing, etc.

6. We set our own priorities.

7. We can take a flyer—go for the big jackpot.

8. We can get paid for the same work more than once.

9. We can use our freedom to plug into events, people, occasions, and activities which pay off in money and pleasure.

10. We benefit and expand our horizons through constant exposure to new fields.

11. We are constantly meeting new, significant people through contacts on diverse assignments.
12. We enjoy the sense of our life's work developing along lines we have shaped ourselves.

What freelance writers do and how they do it

Freelancers come in many stripes. There's the *occasional freelancer*—a retired businessman or army officer, a professor, a student, a housewife—who makes a few scattered sales in a lifetime. He or she may be hoping for the one lightning bolt that pays off the mortgage—a runaway bestseller book or series. Conversely, the richest banker in town may pride himself on the articles he has contributed over the years to the local historical society's magazine, the recompense for which, all told, would hardly cover a party at the country club.

Another variation on this theme is the well-known film star, athlete, or other newsmaker who "writes" his life story. Most of the time the writing is done by someone else—a ghost, whose name does not appear on the book's cover but who did the actual composition.

There's the *part-time freelancer*—someone who, by preference or necessity, writes while holding down another job or jobs. Writers may move in and out of this state during various phases of their careers, their marriages, their lives and fortunes. Kurt Vonnegut is but one example. While he was drawing a $92-a-week check from General Electric, he received $750 for one of his stories. The next piece paid even more, and soon he got to the point where he was "a couple of years ahead of General Electric, so I quit and moved to Cape Cod" to become a full-time freelance writer.

The *full-time freelancer* category includes those whose names appear routinely in *Publishers Weekly* with the announcement of a new book, and in issue after issue of national magazines. They're the ones you'll most often see on TV talk shows as regular guests. These are the superstars, like Vonnegut, Erica Jong, Norman Mailer, and others, whose faces beam at you from newspaper ads and magazine profiles. They're invited to the White House. They mingle with royalty. The variation on *this* theme is the hardworking freelancer who makes a living at his or her work but never quite gets the big brass ring of a bestseller or movie version of a novel that boosts him into that superstar class. But, whether they make mammoth fortunes or not, these are the professionals, the backbone of the industry. It's their prose that finds its way into print in every conceivable form. Their names appear on the rosters of such organizations as the Authors Guild and the American Society of Journalists and Authors as well as specialty groups like the Society of American Travel Writers or Western Writers of America.

Actually, everyone who has ever cashed a check signed by the treasurer of a publication has, at least momentarily, been brushed by the wand of success. It may be all the success he or she deserves for a limited investment of effort. It may be all that's wanted by someone with a busy and otherwise fulfilling life.

Some more or less dark clouds

I feel obliged to mention some negative aspects of the business, partly because I don't want to make freelancing so inviting that those who aren't serious about it make it more difficult for those of us who are, and partly because it's a tough business. You have to work hard to succeed and then work even harder to progress. The business details may be annoying, but mastering them is absolutely essential if you're going to make a go at freelancing.

Another freelancing headache is that you often have to convey to others—family, friends, lovers, bankers, creditors—that you're really working. That's because sometimes, when you're *thinking*, say, it just doesn't look like much.

And then there's that huge fly in the ointment—discipline. Once you cut the cord to that salaried position and security, you see days blossoming endlessly. But the end of the month eventually comes and there's no check to pay the rent.

Or the opposite can occur—too many assignments hounding you at once. That predicament may not seem terrifying at the outset of your career. But when you're in the middle of it, it's all too real. (So, too, is the confinement imposed by the necessity of a book to be proofread and returned to your publisher over the Christmas holidays when most of the rest of the world is concentrating on the joys of fellowship and ceremonial cheer.) But of all these considerations (and more I haven't mentioned) the hardest, perhaps, at least for the beginning freelancer, is that first one: treating freelancing as a business. As in any other business venture, there are priorities. There are seemingly endless details. There's unpaid overtime. And there's more. The Small Business Administration puts it this way: "Even in times of economic prosperity, an overwhelming majority of those who attempt to become entrepreneurs fail within the first two years." Freelancers are entrepreneurs—or should be if they want to succeed.

Obviously, there are a number of qualifications necessary to working successfully on your own, aside from the ability to write. not the least of which is the ability to deal with money, management, and marketing. Even though those three words might seem alien to the creative spirit, they are often the ones that spell the difference between success and failure in the independent life of freelancing.

The SBA goes on to say: "The single biggest reason for failure is a lack of expertise in a chosen field. People are attracted to a business for a variety of reasons—almost always without the necessary understanding of the business side." That is, they seldom focus on such things as the need for inventory control, bookkeeping skills, an understanding of what their overhead will be, or the necessity of a healthy cash-flow policy.

So, here are some mean questions for you before you step out on your own. Do you:

- try to make limited capital stretch too far?
- handle creditors too tolerantly?
- let material get backlogged, not getting it to its market in a timely fashion?
- concentrate on markets that pay too little?
- lack training and preparation for particular areas of freelancing you want to enter?
- have an inadequate understanding of the markets available to you?
- wait too long to update your equipment, bottlenecking your productivity?
- lack financial savvy; lack knowledge of sources of available funds or how to use them to the best advantage?
- have little or no recordkeeping skills, little familiarity with accounting methods?
- get so involved in the pressure of day-to-day details you have no time left to analyze the situation?
- fail to seek help when you need it?
- become frustrated by changing competitive conditions; become unable to evaluate or cope with them?
- lack understanding of the basics of management?

To succeed in today's competitive world of communications, a freelance writer must wear a number of hats—creator, editor, interviewer, researcher, secretary, salesperson, public relations executive, bookkeeper, cost accountant, bill collector, general manager, and sometimes designer, promoter, and publisher as well. With such a list of responsibilities (and I'm certain to have left out a few), there is little room for the lackadaisical or nonprofessional attitude. Unlike many businesses, freelance writing naturally attracts creative people who, often proudly, claim they "have no head for business." Freelancing success, however, is based on handling business details in a businesslike fashion.

This handbook covers all angles of that business world, from the initial decision-making phase to the equipment needed to set oneself up in business, the organization of an office, researching and marketing techniques, budgeting, inventory taking, bookkeeping, collections, credits, retirement plans, insurance policies or their alternatives, royalties, subsidiary rights, tax matters, alternative sources of income, and self-publishing.

For those who want to take the plunge into freelancing, either full- or part-time, but need guidance, this book is for you. For others who are already publishing but know they need more techniques to increase their profits (*and* hang onto more of them), this book can also serve as a useful tool.

It is designed to be dipped into at whim and according to one's needs. Not all of the exercises or techniques are for every freelancer. People who find they're most effective with informal work patterns and unstructured methods may skip what they want. One caution, though: Since the freelancing field is becoming increasingly competitive, don't discard the suggested ideas too quickly. Take the time to try some on for size periodically. There may be more profit lurking behind them than you'd at first surmise.

The first assumption this volume makes is that you already know how to write, whether or not you've published. If you need more help with the actual craft of writing, it might be best to check some of the resources for that purpose listed at the end of this book. If you can, attend classes given by established writers. Or get to a seminar or writers' conference where you can have your writing critiqued. If that is impossible, then do look at some of the hints on combatting creative burnout (Chapter 5) and the techniques of reading as a writer and creative listmaking (Chapter 16). Although the emphasis in this volume is on matters related to marketing and improving your freelance business, I do not mean to suggest that *what* you write and how well you do it are not of crucial importance. Of course they are.

Your words can change the world

While it is important to consider the freelancer's place in the tough world of business, at the same time we should never lose sight of mightier challenges. We are writers, after all, and the substance of our writing life is to enhance and ultimately change the world in which we all live and work. By publishing a meaningful story on a controversial subject or an explanation of a new scientific discovery, we help others. By writing a brilliant novel that illuminates human foibles, we change a bit of the world.

True, such altruism may not be uppermost in your thoughts at all times in your career. Not all of you will or should don sackcloth and distribute to the needy those meager wages earned from your first published material. But as your writing career progresses, I think you'll discover how fortunate you really are to have become a published writer. As you do, the real romance of the profession will become clearer. When it does—when it is incorporated into every aspect of your writing day—you'll begin to recognize the most satisfying elements surrounding that overused but still legitimate word "inspiration." Naturally, your ego is involved with the outcome of every writing job. But that need not be an entirely selfish proposition, as the following examples suggest. And, of course, much, much more than mere ego is operative if the writer manages to achieve his most important goals. I think, immediately and indiscriminately, of such authors as Zola, Camus, Rachel Carson, George Bernard Shaw, and Mark Twain to start with. You can add numerous other favorites yourself.

Joseph Blank, long a freelancer and roving editor for *Reader's Digest*, makes a very good living. But Blank, in an interview, emphasized that the best rewards from his work weren't monetary. By writing about human beings in crisis—struggling to overcome incredible odds after their town has been turned to rubble by an earthquake, for instance—he believes he's changed, in some small way, people's attitudes toward many of life's most difficult situations.

If you are saying, "Yes, but there are no frontiers left," consider what areas George Garrett alludes to when asked by *Writer's Digest* editor John Brady why the form of the interview is so popular today. "Sometimes I think it's another sign of the sad necessity of our crowded, lonely lives, an urgent, hopeless reaching out to touch something real, a deep hunger for something authentic when everything seems false, a desire to believe at least in the possibility of the naked truth. And we seem to know, to realize . . . that these people, the characters we encounter in the various forms the interview takes, are . . . really very much like us."

Whatever avenue of freelancing you follow, I hope you'll discover the truly satisfying romance writing offers us all. With that in mind, I suggest you remember two final thoughts, both from Robert Louis Stevenson: "Keep your fears to yourself, but share your courage," and "To journey hopefully is better than arriving."

Chapter 1
Scouting the Territory

■■

On a clear day you can see forever

There's money to be made from freelance writing—lots of it.

Magazine analysts tell us there are around 20,000 periodicals published in the U.S. alone. Each month, it seems, one can spot premier issues on the newsstands. On top of that, there are over 6,000 book publishers in the U.S. The 1981 edition of *Writer's Market* contains 4,000 market listings. *Working Press of the Nation* and the *Ayer Directory of Publications*, to mention but two more directories writers use for market reference, list thousands of others. Excluding some obvious overlap, that's an almost unnervingly vast expanse where whatever one writes might find a home. The diversity of the marketplace is such that there are more ways for a freelancer to strike pay dirt than even some longtime professionals realize.

The flip side of that coin is the horde of writers and would-be writers after the bounty. Over 50,000 people in the United States call themselves writers and have clippings to prove it.

Some major New York book publishers receive over 10,000 *unsolicited* manuscripts a year, out of which they may publish *one* or *two*. The average high-circulation magazine receives approximately 200 manuscripts a month. Some people contend, therefore, that the odds of selling to those outlets are overwhelmingly against it. That's not necessarily so. For the thoroughly competent writer, the chances of selling are far greater. Perhaps only 20 of those 200 manuscripts will be good enough for an editor to take the time to read. Bear in mind that the flood of material that washes over editors' desks in publishing houses and magazine offices, in newspaper and syndicate offices, in television and movie producers' studios, consists mostly of badly written material. Well-conceived, well-written, and well-targeted material is scarce. Currently marketable material is even less available. The trend-setting story or article series is an absolute rarity.

Keep the following thought uppermost in your mind as you approach each new and potentially successful day: The many benefits of the freelance life and riches from your writing efforts, like the gold that lies under the mountains, come to those with the knowledge and ability to dig in the right places, the proper tools, and the overriding ambition to find it despite the often back-breaking, ego-mangling work that's required.

A realistic overview of the publishing world

It's *possible* to publish three books in one year while holding down a demanding full-time job. First novels *have been written* in the wee hours before dawn, long after everyone else has hit the sack. Successful writers can juggle heavy teaching schedules and still find time to give their best to their own writing—Joyce Carol Oates, George Garrett, William Harrison, and Colleen McCullough are but a few who have done so. I know writers who have written entire books in one nonstop week—books which were published and sold reasonably well.

Lawrence Block observed, in a *Writer's Digest* article, that "P.G. Wodehouse lived to be 93, and wrote about that many novels, fitting them in between plays, musical comedy lyrics, screenplays, essays, articles, and, I have no doubt, blurbs for the backs of breakfast cereal boxes and screeds to be tucked into fortune cookies. He did all of this with consummate grace, dovetailing a plot like DiMaggio gathering in a fly ball, making it all look quite effortless."

But looks, as our mothers warned us, can be deceiving.

The possibilities are there, all right. Trouble is, the problems cozy up on the loveseat right beside them. The truth is, it takes good health, energy, tons of discipline, and devotion to one's craft to make a decent living. (It doesn't hurt a whit to have an extremely understanding spouse or family for support.) Freelance writers do rise, phoenixlike, full of vim and vigor from nights of feeling completely burnt out. But juggling the demands of writing and a part- or full-time job elsewhere does take considerable cunning.

Now, you might be asking, why would anyone be such a masochist as to try to do both? Because, though the process of putting the right words in the right place is high art, the reality of a writer's revenue from his creation is all too often low comedy. *So* low you won't hear even a titter from me or any other serious writer I know.

To demonstrate, let me cite a few statistics. The following figures were compiled by Franklynn Peterson and Judi Kesselman-Turkel, coauthors of *The Author's Handbook*. "The average book earns for its author $1,710. The average author writes under two books per year. Each author is owed $68,230 per year in government subsidies." Admittedly these figures are a bit odd. They come from such figures as estimates of the number of titles in bookstores, the number of titles published each year, divided by sales figures for trade and paperbacks and such other figures as the number of members in the Authors League. Regarding the government subsidies, the authors were simply assuming that the government should be subsidizing authors to the same degree it subsidizes publishers of books through such agreements as discounts in postal rates.

Say Peterson and Kesselman-Turkel, "If we encountered the above statistics while researching a book, we ourselves would question the universality of their applicability. But they do shed some light on the all-but-buried foundation that holds up the publishing industry, the workaday author."

That's an incredible understatement, if you ask me. It's not, however, as shocking as their next disclosure. "Figured into these calculations are the few multi-million-dollar book deals that make headlines periodically. Without those blockbuster sales that, once in a while, make an author rich, the earnings of writers would be even lower."

Advances offered book authors are in many cases painfully small. Those handed over for an author's first book are described by professionals as somewhere in the range of pay common in Neanderthal times. (An advance is a sum of money a publisher pays an author prior to a book's publication. The sum, by the way, is later deducted from any royalties—the actual proceeds from the sale of the volume. For more on this, see Chapter 11.) First novelists fare particularly poorly with advances. "A fundamental fact of the writing of the first three books is that they are written at four o'clock in the morning," says James A. Michener, the author of such bestsellers as *Hawaii* and *Centennial*. That's because writers are forced to take other jobs to support themselves. "If writers don't have the courage to do that, they fall by the wayside."

Colleen McCullough, author of the wildly popular *The Thorn Birds*, is a millionaire now. But she was teaching a full load of courses at Yale when she received her original advance for her first novel, *Tim*. It was a mere $2,000—not bad, actually, for a first-novel advance. McCullough told me *Tim* sold over 10,000 copies in hardcover, something of a marvel in itself since that's better than 99 out of 100 first novels sell. With that kind of track record one might think the publisher would have offered her a *lot* more money her second time out, right? Wrong. Three years later she received a $5,000 advance to write *The Thorn Birds*, a 690-page book. It was only after *The Thorn Birds* sold to a paperback house for what was then a record $1.9 million that McCullough says she "became the darling" of her publishers.

Kurt Vonnegut, author of such bestsellers as *Slaughterhouse-Five* and *Jailbird,* pessimistically told a college audience, "Talent is extremely common, but publishers aren't willing to support new authors." According to Vonnegut, who waited a long while for fame himself, "You can't really blame the publishers for their conservatism. They take a tremendous risk. They're not really to be taunted for not throwing their money away—nobody else does."

And if you look at writers' payments for publication in periodicals over the years, the picture is no less gloomy.

Statistics show there are many magazines paying the same rates they paid writers ten to twenty years ago. The group includes major consumer periodicals with revenues that have increased dramatically over those years. Editors of *Writer's Market* surveyed the pay for freelance work and discovered what professionals in the marketplace already knew: "There are some magazines that have cut their pay scale, and one pays just a penny a word more than it did in *1940.*"

Now, before you let that news chase all thoughts of ever freelancing out of your mind, read on. While it certainly isn't *only* the fault of freelancers that their pay is so low, it is true that quite a few writers accept what is offered without question or negotiation, although they'd not think twice about asking for a raise from a steady employer. One of the points of this book is to help freelancers understand that, though it's an unusual sort of business, freelancing *is* a business. Freelancers who handle it like one are more apt to profit.

The many fields open

Books and magazines represent a mere fraction of the writing opportunities that exist today. Subsequent chapters will define these in considerable detail and suggest more. But if you take the following list and multiply several of the categories by four—for local, regional, national, and international versions—you'll recognize the many open roads leading out from your typewriter. Good news? It looks even better when you've developed the knack for utilizing these outlets, moving from one well-conceived project to another.

Television scripts	Company publications
Film scripts	Brochures
Audiovisual scripts	Advertising jingles, campaigns
Newsletters	Political speeches, campaigns

Trade publications
Publicity releases
Promotional booklets
Technical manuals
Medical journals
Scientific journals
Ghostwriting; collaboration
Fillers
Cartoons and jokes
Consultation

Documentaries
Interviews, market research
Teaching, tutoring
Television commentaries
Company histories
Lobbying
Seminar planning and presenta-
    tion
Self-syndication
Self-publishing

Some of these may not at first seem means of making a living by writing. But as you dip into this book you'll see they are. Writers are, after all, creative thinkers, and that specialty can be applied to a broad spectrum of writing and quasi-writing tasks. Of course, some writers confine their major efforts to either fiction or nonfiction, seldom if ever crossing to the other side of the boulevard. But these two areas are far from mutually exclusive. In fact, a scan of the ASJA (American Society of Journalists and Authors) Directory shows that many of the members have, after years of writing nonfiction exclusively, turned their talents to writing novels as well.

Three typical success stories

With that list as a rough map of the freelancer's territory, let's look at three representative sketches. The names of the writers are fictitious. The figures themselves are composites of numerous writers with whom I'm acquainted.

Sara M. sold her first article to a women's magazine five years ago when her youngest son was entering high school. The piece, a personal reminiscence, "Teaching My Husband to Cook," required little outside research—just one quick trip to the library for statistics to sprinkle among her humorous anecdotes.

She received $750 for it. The hoped-for reprint in *Reader's Digest* never came through. Undaunted, she wrote four similar pieces during the following year—wry, homey observations on changing roles in the American family. None of them sold the first, or even second, time out. Still, Sara learned a good deal about herself. Her confidence in her ability to write was bolstered.

She signed up for a continuing-education course in freelance writing, taught by a feature writer on the local newspaper. The next semester she enrolled in photojournalism. From both courses she learned the primary necessity of combining all of her talents imaginatively in seeking markets for her work.

After revisions and realignments of the subject to her target markets, Sara sold the same four basic pieces to a nearby weekly newspaper, a Sunday supplement, a regional travel magazine, and a religious periodical. Her total take that next year, however, was only $850.

However, this taste of success launched her on an intensive study of magazines. She analyzed content and clipped potentially usable information and anecdotes for her files. She learned to write pointed and tantalizing queries to editors. Although none of them paid off immediately, Sara felt she had the beginnings of a semipersonal correspondence with a dozen editors to whom she subsequently sold her new material.

Her photographs, too, began to appear in regional magazines. When she sold two at ASMP (American Society of Magazine Photographers) rates to an oil company magazine, she realized it was time to organize an efficient filing system for her prints and negatives.

She moved her typewriter from the dining table and took over a room for her office. Her fourth year of freelancing earned her nearly $8,000. But her expenses were almost $3,000. At that point, Sara seriously considered taking a nine-to-five secretarial job. But she had learned so much about the publishing business she hated to give it all up too soon. So she cornered a friend with expertise in bookkeeping and accounting for advice.

With that fortification and the friend's encouragement, she made out a strict budget for her freelancing. She began keeping track of her expenses and gathered nerve to bill her clients for them. Now she is aiming for a gross figure equal to what she would earn in that hypothetical nine-to-five position. She knows the net will be lower, but with prudent efforts she expects to hold her out-of-pocket expenses at rock bottom. She feels confident she'll succeed.

Harry T. lives midway between New York and Washington and commutes, on his own schedule, to both cities. He figures he needs to net upward of $40,000 a year from his freelancing and by now can confidently expect it. If his present plans work out, that figure may double in five years.

He began his career in the fifties, straight out of a good Midwestern journalism school. First he was a jack-of-all-trades for a county weekly. Then he became a reporter on the state's leading newspaper. A series of articles on juvenile crime and prison reform brought him to the attention of a former governor about to launch a senatorial campaign. Harry worked not only as speechwriter but as idea man and press liaison.

He went to Washington with the senator, and became an unidentified contributor to a Washington columnist. Under his own name he published substantial articles on the criminal justice system from the Supreme Court on down. He collaborated on a very successful book with a celebrated trial lawyer.

With the money from the book Harry took time off and wrote a novel, which was a minor success—$11,000 total income.

Five years of commuting to New York for an editing job on a men's magazine followed. He moonlighted through these years by writing on his specialties (crime and criminals; political prospects and personalities) for other magazines. The great payoff of this period was being included in the small fraternity of New York editors who share ideas, information, and tips and do each other favors. He developed his own stable of good writers who trust him.

Now his commuting is as a consultant for a citizens' lobby. He provides them with know-how about the ways of government, and keeps them in touch with writers in his stable, who help with their publicity, speeches, and the planting of favorable articles in the local and national press.

Harry still rises hours ahead of schedule to work on his own books before heading out to the train. His plan is to arrange his output so he can enter a working partnership with established publishing houses. He's acquired a word processor, a copying machine, and other equipment that allows him to deliver camera-ready copy. In two or three years he may be delivering finished books, written by himself and the writers in his stable, to the publishers, who'll be responsible only for distribution, sales, and accounting.

Harry has never moved very far away from his lifelong specialties in writing, but from them he has pushed out sturdy branches that have paid off well.

Cindy L. hardly touches a typewriter anymore. But she knows how to make one hum. She served a ten-year apprenticeship as a fashion reporter and film gossip columnist and wrote a syndicated "Advice to the Anxious" column under another name.

Then she became the invisible collaborator and first interviewer for a TV talk-show celebrity. She supplied ideas, deft quips, topical slogans for the weekly programs. But first and foremost she provided personalities. She developed her knack for turning colorful and/or afflicted men, women, and children into *properties*.

Now Cindy rides into the city in a chauffered limousine, dictating all the way. She keeps track of people at the shadowy fringe of society. Her business is to bring them into prominence in the news—and to keep her hand in at all levels of the publicity they generate.

For Cindy, promotion doesn't begin after a piece is written. She initiates a campaign as soon as the ingredients of her stories start to emerge. Cindy arranges interviews with anyone who can give the inside scoop or present a controversial opinion on television. She sees the incipient story and pumps it up. Then she arranges the reportage that follows.

Cindy is, in the world of freelancing, a producer. She makes newsworthy stories, then harvests the crop she has planted. She is nearly the total businesswoman. A major part of each morning's dictation involves correspondence with people who can help her story grow. She cashes in by marketing her own byline or inside information to the biggest TV news programs, the most widely circulated tabloids. When she wants a writer to turn out copy, she supplies a few key words, names, slants. She leaves the typing to others.

Placing the profit motive in perspective

Even if you have been publishing and making a living at writing, you may be guilty of practices that hinder you from making more money. Maximizing your profit requires you to:

- budget time and money carefully.
- set up daily and monthly schedules and stick to them.
- learn as much about the business of business as you must to keep your profits growing.
- master the freelancer's sales multiplication tables (i.e., use of spin-offs, recycled research, quick repeat sales to steady, in-hand markets, etc.).
- review the whole range of methods you're used to, periodically. Weed out the bad ones. (It may have looked like a beautiful garden in the beginning. Is it becoming a briar patch by now?)

There can be trouble spots you aren't aware of. Are you allowing too many interruptions to devastate your schedule? Are you letting too much time slip by before you get an idea and propose it to editors or your agent? Are you learning from your colleagues? Your competition? From publishers themselves?

Successful freelancers periodically review their assets and liabilities. They can never afford to imagine there isn't room for improvement, and they don't believe in giving things away free.

This isn't a stingy thought, but a sound business principle. Sometimes professionals may appear to be giving away freebies. (They, as a group, *are* quite a generous lot, particularly to those who are trying to learn the craft of writing.) However, they're really casting bread upon the waters.

To survive, a freelancer must be versatile and resourceful

A successful freelance writer does any number of things. I've made a list I think covers most of the important bases.

1. *Writers meet deadlines.* This is a slogan many successful writers actually keep posted above their desks until it becomes second nature. Meeting deadlines is the first step toward professionalism.

2. *Writers write something every day,* no matter how little time they have to do it. The product may never see print, but they are practicing their craft and building files for later use.

3. *Writers read, read, read.* They devour everything from cereal boxes to the encyclopedia. Their curiosity never seems to cease. They realize reading is one of their most precious tools and that reading as a writer is a precise art.

4. *Writers make notes on nearly everything.* They are often creative list makers. They realize their notes are a vital part of their business inventory and guard them well.

5. *Writers learn to memorize.* They absorb quotes and pertinent situations. They mentally record conversations, tones of voice, visual details, sensory stimuli, portentous facts. They also realize part of their repertoire should be bits of memorized eloquence, momentous moments, and entertaining minutiae.

6. *Writers learn to systematize, clip, file, and retrieve vital information.* The more skilled at this they are, the more productive they become and the better is their finished product.

7. *Writers use libraries.* They become personally acquainted with librarians. They support their libraries in every way possible.

8. *Writers love words and the language.* They are forever increasing their working vocabularies.

9. *Writers buy books and printed matter of all kinds.* They may own seven different kinds of dictionaries, as well as thesauruses, almanacs, resource guides. These volumes are dog-eared.

10. *Writers constantly study their markets.* They note the changing facets of the market and are quick to spot a trend. They stay alert to the long, cyclic drifts within the culture. They aim to be at the right place at the right time with the right proposal.

11. *Writers learn as much about the editing, publishing, and marketing business as they can.* By being knowledgeable about all aspects of their business, they are more effective entrepreneurs.

12. *Writers take their work and their business seriously, forcing others to do likewise.* The better skilled they are at this, the more successful they become.

Now, anyone can argue that writers do not fit neatly into molds. And yes, some successful writers will be better at one part of their business than another. Certainly there are writers who do all of these things and whose names are still not household words. But with so much stacked against the writer, it's essential for him to sharpen his writing techniques and business acumen.

Writers in general, if they are successful, are using what I call "cave-smarts." Because they have been so long underpaid and overworked, many have been forced to acquire the strategies of guerrilla fighters, those sometimes motley but rugged individuals who have, out of sheer necessity, developed first-rate survival tactics.

I truly believe the more you practice such techniques the longer you'll thrive as a freelance writer. If you need a cohort to do so, get one from the many available around you. Caroline Bird, author of *The Two-Paycheck Marriage*, among other books, told the ASJA:

> The world is full of women who are having babies, or people taking care of aging parents, who are looking for something to do but don't want to work full-time. At one time I had a nursing mother taping interviews of people on the telephone and taking the tapes to another woman (who had to stay at home) to type up. We live near a whole bunch of colleges, and colleges have extremely bright young people who want to be exploited.

(She doesn't exploit them, however, but lets them run a pretty relaxed shop, doing their jobs on their time, earning money in the process.)

So let's make the list a baker's dozen:

13. *Writers are compulsive, impulsive, frivolous, unique, and industrious.* They have "cave-smarts." They know that the difference between the writer and the would-be writer is knowing that inspiration is another word for hard work—theirs most of all.

As for the argument that any number of successful writers don't clip, file, and retrieve, for instance, look again. When you find such a writer, notice how he's compensated in another aspect of the writing trade, similar to the way a blind person may overdevelop a sense of smell or hearing. If the writers made it *work*, that's all that's important.

My husband, R.V. Cassill, author of *Writing Fiction*, put it this way:

> More important than talents or intelligence, luck or strength, is *the knack for using these things and using weaknesses as well.* This knack is a very mysterious thing. Perhaps it is no more than a determination or a strong desire to make use of the good as well as the bad. The creative process, by its nature, can't have any predetermined goals, but a faith in the infinite possibilities for shaping life tends to define and clarify the value of achievement as one goes along.

To *succeed,* a freelancer must pay steady attention to every part of his writing business. This theme song will be played throughout this handbook. I hope it wafts merrily through your head, the way "Greensleeves" or "Joe Hill" runs through mine some days.

Because writers are so good at daydreaming, they aren't always likely to pay close attention to picky details. Account books, budgets, filing, and recordkeeping are all drudge work. Writing promotional copy about themselves and sales pitches about their work either frightens, eludes, or bores them. Still, the ability to strip away your boredom or fear and get the jobs done will turn out to be the key to your financial success.

Luck is a writer's lot. When you learn to cultivate your share of it instead of waiting for it to roll around on its own, you'll have much of the work completed. Becoming your own best teacher, as you are when you devour books like this one, will increase your fund of knowledge. Like dominoes falling against each other, use of that knowledge will improve your writing and writing-related skills, which, in turn, increases your chances at publication and prosperity therefrom.

After all that seems to say the life of freelance writing is a bummer, I say not necessarily so. Everyone likes a good story. Although we live in an era of instant information, a story still captures people's imaginations. Stories are the mainstay of our mythology about ourselves and our world. They are the means by which we capture and reenact our lives—in whatever form they appear, be it a well-told joke, an anecdote, a brief bit of humorous gossip, a well-phrased historical narration, a short story or a novel. We need them. We need good writers to write them.

Saying that, I leave it to you to decide who will do it.

Chapter 2
Taking Stock

■■

Analyze yourself and your situation

Writers choose to freelance because they long to be free of constraints. They want to concentrate on their own writing. Yet the business of freelancing, like any other, has its own restrictions. To keep them from becoming shackles, you'll have to work very, very hard. Start out right. Begin by learning all you can about the perils and pitfalls before you take the big leap. Talk to others who have been freelancing awhile. Read what others say are the hazards in the path. There are no ready formulas, just good and not-so-good experiences. Take some with a grain of salt, of course. There are hacks in this business as in any other. It is quite possible that, with steady nerves, good writing, practical business habits, and luck, you'll be able to improve considerably on someone else's track record.

First, let's look at the inner you. When you were working for someone else:

- What kind of energy did you have?
- Was it difficult to get going in the morning?
- Were you all charged up to work during certain hours and not so sparkling during others?
- Which days of the week could you count on to be your best ones and why?
- Did you take as long at lunch as possible to avoid returning to your job?
- Could you be counted on to work overtime now and then without grumbling?
- Were you easily bored by routine chores even though you knew they must be done?
- Were you an expert at procrastination?

Now that you've answered these questions yourself, do you have the gumption to ask a friend, family member, or coworker to answer them about you? If you can face it, try it. You'll need as much input as possible in this original analysis—you are taking on a lot when you're starting to freelance full-time. But whether or not you get another's opinion, do consider carefully the physical and emotional demands already being made on you. Consider where adjustments will probably have to be made in your living habits and in the time you allot to others. You have only so much energy. What will just have to be ignored when you start your own business? Can you readily adjust to the probable changes? Knowing how you work best—at what hours and under what conditions—will help you chart your ideal course as you continue on your freelance business plan.

Next, look at your current situation just as carefully as you examined yourself. There is no right or wrong time to start freelancing, although many people will try to give you some formulas. Goldie Hawn put it well when she told an interviewer, "I've finally discovered life sort of unfolds and certain things, which you can't plan, reveal themselves at the right time." But if you're the kind of person who needs to approach matters logically instead of jumping off the deep end, you'll be better served by researching all the possibilities. What is your own market potential right now, right where you live, with whom and with what you already know? Which markets can you approach with your current skills? (Later, you'll look at what you'd most like to do, when and if other possibilities show up.) What kind of money can you reasonably expect from them? Will it be enough to cover your expenses with something left over? Where can you find help?

How do you find answers to these questions? The procedure, as any business person will tell you, is this: Take inventory of what's already in stock.

Inventory the resources available

You are your own best resource: who you are, where you live, what you need to survive on, what you want out of life, what you believe in, what you know you can accomplish with ease, what you have to admit is difficult for you. Fig. 2-1 is a rather extended chart of items you might want to consider in your overall inventory of available resources. Some won't have anything to do with your business picture yet. Some may never come up. They are only offered as categories to think about in your exploration of the total picture. You can use the various headings to separate your answers; if you write down as much specific detail as possible at this time, you'll have the start of a thorough analysis on which to base many future decisions.

After you've detailed the necessary information in the first column, you'll need to consider possible outside support mechanisms, as well as the necessary items listed under hardware and software. (This list is extensive because as your business grows so do your needs and your helps. Check off only what is pertinent at the moment and file the rest for later.)

Your next step will lead you to your branch library and any specialized libraries in your neighborhood for resources to help you

Self	Outside Support	Hardware	Software
aims	part-time help	income	market lists
experience	libraries, librarians	typewriter	personal library
track record	newsletters	desk	editorial network
needs	writing experts	file cabinets	account books
impulses	specialty experts	Rolodex, card files	budget
energy, health	subscriptions	office	production schedule
confidence	business experts	car	interview tapes
specialties	researchers	cameras, tape recorders	notebooks, other records
reputation	PR people	telephone, answering machine	photo & negative files
distractions	artists, designers	copying machine	stationery, business cards
other obligations	printers, etc.	other equipment	press credentials

Fig. 2-1. *Sample inventory of available resources.*

discover potential markets. Be sure to take a fat notebook, because you'll want to list every possibility at first, even though you may know in your heart of hearts that some are more dream than reality. Once you've exhausted what you can find, ask the librarian to help you discover others that you've overlooked.

Begin to draw up a list of people you know—your banker, your real estate agent, the doctors, dentists, schoolteachers, and salespersons that make up a part of everyone's life. You probably know them in one sphere only. They, however, know many people who could be possible clients for you. Think about how the lives of the people in a community intertwine and ask yourself, "Could so-and-so be a possible lead? What schools and colleges are they connected with, even peripherally? Are they members of professional organizations who could use my writing talents in some way? Whom do I know in government agencies nearby? What did I hear recently about so-and-so's job change?"

If there is a community college in your area, take a look at the course list. Is there one aimed at helping people develop new careers in midstream? Make an appointment with the instructor. Tell him what you're trying to do. Does he have suggestions you might not have thought about?

Once you've done this homework there is another list you should consider compiling. It relates to the business side of freelancing—not how to make contacts with potential clients, but how to be paid what you're worth, how to control expenses, how to find part-time help to hire, where to find used office furniture, how to save and invest your proceeds. Write down names and telephone numbers of any experts you know whom you think you might need in your start-up strategy: brokers, accountants, librarians, researchers, lawyers, public relations experts, students looking for part-time work, executive secretaries, and bookkeepers. If you don't know at least one good one in each category, ask friends and acquaintances to recommend two. They should be people who might be open to giving you free start-up advice, people who would be sympathetic to a freelancer's goals and gumption. Then write a polite letter to see if you might get some helpful hints. Make an appointment to talk to these people. Don't overlook the local Small Business Administration office. Gather up all their free pamphlets for study.

Consider your start-up costs

I know of no other business in the world where the first question prior to venturing into the blizzard of competition—"What will it cost?"—isn't primary. So many writers start out with just the shirts on their backs to keep them warm, it's a wonder we don't find more frozen bodies along the wayside. We all know about the big successes in this profession because the headlines are dazzling when they happen. What those banners don't report so often is how the ones who didn't make it are managing to survive, if indeed they are.

To avoid calamity, make a checklist of your probable start-up costs for your first two years as a freelancer. Begin with the following list and add to it any special expenses, such as child care, that you know you can expect.

proper stationery and business cards
professional tools and equipment
local transportation
records and bookkeeping
part-time help
postage and shipping
dues for professional organizations
educational seminars and meetings
travel and entertainment expenses
business gifts
taxes
insurance
personal library and subscriptions
office and equipment rental
photocopying costs
telephone and answering machine
office furnishings
special clothing if necessary
promotion, publicity
legal costs
miscellaneous

In your first months you won't need to fork over cash for everything listed. That would be foolhardy. Ask yourself what you absolutely must have to start out. Be relatively hard-nosed about your answers, since you will be competing with freelancers already out there with steady incomes and more or less balanced budgets. You should try to appear as professional as possible in your start-up with the minimum of the essentials you'll be able to afford.

You need a place to work. You need a desk, a chair, a functioning typewriter, paper and supplies, and good-looking business stationery. You should start with a simple but expandable bookkeeping method (see Chapters 4 and 13). You'll discover you need some sort of files. Again, if you arrange to keep track of your papers properly at the outset, you'll reap many benefits later. So make sure the method you choose is easily expandable. When you've toted up the minimum costs for these (after some telephoning around town for price estimates on secondhand furnishings and office equipment rental costs), round out the figures a bit, add ten dollars a month to each category for good measure, and multiply by six months. Now you have a figure to measure by. If your savings or other available moneys match your six-months' figures, you're in pretty good shape to start off. Not that you won't have to hustle to replenish some of that dough within those six months of writing and marketing—you *will*. But with such a cautious start, you'll have far less to worry about.

When considering what you have in reserve, it's not prudent to forget your outstanding debts. They'll be eating away at your budget if you do. So consider what Nancy Edmonds Hanson recommends in *How You Can Make $20,000 a Year Writing (No Matter Where You Live)*:

> You can limit the size of financial reserve you need by cutting down your regular bills. I was able to securely start with much less money in the bank because over a period of three months my husband and I applied extraordinary effort to paying off every credit card, every store charge account, and every other obligation due to come up during my first freelance months—regular insurance premiums, college loan repayments, and the like.

Take your calculations and ask a friendly bookkeeper, business person, or accountant whether the picture seems realistic. Or speak to someone at the SBA. Such people may give advice that sounds all too stern, but remember, they're used to hearing about new business start-ups and subsequent failures. They may know very little about the freelance writing business, however, so also try to talk to someone closer to your field—an editor or a reporter for the local paper who moonlights as a freelancer, for example—about your planned necessary expenses.

If you have no penchant for keeping accounts, be particularly resourceful at the outset. Check your list again for accuracy of your estimates. This practice with figures—receipts and expenditures and hidden costs—will prepare you to better analyze every phase of your business, now and later on. And you'll be much happier at tax time when you discover you've successfully wrestled the financial tiger into line.

Next, prepare a tentative budget for each month, using your estimated figures. Allot time in a regular schedule for review and updating. You may find you have to examine figures more often at the beginning, but as in most anything, practice, happily, leads to perfection.

What route do you want to follow?

The key word at this point is *want*. Before you can settle where you'll be six months or two years from now, you'd be best advised to take care of some wants. Freelancers do not flourish by ignoring their basic natures. They can't help wanting one thing over another, and they do not all want the same things. So fess up. You *do* want to follow in Tom Wolfe's footsteps. You'd really *like* to end up being known as a better interviewer than Barbara Walters, Oriana Fallaci, or David Frost. You know you can *survive* (barely) without foreign travel, but you certainly do want to do as much as possible within the next five or six years.

Imagination is the master of art as well as of life, as Joseph Conrad told us. Use yours to decide how to separate your truly important wants from those others. One approach is to list things in which you excel; jot down your specific talents. Usually those are the areas in which your primary wants will appear.

Now, don't get edgy. Just because you have done something well doesn't mean you want to stay with it, of course. But it's important to get off to a good start in freelancing as in anything else. One writer I know began her career by writing about gardening for the local paper because she happened to know a good deal about house plants. She built up quite a following and turned out reams of copy on the subject before she came to the conclusion that she couldn't write *another word* about Swedish ivy. Okay. But she did get a sound freelancing start and many months of income under her belt, which she sorely needed later. Don't turn away from an overly familiar area too soon.

When you've got a clear idea of your *wants,* and know just as well what you *don't* want, and have the lists to refer to later, proceed to "go."

Which niche is yours?

Understand that everyone can't be selling everything they write to the top markets at the same time. Ask yourself which areas appeal to you most. *Then* look at the competition in your chosen field or fields. (You'll examine them more closely in Chapter 3.) How do you stack up—your education, your current writing ability, your drive, your track record so far, your current financial needs, your probable financial needs a year and two years from now (honestly projected)? You may have a burning ambition to write bestselling novels but may actually be, at this moment, far better prepared to write ad copy and jingles. You may have a solid background in the most recent genetic research but be darned if you want to spend your writing time going over the same material—you want to write and sell your poetry or television scripts!

Before you make a firm decision about which niche is yours, turn to your inventory chart. Think about item number 1 under software—market lists. To get the most complete picture of where you can market your material and ideas, you'll want to use some of the items in the second and fourth columns to jog your memory. (For example, all of the categories under outside support should hold additions to your library-researched market list as well as items 2, 3, and 4 of the fourth column.)

Remember that you need to be thorough in your researching and listing because you'll have to delve into a variety of markets over and over again to make a decent living. And I'm not just talking about writing articles for a variety of magazines. In fact, it's difficult to think of writers who, once embarked on a freelance career in earnest, haven't written for a half-dozen kinds of markets at a minimum.

While the range of writing opportunities is so varied it's impossible to keep current with all of them, here are some you might consider: advertising/marketing/promotional materials of all kinds, book editing, book development/packaging/publishing, brochure and pamphlet production, cartoons, catalogs, collaboration in various forms, conference and seminar organization, consultation, coaching on your specialty, copyediting, corporate communications, crossword puzzles, design and layout, exhibit planning, novelizations of scripts, films and audiovisuals (filmstrips, slide shows, cassettes), direction and production of films and audiovisuals, food demonstrations, gardening demonstrations, ghostwriting, hymns, industrial shows, investigative reporting, lecturing, lexicography, literary representation, magazine editing and development, manuscript analysis and revision, newsletters, newspaper editing, news releases and press kits, photography, photojournalism, plays, poetry, general production, proofreading, proposals (books, plays, programs, or series of coordinated works), public relations and publicity, research, reviews and criticism, speechwriting, teaching, technical writing and editing, textbooks and other educational matter, translations and foreign-language communications, television and radio production and scripts. Even that is not an exhaustive list; it consists of the categories in which the members of the ASJA are experts.

Whether you are just beginning to consider freelancing, are an advanced beginner with a few published works under your belt, or have been at the business for five or ten years, I'll wager there are a number of interesting niches in the above list that might be worth considering. I recommend that you refer to the list repeatedly. There will be times when your budget will require an emergency transfusion, and times when your creative powers will demand just the kind of stimulation an oblique move to another area of writing and writing-related tasks can offer.

Another important point: When weighing which niche is yours, don't make the mistake of picking one you consider "easy" for your bread-and-butter funds with the thought that you'll save your *real* self exclusively for your novel or poetry. You'll never make ends meet in the competitive world of freelancing if you don't consider that every job for each client is worth your *utmost* effort. (When I hear about a writer who has sloughed over a project, I recall the saying on Countess Dolingen's tombstone in *Dracula's Guest* by Bram Stoker: "The dead travel fast." So, too, around publishing circles, does the name of a lazy writer.)

The entrepreneurial hustle

One of the first things you'll discover after the glow of setting up shop wears off is this: There are plenty of inequities in the business world. Small entrepreneurs say the amount of paperwork required of them by the government is way out of proportion to their situation and profits. Not only that, they are continually threatened with more paperwork. To top it all, the freelance writer, as a special kind of independent contractor, is taxed out of proportion to his income (see Chapter 13). Consider these questions:

- Do you handle business details effectively?
- Are you prepared to work seven days a week if necessary?
- Are you willing to forgo vacations and national holidays?
- Can you juggle your personal life around your business?
- Can you live happily without a steady salary?

- Does a sense of isolation bother you excessively?
- Are you a decision maker?
- Can people trust what you say?
- Can you stick with a problem until you've solved it satisfactorily?
- Does your personal checkbook balance at the end of each month?
- Are you immune to anxiety attacks when filling out your tax forms?
- Are you a tough competitor?
- Do you thrive on difficult assignments?
- Do you have the ability to work on a project and see it through even if the axe might fall on it?
- Do you have the business savvy to recognize unprofitable plans and drop them for more lucrative ones?
- Can you be your own best employee?
- Are the methods of sales, management, public relations, and publicity foreign to you?

Now, naturally, I realize none of us can answer all of those questions perfectly. They're not here to intimidate anyone. Rather, they're meant to help you see the possible dangers in the dark. That way you can prepare for the worst of them by applying more diligence than you might otherwise. You'll know *when* you need help from an expert as well as *where* to find it before it's too late.

There's one question I left out of the above list because I wanted to emphasize it. How are your typing and general secretarial skills? I'm continually amazed at how many would-be writers don't know how to type. You don't *have* to type well to write well. But since your writing has to be presented in typed (or printed) form to an editor or any other client, some kind of typing skill is a must. If you don't have it and have no intention of getting it, you'll have to hire a typist. Of course, as your assignments increase and you have a lot of them to get out at the same time, you'll no doubt find hiring a typist for some of them a time- and money-saving necessity. However, if you've started your freelance business on a shoestring, the cost of a typist might be prohibitive. Manuscript typists get anywhere from 65¢ to $1.00 and more a page. Those with word-processing equipment ask and get even more. The cost of a one- or two-semester touch-typing course or a how-to book on the subject might be the better bet for your start-up budget. Not only that, the happiest professional reporters I know (because they are earning top dollar from a very demanding national publication) are those men—yes, they are all males—who were forced to learn shorthand to get their first jobs out in the boondocks. Their boondocks, though, happened to be in Britain, where, at least when they were starting to work, typing and shorthand skills were absolute requirements for beginning reporters. (I can't tell you how many times I've wished I'd taken my father's advice and continued just a little longer in that high school shorthand class.)

With that list of questions about your entrepreneurial talents answered to the best of your ability, prepare some legible notes (names, addresses, telephone numbers) on the experts you can ask for help in the areas of your greatest weakness. Some of these, of course, may be friends who, for a cup of coffee or a lunch, will offer early guidance. In other areas you will want to refer to books mentioned in the Resources chapter as well as other chapters in this volume. You might, to steady your confidence in a particularly shaky area, want to take a course at a community college or trade school.

One last thought here: In any endeavor, we all have moments along the way when our enthusiasm wanes. These should be taken as passing moments, in most cases. (If they seem to be more than that, perhaps the section on creative burnout in Chapter 5 will help.)

Testing the various waters

Although I practically fell into it—certainly it wasn't planned—my first paid job after I graduated from a university writing program was a happy break. It wasn't a staff editorial job, which I had applied for, but a freelance one. I was given a chance to show my stuff by becoming a freelance "first reader" of book manuscripts. That meant that my employer sent me back to my apartment with an armload of manuscripts to read critically and either recommend for publication or reject. Frankly, when I think about it now, I shiver. Who was I to say what should or should not be published? Well, for one, I was fairly well-read. I had just spent four years attempting to write fiction under the watchful eyes of some of the best writing teachers in the country. I had even been published. But I doubt those were the reasons the editor gave me the job. I think now it was my enthusiasm and my optimism that sold him.

Reading slush is often a first-rung job at an editorial office. That's good, in a way, because it offers you a chance to test your editorial judgment at a point where it will probably do the least harm. The company gets an opportunity to see what you can do, and you get the chance to see if you want to do it. That's a fair exchange.

Consider this kind of approach if you want to test the vagaries of that long list of freelance opportunities mentioned earlier. Try to think as the employer is thinking before you suggest a tryout for the top job in his company. You're an absolute stranger to him. He has only your word and a résumé you wrote and perhaps the names of a few references you picked out on which to base his judgment. If you were in his position, I'm pretty certain you wouldn't hand over the best window office and the services of all the secretaries immediately. Though you're not asking for the keys to the safe, you can nevertheless use this opportunity to test out what's in his bailiwick, to see if you want to spend much of your freelance time working for him, so that the two of you can strike a reasonable bargain.

How do you discover which is the lowest rung on his ladder? Ask. First you might want to talk to people who are on a less lofty plane than the president of the company. Listen to their grapevine of information and rumors. If they don't have the answer you're seeking, they should be able to refer you to someone more in the know. The mail clerk, the secretary, the assistant public relations person, or even someone who works in the company lunchroom probably has more knowledge of the organizational structure than you. Ask two or three of them to suggest a path. Then use your very best judgment.

One form of asking is letter writing. If your campaign includes possible clients outside your city, you can take a stab at spreading the word about your interest in an entry-level job on a freelance basis by mail. This may or may not get the kind of response you want. It will depend on your credentials, your cleverly worded letter, and, most probably, a few follow-up calls and personal interviews to assure your correspondents that you are in earnest. Persistence, at this point, is a decided virtue.

Recommendations from highly placed individuals are another form of asking. When you've just published a book, you'll be getting, if you can, writers, reviewers, and experts in your field to supply blurbs for the book's cover. Why not start practicing now by seeing whom you can discover to recommend that a client give you a chance?

Potential assignments besides slush reading at a book publishing company or magazine might include the following:

Companies that publish directories (like the *New England Media Directory*) or textbooks occasionally hire freelancers. Perhaps you'd be asked to do simple library research, then write a report on material you've unearthed, to be used by an in-house writer/editor. Or you might be called upon to gather local or regional statistics, using the telephone, your car, and lots of shoe leather for various sorts of market research.

Promotion departments in a variety of businesses engage large numbers of part-time employees from time to time to write publicity releases, captions, leaflets, booklets, and articles for trade journals. Ask.

Mail-order companies, though they'd probably start you typing labels and doing other clerical tasks, might offer you a chance to try your hand at ad writing. Ask.

Or look into expanding personnel departments at banks, investment companies, and factories. Writing jobs such as analyzing and restructuring employee questionnaires or gathering news for the company newsletter from employees in far-flung satellite plants might be assignments the company would be all too happy to farm out to an enterprising freelancer. Ask.

Now ask yourself what might be wanted or needed in a hospital, government agency, or insurance company. Think about what really makes you mad about how they do things. Do you know a workable solution? Put it down on paper, talk to someone in a decision-making position, and offer to help. A trick that may well stand you in good stead now and later: Try to discover what innovative technique has been applied by one kind of business but has yet to be adopted by your target client. If you spend some time now exercising your imagination, it won't be wasted.

A handy tool for some of your research is probably right in your living room—the television. You can use it during your downtime, when you are too bushed to type another word, face another letter, or pay another bill. Whether they're soap operas, mini-series, or weekly situation comedies, many of the shows will sooner or later dwell on what is happening in boardrooms, business offices, and hospital rooms right now. (The writers of these programs must stay current in order to entertain. So without ever walking into a boardroom of one of the Fortune 500, you and I can get a reasonable glimpse of what does go on.) If you are an astute observer you can see through to the problems that are multiplied many times in the actual boardrooms these dramas are representing. And certainly the books on your own library shelves—the novels and informative non-fiction titles (think of all those self-help books flooding the market)—offer potential problems to solve for others (for a fee, of course).

Though you don't know the solution when you hear about or read about such problems, jot down the gist of the situation in a special section of your writer's notebook. Leave room for the notes you will make later when you are thinking about solutions. These ideas, by the way, will generally come to you when you're doing something else—washing the dishes, driving to the grocery store, painting shutters on the house, or, most often, trying to sleep. Nevertheless, jot them down as soon as possible.

When you get a nibble, be prepared with a well-planned project, a good sales pitch, a strong sample portfolio of your work, and a trial layout or ad series to support your idea.

Picking a territory

In the foregoing jaunts—either by letter, telephone, or in person—you've been doing more than testing to see where the jobs are. If you've done even half of what I've suggested, you've successfully spread the word that a valuable, skilled writer with many other abilities (such as professional reading, researching, editing, organizing, planning, and designing) is available and eager to *help*. If you've done the requisite homework and built a solid presentation, by now you've piqued the interest of several possible clients. From those nibbles ("We like the look of your presentation, and we'll get back to you") and a couple of real bites ("Can you get this research done by the end of the month? If so, you're on"), you'll be able to describe, for the time being, a certain territory of your own in your own hometown or region. Don't be surprised if that territory seems indescribable to anyone else at the moment. A friend of mine who dips into playwriting, jingle concocting, teaching, and speechwriting isn't unusual for a working freelancer. When he needs to call himself by one title or another he does so, fully confident that while he wears that hat that's who he is and his part-time employer will recognize it. Nor, generally speaking, would that employer care about what he called himself at other times. What does he have on his business card? *Freelance Writer.*

As you pass from the testing process to choosing a territory of your own, ask yourself about market potential and your expenses. The following questions are worth listing separately and answering for each segment of the territory you're beginning to define.

■ How much of your freelance time would be required to accomplish this kind of work?
■ What kind of money can you reasonably expect?
■ What are the particular expenses this would necessitate?

- Would it require any special accounting or recordkeeping?
- Would special working space or equipment be required?
- Would travel be required? What kind, how far, and how often?

Finding a specialty and making it pay off

Too often I've been confronted with students who've picked out a special area of concentration before they've even considered the total picture. They do it for one reason—it's easier. All this research—libraries and librarians, telephoning, going for interviews, preparing presentations, and more—is time-consuming. And keeping a bulging notebook of all that you've uncovered is a chore. But keep in mind the fact that you're not just going to use this voluminous research material for your start-up. You'll find some use for the information you've gathered, and for many of the techniques for *discovering* that information, at least ten years into your professional freelance career.

Let me give you an example. I once had to arrange for a family of five to move to another continent for a year. Where to live, how much rent to pay, how to care for the house in the U.S., how to find a suitable school for the teenagers, rounding up passports and pertinent papers, finding contacts for business, medical care, and housekeeping details—these were but a few of the problems confronting me. My first trick: I started early. Second, I kept all the information in one notebook, segregated under the proper headings. It worked like magic. The family breezed through its time abroad and returned having had no major problems. I tucked the notebook away and forgot about it. I continued my freelance business. Suddenly one day the light dawned. All of that work shouldn't go to waste, and I made certain it didn't. I've now parlayed my little notebook (and all I learned from making it) into many related ideas, which have paid handsomely: consulting, magazine articles, booklets for specialized audiences, and teaching the technique itself.

So don't do all of the research if you feel it unnecessary, but if you do it, don't toss your notebook away too quickly. Further into your freelance business you may find it more helpful than you could have imagined.

An example of finding a specialty

Barbara Sunderland found a specialty and made it pay. She noticed how many women working in businesses needed help with language and presentation skills. They were file clerks, stenographers, and waitresses, but they wanted to move on to higher-paying jobs. Since one of her former jobs had been heading a modeling agency, she knew she could help them. She wrote a thoroughly professional proposal on the teaching of proper speaking and writing techniques and took it to the local business school. Suddenly she was in business teaching her specialty. When the school contract expired, she found a classroom to rent and advertised. Eventually she progressed to a mini-lecture circuit, a how-to book, and the possibility of establishing a nationwide franchised network.

Barry Beckham, a professor and writer at a college nearby, teamed up with Barbara at one point. He had long been aware that middle-management officers could use help with their writing skills. "You'd be amazed," he said, "how many people even in well-paying positions really need help. Either their education has been faulty or they're caught up in the jargon of their business. Their reports and speeches are *terrible*." Barry developed short, fact-crammed seminars for these people, who were far too busy to spend much time upgrading their writing skills and intelligent enough to grasp the information in a minimum of time.

Barbara and Barry both did three things. First, they recognized a need within a specialized area. Second, they put their ideas on paper in a fully realized presentation. Third, they took their presentation to the officials with the decision-making power to implement their programs.

Some beginning in a new field find it profitable to write a few paragraphs describing themselves and their potential in a specialty as well as their ability to develop new angles or approaches to it and stash them in their files. This outline is the basis for a preliminary sales and marketing plan. If you do this, consider what you have to offer (your unique personality, experience, specialty, and your view of the world). You have an MBA *and* an MFA? Make the combination, which is very rare, your own bailiwick. You've studied tax law? Think how many people are eager for your information and advice. People tell us there are tired, overused ideas. Mostly there are tired thinkers.

Consider these questions when choosing a specialty:

- What do you know or like best?
- What can you afford to spend your time on right now?
- What areas of your interests overlap with related fields that may offer a clearer, less competitive option?

- Would this specialty require more training?
- Is this area already overcrowded?
- Do you have a new angle or approach no one has thought of?
- Are there some gaps in certain specialties not being adequately covered in your geographical area?
- If you specialize in this particular field, could you develop spin-off material into a syndicated series, a column, a consultancy, a book?
- Are the reprint possibilities strong?
- Does this specialty lead into your overall plan, helping you get where you want to be two, five, or ten years from now?

With a stack of newspapers and periodicals in front of you, try to answer as many of the above questions as you can. If you're still puzzled, continue your search by clipping and filing material into categories for a few weeks—celebrities, sports, hobbies, the occult, travel—whatever stirs your interest sufficiently. Tuck the material away for a few months, then look back over it to see if your interest has remained high or if in the interim you've managed to quell any curiosity you originally had.

Unfortunately, temptations abound to glamorize some specialties. Travel is always to exotic locales. Profiles of celebrities put you immediately in the stars' inner circle of pals. Not so. Both of those specialties require an inordinate amount of painstaking work. I'm not knocking spectacular sunsets and shimmering lagoons. But travel writers have to find a great deal more to write about than that, often while in the throes of jet lag or culture shock.Writing a truly professional profile of a celebrity can take months of tracking down anecdotes from reluctant friends or old-time acquaintances in un-glamorous places. Trying to start out specializing in those two areas could be biting off more than you can chew or than your budget will comfortably allow.

Of course, you don't want to specialize in something that doesn't excite you at all. But look at the wide world of possibilities; stretch that first quick description of your interests to see what else it might include. Have you forgotten that you used to be fascinated with geology? Do you secretly want to redecorate your friends' homes the minute you step into them? Are you a hang-gliding enthusiast? Is consumer advocacy terribly important to you?

Stringing

Stringing can be a specialty, too. The term goes back to early newspaper days when a reporter's copy was "strung together" and he was paid by the inch. It now means working for a newspaper, news magazine, or other publication "from the field," turning in ideas and stories when you find them or when you're contacted by your periodical (in the middle of the night or on a national holiday, as often as not).

Each individual company sets up its stringer network in its own way. Some stringers get small retainers plus their usual fees when their stories see print. In other cases there is no flat fee, only a loose arrangement about acceptance of stories or, perhaps, a certain number of guaranteed stories in print throughout the year. The main point is the newspaper or periodical knows the quality of your work *and* how to get hold of you fast. You know how they want their stories and photos sent to them. You know you can count on a certain amount of work each month. It's possible to be a stringer for a number of outlets at the same time if they are not in competition with each other.

Arlene and Harold Brecher collaborate, specializing in medicine and the behavioral sciences. They have built a lucrative freelance business. Their files hold the names of an enormous number of contacts—doctors, psychiatrists, other experts—whom they can reach on a moment's notice for a quote on almost anything. Editors who use them regularly say they are indispensable. Why? They can turn a story around very fast and can be counted on to be accurate.

How you amass such files yourself isn't nearly as important as what's in them and how current you keep them. Besides names, addresses, telephone numbers, and the subject's expertise, you'll probably need any clips of comments or activities by the expert as well as anything written by others about the expert's work. Certainly you'd want copies of his or her published papers and speeches. What you'll have, essentially, is a studious profile of the person, one which you'll refer to time and again.

To make a specialty pay requires a good deal of early preparation prior to your choice. It requires hard work developing your particular angle. It's probably best, too, to choose a field that doesn't require too much up-front funding, at least at first, since it's unlikely you'll recover those costs quickly. Consider a first-time specialty that can easily be researched at your local newspaper morgue, library, or nearby college, with support material coming from local interviews and telephone calls. Use the education you already have. When your successes build and you manage to make more than the bottom line of your expenses, you can branch out, take a course to start a new specialty, or move from nonfiction to fiction.

A professional who had been freelancing for years found herself in a mental bind. She wanted to switch gears mid-career. Well aware of the vicissitudes of the freelance business (slow payments, unfinished projects, the sudden disappearance of one's best editor or client, etc.), she realized she couldn't get too far out on a limb financially. After analyzing her current situation, she chose to continue taking some jobs writing ads and commercials for radio. But as soon as those assignments covered her fixed monthly expenses, she stopped. By slicing the time spent on them to one week a month she found free time to pursue new creative avenues. The decision turned around her entire career and outlook on life. I doubt if that would have happened, though, if she hadn't carefully planned her gear-switching to guarantee that she'd have enough money each month for the necessary expenses.

One more thought on specialties: Watch out for areas nearing the saturation point. Head the other way. To publish and sell regularly, you'll need to supply what editors and clients (and their readers) want. You'll be competing with the old established pros in the fields, so be as selective and ingenious as possible.

Keeping afloat

Everyone needs a financial base from which to operate his freelance business. Just as you should thoroughly check the foundations of a house you're considering buying, you should spend as much time as necessary (and perhaps a little extra as insurance) considering your financial foundations *before* you sever the cord to a full-time job and strike out on your own. Doing your homework as honestly and thoroughly as possible will give you the confidence to fulfill your writing assignments with ease and to procure those assignments in the first place.

Confidence—especially in this business—is a funny thing. Hardnosed editors will seldom admit that the confident stranger who pops into their office with a good idea for an article or column has the edge over any other would-be writer with the same idea. But, believe me, he has. The assured freelancer is in a much better position to sell to that editor because confidence is infectious. If you have that sense of yourself and your abilities, as well as your idea, the editor is far more likely to be confident of them too. If you have the surety that a small but regular check (from anywhere) gives you when you start out, you'll be in better shape to venture further into the freelance world. (For more on confidence building blocks, see Chapter 5.)

The aforementioned stringer jobs can be beneficial for a freelancer, but they aren't easy to come by. You might have to start your freelance business by working at it only part-time, keeping that weekly paycheck from a current job, no matter how small, as you build your business.

What kind of part-time job you take depends on you. But it will undoubtedly affect the energies you have left for writing. Some people turn their full-time job into a part-time one. Talking your employer into such an arrangement may not be as difficult as you think. The employer gets the same quality of work from you for the hours you spend on the job, and you save him money on his contribution to employee benefits (Social Security, medical insurance, etc.). Some freelancers try to hold a full-time job while freelancing nights and weekends, which is fine unless their job involves the same sort of work they are attempting to do on their own time. Then the paid position can be too much of a psychological drain. Joseph O'Connor, for instance, was a promising playwright who, after three years of study at the Yale School of Drama, looked for a job. "It is, inevitably, difficult to earn one's living as a creative writer," says O'Connor. "The compromise I reached was to go into advertising." The full-time position made its own demands on him, leaving little time for his own writing. "What minor talents and energy I had were pretty well used by my work."

If you think this could be a problem for you, perhaps you should head straight and fast to any menial position that would allow you to protect your creative juices for your own efforts. I know stockpersons, mail clerks, bartenders, taxi drivers, and chauffeurs who write. The latter, by the way, think their part-time jobs are ideal, since they allow them a lot of time in which to read and make notes if not actually to write.

Besides part-time jobs, you'll no doubt want to consider bartering as another form of life raft. Barter for the large and small items in your budget. Can your expertise be useful to someone or some organization? Exchange your ad-writing talents with a commercial artist who's just beginning in business for some well-designed letterhead. Or you might offer to write promotional material for a printer in exchange for slicing your printing costs to the bone. Barter, too, with students and potential researchers to cut your biggest expenses.

Don't be proud. Accept any freebies that come your way as long as there are no strings attached. People are kind; they do like to help others. Be grateful and let them know when they've helped you further your business.

Apprenticeships and sidelines

Just as you're not likely to get a writing job without good craftsmanship, you won't be paid much unless you have writing experience. If you don't have that, you'll have to find ways to get it. Almost *any* position in which some of your time is spent writing *anything* will be useful on your résumé. Jobs at retail stores, banks, hospitals, manufacturers, distributors, public utilities, even menial work at a radio or television station, hold the potential for an entry-level writing chore. You're on the spot when an emergency comes up. You're also around daily (answering the switchboard?) to remind the powers that be you'd like to be given a chance.

You can take a look at the form in which material in your business is written and, at night, draft your own version. Then attach a nice note to it and give it to the boss, asking when he has a minute to give you his comments. Or you can drop in at the office where the company's publications are prepared. Show interest. Offer to be an unpaid reporter for the company newsletter.

If you've headed for your neighborhood newspaper for a job, even if it's just handling low-level tasks such as taking want ads, you still might get a good chance to practice your writing skills. And you'll learn about deadlines. Writing against one, over and over, can sharpen your creative power with the written word as nothing else can (unless it's actually seeing your words in type).

If you don't need the job for the money but for the writing experience, you can even put together your own sample newsletter or small booklet on your area of expertise. Ask a professional (reporter, teacher, editor) to critique it for you. What they say might start you in the publishing business, albeit in a local manner. On the other hand, it might send you to the best writing course you can find.

Courses *can* help when you need it, so don't shy away from them. Take what you need and be grateful for any friendly criticism of your writing that the instructor and fellow students give you. Face up to and *repeatedly practice in* the area of your *greatest* weakness. This is the only truly helpful technique for learning more about writing creatively.

Consider the network you already have

Once you've done even a fourth of the tasks this chapter has suggested, you will have established a working network for your business. Put your newfound information on people, places, markets, jobs, and possible specialties side by side with your personal list of friends and family (near and far). Record the names, addresses, and telephone numbers in a handy Rolodex if you haven't done so already. Set the file beside your telephone. Think of it as a living thing—it grows with you and your business. It needs to be watered and pruned occasionally. But more than anything else, it needs to be used.

Chapter 3
Assessing the Markets

■■■

A world of possibilities

It *is* exciting to discover the wide variety of markets for your talents. You will, as you progress in your freelancing, find even more markets than I've mentioned, markets not listed anywhere. You may turn up someone or some company in your own neighborhood that becomes a freelance market simply because you approached them with the idea that they could use your services. New technologies create new markets as well—for instance, educational and recreational material for home and business computers. Whether markets appear to be a widening gyre or a row of locked doors is entirely up to you, your energies, ambitions, and talents as writer, promoter, salesperson.

The Yellow Pages for freelance markets are *Writer's Market, Working Press of the Nation,* and *Literary Market Place.* (For even more market information use the resources listed at the end of this book.) Investments in one or all of these are well worth your while if you're serious about making your living freelancing. You'll also have to decide how often you can afford to replace them, since they are all annuals. The answer will depend on a number of things: how well you are repeatedly tapping certain markets, how deft you are at selling spin-off material, and where you wish to focus your efforts each year. If you can't afford to buy books at the outset of your freelance career, be the first to pore over them when they arrive at the library.

It's probably false economy to purchase these volumes only once every three or four years. Editors play musical chairs, and magazines, rates, and requirements change regularly. It is essential to know the exact name, spelling, title, etc., of your client. If you are going to impress him, you must follow the simplest of professional rules—get his name right. These details become increasingly important when you must query an editor who knows nothing about you or your work.

Changes *during* the year can be caught by watching the market columns in *Writer's Digest* and *The Writer.* If you are a member of the National Writers Club or similar organization, you will get monthly newsletters detailing news about the markets. When you run across a significant change (new address, new editor, changes in specific requirements, etc.), reach for your *Writer's Market* and note it before you file the periodical away and forget about it.

Keeping up with the publishing industry's periodicals is a more expensive proposition. But even without taking out costly subscriptions to *Publishers Weekly,* the bible of the book-publishing industry, and *Folio: The Magazine for Magazine Management,* you can regularly check these at your library. Many freelancers also subscribe to one or more of the large metropolitan daily papers, such as the *New York Times,* the *Washington Post,* the *Wall Street Journal,* the *Los Angeles Times,* or the *Chicago Tribune.* They give far more extensive coverage of events, which is helpful for your clippings files, and can be rich in ideas for queries. This way you can keep up with what the editors you'll be querying are also reading.

If you've decided on a specialty, you'll subscribe, I'm sure, to the best publications in your chosen field, or track them down regularly wherever you can. I also suggest you listen to an all-news radio station from time to time for possible story leads. A local story may have national interest, given a slightly different slant. And trends can be spotted more easily, sometimes, by freelancers who aren't in metropolitan centers.

The following is a list of magazine and newspaper feature articles broken down into types of approach. This list is not exhaustive, but it does cover most of the material you'll be reading in periodicals of every stripe. Occasionally there will be some overlapping.

According to subject matter:	**According to treatment:**
academic	as-told-to
adventure	book review
art of living	controversial essay
business	exposé
family relations	how-to
finance	humorous
historical	inspirational
literary	nostalgia
medical	personal experience
professional	profile
psychological	protest
safety	question-and-answer
science	round-up
seasonal	subjective essay
sociological	think
sports	you
success	
trade	
travel	

The aforementioned material fits into the following markets:

■ Magazines, newspapers, Sunday supplements, both national and regional. These can either be *consumer-oriented* (directed toward the general public, such as the national "slicks" with readers in the hundreds of thousands), *specialized* (directed toward a special-interest group), *trade* or *professional* journals, *company publications, literary* and *"little" magazines,* or *alternative-press weeklies* or *monthlies.*

■ Books, booklets. Fiction, nonfiction, textbooks, children's and juveniles, historical, gothic romance, science fiction, religious, arts, crafts, how-to, etc.

What should you do with these lists? On the face of it, it's obvious. Try to match the outlets with the kinds of material they publish, and you automatically come up with an infinite variety of opportunities. Add to the lists the freelance jobs I've suggested you look for in your own area, ones that aren't *listed* anywhere, and the market basket overfloweth.

Analyze your competition

Let's get the worst out of the way first. In one sense, the top competition will be all those writers out there who, like George Garrett or Isaac Asimov, have been practicing their craft for many, many years. But it's folly at the beginning of a freelance career to worry about the ones who are that far out ahead of you. They should be regarded as guiding lights, not as intimidating roadblocks. So study your favorite special "stars" and learn from them. You've got plenty to do just dealing with what I consider your real competition. And for each one of you the competition will be somewhat different, depending on where you're starting from, and where you want to go.

When you examine periodicals, books, or other markets, pay special attention to the writers who appear in print over and over. Make note of those who seem to get the most mileage out of an idea or have the most prominent articles—the largest display, the longest stories. If one or two names appear in a number of markets, jot down where they're selling their work. Also see what specialties these writers seem to be known for. In most magazines there is often some explanation about the background of the article on the editor's page or a biography of the author with the story. You should read these as well because they help acquaint you with the writer behind the byline. Then, with your list of, say, ten to fifteen names, head to the

Readers' Guide to Periodical Literature. Look up these authors' names, going back perhaps as far as six years. Jot down the other titles of articles or stories they've published. Read them. Then make a few notes analyzing the careers of these people. Have they stayed with the same markets over and over? Did they progress from a bylined story to a spot on the masthead? Or vice versa? Have they appeared in competing periodicals and, if so, did they seem to progress? (You can tell this if you have been reading and analyzing the competing markets listed in *Writer's Market,* since most listings describe the basics of their pay schedules. You can also be your own judge of which magazines are probably competing by looking over the newsstand. Which magazines look alike or cover much the same territory? *Time* and *Newsweek* and *U.S. News and World Report,* that's for sure. *People, Us,* and *You* are in the same slot, *National Enquirer* and *The Star* have a similar look. So, too, do *Ladies' Home Journal, McCall's,* and *Good Housekeeping.* Or *Cosmopolitan* and *Redbook.* Or *Family Circle* and *Woman's Day.*)

How does your competition write? Is it slick, sassy, and humorous like Nora Ephron's prose? Is it thoroughly researched by a pro with a solid background in science? Does the writer seem so bright he's probably a member of Mensa? Or do you consider the writer's job of researching and writing to be lackluster—okay, it's publishable, but it doesn't make you eat your heart out?

Another aspect of your competition is *what* is being written about. You must read widely and browse in bookstores and newsstands and in the library's periodicals department. People like Nino Lo Bello, Tom Mahoney, and Robert Dunham, who publish constantly, say they check the market all the time. Lo Bello told travel writer Curtis Casewit, "I believe I spend as much time on keeping up on the market as I do writing."

In fact, I have never yet heard an editor speak before a crowd of freelancers, beginners or professionals, without admonishing the audience to "read the magazine before submitting." If you go back and read six to eight years of *National Geographic* or *Science Digest* or whatever, you will learn two things: what kind of article subject the editors liked (you can assume they wouldn't have published something they couldn't stand) and what article subjects to stay away from in the near future. (They will not repeat a similar story soon. If they just ran a series on solo adventuring, such as rowing the Atlantic, or rounding Cape Horn in an inner tube, don't think, "Aha, here's the place for a story about my friend Ned, who's circumnavigating the globe in a converted bathtub." They won't buy it.)

If you've methodically progressed this far, you've picked out a few periodicals in each of the categories that interest you in the list of markets presented earlier. Do one more exercise. With the names of the writers you've been studying, go back to that list of types of approach and make a note about the kinds of articles they've published. Was it an as-told-to or a bit of nostalgia? A think piece or a profile? Does it look like a protest or an exposé? Beginning freelancers often find it difficult to clearly define which category an article fits into. So study carefully. Some articles are confusing because the lead starts out one way and the body of the article takes quite a different slant. If you are confused, ask the librarian to describe the article, using the category list.

This is not an idle exercise. Not only will you become more aware of what your competition is doing, you will learn to be more discerning in your reading, which will help when you are querying and writing. If you really are bogged down at this point, be honest. Perhaps you need to take a course in nonfiction writing. Also, check out some of the books listed in the Resources chapter.

Nor is the suggestion to thoroughly study the competition meant only for those new to freelancing. You will automatically acquire more knowledge, insights, rumors, and impressions about your colleagues as you publish more of your own work. Still, you will always benefit from a really solid review from time to time of what your competition is publishing, where they're making new inroads, or why they've turned away from a certain market.

Consider major and minor outlets

A good many beginning freelancers complain that they have no hope of cracking the big-money markets—the bestselling book; the national slicks which pay thousands of dollars for a 1,500-to-3,000-word article. That's not exactly true. There's always an off chance. But they're right in a sense; the possibilities are very slim, at least at the beginning.

I therefore recommend that you look at both major and minor markets. Don't think, when I say minor markets, that you won't have any competition to worry about. Some of those same writers you'll find in the big slicks will be selling to your hometown newspaper's travel section or Sunday supplement. Minor markets aren't necessarily less professional. They just pay less. The professionals writing for them are, practically without exception, selling spin-offs of their researched material. Very often the same article you see in your travel section will be appearing simultaneously in ten to twenty other newspapers. (See the discussion of spin-offs in Chapter 9.)

So take down your *Writer's Market* and consider the various divisions. (If there's any chance that you'll be taking photographs to go with your stories, also get hold of the current *Photographer's Market.)* Note as many minor markets as you can that fit your interests. Compile a target list of approximately twenty-five publications or outlets. Label it "A." Then compile two other lists of approximately the same length and label them "B" and "C." Your A list will consist of the best-paying markets, your B list will be made up of those publications paying in the middle range, and your C list will be spin-off markets to aim for when the others have been exhausted. You now have seventy-five places to first submit your queries. You can either tack this above your typewriter or slip the pages into a three-ring binder labeled "Markets." But do make the lists. If you don't want to spell out everything, just note the name of the publication, the page in *Writer's Market,* and the pay scale. And *keep* the lists. They will come in handy when you need to change directions in your freelance business (see Chapters 8 and 9) or find secondary sources of income (see Chapter 10).

Why do I ask you to keep the target market lists after you've got a good start on freelancing? Because the markets are ever-changing. You'll find that out sooner than you think if you continue to freelance. Some titles on your list will have to be deleted. Magazines fold. Or they change direction entirely. Or they move out of your region. The point is, with your carefully compiled original lists you can have a foot in the door many times. You'll be prepared when an editor you know pops up somewhere else. And you won't waste time preparing a query to a magazine that's defunct when you are smack in the middle of another big project but still, for your budget's sake, *have* to get a certain number of queries out that quarter (see Chapters 6 and 9).

You'll start publishing long before you get through the seventy-five notations. If, that is, you *read* what the editors say they want and don't want very carefully, if you *have read* years of the magazine's back issues in the library (or at least requested the free copy offered by some magazines and read every last word in it), and if you *do* some of the exercises later in this chapter. (Be sure to write out your answers.)

With your own article-ideas list in front of you, make note of how many different ways you might be able to approach the material. (Refer back to the list of types of approach.) Your idea is a story on the reconstruction of a Revolutionary War vessel? How many ways are you capable of handling the material *right now*? Keep the list for later.

Now add to your markets lists any material you can garner from other sources. Not every possibility is in a book in a library. The amazing thing about the market basket I referred to is its expandability. You'll discover ways to extend it the same way you stretch your food dollar at the grocery store by hoarding and redeeming coupons.

Unlisted markets will, usually, fall under such categories as: local and regional specialized publications, specialized businesses with a potential need for a freelance writer, local agencies and governing bodies, charitable organizations and nonprofit services, etc.

At this point it will be necessary to do some footwork and telephoning around your community. Call friends to see if they can think of places or publications where your talents might be of use. List anything they suggest. If they come up with a name of someone else who might know, get the address, too, and write the person if you can't afford a long distance telephone call. Your friends and acquaintances have the leads waiting for you to track down, if you would but ask.

Cracking a market

You've already got a hold on the question of what the editors want from your analysis of what they've already printed. They want what they already have. They also want what their competitor is printing, by the same writer or someone with even more renown. They want, in a word, story ideas and bylines they can spread across the cover that will automatically sell copies.

This is what you're competing with. The question is how.

The answer is more homework, more solid analysis of what's really going on. But every minute you spend now in this effort will pay off handsomely later on. It's just like developing a convincing bluff in poker or learning the intricacies of backgammon so that you're a whiz when you start out on the pro circuit.

The next step: Take a few trial runs. Don't aim all your arrows at the same target. Spread them out over a diversified market list. You are after a *market sampling* as well as sales. The reactions will tell you what you can expect from this direction of your efforts.

When you decide which markets you can and want to sell to *right now* (perhaps six to twelve names on your list), set yourself the task of finding the right *angle* on the right story—the angle that is "just for them." Then produce your most succinct query and send it out. If you come close, you'll very likely get a note from the editor suggesting you try again. Do so—again and again. Take heart at this: Even writers who have been publishing awhile and are attempting to break into a new area of expertise have to settle for this technique.

Cracking your chosen market may be easier than you think. It can happen just like this: You've targeted your idea to the right publication and presented your query in the most selling manner. The story idea was timely. The editor said, "Okay, go ahead on spec." You wrote the story, and, lo and behold, the editor bought it. Fine. Keep going along the line you've chosen. It won't be so easy, perhaps, next time. But you're apparently on the right track.

If, however, rejections start piling up, and more and more of your SASEs are being used to return your material, it will probably pay you to go back a step and examine the magazines more closely to see if you really understand what the editors are looking for and if your article ideas fit the market. Think about the probable buying patterns of the magazine's readers, how those readers might have gotten interested or involved in the magazine's subject matter (skiing, jogging, sailing, or whatever), how they progress through it, and if they'll probably still be buying the magazine in later years. Remember, special-interest magazines reach their readers at the peak of interest in the activity and, therefore, at the peak of their buying activity.

For example: A publication aimed at college students knows their main purchases of books will be at the beginning of the school term. With purchases of books go purchases of records, tapes, posters, supplies, and furnishings for their college rooms, as well as their main outlay for clothing. Winter doldrums bring on occasional buying sprees and thoughts of ski trips and weekends at the beach, where the students will spend money on luxuries instead of necessities. So the magazine (and its advertising salesmen) shapes the issues around the buying patterns of the target audience.

The question for the writer, then, is what such readers would most want to read about. When you know the answers to some of these questions, you know when (and when *not)* to query editors with story ideas.

After some study, you should be able to write a brief novel about the typical reader of such a publication. As an exercise I've asked students to write, not novels, but fairly detailed short stories using only their research from a magazine's advertising. An excellent tool to help you "read" the ads and all of their hidden messages is Marshall McLuhan's *Mechanical Bride*.

Let's examine briefly the ads in a recent issue of *Next*. As soon as you open the cover you discover a two-page color ad from Volkswagen, stating "We Improved the Best Mileage Car in America." The appeal is to economy (A Rabbit Diesel), safety ("More visible directional signals," etc.), and, nevertheless, luxury ("Whole new sleek instrument panel, plusher . . ."). The next ad is a one-page color pitch from Benson & Hedges Lights ("B&H, I like your style." Photo of young, good-looking couple in their twenties frolicking in the snow with three Alaskan huskies). Another ad: four color pages from the Easton Press for The 100 Greatest Books Ever Written, with the luxury of "full leather bindings" and priced at only $33.50 each. The following ads are for TDK videotapes, E.F. Hutton, Banknotes of All Nations from the Franklin Mint, Subaru, Kent Golden Lights, and Litton microwave ovens. The articles and other copy deal with ecology, science, media, parenting, financial hedges, and so forth. The appeal is to the college-educated, affluent, upwardly mobile, socially concerned reader.

Okay, you know that the consumer magazines on your list want great articles with possibilities for cover lines and "name" writers whenever they can get them. You may not be able to supply the second element yet, but you can work to supply the first. Examine the four sample covers in the following list.

1. Exclusive! LHJ's New Diet for Women who Work
   Compare Your Marriage: How 30,000 readers deal with sex, infidelity and new rules for sharing love
   25 Ice Cream Dazzlers! plus Southern recipes, plain and fancy
   Forget Your Age! Makeup steps to keep you looking great
   Summer Tops to Crochet
   "Will We Ever Get out of Debt?" Can This Marriage Be Saved?
   Class Reunion, best-selling novelist Rona Jaffe's compelling look at what happened to "yesterday's girls" [ribbon]
   [The cover picture is of Kate Jackson. "She lost a halo and found . . . a new life!"]

2. Easy Skillet Cookbook, money-saving breads, desserts, whole dinners

Complete novel: When two brothers love the same woman
How diet doctors stay slim
100 best fashions under $25
How to get the most for old gold jewelry
Knit our colorful cotton sweaters
Famous Mothers & Famous Daughters
The Pill Book, the 100 most-prescribed pills, plus *all* their side
  effects [ribbon]
[Cover photograph of Debby Boone ("The most wonderful year
  of my life . . .") plus inset photo of Joan and Kara Kennedy
  to illustrate the mother/daughter story.]

3. Special Report: Big Futures in Small Cities
Ten That are Job-Rich
Why They Work So Well
Where the Hot Investments Are
The Candidates and Your Dollars [ribbon]
[Cover photo of young couple in front of car. "Dick and Judy
  Blinn left Oakland, Calif., for the good life in Olympia,
  Wash."]

4. Cray Research/An Inc. 100 Company: From Start-up to $60
  Million
Save Tax Dollars by Growing Abroad
The Baby Boom: Where have all the children gone?
Will America sacrifice its future to preserve its past? [ribbon]
[Cover photo of Seymour Cray. "Seymour Cray and His Super-
  computer"]

From an examination of the covers alone, see how many story
ideas you can concoct that would please the editors of these magazines. When you see stories such as "25 Ice Cream Dazzlers" or "100
best fashions under $25" you can be fairly certain they are staff-
written. But use them anyway for your idea list, since you may well
want to submit a related story to a periodical that has no in-house
staff for such stories. Service articles are often a relatively fast way
to crack the market.
    What do the cover lines on the first two magazines tell you? Many
of the readers are married, or of marriageable age but not actually
married. They have love interests and related problems. They wonder how their arrangement stacks up to those of others like themselves. They are worried about aging too quickly. They want to look

their best—or better—and are always anxious to learn how. They like to make things with their hands that can be admired by others (and that will save money on their wardrobes). The economy has taken its toll on their budgets, and they're looking for ways to save. They'll read the Jaffe piece because it's always fun to look back to see what's happened to your friends over the years. They watch television and follow gossipy news about people like the Kennedys.

With those for starters, see how many other comments you can come up with that describe the person that each of the magazine covers is appealing to. What cover lines would make him pick up the periodical? What would make him spend $1.50 for it? Which articles is he most apt to turn to first, second, third? Which ones might make him keep the magazine for more than a month? Do the same with the other magazines from your own shelves.

Once you've really worked at this exercise, you'll be thinking like an editor, which is exactly what you're after. Professionals do this automatically, and it keeps the money coming in regularly.

The first two magazines in this exercise were *Ladies' Home Journal* and *Good Housekeeping*. The second two were *Money* and *Inc.* They might well come into the same households and be read by the same readers. Yet a writer who wanted to hit both markets would slant the articles differently. I'm thinking particularly now about the story behind "The Baby Boom: Where have all the children gone?" A story with that title could appear in *Inc.* and either of the first two in the same month. But the slant would be quite different, and the anecdotes and details the writer would use would be different. See if you can add to the following list.

Good Housekeeping	Inc.
"The Baby Boom: Where have all the children gone?"	"The Baby Boom: Where have all the children gone?"
1. Photograph of empty bassinets in hospital nursery	1. Charts by demographers on population python; twenty years of children in the economy
2. Anecdotes: school administrators worrying about empty schoolrooms	2. Anecdotes: retailers tracing the babies through economy
3. Story slant: Impact on children and their education caused by overextension of school facilities during baby boom: consolidation, closing of schools, teachers	3. Story slant: A look at what baby booms do to the economy historically; tips to entrepreneurs for forecasting

out of work, lower level of education for remaining schoolchildren at the same time property owners and parents are faced with increased taxation. areas least harmed by the population python's gyrations; ways to skirt financial disaster caused by them.

Another clue to discovering what editors want is to study their entire magazines. Myrtle Nord, writing in *Writer's Digest*, says, "You don't have to meet editors face to face to discover what they want; you only have to meet their writing needs—and this you can determine by *really studying* their editorial columns. I have done this with a number of smaller markets over the years, and while my checks are sometimes modest in size, so is the number of rejections I've been receiving since I discovered my blue-pencil system. *Modern Woodman* pays only $35 per article, for instance, but after I studied their freelance contributions, I picked off $70 from one submission of two articles, and I'm not a woodman." She happened upon her method after hearing the familiar "read my magazine" from an editor. "And that means page by page, piece by piece, cover to cover, and when you know it exactly, go it one better. Research."

Nord listened to what the editor said she wanted, then went over the magazine with a blue pencil, analyzing every story paragraph by paragraph, anecdote by anecdote. After that she could see very clearly what the editor of that particular magazine wanted, and gave it to her. You can do it, too.

Editors will tell you what they want. They've done so in *Writer's Market*. Such magazines as *Writer's Digest* and *The Writer* often feature interviews with editors. And again, knowing what editors are thinking about by reading *Folio* and *Publishers Weekly* will answer some of your questions. But there's more. Most editors have a sheet of writer's guidelines for their publication, which you can ask for. And if their publication isn't on the newsstands, they will often send a sample copy for a writer to peruse. Editors also appear on panels at seminars for writers such as the annual writers' conferences put on by the American Society of Journalists and Authors and by Women in Communications, Inc. (See the May issue of *Writer's Digest* for an annual summary of other seminars.)

With local publications, it's probably best to make an appointment to talk to the editor about current needs. Make the discussion brief and to the point because the editor is most probably very busy, though it may not look it when you enter. But do ask to talk to an editor. Speaking to one face to face is good for your sense of yourself as a writer. Your commitment to your writing will be strengthened. You'll discover editors are human—they're people, and sometimes very nice ones at that. You might even discover you've met a fellow writer, one who understands all too well how difficult it is to follow the freelance course you've chosen.

When you attempt to analyze a company's in-house publications, you have no ads to guide you. Instead, get their annual report and any other material they publish for their employees or customers. Read what the editor asks for in *Working Press of the Nation.* Who are their stockholders—the much-maligned and probably nonexistent little old lady in tennis shoes, or overachievers in the upper echelons of the investment business? What are the readers' age range, income level, hobbies? Does the company have subsidiaries? What are they? Magazines like *Fortune* and *Forbes* often publish articles on such companies. Ask the PR department for handouts. Establish a relationship with the PR personnel—they'll be glad to know you might be interested in writing about the CEO (chief executive officer) or new programs the company is implementing.

And, of course, establish your contacts with the house editor through well-constructed, well-targeted queries. If you live near the home office, arrange an interview. Take along your list of article ideas and/or a portfolio of your slides. If you don't connect the first time, ask what the editor will probably be needing in the next six to twelve months. Then get back to him in that time with on-the-mark suggestions.

There is a broad range of needs and of pay for material in these markets, as you'll discover in *Working Press of the Nation.* There are freelancers who regularly photocopy their articles on such topics as tax or safety tips and ship them out in bulk to these markets, receiving numerous checks of $15 to $30 for their trouble. Larger corporate publications, such as *Exxon USA, Marathon World,* and *American Youth,* publish full-length articles on a wide variety of subjects (sometimes with a company tie-in) and pay from $500 to $2,500 or more for especially difficult articles. Many of the editors of these publications are among the finest in the industry to work with. And there is another advantage to writing for them. The article you publish in their magazine reaches a large but very specific audience, thus leaving you free to reassemble and publish the material elsewhere if it is of general interest. If you are a top-notch photographer as well as writer, you will discover these publications pay well for pictures.

If editors will tell you what they want, why go through the time-consuming exercises I suggested? Because, in spite of writers' guidelines and seminars, I've found that editors don't always know *exactly* what they want. They are kept extremely busy trying to please the boss, trying to make next month's issue better than the last, trying to figure out what their readers will be wanting six months or a year down the road. They're keeping a steady eye on ad revenue, subscriptions, newsstand sales, and all the other vital signs of their publication's survival. On top of all that, they also have to worry about the amount of editorial space they have to fill each month. (What in God's name am I going to use to fill that hole? Writer X didn't meet the deadline, or We were going to run a story about The Pill and the new statistics from the FDA make us look like Chicken Little.) So editors don't always know exactly what they want—not until a sharp freelancer comes up with a terrific new idea. As a freelancer you are an involved, dynamic person. You, of necessity and genius, have your fingers in a number of pies. You're keeping up with many new trends and people. You're out in certain kinds of specialized worlds picking up nuggets of information and putting them together with others gathered elsewhere. You, if you're working hard at freelancing, are an absolute gold mine of ideas. That is precisely why editors need intelligent and hardworking freelancers.

The other reason for the exercises is that you *need* to know how to analyze magazine's needs so you can keep up with the changes, spot an editorial rearrangement or a shift of emphasis in editorial matter being published. To survive and prosper, magazines must change with the times.

One more point: Editors think ahead. On a Tuesday in January she may be worrying about June brides or July alfresco lunches. If you are submitting a suggestion for a Christmas story in November or December to a magazine with a three- to six-month lead time, you're wasting your postage. Length of lead time is one of the questions you'll want an editor to answer for you if the information doesn't appear on the writer's guideline sheet or in the publication's listing in *Writer's Market*. It simply takes some magazines longer to get the issue assembled, printed, and on the newsstands. (If you become involved with book publishing you'll discover, too, that some publishers need far more time than others to edit your manuscript, have galleys made and sent to reviewers, print the book, and have it nationally distributed.)

The only surefire way to find out what an editor wants is to give it to him. Don't query once and then stop after one rejection slip. Do your homework thoroughly. Hone your querying techniques to the sharpest possible point. Then query repeatedly with different ideas until you hit your target. No professional writer I know is exempt from this. Not all of their ideas or queries hit pay dirt the first time out. So query. Then query again. And again.

To recap: Editors want (or wish they had) what their competitors already have. They also want big names for bylines. They want what their readership surveys tell them their readers want. They'll tell you what they want, but you have to ask. You can discover some things they want by cleverly analyzing their magazines and reading the editor's pages as well as going to meet them. To make sales to them you must submit your suggestions at the proper time. And you must keep trying, over and over again, by repeated querying.

What kind of pay can you expect?

The range of payment is nearly as wide as the market itself. Nancy Edmonds Hanson's book title *How You Can Make $20,000 a Year Writing (No Matter Where You Live)* is for starters. Some professionals I know have years when their incomes dip below that. Many more make comfortably more—say $40,000 to $60,000. And the figures reel further upward with a bestseller or two. But I don't know anyone who is making those higher figures on magazine sales exclusively. They are putting together a business that includes all of the various avenues mentioned in Chapter 2. One year a writer's income may come from royalties from two books (written earlier, naturally), a teaching job, some magazine sales, and an advance on a projected book. Other years this same writer might be concentrating on raising magazine sales by pushing harder for spin-off sales from material already written. The story is as varied as each writer's life and business prowess allow.

Let me describe some typical figures. You can find many, many more in *Writer's Market* yourself. Starting at the top are publications such as *Reader's Digest, Playboy, Geo, Woman's Day,* and so forth, which pay $2,500 to $3,000 and more, on occasion, to writers whose work they know. Beginners who write very well on the right subject can, of course, crack *Reader's Digest* with a First Person feature, for which the current pay is $3,500 on acceptance. But competition is very tough. The market drops drastically from those figures, however, with professionals getting from $1,000 to $1,500 for full-length 2,000- to 3,000-word articles requiring heavy research.

Then there is another drop to the $750 market (*Chicago, Modern Medicine, Seventeen*, etc.), and a large group of periodicals seldom if ever pay over $500, if that. Below that are typical payments of $250, $350, and $400.

Payment depends, of course, on many factors: the length of the article, the importance of the subject to the editor, the amount of research and legwork involved, the writer's track record, and his negotiating skills. (See the section on negotiating in Chapter 10.)

The above figures may sound grand to you, but in reality many professionals consider themselves terribly underpaid. By today's standards that's true. Some magazines' payment rates haven't changed in years, even though their ad revenues have risen astronomically. Actually, at the start, you'll be happy to get even a small check for what you've written. But if you're putting together a business, you need to consider the time required to research and write your article or book. How long will that check cover your expenses? (Your hourly rates and other financial questions are discussed at more length in Chapter 10.)

Still, before you get your hopes too high in the beginning, see it from the editor's side. The pay may not be fancy, but it may be the best the editor can do. If you're just starting out, you need published clips of your work. So it's foolish to quibble about rates at that point. Take what the editor offers. Give him your best work, too; write, edit, and rewrite your piece. When you've provided the editor with a publishable and timely article and he's accepted, it is time enough to ask for more money your next go-around.

For newspaper sales you can expect anywhere from $10 to $35 for articles of around 500 to 1,000 words. Some of the larger ones pay more—up to $125. (But you can publish these many times and multiply that figure by five or ten or more. See the section on spin-offs in Chapter 9.)

You've figured out by now that you're not exactly going to get rich on magazine sales. That's why you'll have to consider the other markets—books, for one. And any of those in that long list mentioned earlier that appeal to you.

The money you can earn from publishing a book varies extremely. Most of the books published today earn the writer nothing more than the original advance. Depending on your writing ability, your book idea, the sample you've presented to an agent or publisher, and many other factors, you may find you're being offered anywhere from $1,500 to $15,000. Of course, the figures spiral upward for well-established writers. They also go lower. Some writers have accepted as little as $500 for an advance because they negotiated such a marvelous contract on a book that it eventually paid them many times more in royalties. Generally speaking, though, such minuscule amounts as that are in the minority, thank heavens.

About that advance: Although it may be considerably larger than several magazine sales, don't forget that writing a book is going to take a monumental effort. That advance must be stretched over a long period of time and many expenses. The most reliable income-producer, except for a blockbuster bestseller, is usually a text or similar book which is kept in print for a long period of time. If it becomes required reading for students or is adopted by school committees throughout the country, your sales naturally soar. Then your royalties continue to roll in long after the book is out of your typewriter and you're busy on other projects.

Now a word about the waiting game. After you send your manuscript or query, turn quickly to other matters (including more queries). Besides the time for delivery, the editor needs time to process your material. This varies considerably among periodicals and publishing houses. The average reporting time for magazines is three to six weeks. Some take longer, but they shouldn't. Book publishers require from two to three months, minimum. Horror stories abound about authors of book manuscripts waiting a year or more for a reply, but this is unusual. Literary agents and literary critics require three weeks to two months for a response.

It's difficult to rush the acceptance/rejection process. But if you've waited long enough, write a polite note to the editor to jog his memory. If you get no reply, write again. (For further tactics, see Chapter 10.) For dealing with book publishers regarding decisions on manuscripts, the process is the same. (Regarding pressuring them for payments, see Chapter 11.)

Quick routes and slow but steady paths

Theories on which path to success is best are legion. Which one a writer espouses usually depends on how he got his own start and/or how well it worked. In Chapter 1 I mentioned some typical but varied avenues.

There are others. Quick routes to the pinnacle include those noted below. The list isn't all-inclusive, nor open to just anyone.

1. Publish in at least six top markets within eighteen months, apply for membership in the ASJA, be accepted, meet regularly with New York-based editors, and peddle more books and articles.

2. Get a jazzy new idea for a book which will inevitably start a trend in publishing and convince an agent to raffle it to the highest-bidding publisher.

3. Take your idea to market yourself—publish and promote the hell out of your book and wind up with a bestseller on your hands.

Enterprising freelancers have done each of these. For the right writer at the right time with the right idea, there are no holds barred. So if you have the courage and the confidence in your work and you write well enough, take your pick. It just might work. Another quick route is to be lucky. You write the First Person story for the *Reader's Digest*. They purchase it. You quickly sell them four or five more articles. Suddenly you're in the *Reader's Digest* stable of writers with regular checks to prove it. (For *Reader's Digest* also read *Playboy, Cosmopolitan, The New Yorker,* etc.) Joan Mills was one of those who sold to the *Reader's Digest* right off the bat. William Styron, F. Scott Fitzgerald, Ernest Hemingway, J.D. Salinger, and Colleen McCullough are other authors who hit the jackpot early in their writing careers. Occasionally a writer living in a small Southern town will win a short story contest run by a magazine like *Redbook* or *Mademoiselle*. Before you know it she's got an entire book of short stories published and is on her way. It's true, as Shakespeare said, that fortune brings in some boats that are not steered.

But those who are more confident with someone at the tiller had best seek the slow but steady paths. Here are some ways to do just that.

You can write service articles. Author George Campbell wrote in *Writer's Digest* that he discovered the usefulness of the service article just as he was about to give up freelancing. Two years later, he says, "I'm working on assignment for magazines like *Seventeen, Kiwanis, Discovery,* and *Working Woman,* doing an article a week and feeding my hungry bank account with checks ranging from $50 to $400."

Campbell discovered what you'll find out with your thorough magazine analysis. Editors like service articles. Says Campbell, "Trying to decide exactly what *is* and what is *not* a service article can be like attempting to untie the Gordian knot. Basically, any article that will help a reader make a wise consumer decision, avoid a potential problem, or otherwise cope with our complex society, can be classed as a service article." That's pretty wide territory when you think about it. (Some examples: "Some Ways to Ease That IRS Bite"; "How and Where to Find the Finest Clothing, Jewelry, Appliances"; "New Ways to Save on Energy"; "Double the Life of Your Car"; "25 Plants That Thrive on Neglect.")

Or you might want to start out writing travel articles. These, as I've suggested, don't pay much individually when sold to newspapers. You have to make repeated sales to many outlets. In a sense what you're doing with those articles is self-syndicating your work (see Chapter 15).

Along with the short travel piece comes the short feature piece that can be sold to local and regional outlets (newspapers, city or state magazines, or regional magazines like Yankee, for instance). Dan Carlinsky is another prolific writer who is a past master at this. Nearly every other week I pick up my local Sunday magazine section and there's Dan, telling me about humorous new ways to look at the month of October or giving me a test to see if I'm really happily married. Consider also the trade, business, and religious magazines and ones in special markets, like Sail.

You can write fairly regularly for some syndicates by finding timely, newsworthy feature material in your area that has national or even international scope. And a more interesting approach to this is to leave your area. Anne Perryman, for example, put herself on the spot—she went to Southeast Asia very early in the Vietnam war days without any real idea of what she would do there. Soon she was writing timely, interesting features for newspapers back home. "There wasn't much of a trick to it," she says. "Editors were beginning to get very interested in the area so almost anything I turned up was bound to scratch a nerve somewhere. I just sent the material back to the States and it was published."

Alan Levy and Arky Gonzalez are prolific writers who, because they were working from Europe, were uncovering interesting feature material for U.S. audiences constantly. These writers self-syndicated their material by sending it simultaneously to multiple, non-competing markets. (For "non-competing" read newspapers in different geographical areas or magazines with entirely different readerships. For "multiple markets" read Sunday supplements, specialty magazines, etc.) They received duplicate payments for the same material.

Another writer described in Writer's Digest how he operates his own "wire service." He writes a story about an out-of-town tourist who is newsworthy, then calls the story in to the subject's hometown newspaper. They print it and send him a check. If he can, he also spins the brief news story into a follow-up feature for that same paper's Sunday supplement, and he occasionally sells to radio and television stations in the same area.

These and other paths you devise may seem slow at the beginning, but they can be quite steady when you get the knack of it. You have to be able to absorb your research information, organize your notes quickly, and churn out the gilded words and telling anecdotes as fast as your typewriter will allow you. You have to be timely with your queries and keep them going out constantly. But then, the more your material is seen by editors the faster the odds improve that you'll publish and publish and publish.

Alternatives to consider

A report from the *Washington Post:*

> The handwritten notes in the margin of the legal brief were brutally direct. "You have to make your point more clearly," one comment said. "What does this mean?" another asked. A third began with "Awful."
>
> They were scrawled by an aspiring actress and film director who holds one of the most unusual legal jobs in the country— full-time editor for a California law firm, charged with trans-forming the incomprehensible jargon that most lawyers love into understandable English.
>
> She reads every piece of paper that goes out of her firm, every brief, every legal argument—even "the littlest letter" that leaves the office.
>
> In addition to editing legal documents, she tries to package them attractively. She leaves plenty of white space on every page so they do not look crowded and are easier to read. She believes such clear writing and attractive packaging wins cases for her firm.

Now, there's an idea for you. And you don't even have to be working for the largest law firm in your state or even full-time. Think of the satisfaction, straightening out all that legal jargon, getting paid for it, and being able to tell lawyers a thing or two!

How do you get such a job? The way you do any of those hidden in your locale: ask. Speak to lawyers you know to see if they know anyone who would be interested. Be prepared, when you do, however, to have a portfolio of clips and other writing samples, and a solid résumé.

Let's say you're a budding playwright. Local and community theaters seem naturals to try for starters. But what about the social agencies that put on programs for special groups—children's puppet theaters, shows in prison, youth organizations, entertainment for senior citizens? Often schools, colleges, and universities will consider original drama. Brief skits can be sold to radio stations and educational television outlets as well. Many aspiring playwrights are discouraged too quickly from dramatic writing because they've set their sights too soon on the Great White Way.

Breaking into national television or film nearly always requires either living close to Hollywood or having a gung ho agent who does. As a beginning freelancer you might as well forget that angle, unless you like living out on a slim and creaky limb. If that's the way you want to go, however, by all means familiarize yourself with the technical terms and forms. A trip to a bookstore or library will provide you with several good volumes specifically designed to help you. (See the Resources chapter for some titles.) True, material is purchased that is not written specifically for television (rights from magazine articles, nonfiction books, novels), but that material is almost always being handled by an agent who can sell the writer's talents and is familiar with the television market's specific needs and demands.

Why is living in or near Hollywood such a necessity? Most experts agree that producers essentially want to buy writers, then assign stories to them, and not the other way around.

Two other tips, if this is the path you're determined to follow: Be well bankrolled so you can cover long periods without income. (Your expenses, you'll recall, continue in spite of that little detail.) And as quickly as you can, connect with a small, local film producer to learn as many of the tricks of the trade as he can teach you. You'll be a quantum leap ahead when you are ready to start submitting scripts to big-time producers. (To find a local film producer, check with colleges and universities where film writing and production are taught. To find those radio and television outlets, see if your region has the equivalent of the *New England Media Guide*.)

Could science, medical, or business writers in your area use your talents? You might suggest that you could string for them, turning up information they haven't access to or time to gather. You might be helpful during interviews with scientists (while they're conducting the actual interview, you could talk with the secretary or make notes about the lab), or doing research further afield than they are able to. This and other foot-in-the-door approaches to your freelance business are not, by the way, just for beginners. The apprenticeship method of learning new techniques is a valuable one throughout your freelance life. It may not put dollars in your bank account immediately, but it pays off in experience and contacts.

One writer I know seems to spend half of his working time at conferences and association meetings. He takes careful notes, often tape-records informative sessions. He then condenses and refines the information and offers it through a newsletter to corporate executives who have an interest in that particular subject. This writer's pitch is that he digests the information and presents the busy executive with only what's pertinent to him. Many such meetings are tape-recorded now, and, for a price, you can get the entire meeting or meetings, mumbles and fumbles included. But most people don't want or need that much.

This writer also thinks of ways to spin off the material into articles for trade publications. He's sort of a one-man band, a news-and-idea-gathering source for CEOs, public information officers, and employee-relations personnel. He figures that such people can't possibly attend all the meetings that would interest them. He has a warehouseful of sources they haven't. He's turned his freelance operation into a thriving business by not thinking in traditional terms.

"As a writer I figure I'm sort of a creative machine," he says. "Ideas are my business, and ideas being what they are, their impact stretches out in ripples, overlapping unusual waves many people just don't think about. I do that thinking for them. The way I see it, my total operation is a very efficient idea factory. That's what they pay me for."

You might also try selling to the college, school, and university market. They put out periodicals, newspapers, yearbooks, newsletters, alumni magazines, fund-raising and development-office material, and admissions flyers, among other things. Find out which are staff- and student-written and which might be open to outside help. Many of those staffs are small. You might be able to find a freelance assignment with them, putting information together for in-house or outside consumption. If you can, get on their mailing list for news releases. Once you let the staff know you're around, they'll be glad to pass on information to you that you might be able to place in the general market. Speak to the faculty and professors doing research. They can be great sources of leads for stories.

Other alternatives that freelancers have devised include helping a meeting planner develop a conference and handle the publicity; using a knowledge of the history of a city to produce slogans and brochures for the Chamber of Commerce, bumper stickers for the Lions Club, and a series of posters for the tourism bureau; a family history made to order, with photographs; and mail-order book sales (see Chapter 10).

Creative thinking builds business

In any business with foresight, creativity is highly valued, because it helps diminish losses and increases profits. Major corporations conduct creativity-stimulation programs for their research employees, and universities offer creative problem-solving courses.

Since you're in business yourself as a freelancer, you'll want to be exercising every creative "muscle" you have, not just to write creatively but to operate your business that way. Actually, it doesn't become more difficult but far easier. If you practice thinking like this as you go along, pretty soon it becomes second nature. Primarily because it's just plain fun. The puzzles we freelancers have to unravel each week are what most of us thrive on or we wouldn't be writing.

According to *Folio* magazine, James B. Kobak is a living example of someone who put the study of the publishing world to work for him. Trained as an accountant, he has become a much-sought-after consultant. He's the current "high priest and family doctor" of the sometimes disabled mass-communications industry. He's left his mark on hundreds of magazines, radio and TV stations, and publishing houses. And he's a writer in his special field. While a student at Harvard, however, he worked for the *Boston Herald Traveler* as a "paid-by-the-line" reporter. He persuaded the paper to publish the list of graduates from Harvard in 1942. The payment for each line was not overwhelming, but then the list of names was long. He pocketed $400 for the job. That's when he decided there was money to be earned in the communications business. The vast *Playboy* empire is just one of the businesses Kobak has since reorganized for increased profits.

With courage and a brighter idea than the next fellow you can move forward rapidly in freelancing. The point is, never accept an apparently closed door for what it seems to be. Move in closer, push it a little and you may discover it was simply an optical illusion—the entrance to freelance riches is wide open.

Chapter 4
Space, Tools, and Equipment

■■■■■■■■■■■■■■■■■■■■■■■■■■■■■■■■■■■■■■■

A room of one's own

Most freelancers start out with a modest investment in equipment and material. Some of the most successful novelists describe their start-up as a "me and my typewriter" operation. Often as not, those hardy souls holed up in dark hotel rooms in Paris or London with nothing more than their inspiration to keep them warm.

That romantic approach is fine *if* you can make it work. But the freelancer starting out today will be better equipped to face the competition by taking a more practical approach. Certainly this holds true for the writer preparing to work in the multifarious world of nonfiction.

Start, if you possibly can, with your own office, no matter how small it might be—a space entirely yours (preferably with a lock on the door), a space satisfactory to your creative needs, available to you at any and all times.

I don't mean to suggest that it's impossible to freelance without an office, but it's harder. I've freelanced for years, and I've worked under nearly every conceivable condition, including that dingy Paris hotel room. But when I managed to set up an in-house office all my own, my productivity *and* assignments increased manyfold. All of the most productive writers I've ever known have had at least one office reserved for their days and nights of creativity. (I say at least one because once writers have considerable assignments coming in, they often feel the need for more space. Ray Bradbury is but one of the many who have two offices. Bradbury doesn't drive. So while waiting for the cab to take him to his official office, he squirrels away in his basement hideaway to write, not wanting to waste a minute.)

Once you realize you need a special place, the question is where? The choice of an office in your home versus somewhere outside is up to you. Some writers borrow an office for a month or two to feel out the possibilities of working in a corner of a loft or in a building downtown. This technique is helpful if you need to examine more closely your specific creative needs. Some people need more creature comforts to work effectively than others. The following are some thoughts to help you balance the scales on the two kinds of office space: in the home and outside it.

The home office allows more flexibility. You don't have to worry about commuting. You'll be able to laugh off bad weather. When you're not feeling up to par, you can pick away at those necessary office chores—billing, letter writing, filing—while still obeying the doctor's orders to "take it easy." Then, too, if you're working at home you may be less prone to catching those nasty bugs in the first place. You can keep up with the news by radio or television if you want. (This morning, for instance, I taped a television interview that was necessary for one of my projects while I continued to work at my desk.) You'll find you need a less extensive business wardrobe. And there's less wear and tear on your car or transportation budget.

Of course, there are drawbacks at home as well. You'll discover you have to counteract interruptions of all kinds—charity seekers, itinerant salesmen, proselytizers. The opportunities to procrastinate will multiply. You may never have had an interest in washing the car or cleaning the basement, but when you're faced with writer's block the necessity of completing those chores will seem urgent.

Then, too, people question the stay-at-home writer. They conveniently forget the hours you've asked not to be interrupted. When you try to hire part-time help you may discover that temporary agencies are reluctant to send employees to a home office, no matter how fancy or separated from the living quarters it might be. That problem falls under the heading of convincing the business community yours is a legitimate business. It shows up again when you're applying for credit with suppliers or subcontractors of all sorts. And in particular it rears its ugly head when you're settling accounts with the IRS (see Chapter 13).

The office outside the home has its cons and pros, too. First, the rent and utilities bill come due every month, whether your income is regular or not. Freelancers in an outside office have the cost and inconvenience of commuting. When they're at the office the material they need is back at home, and vice versa. They may spend more time and money lunching out than is necessary. They may attend more meetings than they need or enjoy. And the distractions of friends or nearby office workers may eat away at their precious hours of creativity.

On the positive side, however, an outside office can be a real boon. That rent due next week spurs you to increase your productivity. If you've been fudging on some chore out of lack of confidence, you may find it easier to grapple with just knowing the wolf (i.e., the landlord) is at the door. Some writers feel that going to an office the same time each day is a way of putting on proper work habits rather like a uniform. James Joseph declares in *A Treasury of Tips for Writers,* "Nothing spurs a writer to writing more than does an office. When he leaves his house he is on his way 'to work.' When he arrives at the office, he is 'at work.' The demarcation is clean and clear. Plain or fancy, an office for the professional writer is a place of work—writing." (The office Joseph describes is a fancy one—a four-room suite in a business neighborhood in Los Angeles—but then Joseph has been a highly paid, very productive freelancer for a long time.)

Not only does an outside office allow the freelancer to take his work seriously, it reminds others to do so. Another writer told me, "I get out and around in the business community, and it keeps me on the ball. I see the entire scenario each day. It gives me the perspective I need to speak directly to a client's needs."

Many writers who pay rent for offices outside their homes make the additional point that the out-of-the-house office precludes the depression caused by being too cloistered that stay-at-home writers know so well.

Once you've analyzed your own needs and your financial situation scrupulously, make your choice and get to work. The opportunity to change your arrangements will always be there. That's another advantage of the freelance life.

The start-up kit

The variations on this theme are amazing. What one writer finds essential will be utterly superfluous to another. Yet I've never failed to learn a new trick whenever I was allowed into another working writer's office. So stay alert to alternative solutions to your changing physical requirements.

The most obvious requirement is a sturdy table or desk (or both) on which to lay out the current project. Some writers feel the bigger this work surface is the better, because no matter how hard they try to maintain order, in the heat of creation the thing will inevitably become cluttered. I've tried many variations myself and find I work best at a regular office desk with drawers to hold the most immediate needs such as stationery, pencils and pens, paper clips, labels, etc. One drawer is actually a deep file, which I've found very convenient. It holds my tickler file with all the most current information I need for a month's projects. A couple of large tables are adjacent to the desk. Bulletin boards and plastic holders for "hot" files extend two feet above the entire table/desk area on two sides of the room. The "hot" files on the wall are exceedingly helpful, since they keep material I must check daily before my eyes but off the desk top. Above all this are bookshelves—my own reference library (including the telephone books of cities I call most frequently). Directly over the typing area is a space reserved for the pages of any current writing project.

The next essential in a writer's office is a good, durable typewriter. Although some diehards cling to their trusty old manuals and still succeed as writers, they are a small group, and their numbers are getting smaller every day. Most writers I've been in contact with who are full-time freelancers have discovered they are better off purchasing the best electric typewriter they can afford. Many have more than one, with different projects going in each.

Electrics allow you to turn out more words per minute and far better looking copy. Editors and other clients have become used to the marvels of the electronic age. If you're just starting out, remember, you'll be bucking competition that already swears by their expensive equipment with its sophisticated correcting features.

You don't have to have a *fancy* electric typewriter, though. Find something within your budget and one that you feel comfortable with. You'll want a model that doesn't need servicing constantly. And you should consider the advantages of a service contract compared to expensive one-time service calls, especially if you've purchased a rebuilt, secondhand machine.

The next two items on your shopping list—a back-supporting chair and good lighting—you shouldn't pinch pennies about either. Since you'll be spending a great deal of time at your typewriter, an adjustable stenographer's chair, with firm back support, that keeps your feet planted firmly on the floor is a must. The lighting you choose will naturally depend on the amount of natural light available to your desk area. Most doctors agree that flourescent light is less desirable for long periods than incandescent light. Goldsmith Brothers, an office-supply firm in New York, has a free mail-order catalog as do numerous other businesses around the country. For more information on office furnishings—what to look for and what to avoid—look into *By Design*, by Jon Goodchild and Bill Henkin. Although slanted toward the graphic artist, it has many useful tips for freelancers. Be sure to ask questions of the dealers with whom you discuss possible purchases.

Be sure, as you shop around to get the best price (new or used doesn't matter), that your bargains are real ones. You'll be spending a great deal of time with this equipment. Not only your business but your health will depend on its quality. If you have reservations about purchasing any of these pieces, you might want to consider leasing them first.

Your telephone is another essential. Although I've known beginners who thought they could get by without one, I've yet to see anyone make a go of his business lacking such a crucial tool. The telephone is your arm out to your clients. At the outset of your business, particularly, you'll spend a great deal of time on the phone.

There are merits to converting your phone at home, if your office is there, to a business one. The monthly rate for a business phone is higher, but by eliminating the home phone instead of adding a second line you'll save money. The main reason for doing this would be to get a Yellow Pages listing. I've never found it necessary, but you might. If you've opted for that office away from home, you'll definitely have to add the cost of a business phone there. The telephone company offers many special services that you should investigate: call waiting, call forwarding, etc. But be certain to read the fine print and ask questions, because the added costs for these services are not always as clear as they might be. Purchasing the phone instruments elsewhere and just renting the service from the phone company is an added plus, but as with any long-term purchase, it will take some time to earn back the money invested. (See Resources for more telephone information.)

Your next investment will be at least one sturdy office file. Actually, for most writers, these items multiply nearly as fast as the books in their libraries. You can do without one for a short time, but I don't recommend it. Files can be purchased at discounts, secondhand, or by mail order. Keep in mind that your entire inventory of ideas, clippings, correspondence, and manuscripts is going to be stored in your file. Buy a good one that is meant for rugged use. If you get it at the beginning and start your filing system out right (see Chapter 6), you'll be money ahead and save yourself stressful moments hunting around for that important document.

Setting up a basic reference library needn't be expensive. Many of the almanacs, dictionaries, directories, and word finders can be purchased in paperback. To fill gaps in your basic library, keep on the lookout at flea markets, the Salvation Army, and secondhand-book stores near college campuses. Scan the catalogs of mail-order distributors, such as Publishers Central Bureau (1 Champion Ave., Avenel NJ 07131), for publishers' closeouts at hefty savings.

There are two other items I've found to be absolute essentials to a businesslike approach and a high output: a Rolodex card file and a telephone-answering system (either a service or a machine, depending upon your preference). Set up properly at the beginning of the freelance venture, the Rolodex, like the file cabinets I mentioned above, saves time, energy, and temper when you need to call a client, a member of your network, or a supplier. Whatever system you use should supply information to you quickly and easily.

I lived without an answering system for a while, thinking that because my office was in my home and there was almost always someone there, I didn't need one. I was wrong. The machine never makes mistakes and never forgets. The only problem—and it's an easy one to overcome—is forgetting to turn it on when you leave the office. A notice on the office door will remind you to push the button before you leave. Some of these machines have features which allow you to tape telephone interviews or dictate information onto tapes. Some let you listen to a caller before you decide to answer the phone. The value of such features depends on your needs, but consider all the options before you buy.

The next item you'll need is an accounting ledger (see Chapter 13). The rest of the supporting elements of your business have already been listed in Chapter 2, where you were figuring possible start-up costs. But I'll mention them here in the order in which they become necessary in the normal freelance business.

The tape recorder (or recorders) is an item that most freelancers find not only handy but essential in a variety of situations (see Chapter 7). A recorder is a helpful tool in a library if you want to note information quickly, and driving between interviews you can record your own thoughts and observations while they're still fresh in your mind. And you can use a recorder to monitor a segment of a television show or for dictating parts of a project to ship back home to a typist while you're away on assignment.

The drawbacks are there, too. Even the best tape recorders tend to go on the blink when you most need them. (For that reason I *always* take notes at the same time I'm tape-recording an interview, either in person or on the telephone.) Or you can accidentally erase important material. (Who can forget the eighteen-minute "accident" in the White House tapes?)

But after you consider all the arguments against tape recorders, remember that even the best scrawl or note can become nearly illegible once it's grown cold. Few American writers have the benefit of shorthand techniques. Even the best-trained memories are occasionally faulty. Most people who are nervous about recorders at the beginning of an interview eventually relax and forget they're on. I recommend using tape recorders, especially for the beginning writer who needs to be able to carefully verify quotes to establish his reliability with editors.

Those of you who want to add photography to your writing skills should consider the purchase of camera equipment at this point (see Chapter 9).

The next two pieces of equipment freelancers find true assets are a copying machine and a calculator. Depending on the amount of business you're doing, you will want to look into either purchasing or leasing the first. Once you've reached a reasonable, steady assignment rate and can estimate the yearly cost of sending manuscripts out to be photoduplicated, compare that figure to the cost of your own copying machine. Your accountant can help you figure the advantages (such as depreciation at tax time). The second, a calculator, is relatively inexpensive and should probably be included in your start-up even if you're a whiz at math. Those ledgers should be correctly balanced every month.

A last thought about basics: One cold winter I was under pressure to complete a particularly difficult assignment and needed space and a chance to concentrate totally. I decided to borrow a spare office from a friend just for this one project. It turned out to be the smartest move I could have made. This office was plush, the furnishings more than adequate, the view of the river splendid night and day. There was even an oriental rug on the polished floor. But, best of all, the room had a charming colonial fireplace, in which I kept a small fire going. That fire cheered me through the completion of the job during one of the worst winters I can remember.

Although you may not be able to outfit your office at this level of luxury, there are some affordable creature comforts you should be able to count on—an overstuffed reading chair, a favorite painting or photograph, a bright rug at your feet. The point is, there is *no* point in making your office so barren that you are subconsciously repelled by it. If you do that, you may find yourself running away from the office when you should be sticking to an annoying but necessary task.

Supplies

The most important and expensive supplies, at least at the beginning, will be your letterhead and related stationery with your logo or business address on it. These will carry your business image to the larger business community, so consider carefully how professional they look. They need not be embossed or grandly baroque. In fact, they shouldn't be. But you'll be off to a good start if you have a professional design them and help you with the choice of paper.

Once you have your letterhead, labels, and business cards printed, use them to get competitive bids from a variety of office-supply merchants. If you've had that business phone installed and are now listed in the Yellow Pages, or if your new company got a two-line write-up in the local paper or the advertising community's newsletter, you'll be receiving calls from suppliers attempting to snare your business. Ask them what sort of discount they'll allow you on bulk orders and what their credit terms are. Also check the possibility of ordering your supplies from mail-order companies such as those mentioned in the Resources chapter. You can save a sizable amount on your yearly supplies by such maneuvers. Be sure also to plan ahead and estimate carefully on such items as staples, paper clips, typewriter ribbons, calculator rolls, pens, pencils, index cards, various kinds of paper, and filing paraphernalia. Purchased piecemeal, these may seem relatively small items in your budget, but they mount up over a year's time.

"I purchase supplies in bulk but I also keep a small account open in a local office-supply store for emergency purchases," a writer told me. "I discovered establishing credit in one's own home territory helps to immediately verify one's business as legitimate." Another writer found that bulk purchase of rolls of stamps and the use of a postage meter saved her lots of time and money. "I hate to stand in line at the post office, so I've even scouted the best one in my area and the best times to go so I won't have to wait long. I purchase postage with my business check and thus have a receipt for my records. Even if my stamp purchase is small and I've paid cash, I always ask for an official receipt." A smart idea, since for most beginning freelancers postage is a large chunk of the monthly budget.

Supplies become a problem when you're away from your office, whether you're doing extended research in a library, off for a day of several interviews, or out of town on assignment. One writer told me she keeps a "travel desk" always ready to slip into her briefcase. She travels a good deal, so now she's developed a second "desk" that stays in the trunk of her car. The first one is simply a plastic insert with a zipper. In it she keeps the essential supplies she may need: stationery, envelopes, prepaid postcards, stamps, a Clip-it, a small business card file, 3x5 cards, paper clips, a tiny stapler, and rubber bands. The larger travel desk is a plastic file with a handle that holds a few file folders, scissors, a small flashlight and batteries (for reading maps and finding her way in darkened motels), tapes for her tape recorder, extra batteries, an extension cord, cellophane tape, glue stick, and felt markers. "I'm always ready to take off for research work or an assignment," she says. "I don't lose valuable time in a strange city hunting for the things I need."

Build in overhead control and room for expansion

In order to set up a system that allows you to control overhead, observe how other businesses do it. They keep careful records of expenditures on every item and review the figures regularly. They keep an eye out for bargains and buy in bulk at discount. They utilize credit. They set goals for their budgets and keep to them. They update equipment when they can afford to.

You'll want to measure your success against the cost to see where you could cut corners and still maintain the needed writing routine. Let me give you an example. For a long time I was certain that I wrote best when I used a sheet of carbon and a second sheet behind the white bond. Somehow the procedure worked subconsciously to command me to "type a perfect copy." I believe I worked harder to write well with this setup. It took me a long time to change my habit and still get the same results. But until I did, the paper wasted this way mounted up. I finally started using the copying machine instead of carbon, and I've saved money in the long run.

How you handle the basic materials of your trade is a matter too important to ignore. However the thought process may begin, the writer soon finds himself composing and refining his thoughts on paper. Some writers start in longhand. Others go directly to a typewriter and compose. In the early stages you won't know which methods will serve you best. But keep an eye on yourself as you continue, learning by self-observation how you use paper (and other materials) to produce the best final manuscript you can. By trial and error you will come to the routine that produces your best work with a minimum of wasted time. If this requires an *apparent* waste of paper or roundabout approach, that doesn't matter. What counts is the excellence of the result. Eventually, too, you will learn to refine and rid yourself of the seeming wastefulness of matériel *after* you have refined your writing.

Just as you recycle story ideas to additional markets, so you should learn to use and reuse other pieces of your matériel: using the backs of PR handouts for filing notes or carbon copies, applying new labels to old folders and envelopes, etc. For the final copy that will be sent out to a client, you don't want to stint. Good (but not fancy) twenty-pound bond paper and clean new envelopes are what you'll use. But the materials that will stay in your files needn't be so pristine.

You'll be dollars ahead if you study religiously every tip that comes your way regarding items you can get for less or, better still, for free. For instance, professional writers can receive the *Reader's Digest Index* gratis every year just by sending in a request. The same holds true for free tearsheets from magazines, which will save you having to buy an entire copy when you don't need it. Many more items that won't cost your business a cent will turn up throughout your research into your own community. But you must take the time and trouble to search them out.

Look at each item on your budget and examine alternatives. Can you use another service, such as United Parcel, in place of the U.S. Mail and save money? Bus lines often carry packages between cities for less. Consider the many ways you can accomplish your research and compare prices. Don't stick to one method just because you're most familiar with it. It may be costing you more than you realize.

One writer I know was stymied by how to conduct a long series of interviews for a book when the interviewees were scattered all over the country and she had not received a large travel allowance. She suddenly remembered a public relations firm that had wanted her to drive a camper for a couple of weeks and write about it. Originally she had turned them down, but now she called them and arranged for the free camper for a month. With a kindly helper to split the driving, she managed to cover the territory and write on the road. She saved both time and money in the process. And the company promoting the camper got several stories in print in exchange for the loan.

Of course, another alternative would have been to conduct the interviews by telephone. This is also costly. One way to hold these expenses down is with a telephone log book. This provides a daily record of the outgoing calls, so you can see at a glance more or less what next month's phone bill is going to be. If your budget is tight one month, be more meticulous about which client is called and which one gets a letter or postcard. It's far too easy for the writer caught up in the excitement of an assignment to forget how those calls add up. Speaking of postcards, in many cases they are just as efficient as a first-class letter, and they cost less. (When you use them, though, you may find it a good trick to make a brief note on the letter you're responding to before you file it. Just note the date you answered and some reference to the kind of response you made. For example: "7/6/81—can't attend; will call next month." Then your record is complete.)

In addition to saving to control overhead, there's also selling to control it. Here you might want to use your writers' club or professional organization's newsletter to alert potential customers to what you have for sale. Let's say you've saved a lot of back issues of a journal but no longer want them. Either sell or exchange them for something of value to you, generating small amounts of income that can keep your overhead down. The same holds true, naturally, for outdated equipment. (See the last section of this chapter.)

In this regard I must say I'm fondest of the story told by the indomitable Tom Mahoney. He needed information on a company for a magazine article. He bought stock in the company so he could attend a few stockholders' meetings and ask questions. Then "when a struggle for control developed, I sold my ten shares at a profit of $300," says Tom.

If there's one thing you can count on in this business, it's expansion. Your clippings multiply. Your completed manuscripts, as well as all the false starts, multiply. Your files, books, bookshelves, correspondence, rejection slips, and, I hope, acceptances, all multiply at a rate that may alarm you. Be prepared. I promise you, if you buy two office files instead of one at the outset, that second one won't be empty for long.

Better to control the mass of paper and other matériel early, then. Outline your storage needs as you do your start-up costs. Consider immediate needs, but also look six months and a year down the road. Don't make the mistake of underestimating your business too drastically. If you're any good and have any luck, the demands on your space and equipment will be heavy.

You probably won't believe me until you're in the middle of such a situation. For a while you'll just be getting by, then suddenly you'll have two, three, four or more assignments at once. You'll not only have to be prepared psychologically to handle a number of jobs more or less at the same time, but your physical surroundings will need to help, not hinder, you.

While you don't want to make the mistake of getting heavily in debt for equipment you won't need for five years, you would do well to look occasionally at brochures that describe new equipment. You won't be buying yet, but by the time you are ready to you'll know more about which product you may want. The same goes, too, for what others in your business community are purchasing. Occasionally ask about the merits and faults of new equipment you see in a client's office or another writer's den. Make a note of it and keep all your jottings together in a "future" file. This holds true for all kinds of office tools and equipment, from home computers to word processors, from the simplest new gadget at the art-supply store to IBM's latest electric typing wonder. You simply won't know what's out there that can help you save both time and money unless you look around.

Expansion doesn't always mean buying new, though. Look for bargains in secondhand sources. Remember, too, the possibility of borrowing or leasing for a specific temporary project.

Office sharing and time sharing

Covering the costs of a freelance operation may be easier for you if you band together with others. This is worth trying if your start-up is particularly modest. Let's say you've decided you simply cannot work at home, but you can't find a suitable office space within your budget's limitations. In this case, look for an even larger space that can be subdivided easily. When you spot one, start looking for office mates. You can share office space, some equipment, the telephone, even a secretary-typist. Writers grouping together might even consider adding a word processor or a part-time researcher. Two or three writers in one area might want to find a freelance photographer to work with them on a continuing basis. (If having another writer in the office isn't practical, consider sharing with other creative people, like photographers, artists, designers, craftsmen, etc.)

Whatever you do, consult a lawyer and have a simple contract drawn up among participants that spells out all the details of use of space, time sharing, office chores, payment of bills, and so forth. Be sure you have a dissolution clause in the contract, as well as a stipulation about the manner in which any changes in the contract must be made.

Authors more often collaborate in the writing or researching aspects of their business (see Chapter 12), but there's no reason they can't collaborate in this manner. They can conceivably save money on office overhead, add benefits, such as a secretary-typist, they couldn't otherwise afford, and have the companionship of other writers to help them fight writer's block or the blues when they need it. This sort of grouping together, in one way or another, is probably at the heart of the numerous writers' organizations and publishing efforts back through recorded history. You can start out in your own area putting the theory that two heads are better than one to your own good use.

Update when you can

Automated equipment and other changes in the wind will revolutionize many segments of the freelancer's business, whether or not he's prepared. Anything he can do to improve his own setup and still remain cost-conscious will ultimately increase his income. The tape recorder is one example. When recorders first appeared on the market, they weren't exactly grabbed up by writers as an essential tool. But now even the hard-nosed reporters who rely on notepad and pencil for the short interview are turning to recorders for longer sessions with interviewees, for dictating notes while on the job, or for dictating first drafts of long articles or chapters of books.

For that last chore, by the way, I've found an office dictating machine to be far superior. Typists who transcribe material from it also claim it makes their work easier and faster. (With the dictating machine there are ways to indicate that the typist should prepare for a change coming a few sentences ahead. If you're dictating letters or a series of graphs you can mark where the breaks are, and the typist can see at a glance how long each section is. Some machines use a mailable disc, too, in case you need to ship it elsewhere.)

While many writers aren't using this kind of equipment (mainly because they are still not quite ready to employ a typist, either because of temperament or finances), I strongly believe this is a machine most of them should add to their arsenal of mechanical helpers. It does take some getting used to, however. Seeing a word is quite a different process from speaking or hearing it. When you're accustomed to creating one way, as I mentioned earlier, some prodding of your creative talents will be required to shift to another form.

Robin Perry is a writer/photographer who managed to modernize some of his methods, and he's never regretted it. I visited Robin's office and must say I was impressed. On the wall were sheets of paper approximately five or six feet in length—an entire book-length manuscript in the process of being revised. At his desk Robin had, instead of a typewriter, a word processor. He'd devised a rack that fed large rolls of white paper into it. As he typed on the keyboard he received his printout on the roll of paper and on a memory disc as well.

"I thought word processing was a phrase used by large corporations and nothing I, as a small businessman, would ever use," Robin told me. "It turned out I couldn't have been more wrong. I was aware of automatic typewriters for years and watched them turn out typed letters. Then a sales representative from a word processor company called on me and suggested I try one. I was impressed with the demonstration, but I couldn't see why a one-man business should spend $4,500 for this kind of aid. He let me play with his demonstrator for a few days. When he returned, there was *no way* I would let the machine out of my sight. My word processor has been going every day since I bought it. I don't think I could function without it any more than I could without my typewriter."

He's right—it *is* going all the time. The marvelous thing about it is he doesn't have to be there hitting the keys. Of course he sits at the keyboard to put the original words, as well as all of the revisions, on the paper and disc. But if he needs a section or the entire work typed up after his input, he can push the right buttons and go off to dinner. When he comes back he has a fresh, perfectly typed and spaced manuscript waiting.

Other writers have reported they've installed word processors and would never go back to the typewriter. The range of word processors and their costs is varied. And some writers, having tried the machines, have rejected them, declaring they inhibited their creative juices. It's obviously not yet time for *all* writers to turn in their typewriters, at least not until prices come down and the machines become more uniformly usable. Still, they may be the wave of the future, as Robin and others proclaim. They would seem to me to be just one more item to thoroughly research and mark for possible consideration in your "future" file.

As for myself, although I haven't moved up to a word processor, I did take away one idea from Robin's office and put it right to use: that ingenious continuous-feed system. A former art student supplied the rolls of paper. Now I too can type an entire chapter on one long sheet and pin it up where I can read it easily to revise and edit.

One more note. When you are considering updating your equipment, get several bids on your older equipment at the same time. Some suppliers will take your equipment as trade-in and allow you a better price; others will not. But, when a merchant wants your business and knows you're shopping around for the best bid, you're in a better position to bargain. If a trade-in isn't in the cards, look around for bulletin boards in shops, photographer's labs, or nearby colleges and schools, where you can post notice of your equipment for sale or exchange. As another resort, you can, of course, donate outmoded equipment to a nonprofit organization and take a deduction for its current market value from your income taxes. When you give the equipment away, be certain to get a receipt from the organization with all of the pertinent information on it, though.

While a freelancer is a writer first and a business person second, how he sets his office and tools up is of vital importance to his productive capacity in the long run. You need not pour months of your time into the project, but if you do it with care, applying the tips suggested in this chapter, you'll be able to move forward more nimbly into the work before you.

Chapter 5
Getting Yourself on Your Side

■■

Staying competitive

In Chapter 2 you mapped the plan (with the prime ingredients—yourself and your aims—up front) for the start of your small new business—the bare essentials you needed to consider before making the big leap. That was fine to get you going; it's not enough, however, if you are bent on profit. Whether you'd just like to sell your work steadily to quality markets without too much hassle or whether you like the idea of making enough money to be annually invited to test-drive the latest Rolls-Royce, you must look to profits. If you don't concentrate on having a surplus at the end of your year, you will in actuality fall behind. Profit requires knowing how to compete with the professionals so you may join their ranks.

The basics of getting and staying competitive are:

- Discipline in the craft of writing
- Financial reserve
- Well-managed energy and time
- An organizational plan with established priorities
- Business acumen
- Techniques for problem solving
- Ability to take calculated risks
- Expansion plan

Confidence building blocks

All the above depends on confidence. Whatever kind of writing you do, you probably won't feel supremely confident all the time. Some days you'll be up, ready to take on anything. Other times you'll wake not willing to drag yourself through the day, let alone out on a risky limb. Chances are, especially when you're just beginning to freelance, you'll have moments when the mean spirits whisper you were a fool to let a good, solid, boring job get away from you.

What you need—whether you're a beginner or an experienced freelancer—are steadying influences. Think of them as confidence building blocks, and don't be remiss in laying them down as foundations for a long career.

In the very earliest phases of your career, when you've had no more than a letter to an editor in print and you know you need help with the craft of writing, you can build confidence from writing courses. The feedback you'll get from your instructor or other students can be a strong buttress to your ego. You already have readers, when your work is being discussed (and praised, perhaps) in class.

Conferences and colonies

Writers' conferences and seminars on all aspects of writing and marketing writing abound. Some are well worth the money and time spent on them. Others, frankly, are duds. Matching yourself and your own business needs to the right one in the right place takes planning, plenty of research (especially if you're working more or less alone and aren't in touch with other working writers), and money. Trial and error is required here, too. What was a superb conference one year may slip down to another rung a few years later, depending on the way it is managed, the kind of publicity it receives, the level of faculty expertise, and the state of the economy. Some very popular conferences I've attended over the years turned out, in the long run, to hold lots of promise for the few and less for the masses. You'll certainly hear lots of "insider gossip" about publishing. But you should get more than that for your money.

If you're considering a conference coming up in your area, ask yourself some questions about it first. Can you tell from the flyer who the primary audience is? Is this a conference for all writers—poets and novelists as well as nonfiction writers? Is it aimed at college students exclusively? Who will be the speakers? Do you recognize the titles of their work? Do you know if they'll be criticizing work at the conference? One-day or weekend conferences seldom offer this service; there simply isn't time. Week-long or month-long conferences, with sizable fees for room, board, and meetings, usually do. Will publishers and agents also be present? What are the accommodations? Will you have a chance to mingle casually with the experts? Try to find someone who has attended the conference in the past and question him as thoroughly as possible about its good and bad qualities. (For some listings on conferences, see the Resources chapter.)

Writers' colonies, too, have their merits, especially if you've come to a point in your career when what you need most is to complete a long project with time off from the hectic realities surrounding your home base. For some writers, these communities of writers in tranquil surroundings are the panacea they've been looking for. For others, being cut off from the bustle of humanity and business they're accustomed to is a scary proposition. In some colonies, substantial social life prevails, at least around the dinner table. In others you'll see nary a soul from the beginning of your stay to the end. Some take beginning writers, others do not. Check thoroughly before you apply. Talk to people who have spent time at the one you're contemplating before you make the leap. If you don't know anyone who's been to one, write to an author listed in the colony brochure for advice.

Write for an application form. You may be asked to send samples of your work. For most you'll need the recommendation of a former visitor or other references. You may be expected to send a work plan or explanation of what you hope to accomplish at the colony.

If you're a professional with a good track record and want to expand your writing operation and begin teaching writing, you might apply for a position at a conference. Conference teaching can be a springboard into teaching at a community college, university, or school (see Chapter 10). The application procedure for a part-time position is relatively simple. All it takes is a letter explaining what you are looking for, your résumé, and perhaps some of your published works. Spread the word through your agent, editors, other writers, and people living in the area where the conference is held (if it's not nearby). Do it early, though, since many annual conferences are set up at least a year ahead. If you don't make it onto the faculty your first try, send a reminder that you'd be interested later. Keep after them, the same way you keep after other elusive freelance assignments.

The step-by-step approach

Once you've made it into print, you'll need to keep moving farther out on a limb—without falling. Let's say you've published several times in the local paper. Your next step might be to query a regional magazine, suggesting to them that you write on a subject you know well. To make a dry run on such a venture, why not write up a query as if you were going to send it off to an editor, but try it first on friends whose judgment and tastes you trust. Are they fascinated by the article idea you are proposing? If not, what is there about your presentation or choice of subject that turns them off? Have they seen too many similar pieces already in print? Do they find too little information supporting your query? Whatever the amateur verdict, it may be very useful in revising your query before you actually put it in the mail. What you've done is a tentative survey of your market.

You will earn, too, whatever confidence you build by conscientiously doing your homework—studying the magazines in which you hope to appear; scouting for possible clients among the publications, corporations, ad agencies, in your immediate vicinity.

Nothing builds confidence like money in the bank and words in print. Until these accumulate in sufficient amounts, writers rely on substitutes—encouragement, hope—and, sometimes, on counterfeits. Several young writers I know treasure the letters of rejection that come back with manuscripts that have been submitted on speculation. If the letters contain any expressions that can be interpreted as praise, the writers ponder them as if they were golden eggs laid by some miraculous goose. They pore over rejection letters for clues as to how the manuscript might be revised to become a winner. The trouble with this is the editor's words are often being stretched far beyond their intent and beyond any implicit promise that may be in them. It's better—and more professional—to quickly submit the rejected manuscript to another possible market, or to revise and submit.

On the other hand, when an editor's letter of rejection indicates some interest and admiration, do make plans to keep ideas and manuscripts flying his way. Put his interest in the proper perspective, realizing that in making a potentially valuable new contact you have added one more small link to your network—a network that will expand and grow stronger as you continue your career.

Many struggling writers *feel* that their work is better than comparable material they see in print. Sometimes they're wrong, but sometimes they're right. Here's my tip: Work toward a realistic, detached, objective comparison of your unsold manuscripts and those which appear in your target periodicals. Grade your work honestly on several different aspects as you grade the published material. Is yours superior in (1) research; (2) language; (3) interesting organization; (4) timeliness; (5) economical, hard-hitting, and clear presentation? If you can give yourself good marks on all of these counts, you deserve to be confident. It's only a matter of time until you join or replace your competitors in that magazine's pages. On the other hand, if you honestly find that your work is superior on only one or two of these counts (or perhaps fails altogether in some aspect), then you can set about repairing the deficiency, with increased confidence that you've remedied a blind spot which need never handicap you again.

In this exercise, as in the case of practicing how to write an effective query, the advice of friends and teachers can help keep you on the mark.

At the beginning of your career, particularly, it's important to see that you get credit for *whatever* successes you have clearly achieved, from good grades received for student writing on up to rave reviews for a first book. Remember that you're planning for the long haul. In the years ahead, your fellow students just might turn up in editorial positions, where they'll remember your past performances and call on you for an assignment. Word-of-mouth credits can be crucially important at key moments in your career. Reputation may be a bubble, as some skeptics have said, but it is what careers are made of. And the quiet reputation you may be building among writing associates and in editorial circles is something you can justly have confidence in.

Discipline as a creative tool

After completing his book on the French Revolution, Thomas Carlyle gave the manuscript to his friend John Stuart Mill for proofreading. Mill's maid accidentally used the papers for kindling. Undaunted (according to history), Carlyle sat down and, without notes, completely reconstructed the book. This time, however, he cleverly refused to submit the work for proofing. Aside from the facts that I find it hard to believe anyone could be *undaunted* in such circumstances and that with the availability of carbon paper and copying machines such a problem should never arise for us, the story is still applicable. Such courage, fortitude, and persistence are the stuff of which successful writers are made. Overcoming catastrophes takes stern discipline, as do other aspects of the freelancer's life.

Today self-discipline sometimes seems a lost art. It isn't, of course. The freelancer who means to get ahead takes great pride in maintaining control over the elements that would play havoc with his work schedule. How is this done? First, by anticipating problems and preparing ways to counteract them so work won't suffer. The primary way to anticipate is to recognize patterns.

Professional writers will tell you about the pattern deadlines follow. Like cars on a superhighway, they seem to like to clump together. It doesn't matter that you've planned them to arrive at intervals. They overtake each other—and you—if you don't remain vigilant.

Knowing this, the professional builds into his planned writing time tricks to minimize deadline crashes. When he has three simultaneous deadlines, the professional writer wastes no time getting to work, in some way, on all three at once. He may actually start

writing a finished draft of a relatively easy article while he orga-
nizes his research material for another and puts in telephone calls
for preliminary interviews on the third. The professional knows the
cardinal rule: As soon as you have a firm assignment to produce,
take the first step immediately. By doing so he's made a *commitment*; like a best friend who won't let him off the hook once he's
promised his word, the act of commitment steels his nerve. The
second and third steps follow without requiring anywhere near the
effort of the first.

Once you've recognized patterns in your own working habits, you,
too, will be able to do as this professional does. For instance, he may
well devote his early mornings to the toughest writing chore because
he knows these are his most creative hours. At such time he brooks
no interruptions. He allocates time later in the day to the necessary
phone calls, trips to the library or correspondence and bookkeeping
because he's sure to have run dry of literary brilliance or clever
turns of phrase for the time being.

Another trick to help your self-discipline is to set a timer or alarm
clock as you approach your chores. Break the job, whether it's actually typing a manuscript, cutting and pasting, revising and editing,
or diving into a mound of accumulated research, into reasonable
segments, then set your timer and work against it. You'll be amazed
at how much you can accomplish with the clock ticking away.

What are you really doing when you set such an artificial mechanism to work? You're competing. You've pitted yourself against a
clock and you're determined to win. Writers can also mentally pit
themselves against other steady producers to spur themselves on.
Some beginners I've known decided at the start to regularly compare their output with that of a more successful writer. If he lives
just down the block instead of in a distant city, it's easier to see when
he's out jogging instead of pounding the typewriter, but actual sur-
veillance is not essential. As a professional, you are constantly keeping up with what's going on in the business. You can keep track of
how often his byline pops up—not just in the markets where you'd
expect to find it, but elsewhere, too. Is he getting into a new and
promising field? Isn't it time you considered opening up new horizons yourself?

I said commitment was like a friend who won't let you off the
hook. But actual friends who won't let you off the hook are valuable,
too. Getting them to put you on the hook in the first place is the trick.
If you're the sort who works better when the thought of public
embarrassment is your doom if you don't (nightmares of stand-

ing in front of a large audience and not being able to remember your own name, let alone the speech you're supposed to be delivering?) you might want to tell a friend about a particularly ambitious project you're contemplating. Explain you're going way out on a limb and that you may need reminding, now and then, how you believe you can accomplish the work. Actually telling someone will act as a monitor in itself to keep you plugging away until you achieve what you're after. Be careful, though, to pick the right friend or friends for this coaching task. Otherwise it's all too easy to *talk* big plans instead of actually doing them. Look for circumspect and action-oriented friends to confide in and you'll skirt the problem of endless bull sessions that usurp the work.

Perhaps this is the time to admit one of my secrets of steady production. I use an electric typewriter. There's something about the sound of that motor running (the cost of electricity, I suppose) that actually helps speed my fingers over the keys like magic. And the sound keeps me company in an otherwise quiet room.

I mention this only to suggest that we all have ways of tricking ourselves into the proper mental and emotional state for high production. Some people require the wolf at the door, others just the opposite. Whatever you need, it's up to you to find the best scheme. Then use it properly and often.

One last point: The methods you devise to juggle your time and work load may work fine for a while, then suddenly you find they're no longer adequate to your changing professional situation. If deficiencies develop, your bank balance will register them immediately. Once that happens you'll have to do some fast shuffling of priorities and techniques to keep from going under. So maintain as much flexibility as you can. Realize that patterns lead to other patterns until whole skeins of them will help you decipher the mysteries of the writer's discipline. In order to examine these more closely, prepare by answering the questions that follow.

Establishing priorities

Days

What are your hours of peak productivity in actual writing? Mornings? Middays? Evenings? How many hours of each?

What hours do you have available for preparation for writing, for research?

When do you take care of your correspondence? (Do you do it all in a bunch, making use of In and Out baskets? Do you handle it by priority items? Or do you do it as the spirit moves you?)

Do you know what hours (or fractions thereof) produce the most results when you must phone for assignments, interviews, information from the library? Do you waste or lose time by inefficient transmission of material received by phone to your files or your manuscript?

Are you negligent in fitting other obligations (or irresistible temptations) routinely into your working day? If you can, reschedule them to your advantage.

Do you meet the procrastination problem head-on? Do so and you'll increase your production and your income immediately.

Weeks

How many days do you schedule for actual work that will pay off in writing? How do you divide your time among important projects? Do you keep to this schedule, or do you dump everything else to make a furious effort to hit a deadline? Do you drift and wait when there is no pressure from a deadline?

Do you have a calendar of "Top Priority," "Secondary," and "Do at Leisure" tasks for each week?

Do you clear your desk regularly of the first two categories? (Every Friday afternoon, for instance, just as if you were in someone else's office. If not, do you take care of them on Saturday *for sure?*)

Months

How is your cash flow? Are incoming checks matching expenses? Are you sending out invoices on time? Do you regularly rebill late-paying accounts?

Are you scouting *now* for new assignments to fill in the weeks and months ahead?

Do you have days or evenings when you are systematically building your files, increasing your contacts, beginning speculative new ventures, adding to your catalog of possible topics, promoting yourself? These may be your "Do at Leisure" items. But you must fit them into days of building your substructure to produce a steady flow of work and sales.

"I have six hands," says a middle-aged writer of my acquaintance. "Two of them are just as good as yours. The thumbs on the others aren't so bad. Good enough for some of my chores."

What he means is that his career came all at once to a potentially profitable climax. His years of struggling were over—if he could handle all the assignments he was being offered. He could well afford to pass some of them up, but he saw clearly that the more he could handle when the time was ripe the easier his future would be.

So for a crucial year or two of hard work he is dovetailing the demands of a lecture tour with finishing two books and up to a dozen spin-off articles. Material for all these is coming from files he built over ten years when he had little direct use for them. Public interest has peaked in a subject he kept in view while no editors thought it worth their attention.

He is fortunate in that he has studied the priorities throughout his writing career and has learned from a careful sifting of his experience how to juggle and allot his whole array of resources. Though he has not been able to grab all the goodies he might have if he literally had six hands, he has made a good grab at an opportunity that might not come again. The moral here is probably that he is now able to arrange his priorities advantageously because he never neglected to keep priorities in order through the lean years of his career. That is, the research and maintaining contact with editors, which must have had secondary status when they were not paying off, stood him in good stead when the priorities changed. If he had always gone for the main chance of the moment and let other considerations slide, he would be in no position to handle all that he is doing now.

Time and energy management

Next to a total failure to budget your time, the worst mistake is budgeting it as if you were a machine. This is where sensible energy management comes to the fore. As one writer says, "I try to get myself going every morning by 8:30. Sometimes it doesn't work. When nothing comes, I give my dogs a run on the beach and watch the gulls sailing with motionless wings. Or I drop in for coffee and doughnuts at a place where commercial fishermen hang out, and just listen to their morning jabber. As often as not when I 'waste' part of my morning this way, it actually speeds me along." He's right, of course. He knows *himself* and his *work habits* well enough to make these diversions work for him.

Particular diversions will work for you as well. *Plan* them into your time and energy budget, and be thankful for them. (After all, only workaholics think it's fun to work *all* the time.) But do so with care. It's too easy to take time to have that extra cup of coffee.

Especially if a thorny business decision or writing problem has you entangled in a nonproductive maze of guilt, anxiety, fear, and simple laziness. Letting the job slip until it becomes colossal often proves disastrous, most especially to the creative part of you.

Never forget that your physical and mental energy is one of the major resources you intend to convert into dollars and other satisfactions of the writer's trade. You, too, have to make hay while the sun shines. You can't afford to lay off when it rains, or the energy level fails for any reason; therefore, it's up to you to find ways of distributing your tasks so that those of lesser priority can be advanced when you're not up to giving your best shot to others.

You need to study, in an informal way, the actual patterns you follow through the day, the week, the month, and the year. And to make an accommodation so that you don't squander those periods of peak creative energy on what could just as well be accomplished when you're fatigued and less productive.

Learning what your best pace is and then fitting that pace to the writing obligations before you is much too important to be neglected. And it's such a subtle problem that you can't expect to settle it on the spur of the moment, or settle it once and for all. But get on with it, starting now and constantly refining your study of yourself as you work along.

A couple of notes of caution: Overachievers should be recognized for what they are. Don't let them get you down. They seldom believe in lists or time management as it's taught in schools. If their levels of energy are high in the middle of the night, that's when they work. Just because a bestselling author reports that for weeks on end she can sit and write sixteen hours at a stretch shouldn't discourage you. If you can't operate that way, don't even try. There's absolutely no sense in attempting to be what you're not.

Also, allow yourself time with your friends. Not only are your friends important to your emotional well-being, they often offer creative dividends, too, since they can become guides to new information, story ideas, and essential business contacts. Developing and maintaining good friendships, as in any business, is an important part of your job. (But remember to keep the occasional lunch out to a specific allotment of time, as if you had a typical nine-to-five job.)

Edwin C. Bliss, author of *Getting Things Done: The ABC's of Time Management,* speaking to a group of communicators, said, "Work is only fun when you have it under control—when you know what your objective is and are moving toward it. And leisure is fun only when you can relax without feeling guilty, knowing you've earned a good rest." Bliss's suggestions for achieving this include (1) assessing yourself and your situation truly instead of fantasizing and procrastinating, (2) taking baby steps before attempting to take big leaps, and (3) reinforcing your learning by rewards along the way.

The best managers control their time by thinking in terms of objectives rather than activities. They make decisions quickly, avoid procrastination, and treat their time as the precious and limited resource that it is. They learn to set priorities in relation to their own goals *rather than someone else's*. They screen themselves from unwarranted interruptions. They delegate, plan, and concentrate on important things, disregarding trivia.

Certain peculiarities of the freelancing business can add insult to injury. Samuel Taylor Coleridge was writing "Kubla Khan" directly from a dream. In the midst of writing it, he was interrupted. When he went back to work he discovered he couldn't recall the rest of the dream. The manuscript is unfinished to this day.

Your time may be your own when you're freelancing, but there's a finite amount for us all. Think about it realistically. You can't do everything. Yet you must accomplish a great deal. You can learn to do it better by *managing* your energies and time. Think of them as two more of your most precious commodities.

Situation summaries

Seeing a problem clearly—laying out in black and white the goals to be reached, the obstacles to be overcome, and the resources you can use singly or in various combinations—is almost the same as solving that problem.

Think of a military situation map. Battle commanders must have, for quick and effective decisions, a map marked with all the different units and weapons they can call on to attack the enemy. *At a glance,* the attacking officer can assess the entire situation and concentrate on filling in whatever additional forces he may need.

Of course, you may say that you do this, too, but that you "do it in your head." However, *writing down* your situation summary has added benefits. It clears up sloppy or wishful thinking. And it's far easier to review a written summary later to see if you've achieved your goals. You can use one when you're considering updating a lot of expensive equipment or if you're applying for a loan or large advance or need to write a business proposal for a corporate client.

(A succinct, persuasive proposal, by the way, does these things: It gets to the point quickly, it covers all known contingencies and rules out alternatives, telling why they wouldn't work as well, and it demonstrates cost-effectiveness and benefits to be derived from the proposed step.)

At the very least, a situation summary, used at crunch points in your freelance business, should allow you to resolve some of your most difficult business decisions. Let's say you are in the following position: You've been freelancing for one year. You've placed several articles with local newspapers and regional magazines, all of which pay too little for you to live on. But the satisfaction of seeing your name and writing in print has boosted your morale considerably. You want to continue freelancing, but you also want to break into a higher-paying, reliable market. How do you do it?

Spell out the specifics in a situation summary for yourself. Once you state the problem, you need to become quite specific in detailing the next step—recommended action. Pick your target markets as carefully as possible. Choose one or two magazines that pay a little above those you've sold to already. You should also include other writing jobs—revitalizing form responses for state agencies and college and university departments, for instance. By listing the names of persons and organizations who might be interested in your services, you've already taken the first step toward increasing two important interrelated items—your writing output and your income. It's too easy to think vaguely that, yes, there must be someone out there who needs what you do. Forcing yourself to write down the details and organize an approach toward them will help you to quickly make inroads into your problem areas.

Make a situation summary even if you are not going to use it as preparation for a business decision or for assessing relative financial profits. If your problem is merely how to improve your writing, laying out such a summary can clarify your thinking. The summary I have devised might be likened to the process of diagramming a sentence. Diagramming clearly shows how the parts of a sentence work with each other to present and qualify a thought. This is very much what the layout of a situation summary can show about the various resources you have as a writer.

Here is an outline of a situation summary that can be adapted to your particular needs:

The Problem as You See It
    [Enter a short, concise, statement of the main point.]

Recommended Action
[Be specific. Generalities are no better than good intentions. Support your recommendation with a plan that includes relevant dates and resources required. If your plan follows the action of other freelancers you know, you can note here their names and their resolution of the problem.]

Benefits from Recommended Action
[List financial benefits, improved mental state, increased flexibility—whatever is worth aiming for.]

Cost of Action
[Include here financial costs, time required, other resources spent or committed to complete the action.]

Alternative Solutions
[List these in order of your preference, without too many details. Note best reason for *not* taking each of them.]

Markets and Contacts to Approach
[Who and what can be relied on to advance new plan. Note sources of information to be called on, reference material needed, editors who need to be informed of your new direction.]

Date to Review Action
Dates the Action was Actually Reviewed
[These, obviously, will be entered at later times, when this and other situation summaries have become part of your continuing record. Most useful in seeing where you were and how you were thinking as time went by.]

Decision making

Any good decision springs not only from a thorough assessment of the current situation—of the sort you laid out in your situation summary—but also from educated guesses about the short- *and* long-range effects of the action you are contemplating.

In lieu of a crystal ball you can only map out the probabilities, the likely consequences of mortgaging your house to buy word-processing equipment to increase your productivity or of turning down an assignment to clear your desk for work on a more attractive subject. Though this projection of the future cannot, by its nature, be as definite as your situation summary, it is no less important.

My young friend Arnold K. finished college last spring with every intention of making a lifetime career as a writer. He was lucky in getting a summer internship to work as an editor on a respectable national magazine. I was very happy for him, because editorial experience at almost any level can be invaluable as part of a writer's preparation.

He came back this fall to tell me he had found the work boring and disillusioning. He had been given no assignments at the magazine beyond filing and continuing some correspondence on business matters. He had been given no voice in magazine policy or in the acceptance or rejection of manuscripts. Therefore he had declined to stay on when his internship was finished, though he had been offered a small permanent position. He said he was going back to graduate school to "learn some more about the art of writing."

Since by this time his decision was already made, I was not about to comment on the wisdom of his choice. I said only that I hoped by the next time he had to make a major decision he would have reflected on this one, would have considered what difference it might have made to his writing career if he had stuck with his presently unrewarding job at the magazine. He may always be glad he left. I hope he is. Even so, to ponder what might have followed from different choices in the past is one of the best bases we have for guidance in decisions about our future.

One further note: The experience of others is never a rigid guide. It is part of our privilege as freelancers to take a chance. So, after sizing up the situation and the probable consequences, always consider what you *want* to do, and take your chance at it.

To firm up your policies and establish consistency in your performance, whenever you've made an effective decision you should review the other decisions that will be coming up. This leads to an ongoing review of the cost of equipment and supplies, time that must be set aside from production, when and whether to hire expert help (accountants, lawyers, public relations persons, secretaries, researchers), how to schedule savings into an already excruciatingly tight budget, how to keep the operation rolling without going broke.

Procrastination problems

Thomas Huxley said, "Perhaps the most valuable result of all education is the ability to make yourself do the thing you have to do when it ought to be done, whether you like it or not."

Alexander Woollcott said, "Many of us spend half our time wishing for things we could have if we didn't spend half our time wishing."

Procrastination makes problems for all of us. Abulia, the abnormal lack of the ability to act or make decisions, is a force to be reckoned with.

Knowing when, how, and why you are procrastinating is the first step toward improvement. Define the stumbling blocks in your path. Then tackle them *one at a time.*

One can hardly mention procrastination without recalling Norman Vincent Peale—and his wise, if somewhat oversimplified, technique for attacking it. Peale suggested the following six points:

1. Stop regarding procrastination as a harmless little hang-up. Don't reward it.
2. Pick one specific area where it plagues you and conquer it.
3. Learn to set priorities, then focus on one problem at a time.
4. Give yourself deadlines.
5. Don't duck the most difficult problems.
6. Don't let perfectionism paralyze you.

In spite of the warnings from eminent men about the evils of procrastination (and the admitted necessity for controlling it), this remains to be said: If you can't lick it, *make use of it.*

Procrastination is not always what it appears to be. A writer should always suspect that his subconscious is wisely keeping him back from something he is not yet ready to do. This "something" may be only a segment or section of an article on which a good beginning has been made, or it may be the approach to a better-paying market.

Though deadlines are pressing and the bank account is drying up, the tendency to think "not yet" oftentimes ought to be heeded. The sky may not fall if you miss a deadline. If it does, there will be another one up there tomorrow, and your procrastination may be precisely the factor that has left you in position to meet opportunities better than the ones you let go by.

You make good use of procrastination when (but only when) you are able to persist until you find a *better* way to accomplish what procrastination avoided. It can be a blessing in disguise, but it won't be unless you *make it so.*

For the writer who works alone, there has to be some voice restraining her from crossing her bridges before they have been built, or from submitting work before giving it time to ripen in her mind. Since we are not machines but complex individuals who must depend on the always mysterious contents of our own imaginations we have to learn as best we can to work according to the whole law of our natures.

Don't spare the whip—except sometimes.

An experienced novelist of my acquaintance "almost finished" a novel two summers ago. His agent knew (because he had told her) that the manuscript would be in her hands by Christmas. Christmas passed. She called to ask what had happened to the promised novel. She reminded him that he was the one who had been so anxious to get another book in print to keep his name and work before the public. She had a number of queries from editors about when the new work might be submitted. The time was ripe and overripe for successful negotiating. Why was he procrastinating?

Not because he lacked the craft to finish the novel in a way that would be perfectly satisfactory to the editors eager to publish it. Nor because he had more money than he knew what to do with. He merely felt that something he couldn't name was still missing from his conception of the novel, that it wasn't finished and couldn't be finished until the missing something popped into his mind.

Another year passed. Then with what appeared to be minor revisions, the novel was finished. The publisher who bought it loved it. It was very well reviewed, and the sales were excellent. The author got numerous fan letters. Wouldn't all this have happened if he had turned the manuscript in when he first promised it? Since his revisions weren't on a large scale, the novelist can't be sure. But he has the healthy suspicion that the delay enabled him to get a better feel for his characters so that each of the touches he added later were definitive. He is convinced that his procrastination worked for him, slowing him down until his imagination refined the ingredients which accounted for the success of the book.

What's the cost of goofing off?

Every minute wasted costs you money. If you earn $16,000 a year, every hour goofed off costs you $8.58, at a minimum. Every minute is worth 14.3¢. If 15 minutes a day are wasted, you're out $500 a year. Fig. 5-1 shows you how to calculate what price procrastination.

And that's not the worst of it. Those figures are calculated for someone working for someone else. If you're freelancing, your hourly and daily rates should be calculated higher, since you can't count on being paid for every hour worked.

If you earn	Hour is worth	Minute is worth	15 minutes per day over 1 year are worth
$ 8,000	$ 4.29	7.2¢	$250.00
10,000	5.36	8.9¢	312.00
14,000	6.42	12.5¢	437.00
20,000	10.72	17.8¢	625.00
30,000	16.09	26.8¢	937.50

Fig. 5-1. *What price procrastination?*

Creative burnout

Creative burnout can bring your productivity to a standstill. Freelancers are most prone to it when severe isolation, inadequate feedback, and the necessity of long workdays and workweeks get to them. Spontaneity, joy, and energy fly out the window. The victims become detached, depressed. According to William Saroyan, "When we say we run out of ideas, we run out of faith in the mysterious kind of energy that tells us the story was worthwhile."

A writer is not a machine that can be kept going by replacing worn-out parts. The problems of beginning again will only be resolved by restoring the health of the whole bio-psychic complex. Here, if anywhere, you are up against the challenge: Know thyself. Know thyself—and remember past instances in which your imagination went into hibernation, when you thought it had rolled over and died. You know that you can't get going again by kicking yourself. Sermons and analysis won't necessarily help, either. In such situations it's well to see that our dry seasons are misfortunes that others, too, have experienced and recovered from. Much as we hate to admit we are like other people, the return to productivity just might begin by admitting our plight is a common one.

According to psychotherapist Thomas Wright, who spoke at a Women in Communications conference, creative blocking is caused by:

1. Forcing work to fit a preconceived structure.
2. Talking before listening.
3. Paying too much attention to technique at the wrong time.
4. Setting expectations too high.
5. Evaluating too soon.
6. Taking too little time to play.

At such times, Wright says, one should revive one's spirits by indulging in guilt-free playtime. "Listening, seeing, and being open to expression are parallel to creative perception," he says, "which is the creative process in the most critical stage of all. Creativity means taking a fresh look and seeing things that aren't obvious."

Maybe burnout time should be autobiography time. If you can no longer produce, do the obvious thing first: start writing *about* someone who can't produce. Write critically but lovingly. Above all, write as if you had all the time in the world. Write about all the sorry and wonderful details that always seemed too trivial for you to write about before. Forget, for the time being, all the strictures of laying out a situation summary or planning for career decisions. Let the pages, or notes, or vignettes of autobiography accumulate without any specific design for shaping them into a unified work or finding a market for them. Search for yourself when you reread and revise what stacks up around your typewriter.

Why do I recommend writing as a cure for creative burnout when it was writing that brought it on in the first place? Why not a month in Bermuda, or a year working as a dishwasher? A *different kind* of writing is the natural way for a writer to come out of the trap he's dug for himself.

When he was old, W.B. Yeats wrote a poem about this problem, which geniuses share with the rest of us. The poem is called "The Circus Animals' Desertion." In it he wrote: ". . . Now that my ladder's gone,/I must lie down where all the ladders start,/in the foul rag-and-bone shop of the heart." The ladder was his creative imagination. To paraphrase the rest: He knew he had to start it again by wallowing in the rich but messy territory of autobiography.

Anticipate. If you prepare for the unexpected, you've won half the battle. Like everyone else, you are sure to come to periods of drought. Anticipate them with the confidence that by learning more and more about yourself you will find your way through them. I hesitate to say you should budget for such periods. In matters like this such stringent words are out of place. *Anticipate* is a better word. And never despair when such times come on you. They really do have their purpose in your writing life.

(More) Problem-solving techniques

Before the days of the automobile, people lost in blizzards or too drunk to drive let go of the reins and counted on the instincts of the horse to get them home. That's what is called a calculated risk. Developing your understanding of your instincts, hunches, intuitions, and other emanations from the writer's subconscious to a fine point so that you are in position to take the necessary calculated risks will be one of your more important jobs. These have to be relied on many, many times for guidance in the management of a career just as they do in the shaping of an imaginative work. The trick is to *induce* the subconscious to work smoothly with the rest of the mind. Since there's a bit of Walter Mitty in all of us, we need, as writers, to learn to enhance our situation by letting our daydreams surface so they can be of use. This is what Hayes Jacobs calls daydreaming on schedule, a fine technique for increasing creativity.

On the other hand, inspiration, intuition, and revelation are notoriously hard to schedule exactly. In spite of our wooing of them, they are all too often laggards, content to doze in some dark corner of our subconscious. Perhaps the best way of luring them into a helpful stance is to lay out a rational game plan just as you would build a birdhouse to lure birds to nest and lay eggs in your backyard. Rationality has to design the strategies of problem solving, though sudden flashes of intuition determine how the strategy will be executed in any given situation. As you have done in past exercises, divide the problem into its components and, instead of trying to solve the whole thing at once with luck, intuition, or shrewdness, solve a part at a time until the whole thing yields.

An example is a writer who told me recently how he plotted his course for the year (see fig. 5-2). He stopped early in December of the preceding year to examine and prepare for the upcoming twelve months. He listed firm article assignments as well as what he'd be paid for them. Alongside the list he put the probable production time required, giving *himself* a deadline in each case. Then he divided the remaining dollar figure (his break-even point plus the minimum amount he wanted to earn) by twelve. With that picture in front of him, he listed the specific markets he'd aim for and the minimum amounts they would pay.

He knew better, however, than to rely on just a monthly projec-

	Target	$15,000.00	
	Gross	Less	Net
Royalties, 2 paperbacks (4 pmts.)	$ 6,000	(Keogh) $ 1,500	$ 4,500
Automotive column (1/mo.)	1,200	–	1,200
Firm assignments	2,500		2,500
Probable reprints, photo sales, etc.	800	(commissions) 80	720
	$10,500	$ 1,580	$ 8,920
	Approximate need		$ 7,100

TARGET

Category:	Fee	Date Due	TIP*
Sunday supplement	$ 250	1/20	2 days
Custom Vans	150	1/30	1½ days
Modern Maturity	500	2/10	4 days
Golf Journal	300	2/28	3 days
Sunday supplement	250	3/5	2 days
Parents	500	3/15	3 days
Sunday supplement	250	4/18	2 days
Ford Times	250	4/30	2 days
Sunday supplement	250	5/7	2 days
Car and Driver	1,000	5/25	3 days
Golf Journal	300	6/6	3 days
Trailer Life (package of 3)	1,000	6/15,7/15, 8/15	10 days
Oui	500	7/30	4 days
Kiwanis	500	8/31	3 days
Sunday supplement	250	9/15	2 days
Car and Driver	1,000	9/30	3 days
Bestways (4 shorts)	240	whenever	1½ days
????	150	10/30	?
	$ 7,640		51 days

* Time in progress.

Fig. 5-2. *Sample projected income and production plan.*

tion, so he also made a quarterly projection. What if he didn't get the assignment from Magazine X? He sketched in a contingency plan for that period of time. He marked on his calendar a list of queries and markets to direct them to a month or two prior to the "soft" months.

"It really worked for me," he said. "I cleared $5,000 more than I ever expected because I kept right on the track."

His working papers were simple but firm enough to prod him into focusing on his situation. He projected a plan that would net him slightly more than his target because he wanted to put some money into his Keogh Plan (see Chapter 14), and he knew the amounts from royalties, reprints, and photo sales could vary. This does not mean he sold to the exact outlets he targeted. But he knew the *kind* of magazine his ideas would fit, and he had a working relationship with some of the editors. He was aware of how much time most projects took him. He projected around his monthly column's requirements and already firmed-up assignments. Planning helped him locate the right ideas early enough to query the editors well in advance. He did make $5,000 more than anticipated (a large reprint sale helped), and felt jubilant about carefully planning as far ahead as he did.

What he hadn't spelled out was *when* the payments were likely to come in, an all too common mistake. Fortunately, because he had projected reasonably well in advance he could check his course in time to try quickly for fill-in dollars at his established market (the Sunday supplement) if he needed them. He had stopped short of spelling out the details of markets toward the end of the year because he figured if he could keep close to projections, he'd be able to market another book proposal if he gave himself a little time to put it together.

With the reality of your own picture before you, and with all details spelled out, shuffle items around and arrange what you can. Note those items that can't be pinned down completely, but don't rely on them. The *coordination* of all items is the payoff, whether your resources look skimpy or they run off the page as you jot them down. Put the pages in your tickler file for a special review date. And get to work on the most pressing assignment.

Chapter 6
Organizing
for
Profit

■■■

The plan

Successful businesses start with a master plan. Sketch yours out on paper. This method has three advantages: You'll be able to review your progress periodically; the need for a change in direction will be obvious when the original plan and your checkbook balance clash; and any business loan, whether from bank or guardian angel, is more likely to materialize when a clear, concise, well-thought-out plan is provided in written form.

A general plan keeps your eye on long-term goals. A complete one will detail priorities in a sequence that saves valuable time and energy and helps eliminate worry.

When you draft your plan, stick to facts, realities, and valid assumptions. Don't overlook the obvious pluses. Your spouse has a good job which, God and the economy willing, will not disappear overnight. Or you know that you'll be coming into a small inheritance two years from now. Or you have expertise that editor friends have told you could become a specialty resulting in reliable assignments.

But do keep daydreams to a minimum. Frustration catches the writer whose plan is built primarily on wishful thinking. Also remember that *too* much time spent planning can be just another form of procrastination. Don't overanalyze, or you'll drown in a sea of data you won't be able to use. The plans in this book are only *suggested models.* Devise your own if you wish, but allot yourself a certain amount of time for the project and then *stop.*

If you are dealing with different kinds of markets, you might need separate plans to weave into your other calendar notations. If so, be sure you jot details of them into your tickler system, calendar, workbook, vertical files—whatever you have and use well. Some writers use color-coded ink or paper to flag different entries in such systems.

Your plan should include:

■ A basic analysis of your business, including a list of your specialties, the markets for them, and a paragraph on why *you,* above others, can give a client a special or unique angle.
■ A list of opportunities (see Chapter 3). Be specific about market areas, names of magazines, publishers, editors, and other clients.
■ Market objectives (realistically outlined) for one year, eighteen months, two years, five years. With these in front of you, *briefly* outline your strategy—specific work you'd like to be able to cover in

the year to come; research already available to you; what you'd need to research further and probable places where information might be found; the time and cost to get same.

■ Marketing tactics. A breakdown of material your agent (if you have one) will handle versus that which you'll sell directly.

■ Bookkeeping requirements: profit-and-loss statement or budget; statement of net worth; depreciation schedule of office and equipment.

■ Contingency plans and list of possible outside help to implement them. Projection of future equipment that could increase your productivity.

The long haul

Big assignments call for longer-range forecasting. Break them into daily, weekly, and monthly segments. Make notes on your calendar at the proper intervals.

Know where you hope to be in five years. How much money do you want to be making? What kind of writing—articles, stories, books, brochures, or a combination of these—do you anticipate selling? Projecting further into the future gives you a push to start acquiring the skills you might need.

For one thing, you'll start to keep track effectively of the people and places where you'll find help in accomplishing your goals. You won't veer off into sidelines that aren't financially rewarding enough. A five-year plan maintains vigilance over your best, most lucrative and satisfying ideas. Be both realistic and ambitious—five years can be a very short or a very long time. But if you don't look that far ahead, you'll discover you've lost much more than *just* five years of your time.

Guide to a five-year plan

1. Where do you want to be at the end of your career as a freelancer?

2. What is your definite target two years from now?

3. What kind of assignments do you want to receive on a regular basis?

4. What do you need to know to get them? (education, experience, kind of people for contacts, etc.)

5. What have you done so far that will help you? (Note every assignment, how you did it, with whom you were in contact, etc.)
6. What barriers do you see between where you are now and where you want to be in five years? (Be specific.)
7. What problems in the current publishing situation suggest ways your long-term plan will fit into upcoming industry changes?
8. How well do you present yourself and your talents? Are you too timid or too difficult? Do you overreact to criticism? Are you trying to handle everything yourself instead of looking for the right kind of help? What warnings have been coming back to you that you've ignored?

The days and weeks unfold

Take time to organize the working day before you begin it. Use a standard form or checklist of items in your usual routine. In five or ten minutes you can outline priority chores (with phone numbers beside them if necessary), which will spur you into speedy production. (I like to prepare this list the night before, which saves time getting started on the jobs at hand.)

The following example comes from a writer who does a lot of celebrity and expert interviews for his articles, but his way of tackling his work gives a number of clues that can be applied to any form of freelancing.

"To begin work and to ward off a tendency to procrastinate on any project, I follow a list of steps as soon as I get an assignment," he states. His checklist:

1. I note the assignment (by phone or letter), date assigned, by whom, length and due date, etc., in my assignment diary *at the time I get it.*

2. I reach immediately for a mailing label, type it out, and stick it on an envelope. Then it's ready when the story is.

3. I send off a letter of assignment form (see fig. 6-1) *that day* to the editor.

4. I type out very rough paragraphs on what I think the story might say, leaving lots of space for the quotes and anecdotes I'll get later. My preliminary research (the stuff I used to draft the query in the first place) provides this material. In fact, I often write my query so that it forms the first three paragraphs in the story.

Date_____

Dear_____:

     This will confirm our agreement whereby you have commissioned me to research and write an article of approximately _____words on _____, tentatively titled _____, which I shall deliver to you no later than _____.
It is understood by us that my fee shall be $ _____.

     It is further agreed that you shall reimburse me for routine expenses incurred in the researching and writing of the article, and that extraordinary expenses will be discussed with you before they are incurred. Against such reimbursement we have agreed that you shall advance to me the sum of $ _____.

     This letter is intended to cover the main points of our agreement. Should any disagreement arise on these or other matters, we agree to rely upon the guidelines set forth in the Code of Ethics and Fair Practices of the American Society of Journalists and Authors. Please sign one copy of this agreement and return it to me.

                Yours truly,

                _____AUTHOR

PUBLICATION_____
BY_____EDITOR
DATE_____

Fig. 6-1. *ASJA standard article-assignment agreement.*

5. Then on another sheet I type out ten to twenty-five questions I will probably ask my interviewees. I try to prepare for the "no comment" types by anticipating their reluctance and preparing a question that will get them talking in spite of themselves. That way I haven't wasted my time and phone call. Most stories can absorb a negative or slightly negative comment or two, anyway, if they are strong enough. I do all this while I'm still feeling very "up" about getting the assignment.

6. My next move is to place my calls. I set up appointments for the interviews. I explain to the secretaries what my story's about and ask them for data on their bosses—correct title, age, hobbies, and any little personal details they are willing to provide. If they are chatty, I chat. If they are extremely business-like, I play it that way, and hope I can get the data later—once we've established an acquaintance via the phone. Sometimes I tell them about the difficulties of getting a story, the problems of a freelancer. When I do, I sometimes find a secretary will commiserate. You have to be careful, though. Occasionally, the word "freelancer" spells "amateur." When I think it might, I say "writer" or "reporter." I like to be prepared with alternative terminology.

Whatever you find to simplify your interviewing, your querying, your billing procedure, your research needs, the better. Of course, how you line up your weeks of writing, researching, and carving out a freelance life will depend on whether you are spending full or part time at writing, whether you have a sound business plan to guide you, and whether you have made provisions for downtime. Also, some efforts will depend on the reliability of your support mechanisms—whether those are coming from others or from within yourself. You must have time to lounge and relax, to exercise, to read for pleasure without feeling guilty, etc.

Here's a sample of how one freelancer's weeks progress:

Five mornings a week (from 8:30 a.m. to 1 p.m.) are spent at the typewriter, either writing articles, typing up queries, or editing a book project. After a quick lunch the writer spends the next two hours either delving into new research at the library, placing phone calls to editors and sources of information, or heading out to scheduled interviews. Downtime includes all necessary errands (to photo labs, copying companies, stationery stores, etc.). One night a week she faces up to filing and correspondence chores. (She uses postcards for much of her correspondence, because she maintains it saves both time and money.) Another night she spends with account books and bills to be paid or bills to be sent to clients for out-of-pocket expenses. Some evenings she does general research, scouting the possible new territories in her neighborhood by meeting with friends, stopping in at the radio station, checking the local programs on television. (She always watches TV with a pen and tablet beside her.) Monthly she meets with her accountant to review the overall business picture, attempting to eliminate problems before they occur, seeing how she can update procedures or equipment and prepare for tax time. The questions she keeps asking herself include "Am I keeping afloat? Am I getting ahead? Are there some signals in my five-year plan that call for action now? At this rate will I have enough money tucked away five years from now to take time off to write my book?"

Organizing your ideas

Everywhere you look these days you discover business people trying to enhance profits by increasing output per man-hour. Should you do less if you want to get ahead? Learn to identify critical production bottlenecks in your overall operation *before* they slow you down. Then act to change the way you've been doing things. If you make this a high-priority effort, you'll soon discover you're reaping additional benefits: You'll accomplish your short-term goals more quickly, you'll receive better assignments (and more of them), and you'll be completing them in fewer hours at the typewriter.

Let's examine your ideas file. When you first began to consider freelancing, you diligently clipped articles from the *New York Times, Newsweek, Smithsonian, Reader's Digest,* and your local newspapers. You were clipping information that interested you specifically, as well as material about broad trends in general. Let's say you had an abiding curiosity about certain medical subjects, a life-long enthusiasm for circus clowns, and a love for all kinds of travel. So, you slipped those clips into folders labeled "Medical and related," "Clowns," "Travel," etc. You spent hours reading *Writer's Market* and marking any markets that seemed attractive. But then you may have found you were collecting clippings by the pound, and not really acting on the ideas they inspired. And you hadn't looked at those regional markets listings for months!

Or perhaps the contrary was true. You *doggedly* insisted on staying with a few favorite story ideas in spite of the obvious fact that absolutely no editor on the globe thought his readers would care a whit about them. Lord knows, you tried everyone you could think of. You even remembered that editors play musical chairs, and went back to the magazines you'd approached earlier, hoping against hope that there'd be a new and *sensible* editor in charge this time.

Organizing your ideas into marketable form isn't easy when you're starting out. So if you're having trouble, approach another writer and ask his opinion. (If you don't know any personally yet, you can meet them at writing seminars.) Don't expect him to take you under his wing—he hasn't time if he's leading the busy freelance life. But chances are he'll have a helpful hint or two for you. Writers are approachable, generally. They *know* how difficult it is getting started.

Or, if you know of an editor who, though extremely busy, is reputed to be kind to beginners, ask him *why* you haven't seemed to hit the mark with the ideas you've presented him, *how* you should rearrange your proposals to sell to him, *when* he's most likely to be interested in material in your pet area. As I've noted before, editors are people, too, and I know many who have been available, briefly, for such advice. If you are aware of their time crunch and approach them in a businesslike manner, they just might surprise you and give you a valuable bit of advice. If they do, take it to heart and act upon it immediately.

Perhaps it's time to sit back and take a good, thorough look at the ideas you've been percolating, to check them against what editors say they want and need (rather than what you want to give them), *and* to reexamine your territory to see if markets you once thought held promise still do, if you'd only buckle down and present them with reasonable queries.

Apart from those suggestions, I'd recommend that you closely reexamine a few markets to see if the publications themselves have changed direction. Are they losing ad pages or taking different kinds of advertising than before? Are there articles in them now that a year ago would have been unthinkable? What big names are they publishing? Have you been aiming too high or too low?

Reexamine what you're sending them, as well. Are your queries written in the most exciting fashion possible? Is your writing as polished as you can make it? Be honest now. It's all too easy to get a slightly swelled head as you start to sell. Writing is still *hard* work. Perhaps you should be rewriting or cleaning up your act in other ways.

Your queries

There are many ways to query editors and other clients. *Writer's Market* and volumes such as *Working Press of the Nation* will give you tips to follow, as will other printed sources (see the Resources chapter). And you can usually pick up several tips worth the cost of admission at conferences and seminars where professionals present their pet strategies to aspiring freelancers.

One way to brighten your financial picture is to take stock of the *volume* of queries you get out each week. This is true when you're first starting out in freelancing, and it's also true when you're attempting to change your course. Have you tried multiple submission of the same idea to a number of different, non-competing markets? (For more on multiple submission, see Chapter 9.) Many editors don't mind receiving photocopied queries if they're clean and readable. The new duplicating machines, by the way, produce copies that are nearly as good as originals. Some writers carefully type queries to fit one page of stationery (a nifty, eye-catching title, a short but powerful lead, two or three succinct paragraphs of backup material explaining the story), leaving out the line that refers to number of words, photographs available, or specifics that would vary to fit different magazines. They have these copied ten times and send them out with the last part added to fit each publication they're querying. Cover letters, too, can be done as forms—if your query is specific, you don't really need to say much in the cover letter anyway. Having your material ready to quickly pop into an envelope definitely helps to speed the flow of your queries to possible markets. Getting more than one assignment on the same query need not worry you. You've sent the suggestion to non-competing markets, and you are free to rearrange your material or sell the same idea with a different angle or twist to many markets. You are, that is, if you are careful to sell one-time rights.

One way to keep track of your queries is to use a query card for briefly noting where they went, and when, and the decision by the editor to reject or assign (see fig. 6-2). The back of the card can contain a list of future possibilities. Just list the title of the magazine and key that to the page in your *Writer's Market* where you'll find the description of what the editor is looking for. Especially as you're getting started in freelancing or developing your credits in an area new to you, you'll find this system a timesaver.

Another query technique requires money, time, knowledge of the publishing world, and guts: the once-a-year jaunt to meet the editors

```
TITLE:_____

QUERY:      Magazine              Out      Ret'd
   1.  _____
   2.  _____
   3.  _____
   4.  _____
   5.  _____
   6.  _____
   7.  _____
   8.  _____
   9.  _____
  10.  _____
```

(front)

```
POSSIBILITIES:
Magazine            Page    Magazine      Page
_____
_____
_____
_____
_____
_____
_____
_____
_____
```

(back)

Fig. 6-2. *Sample query card.*

in person. Most writers who live outside the hub of New York and far from cities where other publishers ply their trade (Boston, Chicago, Denver, L.A.) know the value of this strategy. One of the guides I emulated when I was starting out was a fellow who flew in from London once a year. He covered the territory in exactly ten days and returned to England with enough assignments for the year ahead. But he planned every minute of those expensive business trips, believe me. He wrote ahead to let editors know he'd be in town precisely ten days, picked times *he* wanted to see them and suggested them to the editors. He drew up a mental map of Manhattan publishing offices and planned visits to editors on Madison, Lexington, and Third Avenues for a couple of days, editors on Sixth Avenue or 43rd Street for another, always allowing himself walking time between appointments. Then, with firm appointments arranged, he carefully drew up a list of about thirty of his top ideas. He photocopied these pages, making sure he had a few more copies than the number of editors he was going to see. Each editor got a look at all his ideas (and could keep the list to mull over when he was gone). Before he left town he called back to some editors who "weren't quite sure" on some ideas. He continued to pitch the strongest possibilities, pushing, like the salesman he was, for a decision before he was out of the country. The result, as I said, was that he filled his assignment coffers for a year at a time. I tried the same technique and was amazed at how well it worked.

Of course, it can happen that two editors want the same story. Seldom, however, will they want the same slant to the same story material. When that did occur he simply told the second editor who asked for it that he had just sold the idea elsewhere. (All of the editors he talked with knew he was in town for a few days on a selling trip and was seeing every editor he could fit into his schedule, so none of this would come as a surprise.)

Whichever way you consider approaching the querying part of your business, though, sooner or later you'll probably find you need to make that New York jaunt. If you build the cost of it into your plan at the beginning, it need not be traumatic for your budget. And you may discover that editors are actually quite open to occasionally seeing a new face and always on the lookout for fresh ideas. Take them up on that line when you are sure you are ready.

Your office

In Chapter 4 we looked at the basics of setting up a freelance office.

Let's look down the line to see what has happened now that you're working steadily.

Too much paper (files, clippings, manuscript drafts, correspondence) on your desk at the wrong time clogs the wheels of efficiency and slows the cash flow. It may, if you don't watch out, bring the latter to an abrupt halt.

What to do with it all? What to throw out? What to retain? How to file it so it is easily retrievable? A home computer system, a phalanx of efficient secretaries, accountants, researchers, librarians, and miscellaneous file clerks could be a dream come true. But your share of the pie—bigger and better assignments—will make some of these organizational details fall into place. As you progress in your planning and budgeting, the picture does brighten. There's more to spend on help of whatever kind you need most. But be aware of what you don't need, too.

Some simple rules to start with: Keep the tools of your trade close at hand. Keep the things you need only sporadically farther away. Attempt to understand *space*, the importance it has in your life, the manner in which you do your best creative thinking. If you require room free of distraction while working, clear the decks. If you like to be cozy and warm with the fruits of your labor within sight, head in that direction.

Your files need updating? You haven't any idea where to find those 35mm slides on Romania three editors are willing to purchase? You've missed too many phone calls lately? Hire temporary help to reorganize trouble spots. The money spent will be worth it in freeing you to produce.

Examine your entire work space, the flow of paper, storage facilities, comfort of necessary equipment, color of the walls—everything. Coordinating the essentials need not be an expensive proposition. But it does take careful consideration and planning.

Discard any items that you learn are hindering your progress. The round file *may* be the most important and creative one you have. However, if you use it indiscriminately you'll have to trust your memory and your librarian more than ever.

Filing and retrieving

As you become more professional, the overabundance of paper—around your desk, in closets and files, on shelves all over your work and living space—will cry out for organization and constant scrutiny. Integration is a key. And separation, too.

The tickler file, with current chores divided by days of the month (or weekly if you prefer), is a beginning. It can become your own private secretary. Although I have many filing cabinets for articles I've written and correspondence and background material, my tickler file for current chores for a month is in the file nearest to my desk. There's a thirty-day divider for correspondence to be answered, queries to send, and other necessary chores slipped behind the proper day of the month I've allotted for the work. This material is turned over daily. It gets moved to a permanent place elsewhere when it has been completed. Also near at hand in the tickler drawer are folders for current bills and moneys due.

I also have files divided by the client's name, containing all correspondence (queries, letters, assignment notes, contracts, notes on telephone calls, etc.). When I no longer work with that client or magazine, I keep the file for several years (in another room), then pull any items that seem necessary to save (like contracts) and toss the rest. I maintain separate files for professional organizations I belong to, and clean them out regularly.

Much that I used to save religiously when I was first beginning to freelance never makes it to a permanent or semipermanent place in my files anymore. I've learned to discriminate. You should too. When necessary I slip a colored cross-reference card into one file, leading me back to my main source. While I might remember for quite a while where the material is, I've learned that the part-time helpers I occasionally employ can't read my mind.

The best way to think about organizing your material is to list the categories you want to keep track of. Then head to a stationery store, which should have all the latest equipment that well-organized corporate secretaries demand. If you can't see the purpose of the tabs, systems, notebooks, and so forth, be sure to ask a knowledgeable clerk for clarification. It may be something you'd never use in a million years of freelancing. On the other hand, it just might be incorporated into your situation with ease and make filing and retrieving an almost enjoyable chore. Ask librarians, too, how their files and materials are organized. (See the explanation of the Dewey decimal system in the Appendix.)

One other caveat: Keep current with your filing chores. While time-management experts say it's best to handle a piece of paper only once, there are times when I can't make myself adhere to this rule. Naturally, then, there is a basket at the end of my worktable marked "to file." But I keep a watch on that basket, never letting it get beyond a certain height. Whenever I've slipped up, I've discovered I can't face the job of filing at all. So build into your weekly schedule a special time to clear up filing on a regular basis.

The primary purpose of a filing system is not *convenient storage* but *quick retrieval*. What seems elaborate at the outset may soon prove inadequate when the flow of assignments increases. Think ahead.

Some files you may want to consider:

1. Markets (subdivided by geographic area or kind—slick consumer magazine, trade magazine, newspaper, syndicate, children's book publisher, etc.).

2. Telephone Rolodex (business numbers only).

3. Files of business calling cards you collect through interviews, business lunches, and conferences.

4. Resources (public relations people, government agencies, libraries, specialized collections, organizations, universities, experts in specified areas, etc.).

5. Ideas (clipping files, idea lists, copies of queries).

6. Tickler (queries out, correspondence held for reply, billing, accounts receivable).

7. A separate tickler file for copyrights by date due for renewal (see Chapter 11).

8. Contracts and royalty statements.

9. Paid bills.

10. Clipping file by category (medical, sports, family relations, etc.).

11. Production schedules/situation summaries. (It may be handiest to keep these in a ring binder.)

12. Statements (income, expenses, profit and loss, tax data, equipment purchases and depreciation schedules, etc.).

13. Stories in inventory (those not sold or to be tried for reprint, updating, etc.).

14. Form letters; query cover letters; forms for other activities. (Successful writers who can afford the hefty outlay can use word processors to store these.)

15. Copies of your published work. (Portfolios are a useful way to keep them.)

16. Photos in inventory: a card file with numbers and descriptions, where sold, and so forth; a photo tickler file if you have many going out to clients.

17. A tickler for lecture ideas, contacts.

18. Promotional possibilities; a graphics scrapbook; slide presentations.

19. Grants and possible alternate sources of income, with dates for application.
20. Work by others—at least a list of names, dates of their publication, and so forth—if you were in any way instrumental in helping their work into print (students' work, or work you inspired, etc.).

Although you can keep your files simple to begin with—one folder per story sold—as business escalates, so too does the need to refine and separate. When you subdivide and sort, try to work out a simple system you can rely on for cross-reference to keep you on course. A sheet of paper or a card labeled "See also: File on X" can save precious time.

Consider using color-coded paper (white for manuscripts, yellow for copies, blue for interview lists/phone numbers, green for research material lists, for example) to aid in filing, and color-coded cards that correspond to the paper if you need the information in permanent form. This also works well for a card file of photographic work (white for black-and-white, orange for 35mm slides, blue for outsize negatives, etc.).

Setting up your files will be one of the most important aspects of your business. Get off to the right start. Build in time for a periodic review. If your papers appear to be eating you alive, and you realize you're spending more time retrieving information than actually writing, do something about it quickly.

Production planning

Anyone can get caught in the bind of too many small projects that are interesting but don't pay their way, let alone create a profit. Worse, you may on occasion work for markets that don't keep their promises to pay. At year's end, though you've been writing constantly, you find yourself in the hole.

Be realistic about what you can do. Include in your analysis the drift of current publishing trends. Are you heading the same way? If not, what should you do about it?

When Ann R. decided she had to take in $20,000 in the coming year in order to show a reasonable profit above her expenses, she was making a huge leap from her previous year's earnings. She analyzed what she'd accomplished and what she hadn't, and decided that a formal plan was the only answer. She devised a detailed production schedule for the coming year with a built-in review time each month. She also marked specific billing dates (in red ink), since she knew she had to be reminded to do bookkeeping chores. That was the year her productivity and income amazed her as well as her agent.

Ease into systematic production planning by starting with a desk diary—any good executive diary will do, or use the one produced by Writer's Digest Books. You'll be looking for one that allots a page to each day, perhaps subdivided into segments, with plenty of space for notations on your production and billing schedules, and which will also allow you to note expenses and a list of important telephone numbers.

The production schedule entered in such a diary would begin with assignments already nailed down and would include:

■ Deadline and basic specifications (photos to accompany text; sidebars; acknowledgments; graphs or charts).

■ Schedule for initial research. Library work to be completed by a fixed date.

■ Dates and hours for interviews and telephone numbers. Are your interviewees going to be available when you need them? Don't forget time differences if you must make calls abroad.

■ Date for progress report to your editor. (Or to check desirability of new material you've unearthed in the course of research. You don't want to leave the editor high and dry until the last minute if the project isn't going in the direction first contemplated. It may be salvageable—up to a point. If not, let your editor know.)

■ Dates permissions, quotes, supplementary material should be requested. Dates they're due in your hands, ready to be assembled in the package you've agreed to submit.

Set up that production schedule before you have assignments—a sort of sketch to see how you can fit in trips, interviews, writing time, research time, and so forth, at the beginning of any major period. Laying queries out into groups works for some writers. (Scheduling several interviews in a certain region, for instance, saves time, effort, and money.) It's wise to schedule your own deadlines. *Don't wait for editors to schedule them for you.* If you seem to be running sixteen different places in one month, look things over. Perhaps you could do your work in the future in, say, four *planned* trips.

Your billing schedule is a somewhat different matter. Of course you will send your bill when you've done your job. Since many publishers are slow in paying, don't be hesitant to let them know what they owe you. Send the bill with the completed manuscript. (Unless your editor tells you otherwise. Some say they want your complete bill—fee and expenses—in one invoice.) If all figures on expenses aren't in yet (telephone bills seldom arrive so conveniently), a note on your bill to the effect that those will come later will cover you. Then when they do come in, send them off promptly on an additional invoice.

The basic schedule for billing should be entered in your diary. It shows you roughly *when* you can expect your money. Naturally you'll want to match that against the schedule of foreseeable expenses.

Check your projected expenses scrupulously when each new assignment comes in (with new requirements for an outlay of money) as well as at periodic review times.

Basic manuscript preparation

This may seem a strange section to include in a volume written for people who presumably already know how to write. But you wouldn't be surprised if you were sitting on the editor's side of the desk. Even many professionals I've encountered are guilty of beginners' mistakes when it comes to submitting their material. That's not because they don't know better, but because they are rushed, running behind schedule, never learned to type with more than a couple of fingers, or because they feel that since they've reached a certain plateau of professionalism, the editor will overlook a degree of sloppiness.

They're right. Editors who know them will overlook it. (But they don't like to.) If the editor doesn't know you from Adam, she'll get a pretty poor first impression if you send her a dog-eared, hastily prepared manuscript or query. The old cliché is still important: Neatness counts. It shows you care. Think of it this way—if you don't care about how your initial presentation looks, what guarantee does the editor or your client have that you'll care about anything else?

■ Your material should always be typed. Pica type is preferred because it's easier to read, but isn't an absolute necessity. Make sure you use a good, dark ribbon and keep the keys of your typewriter unclogged. For corrections, use any of the materials on the market that make almost invisible corrections (correction fluid or paper). Don't use erasable bond. It smears. Don't use onionskin paper or colored paper. It's possible to use perfectly good, cheap (if only relatively so) paper of a sixteen- to twenty-pound variety.

■ Be sure your name, address, telephone number, and the word length are on the first page of the manuscript. The page number and your name and a word or two identifying the manuscript title go on *every* subsequent page. (See fig. 6-3 for an example.)

■ Always double-space your manuscript.

■ Don't staple the pages together; use a paper clip. No fancy binders are necessary. They only add to the mailing weight.

■ For book manuscripts or proposals, number the pages consecutively. You can ship long manuscripts in a box a ream of typing paper came in.

■ Use envelopes approximately 10x13. Always enclose an SASE (self-addressed stamped envelope) for the return.

■ First-class is the best way to send any written material, since it is handled with more care and gets to its destination faster. It's more expensive, but safer—the post office isn't required to return undeliverable fourth-class mail to the sender.

■ If you have enclosed photos, always use a stiff backing of cardboard that is slightly larger than your sheet of contacts, photos, or plastic sleeve holding 35mm slides. Mark the outside of your envelope "Photos—Do Not Bend" (on both sides).

Managing your mail

The daily scenario: You're trying to work on an article, and you keep jumping up to see if the mailman has arrived. You spend so much time worrying about that mailbox that you can't begin to concentrate on writing.

The only way to keep from falling into this trap is to prepare ahead. *Know* that's your reaction and consider the villainous truth: If you don't ignore the mail and get the article written, you'll not have money or time for new assignments. Start long before the mailman is due. Allow yourself an exact amount of time, when the mail does come, to check it over. Then get back to your writing. Or promise yourself you'll read it when you have the first draft done or on your first scheduled break. It holds a rejection slip? Don't let the depression ruin your workday. Pop the query into a fresh envelope and send it off to another market *that same day*. You'll have it off

Approx. 3000 wds.
First rights only

Jane Smith
809 Elm St.
Denver, CO 80902
(303) 551-6827

THOSE OLD-TIME POSTCARDS

by Jane Smith

The body of the text begins here. Be certain to leave
reasonable margins on either side and at the bottom of the
page. Double-space the text. Remember, if the material is
purchased the editor will need room to make editing marks and
flag information for the printer. As you end each page you
may add "more" at the bottom if you wish to alert the printer
to look for another page. At the end you can simply type
"End" or "30" to signify that is all there is.

-more-

Fig. 6-3. *Sample first page of a manuscript.*

your desk and on its way to another possible sale. You won't sit around feeling dejected, and the current project won't have suffered from the interruption.

When I told one writer I advocated sending off a new query the same day a rejection came in, he said, "It seems to me there is a potential here to sidetrack the whole time-management process. The distraught freelancer moons over the rejected manuscript for a minute, then resolutely prepares to mail it out. But there's the time taken to find a new market, the time for a new query, or at least a cover letter, and so on, which equals wasted time—time not being spent on the manuscript at hand." That can be true, of course. But if your queries and forms and query card file are already researched and prepared (or partially so), it won't take more than a couple of minutes to get it ready again. You can also set aside a certain time each day (after you've completed your current writing assignment) to send queries out. The main point is, if you're certain your queries are written in as exciting a manner as possible and are aimed at the proper market, keep those queries going out regularly. Time is precious for pertinent ideas. Don't waste it.

Telephone tricks

I mentioned earlier that you can use the *Writer's Digest Diary* or its equivalent as a supplementary telephone log book wherein you keep the names and numbers of your clients. That may seem an unnecessary duplication, but it's not. Keeping the numbers where they are needed can be a big time saver when you are hot on the trail of new informants, new leads to jobs, and so on. And it can be crucial when you are billing clients for long-distance expenses.

For writers with too much to keep track of to fit into a desk diary, I suggest a separate telephone log book. Keep it adjacent to your phone or on top of the phone-answering machine. Each day jot down incoming and outgoing business calls of importance by date, name, and telephone number. If an editor is calling regarding an assignment, adding a brief note saves scrambling through piles of papers for the answer to "What was it he asked me specifically to find out about for the manuscript on old-time radio drama?"

One busy writer I know who successfully manages his time allots a precise segment—one hour—for an agreed-upon appointment. He knows his attention span. He turns on his telephone-answering machine and allows no interruptions while the discussion is in progress. When it's over, he returns any calls he might have received in the interim.

He uses his machine to cover for him especially during his planned writing hours—four hours every day of the week—so the telephone becomes his best tool and not his worst. "At first there was always a temptation to answer and leave that damned contraption alone. But when I got used to it, I found my straight, uninterrupted stretches at the typewriter made a huge difference in my bank account."

Sylvia Auerbach, a writer who does a good deal of lecturing, found that clients were often catching her off guard. They'd call to ask her to make a speech somewhere and immediately ask what she charged. To stave off stammering something before she wanted to commit herself, and to give herself time to figure out which fee to charge, she put a list of pertinent questions right over the phone. How large is the audience? What sort of organization would she be speaking to? How long would she speak? Will expenses be paid? And so on. She can reply with firmness as to what her rates are (calculated on the basis of the answers to the above) and what other conditions she requires before committing herself.

Faced with a problem with an editor, another writer says she mentally prepares herself before making the fateful call. She jots down all the important information—what and when and why not, how much, etc.—before placing the call. She *stands up* to telephone when making a difficult call, because she learned in a public-speaking course that her voice carried more authority that way.

As soon as you are working steadily (or even now and then successfully) with a client, ask if it's all right if you call collect. Most businesses realize that is part of their overhead. When you do, of course, do so with discretion. Don't spend too much time on the phone chatting about insignificant details that could as easily be handled by mail.

Mort Weisinger, former president of the ASJA, was famous for his trick of calling celebrities for needed quotes from a phone booth. With a huge stack of coins, he'd place his calls (often during the lunch hour, when the secretary was out of the office but not the boss). When the celebrity heard this freelancer plunking down all those coins, he would often take pity and give him the time needed.

Employees

Sooner or later you may find yourself hiring others to help you. Since you may have chosen to freelance to get away from the problems of being in someone else's employ, try to avoid the mistakes you remember employers made.

Give instructions clearly. Acknowledge the limits of energy and time of others. (Just because you respond to the pressure of a deadline doesn't mean they will. Try to plan what you'll need in advance so your typist or other helper can complete the job properly without feeling too pushed.) Remember to reward extraordinary effort in some way. Try to take the time (it doesn't take much) to show interest in helpers' problems and lives without getting involved in them. And ask them occasionally if they know of a better way to do what you've asked to be done.

Stay up to date on IRS rulings regarding freelancers and any independent contractors. Your accountant should alert you to any changes in the law and the new requirements affecting you.

Don't take employees for granted, or they will very quickly (unless they're members of the family) find other employment.

Ten timesaving tips

The Center for Creative Leadership studied managers and how they work:

> The work of managers consists of numerous brief episodes in which the important and unimportant are capriciously interspersed. Much of it involves giving and receiving information, mostly through oral communication. *It is not clear how much control managers have over their own activities.* Managers work long hours; they are busy doing a lot of things; their work is fragmented and episodes are brief; the job contains a lot of variety; the work is predominantly oral; managers have contact with a variety of people; managers are not reflective planners; information is the core of their job; managers really don't have an accurate picture of how they spend their time.

Sound familar? Busy managers have much in common with busy freelancers. Here are some tips that help:

1. Work at as clean a desk as possible. Move projects, important correspondence, etc., off your desk each week *on schedule*.

2. Aim to handle routine paperwork, such as correspondence, only once. (This seldom can be achieved unless you have an army of full-time secretaries, but make it a primary effort.)

3. Make "to do" lists daily.

4. Use the A-B-C priority system. Write an A on items with high value, B for those with medium value, and C with low value. Save the B's for later. C's may not need doing at all.

5. Ask yourself, "What is the best use of my time *right now*?"

6. Allow yourself rewards upon completion of a job.

7. Plan review time. Look at what happened yesterday, what will happen today, and what needs you have for the future. Keep reviews short—five to ten minutes.

8. Delegate low-priority jobs when you can—typing final drafts of manuscripts, doing preliminary research, telephoning to set up interviews, ordering regular supplies, etc.

9. Force yourself to make *action* decisions. Many important jobs are delayed simply because people avoid making decisions.

10. At the end of each day, take fifteen minutes to *plan* tomorrow. The next morning you'll have a tentative schedule of the day's activities.

Just as the successful business starts with a master plan, the masterful business person keeps uppermost in mind the priorities which evolve from it. The time saved by using this modus operandi is the bonus you will be looking for when your business increases.

Chapter 7
Research—
Jackhammer
of Your Trade

■■

The many kinds of research

The term research is often misunderstood by neophytes. They equate it with the vision of scholars holed up for years in musty corners of specialized libraries preparing the definitive work on an obscure regional poet. Research done by successful freelancers is quite a bit more varied than that. It keeps them on the move and often as not out of the library stacks as in them. Research consists of such activities as clipping newspapers and magazines; studying specialized newsletters and public relations handouts; making an ongoing check of specialized material printed for a particular profession (for instance, the latest psychological abstracts); examining scrapbooks, photo albums, and diaries; investigating police reports and records relating to business consolidations or real estate at city hall; placing ads in a broad spectrum of publications; continuous correspondence and telephoning; using computers to track the most revealing data base; listening to tapings of oral histories; looking for trends in all areas of human endeavor (by keeping one's eyes and ears open when buying the groceries, attending a concert or lecture, or gathered around the fire with friends); and all manner of interviewing.

Jackdaws love my big sphinx of quartz. (Shortest English sentence yet devised to include all letters of the alphabet. Source: Evening newspaper quoting *The Book of Lists*.) It's helpful to stash away such silly or dramatic bits of random information, strange anecdotes, or revealing statistics for later use. Even before you begin to sell what you write, clip items that interest you. (A Clip-it, which is essentially a razor blade with a handle and can be found in most stationery stores, is handier than scissors for the purpose). Paste the clippings onto cards and file them according to your interests (or areas of weakness you wish to strengthen).

Other than the random clipping outlined above, there's clipping (or photocopying) printed material that falls into broad, general topics. In order to see the necessity for this you should consider your writer's research on the widest possible scale. It separates into three categories: that done *right now* for a specific assignment, your *general* reading to discover new subjects and angles on subjects which you'll turn into queries for articles and book proposals, and that which you'll use to *update* your entire freelance operation (conferences, professional meetings, network building, training sessions, etc.). Even some of the pros fudge the research in the third category as their schedules fill up with work related to the first two.

You can bet your first royalty check that many of the suggestions in this chapter are time-consuming. But, if you look at them *only* as nibbling away at your precious hours, you'll soon enough find yourself falling steadily behind.

Your job, then, is to refine your methods of research, keep them suitable to their eventual use, and expand your flow of work in the process. Since each new research project has its unique qualities, stay open to fresh possibilities wherever they might be. Heading doggedly to the same library shelves or other sources for each successive project is wasteful and often frustrating, and can, in the long run, be counterproductive.

The professional approach

First, consider this. The best kind of research is what writers have an abundance of—their own experience. Angus Wilson claims his early experiences, growing up in seedy hotels and near gambling tables, developed his imaginative powers. "Telling lies is the basis of fiction," said Wilson in an interview in the *Iowa Spectator*. His father was a gambler and "in some degree a confidence trickster." Most of the people he lived among at London's Kensington hotels were "failed people." They talked to the boy Wilson, telling him "long stories I don't believe they would have told people their own age. They wanted to talk and they felt free because they thought I wouldn't understand. They were right, because the key to those stories was sex, of which I understood nothing, and money, of which I have never understood anything."

The importance of this cannot be overemphasized. Many beginning freelancers have a tendency to downgrade their own experiences, not seeing in them the germs of their best writing material. Others, aware that the caveat "Write what you know" is pronounced often at writing seminars, make the error of trying to write *only* from their limited viewpoint instead of incorporating their specific personal knowledge of a subject with quotes from experts, statistics, and the results of legwork.

Start, then, with your own experiences—your life research—and blend it with specific research for each project you do. As your writing career progresses, you'll be struck by how many times the research for one job will overlap the research for another.

Be aware, too, that freelancers take any number of different approaches to specific research, depending on the subject itself and their knowledge of it, their expertise at both writing and researching and their personalities. Some pros admit research is the most trying part of their jobs, while others consider it the most appealing. By and large, beginning writers seem to fall into two categories—they either over- or under-research. The over-researchers often lack confidence and are procrastinating about writing. These are the ones who talk endlessly about the new material they've dug up that necessitates even more digging (instead of writing). The under-researchers, on the contrary, gloss over huge holes in their material, hoping their flair with the written word will camouflage their neglect. Recognize both extremes as you go about your own researching, since you must be the judge of how much research is necessary for each project you tackle.

Your research and how you approach it should be keyed to the amount of *time* you have to get the job done, the *costs* involved (are some of them being covered by the publisher?), and the *scope* of the work. Since the amount of research needed to do a professional job often seems out of proportion to the pay offered, most inexperienced researchers will want to be especially careful recording time spent on the job and out-of-pocket expenses. As you land more lucrative assignments, you'll want to know what sort of time and effort will be required for a given project so you'll be able to negotiate a reasonable fee. (See TIP sheet, fig. 7-1.)

Aside from the fact that you have only so much time or money to research and write any given project, everyone has only so much energy and interest to give before reaching the saturation point. Cutting the research task to fit appropriately is an essential first step. It doesn't matter whether the project before you is a short, chatty piece for the local weekly on the oldest man in town, a novelized version of Howard Hughes's life, or an interview with a prince. The methods are the same; only the time spent on total research and the volumes of backup data you accumulate will vary. The preliminary procedures for slicing the job to fit are:

Think through the project from beginning to end. (Sherlock Holmes sets the perfect example. He never made a false move because he took time to analyze the problem facing him first.)

Decide *what* you need to know and *how much* information you think you'll need. By doing so you'll discover the *kind* of material you're seeking—statistics, expert opinion, colorful anecdotes, historical synopses, and the like. *Make a list* of pertinent questions that must be answered as well as a secondary set of beneficial but not absolutely crucial queries.

Subject:_____

Client:_____

Production Period:_____

Payment:_____

Total Research Period:_____

    Library work:_____

    Telephone interviews:_____

    Travel time and interviews:_____

Total Writing Period:_____

    Organizing notes,
     tape transcription:_____

    Writing period:_____

    Rewrite period:_____

    Additional editorial work:_____

Extra Requirements:

    Illustrations, photographs:_____

    Assembly, layout, permissions,
     verifications, etc:_____

Total Hours per Project:_____

Income per Hour:_____

Fig. 7-1. *Sample TIP (time in progress) sheet.*

List your *probable sources* of information in the order in which they most logically should be tapped. This list will include names of those persons locally who just *might* have some interest in your subject. Here's where your general clipping policy comes in handy. Your research topic is numismatics. You've clipped a story about a businessman in your community for another purpose. But don't you recall the story mentioned in passing that the man had a hobby of collecting old coins? Here's a local authority at your fingertips. Other people keep files, clippings, photographs, scrapbooks, etc.— hobbyists especially. These are often the people who become a wellspring of colorful stories and anecdotes. At the very least, they can lead the writer to other people with private collections or primary-source libraries. Considering your schedule and research budget, *realign the order* in which you might best tap the sources.

Simultaneously, as you're checking any clippings you might have saved, you should examine thoroughly your own library, your children's schoolbooks, and any neighbor's cache you might have access to.

The next shortcuts are the telephone and telephone book, especially the Yellow Pages. Using them creatively is a modus operandi that often leads you past the public library to special libraries of organizations, universities, museums, companies, service clubs (Kiwanis, Rotary, Elks, etc.), or helps you bypass the main library for the correct branch with the specific holdings you're seeking. Some libraries are prepared to answer brief, factual queries by phone, too, a decided timesaver in many cases. If yours doesn't offer this service, make a point to discover the nearest library that does.

Ask, too, what your government can do for you. The Library of Congress, particular departments and agencies (Department of Commerce, Agriculture, etc., FDA, FBI, and state and local agencies, for example), congressmen, senators, organizations or lobbyists, and more—all are prepared to provide answers to queries. Here again, preliminary scouting is essential. The Washington, D.C., phone book is available either at your telephone company office or library reference department.

Search for data on microfiche. Look around for an available computer to do some of the searching for you. Not everything is indexed on computers yet, but there may be just the information you need. Some major libraries have the computerized Magazine Index Data Base, which is beginning to make the *Readers' Guide to Periodical Literature* obsolete. Specialized libraries (universities, medical libraries, etc.) often have data available through computer; the fees for their use can vary from minimal to not so. To learn how to use one efficiently, it helps considerably to get expert help, however.

Shorten your research tasks by looking to indexes and clippings maintained by newspapers and magazines. Some wide-circulation publications such as *Time, Newsweek,* the *Washington Post,* the *Los Angeles Times,* and the *Christian Science Monitor* have full-time staff experts who will on occasion help the serious freelancer with a firm assignment. Whether you can get this kind of help or not, you normally can get tearsheets of material they've published simply by requesting it by exact date and page.

Still another source of research help that saves false steps is the local newspaper, television, or radio reporter. Most are approachable (if they're not facing a tight deadline). When you've hit a snarl and need a minimum of information, give one a call. The person behind a bylined article has a file of research—more material than the printed story might indicate. While no reporter will have the time to read it all to you, most are willing to relay a few names, addresses, or telephone numbers to a fellow writer.

Don't be dismayed if the first writing ventures require more research time than you think should be required. There *is* a time balance between legitimate over-research and procrastination. But you're getting your feet wet. As your expertise grows—both in writing and researching—so, too, will your confidence. And these early forays into researching for a writing project will inevitably increase your knowledge of the many sources of vital information available. Just try to keep from becoming so enamored of your subject that you're sidetracked from your goal, which is to get as much information of the right kind as efficiently as possible.

Systematize the search

Sometimes there's a good reason to over-research. Nora Ephron says she prefers to; she has been known to gather data from more than fifty interviews before she sat down to write a long article. The extensive interviews with celebrities in *Playboy* and the three- or four-part series that occasionally appear in *The New Yorker* require an inordinate amount of research. Given the task of writing about the use of satellites by Norway's offshore oil community I discovered I had to research both oil-drilling technology and the intricacies of recent innovations in satellite technology. Not the least problem of the on-site investigation was deciphering the technical information relayed by a Norwegian technician whose English was heavily accented. I was delighted that I'd over-researched when I sat down to review the taped interviews and to write.

But whether you need stacks of material or not, apply a system for *getting* your material quickly, *using it most effectively*, and *retrieving it later* in your career. While libraries may seem to be labyrinths (the New York Public Library's main building has eighty miles of bookshelves), they're also convenient storehouses. Your research for any given project may well begin with a trip to one. Certainly fledgling freelancers, not yet equipped with a large collection of files and clippings, will want to rely heavily on public sources. In approaching them you'd do well to heed the advice of Alden Todd, author of *Finding Facts Fast*, who believes in mixing "techniques that combine the skill of four kinds of professionals: the *reference librarian*, the *university scholar*, the *investigative reporter*, and the *detective*." Knowing how each of these experts focuses on the job of research, what resources they rely on, and what tricks they apply will smooth your path considerably. And of course don't just try to emulate them—consult them.

The *reference librarian's* approach to research is through a knowledge of the vast array of indexes, almanacs, dictionaries, bibliographic titles, and vertical files at his disposal. Getting acquainted with the reference material available to you will be one of your first priorities. A good reference librarian, one I hope you have befriended by now, will be a well of information. If you are as lucky as I was in the beginning of my nonfiction writing career, you'll happen upon a great one like Peg Deignan, who for nearly fifty years *was* the Providence Public Library. Whenever I alerted her to subjects I was interested in, she filed the idea in her formidable memory. She continued to point me in the right direction—often long after my first query to her—until I had built sizable files on my pet projects. Positioned as she was in the library hierarchy, she seemed to know everyone in the city and state who might be of help in my searches. And since most libraries are linked to others in their states and nationally through interlibrary loan agreements, there's little that should not be quickly and readily available to you. Let your librarian help you uncover these sources, and you'll be able to keep your research budget within bounds.

(Since libraries are important to you as a writer in so many ways, it pays to remember them at budget time, too. Contribute funds when you can [your contribution to them is deductible], subscriptions to periodicals, or extra copies of books you might have. Once you've begun to publish regularly, the librarian might ask for a bibliography of your work. If not, offer it for their files on local authors. It's nice to discover they're happy to get material on you—a boost to your ego. You've become a celebrity in your own right. Not only that, the news will get around, which is no small help to the cause of publicity.)

Scholars are another source to call upon. Their knowledge is highly specialized. They have spent their lives developing in-depth comprehension of particular information. They will be cognizant of related disciplines and esoteric facts. And normally they will be acquainted with a great many others in their field of expertise. Ask for letters of introduction to their colleagues at other universities, museums, or laboratories if you see they can help you find your information. From the scholar's technique—concentration in great depth in one subject—you can borrow the discipline of thoroughness, without carrying it nearly as far as he does. An invaluable source to help you find these scholars is *Who Knows—and What, among Authorities, Experts, and the Specially Informed*, which covers 12,000 specialists in 35,000 areas of expertise. If you've tracked down several through this source and want to know more about them, look into the various volumes of *Who's Who*.

Then there is the *investigative reporter*. Contrary to the popular view, his work is far from glamorous, unless you consider wading through ten thousand criminal indictments, police complaints, warrants, arrest sheets, bail applications, and court hearings glamorous. A prime factor in the investigative reporter's research, though, is time. He must complete this thorough research on deadline. The good reporter knows he must check facts and quotes thoroughly (he takes copious notes as he goes along) but that eventually, he must "go with what he's got." Besides the two Leonard Downie, Jr., calls "The Stardust Twins" (Woodward and Bernstein), there are plenty of other scoop artists around and books about the ways they ply their trade—excellent studies with tips you may want to emulate—such as Downie's *The New Muckrakers, The Boys on the Bus* by Timothy Crouse, and Denis Brian's *Murderers and Other Friendly People*.

Detectives and *private investigators* work with probabilities, official documents, confidential indexes, and government resources. Their specialties are the law and human behavior patterns. Some of the tricks they use to uncover information can be particularly helpful to the freelancer in search of anecdotes and colorful copy. They are masters at combining what often appears to be infinite patience with timely impatience. Hollywood to the contrary, a stakeout can be a monumental bore. Talk to a detective and you'll discover how easy it is to gather quite a bit of data about someone on the basis of his driver's license. If you can't find a detective listed in your local telephone book or through a local newspaper reporter, you can contact the World Association of Detectives, Box 5068, San Mateo CA 94402.

Remembering how each of these experts goes about his work is the first step to systematically approaching your material. With your project questions laid out in front of you, *decide which expert's procedure is best.* Often you'll use a combination of them. The next three moves, in order, are: *look at primary reference books first, ask a librarian for assistance,* and *spread the word widely about your quest.*

Basic reference material you'll investigate will depend on your subject. Often you'll want to start with an encyclopedia, either a general one such as *Britannica* or a specialized one dealing with your particular subject, such as the *Penguin Encyclopedia of Places.* Some authors head straight for indexes such as the *Bibliographic Index* (which lists books and articles that have bibliographies), the *Subject Guide to Books in Print,* or the *Readers' Guide to Periodical Literature,* depending on their needs. Almanacs of all kinds can help if you're looking for statistics (for example, the *Information Please Almanac,* the *CBS News Almanac, The U.S. Fact Book, The Naturalist's Almanac, Future Facts,* as well as almanacs compiled for states and regions).

Then, too, many of the books you'll explore on your library's shelves will have two other features of use in your searches—bibliographies leading to other sources and neighboring books nearby dealing with various aspects of the same subject. After you consult a particular source, make sure you note what it provided, or that it wasn't useful, and why, so that you don't return to obvious dead ends. These notes can be kept in a card file (see fig. 7-2).

The juvenile department in any library is also a source not to be forgotten. In many cases a subject will be discussed in a juvenile book with just the simplicity and depth you need without delving into technicalities you might not fathom or want. Because these books are written to appeal to young people, they often provide lively anecdotes or description you won't easily find elsewhere.

Locating anecdotal material and dramatic description seem to stump the novice most in library research. Yet much of what they

```
BLUE BOOK OF BROADMINDED              PPL
BUSINESS BEHAVIOR
Auren Uris                           B174
T.Y.Crowell                          U76b
1968

Good, thorough treatment of business
behavior for everyone.
```

```
MANNERS IN BUSINESS                   PPL
Elizabeth Gregg MacGibbon            B174
Macmillan                            M145m2
new, revised, enlarged 1954

Exceedingly dated for my purposes.
```

Fig. 7-2. *Sample entries from a research card file.*

want might be lurking in unusual places—biographies, particular fiction and poetry, film, photos, travel books, and anthologies. The key here is to know what *kind* of material you need to spark your writing. With practice, the retrieval process eases. To see how a nonfiction book utilizes fiction techniques you'll want to dip into several, examining how each chapter began, taking note of why an author used a figure from mythology to demonstrate a point, and so forth. Such study will be part of your *ongoing* research, since these nuggets are less obvious to the unpracticed eye than conclusions from a set of Census Department figures. But they're there for the finding.

Because there is such a vast array of material in most libraries, I strongly urge you to seek the librarian's expert advice before going further, once you've looked at the basic references and the card catalog. This person's knowledge of the library's holdings, and familiarity with the possibilities of material cross-referenced under headings you might not have thought of, will save you hours of search time.

Ask the librarian, too, about the holdings in the vertical files—the library's own clippings, booklets, and rare documents. Or when you discover a source is "at the bindery" and therefore inaccessible to you for a period of time, see if the librarian can come up with an alternate source. If the material is highly specialized, this expert may well know someone in your region with an interest in it. Such a person might own not only the book you're after but many other valuable volumes you could ask to peruse.

Remember that libraries these days are far more than repositories of books. They hold magazines, newspapers, catalogs, microfilm and microfiche, collections of photographs, films, and tape recordings. Many have computers that allow the researcher access to data stored in other libraries. (If yours doesn't have this service, your librarian will doubtless know where one is available nearby.) Some of the larger libraries have added lectures, classes, ecological tours, etc., to their list of services to the public, which can be a source of information (and contacts) in your research plans.

Spreading the word about your quest may well be the most important part of your research strategy, since no matter how well you research there comes a time when you simply can't find what you need. Then all your casual comments about your search to friends, students, secretaries, the postman, auto mechanic, or hairdresser (as well as news reporters and other writing colleagues) come home to roost.

Obviously, the kind of research that yields the richest deposits of gold for your purposes takes ingenuity and constant practice. A happy fact, though—it gets in your blood. Remember, research often begins in the library, but it doesn't take place there exclusively. You'll be researching when you're sleepily sipping your tea and watching the morning news, as well as when you're catching a glimpse of some late late show. Ellen Goodman, *Boston Globe* columnist and Pulitzer Prize winner, says, "I'm not always writing in my head, but I'm always storing things like a computer. Then one day I press the button and there it is, more than I thought was there." Research for writing is unstoppable. During a particularly arduous writing task, your head will be so crammed with information even your dreams will begin to be affected. When that happens, be *pleased.* It usually means you're well on your way to the solution of your research puzzle.

Systematize storage and retrieval

As the results of a given research project begin to come in, handle them systematically so that when you begin to type up a finished draft, you can work from an already organized sheaf of documents.

One simple system for managing the inflow is the card-file approach—with the cards each having a proper place between prearranged headings and subheadings. This system, with lists of questions under each subheading that are to be answered before one can progress to the next, works well for many projects. Something like it is essential for longer endeavors, such as a book.

Some writers prefer to use file folders instead of card files. All of the clippings or other data for a section go in a separate folder, and the entire bunch of folders fits into a box about the size of a ream of paper. The box, properly labeled, can be filed on a bookshelf along with the backup material still in books.

It doesn't really matter what you use—the important thing is to organize the material as it comes in (set up the organization plan *first*) and keep it all together, properly labeled and/or color-coded. When your project is completed, keep the material together for later retrieval. If there is something vital that must go back into your regular files, make a cross-reference telling where the original can be found with a note or card kept in the project folder.

Another way to organize material is to prepare a dummy booklet, somewhat on the order of the dummy magazine editors prepare when they are working up a new issue. Your dummy would have three or four times as many pages as you foresee for the finished article. Like the card file, it would be marked (with color-coded tabs) for the main subdivisions of your subject.

Nothing fancy is called for in preparing such a working dummy. Staple pages of typing paper together. Give yourself plenty of white space, on which you'll first paste the research findings in their appropriate places. The rest of the space is for notes, revisions, queries to yourself, titles, and telephone numbers still to be consulted. This method is particularly appealing to those with a need to visualize the growth of their project every step of the way.

When the pasting and jotting is finished, you'll have a draft that may only require being run once more through the typewriter before it is mailed. (Depending on your situation, typing skills, and other urgent assignments, you might want to consider using a professional typist at this point.)

Still another helpful tool is the notebook or research journal method. A certain number of pages are given to the data (book titles, articles, contacts for interviews with telephone numbers and addresses jotted alongside) collected for a single project.

Fiction writers faced with numerous characters and complex plots have developed systems for keeping track of them that might interest the researcher.

More than one novelist I know has found a wall map or chart the easiest way to plot ongoing work and to keep track of characters and situations. The advantage of this method is the ease with which crucial ingredients can be reshuffled and yet afford the writer a picture of the whole and its parts at a glance. Robin Perry's long rolls of paper with his manuscript printed out by his word processor (see Chapter 4) serves somewhat the same purpose as the novelist's map—a handy visual tool.

Whichever method you feel most comfortable with (after perhaps some trial and error) should be adopted and developed until it becomes second nature. The point is not which you choose, but that you choose and explore the limits of one. Obviously, the more organized you are at the beginning of any project, the simpler the eventual writing process will be.

Some material you may gather will need scrupulous analysis, sorting, and coding before it is of much use to you. For one of my recent projects I discovered a gold mine—a large file of correspondence on my subject—but the mountain of detail covering the nuggets of true worth was enormous. Much of the correspondence was in illegible scrawl. Deciding I didn't want to wade through it all more than once, I devised a set of symbols to indicate the variety of subdivisions of my subject and wrote them on a code card. I placed a stack of 4x5 file cards next to each folder of letters. As I read each one I numbered it, gave a 4x5 card the same number, then, using my code card for reference, jotted the corresponding code numbers and shorthand on the individual 4x5 card. When I had completed the formidable task I could see, with a simple shuffling of cards, which bits of correspondence I'd need again and which I wouldn't. I then proceeded to put signal notations on them that corresponded to my chapter subdivisions. After codifying it, I quickly photocopied the material I'd need to reexamine and shipped the bundle of originals back to the source.

Some research strategies

Schedule your homework early. The earlier you start your fact, quote, and anecdote gathering the better. If you can tell from your initial probings which segment of your project will probably hold the most difficulties for you—fresh and appealing anecdotes or top-notch quotes, for instance—make a concerted effort to allot a larger portion of time to it. You might be tempted to put these problemati-cal items last on your schedule. Don't. I'm not suggesting you get the cart before the horse; of course you may not recognize a good anec-dote that would fit until you've done some of the other work. But don't neglect scheduling time on your calendar for the hard parts of the job. If you think about them early and regularly review material to see if you're collecting enough, you're ahead of the game.

A former reporter for the *National Enquirer* who is now back freelancing credits the high pressure he formerly worked under for his increased flow of freelance assignments now. The strategy he applies comes from his hectic deadlines—they simply necessitated a workable system. "I don't have the WATS line anymore, but I have a telephone which I use with considerable discretion. I tap sources the moment I have a firm assignment, sometimes before. I make a few quick checks for names and numbers, then hop on the phone and interview fast." His primary homework and research tool is the timely interview (see the section on interviewing at the end of this chapter). Whether you'll be in as confident a position as he, though, you should note how *quickly* he gets down to work. He's learned the skills of the investigative reporter and detective well.

Don't stop in your research efforts, though after your initial probes you have yet to hit pay dirt. Even expert researchers like Alden Todd can be stumped for answers, as he told me:

> Once I got a request from a writer friend on the Pacific Coast. He was writing an article for a national magazine about George Boole, the nineteenth-century mathematician. Standard reference works gave plenty of material. But nowhere could my friend find any human-interest material about the man. Was he tall or short? Red-haired or bald? A believer or an agnostic?
>
> I did some cursory looking for biographical material on Boole but came up with nothing about the human being, only his theories and professional work. Then, suddenly, I solved the mystery. I saw a reference in the article on Boole in the *Dictionary of National Biography* that mentioned he had been a member of the Royal Society, the organization of notables in British science.
>
> Lightning struck me. I had it!
>
> Who knows best and who cares more about the personality who has just died? And who cares enough to put it in print? The members of that personality's fraternity, his professional colleagues, or business colleagues, or close associates. I went to the "Proceedings of the Royal Society" for 1864, the year of his death, and turned the pages for that and the immediately succeeding year, searching for the article of personal tribute I felt certain would be there. It was—five solid pages about the human being that the Royal Society members had known and appreciated.
>
> Moral of the story: When in doubt as to where to find something that you hope is somewhere in print, ask yourself: Who would know? Who would care? Who would care enough to have put it in print?

Let modern technology work for you. This strategy, increasingly important to freelancers in a hurry, is the one Judi Kesselman-Turkel applied to writing a diet and exercise book very fast. She used *MedLine,* a medical computer funded half by the federal government.

> For twenty-six dollars, I got an expert familiar with the computer programming to help me choose my search words, and,

within a few days, a listing of all the articles in the technical literature that were applicable to my topic, going back ten years. By just reading down the titles I could quickly pinpoint the ones most useful to me. Then, still in the medical library, I read and took notes on 3x5 cards *that were keyed to my chapter headings and subtopics*. After ten full days of research I was an expert on exercise and sports physiology, metabolism and diet, and the interaction of the two.

This research in the technical literature was extremely valuable for two other reasons: my knowledge was more up to date than it would have been had I read the popular literature instead of the technical stuff (it sometimes takes years for new theories to filter down), and I knew exactly who the experts were in the field so I could go right for the primary quotes, answers, summations that I needed.

In this same category of applying modern technology to research problems is the strategy of using the *tape recorder* (see the section on interviewing at the end of the chapter) and the *camera*. These are both contemporary tools many successful pros wouldn't be without. Jacqueline Briskin, novelist and short story writer, uses her camera to help her write fiction. She takes pictures "on location" which jog her memory of details of people and places in the territory she's concentrating on in a story. They may be only snapshots, but she doesn't care. The pictures help her remember "the feel of morning-cool sand and hear the laughing camaraderie of the surfers." Days or weeks later she can incorporate the sights and sounds into the plots of her books. The same has always held true for writers down through the ages—before Daguerre, the function of the camera's eye was performed by the words of the writer in his private journal. Some writers still keep journals and, frankly, I'm all for it. But if you haven't the time or the discipline for journal-keeping, at least consider the camera as a possible alternative.

If you can apply modern technology to research purposes, you can also approach the information jungle by the age-old system of getting in on *fact gathering firsthand*, as one student decided to do. Hearing about the four approaches to research (those of the librarian, scholar, investigative reporter, and detective), he lined up four of them, proposed he write a profile of each for the local paper, then proceeded to follow them around through a work day. He discovered they were all flattered to be asked and highly inquisitive about a freelancer's approach to work. Moral: If you want to know for sure, walk a mile in the other guy's moccasins.

Yet another strategy is to *hire research help.* Confronted with the monumental research tasks involved in 1,400-page books like *The People's Almanac* and *The Book of Lists,* the authors, David Wallechinsky, Irving Wallace, and Amy Wallace, had to employ help. So, too, do many freelancers with far less formidable projects. Students and librarians' assistants can be knowledgeable helpers, often at less cost than a full-time expert. How to find them? First, through your network of contacts (see Chapter 2). Second, through notices on bulletin boards in schools, libraries, copying services, laundromats, and third, through placing ads.

Since gathering enough of the right material is only part of the job, be certain your system takes into account *how you'll store it* and *how you'll retrieve it* effectively. The examples already given throw some light on this—my code-card plan for the letters and Judi's when faced with computer information. But there is another point to remember. If you're starting to freelance seriously, you'll find that any given bit of material has many uses, and you'll want to keep that material *alive* in your files. Too often a system that makes the material retrievable for the current project only is hurriedly set up. It pays to take the time initially to devise a scheme that works so well that it still makes sense months or years later. As you will keep your tapes of interviews and background information, as you will find a scheme for coding your photographs and other filed material, find one for this research material that won't kill the opportunity of using it for spin-offs in the future. (See the section on filing and retrieving in Chapter 6.)

A recap:

1. Do your homework early, following a well-laid-out schedule.
2. Don't be stumped because you've checked all the usual sources and found nothing useful.
3. Look for shortcuts through new technology, but don't ignore time-honored or unusual paths.
4. Hire research help when and if you can. Look for chances to barter or exchange research help when necessary. Build your network of contacts early and keep it viable.
5. Research is only as good as your storage and retrieval system. Keep records (notebook or card file) of books and other resource materials that cross your desk. Make certain you note, too, what the source provided, and whether it was useful and to what degree.

Identify and date clippings. Ask others who might be sending you clips to do the same. There's nothing more frustrating than to have good quotable material without a record of the source. Remember to cross-reference, and use color coding when appropriate.

6. For all of your research, apply a system to cut it down to size and to place it where it belongs. Periodically review the system to see how well it's working. If it's not, revise.

Sources of special help

"You can cut costs immeasurably by taking advantage of *PR Aids*, a weekly newsletter for the public relations trade," says Mort Yarmon, whose wife, Betty, edits it. Mort suggests you send her a note with your request. If you have an assignment and want to reach public relations practitioners who may have pertinent information for you—anecdotes, statistics, comments, etc.—she will publish your plea in the newsletter. PR people across the country will be immediately alerted. Don't be surprised if they phone you with just the information or tip you need. There is no charge to the freelance writer. The freight is paid by *PR Aids* subscribers in the PR field. (Newsletters of all sorts can be the answer to many research problems; see the Resources chapter.)

If you're trying to locate a very small town in a large state, as I was once—the kind of wide-space-in-the-road that doesn't appear on many maps—speak to your postman. His books will locate even the smallest dot if there's a post office there. Find out the area code for the dot, then call the information operator (1, the area code, then 555-1212) to track your prey. There is no charge for this long-distance call. (Toll-free 800 numbers can be obtained the same way, using 800 for the area code.)

Information about celebrities can sometimes stump you, especially if you're relatively new to freelance writing. For a fee, Celebrity Service will give you up-to-date information on the whereabouts of a given celebrity. (See the Resources chapter.) They operate on a one-time request or as a subscription service. The latter, which is expensive, will probably be worth it to you only when you are getting many assignments on stars. Then you might want to subscribe, or join with other writers in your locale with similar needs for a joint subscription and split the costs. A less precise source but far more agreeably priced for the novice freelancer is *How to Reach Anyone Who's Anyone* by Michael Levine.

Even your local celebrity story can present problems—how to find out more than the celebrity herself will tell you. So remember to ask, during any interviews, for names of people in her life she's considered important to her development—names you wouldn't know about from your library research, such as schoolteachers, childhood friends, etc. Then you can arrange to talk to those people who will, very often, come up with an entirely new slant on your subject.

For specialized research, such as medical data and tips, a medical secretary or lab technician will often be your best bet, at least for preliminary research. Offer him or her a reasonable retainer for information and tips supplied to you regularly.

If you require a broader picture of a subject—for example, what's going on in Houston—you might want to subscribe to that city's newspaper for a few weeks. "Multinewspapers" is a service that supplies English-language newspapers from over sixty-five countries. It offers a variety of possible subscription arrangements. You can get five different papers from five different countries, delivered biweekly. Or they have what is called a "saturation sub"— newspapers within a given area sent you for a specific period of time.

Get on the mailing list of public relations firms and other organizations that might be helpful to you. You'll receive literally pounds of printed matter, so save a spot on your weekly schedule to glean the best for your files. And budget a thank-you tip for your postman at the end of the year. He'll deserve it!

Use advertising effectively. Place a notice of your special research needs in your local paper, trade papers, the book section of large city dailies, *Publishers Weekly,* and newsletters (*Freelancer's Newsletter,* the newsletters of writers' groups such as the ASJA, Authors Guild, Associated Writing Programs, Poets & Writers, Inc., The National Writers Club, and newsletters of companies or corporations you might have as clients).

Research leads can be found in the want-ad section of newspapers, too. If you find you suddenly need to know something about the technical aspects of electronics, for instance, see if the want ads can lead you to experts at local companies. They will often be flattered to be asked for an opinion.

The D.C. tangle

An information explosion is going on in the U.S., and especially in

Washington. The problem is to find what you need quickly and effectively. Most of the money being spent on information in government and government-related agencies is going more toward gathering and indexing rather than advertising the availability of it. You should first assume your answer is available somewhere, then monitor each research attempt to refine and modernize your own discovery system.

The biggest mine: the mammoth and nearly all-inclusive Library of Congress. It has, for instance, 17 million books, 102,000 newspaper volumes, 32 million manuscripts, 3.5 million maps, 467,000 phonographic discs, tapes, wires, 3.5 million items of music, 178,000 prints and drawings, 8.4 million photographic negatives, prints, slides, 219,000 motion-picture reels, 2.33 million pieces of microforms.

Some additional tips to guide your course in the capital:

Washington Researchers is a professional information service that offers unique guides. They gather and present information to companies about the environment in which they must do business, including markets, the competition, economic conditions, and legislation. They also guide such companies in their own research. They put out helpful publications, and though they charge on an hourly or contract basis, they do give free tips on how to go about your own research, especially through the maze of governmental bureaucracy. (See the Resources chapter for further information.)

At conferences, such as *Folio*'s Face to Face or the American Booksellers Association convention, you will uncover your own leads to the latest organizations in the world of commerce as well as in federal agencies. At an exhibitor's booth, I once picked up booklets from ERIC (Educational Resources Information Center of the National Institute of Education). ERIC was established by the U.S. Office of Education in the mid-1960s, when the literature of education was relatively diffuse; it was designed to correct this problem by providing a more effective way to uncover various worthwhile educational developments for the researcher. At another conference, I met a woman who works for the National Safety Council who had a wealth of information at her fingertips. And from the federal government you can get a catalog of selected federal publications on almost any subject. Free copies of Congressional hearings are also available. (See the Resources chapter.)

Data User News, put out by the U.S. Department of Commerce's Bureau of the Census, for instance, is a federal/state/local cooperative effort designed to improve access to and use of the Census

Bureau and related statistical resources. Each State Data Center provides services to local researchers. The bureau is also attempting to create a user-feedback scheme, an element in research many other resources have ignored.

Gold mines and open doors

Unless you can afford, like Picasso, to fill entire villas with your creative output and other materials pertaining to your work, you have to tame the paper mountain building around you. So look on libraries and other repositories as your villas. Ask for a list of your public library's periodical holdings. Keep in your personal library *only* those magazines the library doesn't subscribe to. Usually writers subscribe to a number of periodicals, clip and file the material they want, then, ultimately discard the magazines. Before you discard yours, though, take the time to take out the tables of contents. These can easily be stored in a ring binder. Then, before you even call or head to your library you can scan your personal index for the precise publication and date you need.

If the cost of subscriptions to many magazines is too hefty a chunk out of your budget, take time to scan carefully at the newsstand before you purchase a new periodical. Learn where secondhand sources for periodicals and books are in your area—Salvation Army, thrift shops, flea markets, and the like. (See the Resources chapter for cheaper national outlets). And ask at the doctor's, dentist's or hairdresser's for periodicals they no longer want. Most will be happy you'll cart them away.

Keep your tape recorder handy if you're driving somewhere. Research information pops up on all-news radio and in disc jockey patter and in all manner of strange places. You don't have to tape directly from the radio, but the machine is great for talking your notes into. This holds true during library research, a visit to a museum, or whatever.

All writers have books in their personal libraries—lots of them. But few take the time to catalog their own library. This is wasteful, since the more books you acquire the more difficult it is to retrieve the information they contain. With a catalog of your personal library you have immediate access to this information in capsule form, saving lots of rummaging through your own bookshelves. An added bonus: The catalog demonstrates what you have for insurance and tax purposes.

You can get a lot of mileage, too, out of the development of your own part-time staff of friendly researchers. Eventually you'll acquire a network of fellow writers and other specialists scattered around the globe. With such a reliable network you become more valuable to your clients and more efficient at garnering information for all of your writing. Some arrangements can add to your income. Handled efficiently, this research method also plays the role of watchdog on your research budget. A freelancer in another city, for instance, may be willing, for a reasonable fee or exchange of services, to do telephone research for you, thus saving you a sizable long-distance bill or the cost of travel. If you don't know how to find such experts, a call to that city's newspaper editor or city desk often helps; try to get names, too, through public relations executives located in that city.

Once you've consciously built your network or research helps (reporters, librarians, magazine stringers, novelists, public relations executives), keep them informed of your needs and offer to reciprocate whenever possible. Most of the time you can use postcards for correspondence with them. But an occasional spur-of-the-moment call to a distant contact can also help enormously when you're in a tight spot, as Alden Todd's friend discovered. A writer working in the area of family relations says:

> I've found that many times my friendships with researchers turn into an agreement for exchange of information on an informal basis. Wherever I am traveling I usually take the time to contact writers, researchers, journalists, or librarians in that area. Although some of them will be too busy to agree to come into my stable of now-and-then researchers or interviewers, they will at least come up with names of others who might be available. Sometimes they'll remember someone who has written and published in the past but isn't publishing at the moment. Or they'll know students who'd like professional criticism of their writing. Since I teach writing, I can offer a second reader's view in exchange for work for me. I keep some part-time writers who live overseas abreast of editor turnover and the demise of magazines. They in turn agree to handle simple research assignments for me—a telephone call, a trip to an obscure museum, library, or tourist office. Each agreement is different. Some are on a tit-for-tat payment basis. Others keep track of hours spent. Whichever suits them best I usually agree to abide by. They are valuable to me because of where they are

living. I'm valuable to them because of my knowledge of the
inner workings of publishing houses. The system seems to
work nicely for all of us.

If you want to try setting up such a system, remember: Keep the
fees for *your* services reasonable and in line with the demands you'll
be making; be prompt and ask them to be, too; never forget simple
courtesy and quick payment.

Another author does his networking this way: "Whenever I read, I
look at the biographical notes on the author. When something
piques my interest about him, I realize I could use that contact
someday. I jot a note for my network file right then. Often I'll write a
card asking for more information. Complete strangers become acquaintances at the very least. Sometimes they become very helpful
friends. I think it's one of my most important research tools."

Interviewing

Interviewing can be troublesome for the novice. My first attempt
turned out so-so. But I remembered my grandmother Adams—the
memory kept my knees from shaking and put a smile on my face.
Gram was somewhat like Barbara Walters; she could talk to anyone
about almost anything. But her best attribute was this: she listened.
Her simple act of caring was so disarming that normally reticent
people spoke to her freely.

There are many interview techniques professionals rely on. Listening well is one of the first. The next is practice—lots of it. Practice
asking questions, practice taking notes, practice observing scenes
and character. Most of all, the best interviews are well prepared long
before they take place. I learned that the hard way, too. In my first
interview I hadn't read nearly enough to prepare intelligent questions. My failure led to the interviewee's controlling the entire interview.

The second time around I went to the opposite extreme, and I was
glad I did. I read every clipping on my subject that was filed at the
local paper's library. I took copious notes, checked dates and names
(the story revolved around a convoluted legal case with many depo-
sitions and several trials). Eventually I tracked my prey. A friend
came along to bolster my confidence, a fortuitous circumstance,
since as I stepped out of the car I was met by three fearsome dogs.
Thanks to my friend, an animal lover, I could head straight to my

man. He'd mistaken me for someone else—a fortunate diversion, giving me time to mentally reconnoiter. Steeped in information about him and his life, I started interviewing on the spot, before he could object. The problem was, we had the interview right there; I had no opportunity to take notes or use a tape recorder. For three hours he talked—and I listened, intently. Without over-research it would have meant nothing. Afterwards I dashed away and wrote down everything I could remember. I was pleased later to learn I'd made "no factual errors and no mistakes on quotes."

In most interview situations, you *will* be able to use a tape recorder—if you want to. Consider the pros and cons.

The positive side, as John Brady lists them in *The Craft of Interviewing*, include:

1. The interviewer can ask more questions in less time than the notetaker.
2. Taped interviews tend to have that crisp ring of truth.
3. The interviewer can concentrate on the interview.
4. A taped interview is reassuring to an editor or publisher if the subject matter is at all controversial.
5. A tape recorder frees the writer on the road.
6. When the interviewer's hands are tied, a tape recorder is of real assistance. (If you are holding an interview during a meal, for instance.)
7. Tape recorders can be used for recording lengthy documents.

I would add these additional points: Using a tape recorder during an interview frees the writer to observe the interviewee and his surroundings more closely. During an interview a recorder captures the words of the speaker but also a good many nuances that you might miss otherwise—how the interviewee spoke certain words, when he paused, or the surprise he registered at one of your leading questions. These are all valuable bits of color for your story, so be sure to look for them and make note of them. They are also good for that crowd interview where you can't get as close to the speaker as you'd like; at such times you may also pick up comments or questions by others that are useful for your purpose.

The negative side:

1. Tape recorders have a tendency to go on the blink when you need them most.
2. Because of the above, many writers are too nervous about the machinery and foul up the interview.

3. Tape recorders are still off-putting to some interviewees, although they're fast becoming acceptable to even the least sophisticated interviewee, thanks to the familiar mike television reporters invariably hold.

4. They can lull the writer into becoming lazy about observation and notetaking, about being up and on his toes during the entire interview. (Always take backup notes at the same time as you're running your tape recorder during an interview, whether the interview is in person or by telephone.) That way not even an accidental erasure of the tape will leave your interview in total ruins.

If you do decide to buy one, what you'll want in a tape recorder is portability and reliability. Since the market for electronic equipment changes rapidly, it's difficult to specify brands or models that are tops. However, you'll do best to buy a standard brand (Sony is very popular with the pros I know), with a good guarantee, and use the same brand of tape. (Don't try to save money or inconvenience of changing tapes by using anything longer than a ninety-minute cassette, since the longer ones tend to become tangled and you can end a two-hour interview with nothing but gibberish for your efforts.) Look for a recorder that has a counter, for convenience in playback, and a built-in microphone that picks up clear sound from a good distance away without producing more static than voice. A good portable with built-in mike eliminates the need for a mike attachment—the part of the tape recorder that puts people on edge about being interviewed. You will want an adapter that plugs into an electrical outlet; it saves batteries and your temper.

Approaching the interview, remember these suggestions:

1. Know what you want to know; check and double-check your facts.

2. Ask questions of *opinion;* you should already have all but the most recent facts available on your subject.

3. If you've missed something, take the time then to clear up the problem ("Let's see now, you said you're expecting thirty-five celebs to attend?"). Your interviewee will not be appalled by the fact that you missed one point and will see that you mean to be correct. Or, as you leave, ask if it's all right to call back to double-check any necessary points. Invariably, your subject will agree.

4. Ask open-ended questions. ("What do you advise a young woman starting out today in your field?") Avoid those that limit answers to yes or no.

5. For dealing with celebrities, don't forget to ask the obvious question. If you're so star-struck that you can only smile foolishly in the presence of a celebrity, you shouldn't be interviewing her—you won't get a good, unbiased story. But of course the really unusual question is also important to remember if you are interviewing someone who has been interviewed all his life. John Brady cites William Manchester, author of *Death of a President:* "There's nothing more insulting than to ask a man like a President of the United States a question that he's answered many times before . . . ask questions that show you have a great familiarity with his life." Manchester asked Kennedy if he were a "generation chauvinist" and got fresh and interesting copy.

6. Follow where your subject leads but try to keep ultimate control of the interview.

7. Keep your eyes open for telling details in the surrounding setting. What books are on his shelves? Does he have a collection of rare guns? How does your subject look when angry? How does he move? What does he wear when relaxing?

8. Get your subject out of her office if you can. At least get her out from behind her desk, catch her off guard at a relaxed moment—after a tennis match, or whatever. Lead her into giving you good anecdotes. Ask if she remembers playing hooky in grammar school, etc.

9. Talk to a subject's friends, colleagues, students, and children for more material on the human aspect of the person.

10. Prepare to find your lead after you've turned off the tape recorder, closed your notebook and have your hand on the doorknob. When the interview *seems* to be over is the time when many people give you the most useful or lively information. A businessman had just moved into his new office when I interviewed him. Throughout the entire session he was cool, calm, collected—and distant. As I was about to leave he called attention to the tags still dangling from the legs of the tables and chairs. (I had noticed but not mentioned them.) "After all that high-flown stuff I've given you, you see the tags on the furniture and I bet you're thinking this is some kind of scam. Come back tomorrow and the office will be empty, right? I assure you, I'll be here." It was a beautiful lead to my article. Such comments will occur during your interviews, too, so be sure you're looking and listening for them.

The benefits of bluffing

Do you think that only the reporters from the *New York Times, Newsweek,* the *National Enquirer,* and *Der Spiegel* land the big interviews? Not so. When George P. Chapman of the *Westerly* (R.I.) *Sun* wanted to wangle an exclusive from Albert Einstein, he pulled a trick that got him past the impatient crew of big-time reporters waiting outside, straight into the genius's living room.

Though he was a reporter, he was also a telephone repairman. Wearing his lineman's boots and work clothes, carrying his tools, Chapman strolled casually to the door of Einstein's summer cottage. "I've come to look over your phone," he said. The maid let him in, saying, "Good. The professor has been trying to get Washington, and the dial is slow." Chapman produced a can of oil and fixed the recalcitrant machine. Then he turned to Einstein and announced he was a reporter for the local paper. Could he have a statement? He got his scoop with a smile.

Bluffing, then, as many writers have learned, has a place in your bag of freelancer's tricks. But use it sparingly, and be prepared to fast-talk yourself out of a corner.

For the freelancer who has the rhythms of his craft in his bones, there is use for everything, directly or indirectly, even bluffing. Emerson knew how it worked. "We say, I will walk abroad and the truth will take form and clearness to me. We go forth but cannot find it; we come in and are as far from it as at first. Then, in a moment, and unannounced, the truth appears. But the oracle comes because we had previously *laid siege to the shrine.*" (Italics mine.)

Chapter 8
Packaging and Promotion

■■■■■■■■■■■■■■■■■■■■■■■■■■■■■■■■■■■■■■■

Graphically speaking

Every product, from mittens to manuscripts, has to be packaged before it can be sold. The size, scope, and sophistication of today's marketplace dictate that you present your wares professionally. How you impress others—in person as well as on paper—is perhaps more significant than it should be, but you'd do well to be aware of it. How you dress, how you speak, and whether you suggest by your entire attitude that you can be depended on to get the job done make the difference between a wealth or dearth of assignments. If every detail about you and your work has an up-to-the-minute look, it will help your overall professional image. The impressions that result matter, so be particular in your presentations. Since much of the freelancer's sales work is done by mail instead of in person, the need for a package stating clearly and forcefully "This is the best person for the job" is vitally important.

Don't let the term "package" mislead you. No one is suggesting you gussy up your manuscript to attract attention. Shocking-pink stationery is simply not professional. Symbols on stationery (such as old-fashioned quill pens) are out of date. Simple is better; less is more.

One editor estimated that only one-quarter of the queries that cross his desk look at all businesslike. He admitted it shouldn't bother him, but it does. Pay attention. This editor is not alone.

Use a good letterhead. If you want a logo (it's not necessary), see that it is well designed by a professional. Select the typeface carefully. Be sure that it is readily legible. Mentioning your membership in a professional writing organization on your letterhead can sometimes be a plus. But leave off all other unnecessary information.

Other elements of your stationery should conform to your letterhead—your bills (print your Social Security number on these for faster payments), memos, mailing labels, and so on. For book proposals some writers like to use an eye-catching cover, but many more book proposals have sold on the merits of what was behind the cover—well-written and -researched material; properly organized, timely topics.

On a scale of one to ten, writers aren't expected to rate much above a two when it comes to expertise regarding good graphics and design. So it's a plus if you come in anywhere above that. Even if all you know for sure is what is really dreadful in graphics—and keep away from it—you're heading in the right direction. If you hire a professional to design all your office stationery needs, that'll spell a certain professionalism about your freelance operation.

If you feel you can't afford to go that route, then you owe it to yourself to study up on currently acceptable graphics. Valuable hints about what's fresh and exciting in the field of graphic arts and advertising are all around you—on billboards, on magazine covers, in advertisements on television. But short of taking an entire graphics course yourself (which probably won't be worth your time unless you are interested in becoming a newsletter editor or have other daily or weekly need for such expertise), head for a friendly expert. If you don't know anyone in a graphic arts department at a college, university, or large corporation, check around to see if any of your friends do. Ask for an introduction. Consult books like Townley's *Another Look* and Craig's *Production for the Graphic Designer* mentioned in the Resources chapter. See what your library offers in the way of recent volumes on graphics. Do be certain that the ones you read are up-to-the-minute. Graphic design is a trendy business. You're not helping yourself if you rely on a book that was first published many years ago and hasn't recently been revised.

A star is born

As a one-person business operation, you should try to keep yourself out front in all public endeavors which can further the cause of your business. You must consider all presentations of yourself as exploratory—the beginnings of friendships and working relationships that you plan to extend. Precede these interchanges with a totting up of your basic qualities as a writer. With every signal you send out, try to imprint those qualities, strikingly and memorably, in the minds of the people you deal with.

This requires energy—lots of it. And it requires a constant alertness to new opportunities, which will appear at the most unusual moments. As you marvel at the stamina of the best professionals, try at every turn to emulate them. This doesn't mean being pushy, however. The real professionals have acquired a forceful, effective, yet graceful way of putting their message across. Research psychologists from the University of California at Berkeley studied what it took to be a creative executive. According to the authors of *Creative Aggression: The Art of Assertive Living,* "Creative ingenuity and innovative capabilities were found to be negatively related to the qualities we typically associate with 'being nice,' such as modesty, mildness, and pleasantness. Instead [it was] found that originality in business management was correlated with traits of aggressiveness, such as forcefulness, toughness, and daring."

Those three qualities must be projected in an attractive manner, however, in order to insure success. Professional promotion isn't bullying. It is effective persuasion. If a client likes you as well as the work you do for him, he's far more likely to return for more of the same. It's as simple as that.

Résumés and portfolios

A pundit once put it this way: "Doing business without advertising is like winking at someone in the dark; you know what you're doing, but nobody else does."

As freelancers, it's all too easy to spend your time winking in the dark. But whether you live and work in a high-rise in Manhattan or on a farm in Nebraska, the time will come to blow your own horn. When it does, a respectable way to accomplish this is by résumé and a portfolio of clippings and/or photographs.

Keep on file an up-to-date résumé, listing the positions you've held, the kind of work you've done for those jobs, the dates, and any other pertinent information, briefly stated, that describes your abilities to a potential client or editor. As you progress in your writing career, you should list your publication history on the résumé as well.

The biographical sketch is somewhat different. A paragraph or two, describing who you are and your accomplishments, is called for here. Occasionally you'll be asked to supply a few biographical lines for the editor's page of a magazine. Then you'll only want to include a thought or two relating to how you discovered or developed the subject of the article ("I never knew I was interested in the Marquis de Sade until I found myself staring at a tumbledown wall of ancient stones in the south of France") or some of the amusing difficulties you faced interviewing Jane Fonda or Robert Redford.

One writer told me, "I keep a working file right behind the folder that holds my professionally printed résumé. As I conduct a panel at a conference on writing or present a slide show for a client, I merely scribble a note with the place, date, title of happening, and my contribution and slip it into the working folder. When it's time to update the bio sheet and résumé, I have most of the job done. There's no need to rummage through old calendars or other files searching for the necessary material."

Some facile writers who work in many different areas have found it profitable to devise more than one résumé. The purpose of each is to focus on certain specialties. Such writers find that these special-ized résumés provide effective introductions to new clients without loading them down with extraneous material.

You might also want to put together a portfolio for various presen-tations. This will undoubtedly also need updating and changing from time to time. So, though you want it to look professional, you don't want to spend the money to have something printed that will only serve the purpose for a short time. Put together a booklet of your best clippings, book reviews, articles, and photographs in the kind of binder you can find at art-supply or office-supply stores. You might want several duplicate portfolios, since you may wish to leave this book with a client for a few days or weeks if you've applied for a lengthy assignment.

You may want to ask that friend with graphics training to com-ment on your layout, lettering, and other details before you spend too much time and money. You want the best-looking presentation your time and budget will allow.

And if you feel you need more guidance in drafting a well-written résumé, by all means check your library or bookstore. Three handy books on the subject are *The Complete Résumé Book and Job Getter's Guide* by Dr. Juvenal Angel, *How to Write Better Résumés* by Adele Lewis, and *Woman's Work Book* by Abarbanel and Siegel (see the Resources chapter).

The lecture circuit

Writers are increasingly required to support their writing efforts by going out on the road. The writer must brave audiences, inter-viewers, and television cameras to push his wares. Not such a bad prospect, actually, when you realize that the more your work sells, the more you are welcome on the "circuit," and that the more ap-pearances you make, generally, the better your sales will be. And in fact, you don't have to write a bestseller to find yourself in some demand for speaking engagements. You can't—and shouldn't—just rely on your publisher to arrange for these appearances, however. Some writers have found, like the now-famous Thomas A. Harris, author of *I'm OK, You're OK,* that giving a series of talks to a large number of small audiences can make a phenomenal difference in book sales. In fact, it can start a snowball effect: as Harris appeared all over the country, his book's sales kept rising until the publisher, impressed with the figures, took over and publicized it even more.

And even if you don't have a book to promote, speaking engagements are a good way to promote yourself and your specialty. Start on the local level at first. After you've gained the needed confidence in your abilities and in the value of such efforts, you'll be ready to speak before larger audiences and receive higher fees.

How do you go about getting your name around to the right people? Be subtle about making arrangements. Charles A. Boyle, author of *Speak Out With Clout,* says:

> Whatever method you use to line up speaking engagements, make sure *never to ask* to be a speaker—always be in the position of being asked. If you ask a program chairman for the chance to be a speaker, you could both be in an uncomfortable situation. In a sense, it's like inviting yourself to someone's party—it could be embarrassing and it would certainly be bad manners and in poor taste.
>
> On the other hand, there's no harm in asking a mutual friend, an employee, or a business acquaintance to suggest to the program chairman of his organization that you be invited as a speaker.
>
> The best, most acceptable, and longest-lasting approach to being sought out as a speaker, however, is by having a good program to start with, letting program chairmen know about it indirectly, and then letting your reputation spread.

Your program can be anything you make it, from a concise speech to a well-integrated slide presentation of your travels. Think about the work you've published. What is there in it that would make a program? Take a topic from your main subject, or look back into the files of your research material to see if there are other angles that, developed a bit further, might be of interest to audiences in your region. Collect 35mm color slides to illustrate your material. Charity groups, schools, businesses, clubs, all sorts of organizations might be interested in the presentation. Program chairmen are always looking for something new and interesting. Let them know what you have.

To seek a broader audience for your lecturing you can use the technique of having a simple flyer made announcing your subjects for either informal seminars or speeches. Post it where influential people might see it. Better yet, have a friend mail it to meeting planners and program chairmen of various organizations. Hand out a few to your business friends asking them to pass them on to appropriate people.

After you have exhausted the search for general audiences, look for others who might benefit from your knowledge. If you have a writing specialty, try to think of ways it might be reinterpreted or directed at specialized audiences. Would a gathering of local physicians be interested in hearing from a writer able to collaborate with them on a writing project? Provided you're equipped to do so, arrange to speak on subjects of interest to them, however informally.

The day you get the speaking assignment, send a letter of acceptance and include a copy or two of your latest or most pertinent published piece, marked to the attention of the person in charge of local publicity. If you do this early, the chances that the local paper will send a reporter to cover your talk, or that the local radio or TV station will schedule an interview, are increased. (In your note that accompanies the copy of the piece, indicate that you'll be available for such interviews.) Be sure to have several good 8x10 glossy photos of yourself ready for publicity purposes. If the publicity person fails to ask for them (many people in this job are volunteers, not experts), suggest that you send them some. No matter how small the occasion, if you give a public appearance, prepare a press release and see that any publications in that locality receive it.

When you're going to lecture, take along several copies of your articles and place them strategically around the room. Keep a couple in reserve in your briefcase to hand to special people you meet. If you have a book coming out, take along order blanks for it. Call attention to the existence of all this material before you leave the podium if the person who introduced you failed to do so.

Saturday night live?

For some people, discovering on short notice they must give a speech or promote a book can be unnerving. It doesn't matter if they must make a formal lecture or whether they're just being asked to fill a certain time slot on a program with clever repartee and snappy answers to questions from the audience. Why not plan in advance for the inevitable? One good way to do this: As you put your book or article series together, keep a journal, notebook or simple file of anecdotes. The bits and pieces will be related to your work as it progresses, of course, but they should also be about you, your life, the broader scope of the writing profession and some of the fascinating people who've crossed your path in the process. These anecdotes will add much to your store of color for your speeches.

Facing a large audience need not be any more difficult than the one-on-one experience of an important interview. Notice, though, that I didn't say *any* interview. As you will prepare your homework for that important interview, you should plan certain techniques for informing and entertaining your audience. In doing so, remember some of the techniques tough interviewers use for celebrity interviews. For one thing, don't pussyfoot around a subject that seems delicate. Your audience will appreciate your candor and empathize with you. You can use jargon to handle delicate subjects, but be certain it is widely accepted, well-understood jargon. You can imply that your comments are playful ones, getting laughs but also getting your point across. And you can also occasionally get yourself off the hook by gently blaming someone else for a comment you are about to make; just be certain to keep that someone an unknown or a general (not identifiable) group. Use terms like "there are those who say" instead of "most Iowans believe."

After months on the lecture circuit publicizing a book, one bestselling author has concluded that she prefers to speak publicly without a prepared text. Her technique is disarmingly—and deceptively—simple. "I'd rather just answer questions. I don't make speeches very well, but ask me a question and I can talk forever." One suspects, on hearing her, that she's developed this method through her years of experience as a teacher, a job that required her to face an audience of demanding and eager undergraduates. This scheme could backfire, though, if you failed to prepare a few questions to start the ball rolling. Your audience could be the sort afraid to open their mouths. You can either plant someone in the audience to ask the first questions or be prepared to bring up some tantalizing openers yourself.

Facing a live audience is one thing; facing the cold eye of the TV camera (or the hot, blinding lights beside one) is quite another. Many writers on the publicity trail find expert help is well worth their money; some even negotiate funds from their publishers for crash courses once their publishers decide to pull out all the stops and put them on the road to push their book. Most such courses are expensive. You can learn some basic tricks, though, without signing up for a course—such things as how to look at the camera, how to hold your hands, and ways to clear up problems in speaking presentations. Observe how others do it. Keep a notebook on the good and bad elements you notice yourself; what is off-putting to you will undoubtedly be bothersome to others. Study the politicians, talk show hosts, talk show guests—their speaking styles, mannerisms, and the cadences of their speech. How does someone cover a mistake? How does another answer confusing or uncomfortable questions? Then take what you've learned and practice on your own captive audience—family and friends. Ask them to honestly critique your performance. When you have a little more confidence and control, try speaking before a more general, though still relatively benign, audience such as people at the library who are interested in books, the local group at the synagogue, or the faculty wives at the university.

It is possible, too, to get professional help in self-presentation through correspondence courses in public speaking and the like. Some of these use taped instructions, and you go through various exercises just as you would learning a foreign language by correspondence. They're not exactly cheap, either. Then, too, with a correspondence course you miss some of the feedback that can be so crucial in correcting such problems as nervousness, nasality, or shrill or too-rapid presentation. Besides, when you're being interviewed on a talk show you're going to be reacting quite differently from times you're on a podium giving a regular speech, which the public-speaking course is aimed at.

When deciding what or if to charge, ask around to see what the going rate is in your area. Consider the size of audience and the amount of time it will take you to prepare. Occasionally it may not hurt your image to offer to speak (briefly) for charity. But develop a scale of fees based on the above points, or you may turn into a charity case yourself. As in all freelancing, you must concentrate to work up to heftier fees. Thrill audiences with your expertise. Then ask for more compensation the next time.

Advertising—discreet or direct?

Even the slightest bit of self-promotion helps. Often as not it happens indirectly, though. Two years after I'd sent an editor friend a copy of a humorous article I'd published elsewhere just because I thought it would amuse her, she called asking me to expand on the subject for her publication. Another article I'd published (and nearly forgot about) indirectly led to a book contract. Since you can never tell when such happy circumstances will occur, it never hurts to prime the pump a little.

If you've published material in magazines that you're certain other editors will probably miss, don't let it stay hidden in your files. Make several copies, mark them "FYI," and send them around to editors who might be interested, however peripherally, in the subject or in the special treatment you've given it. Also send copies to those you may have interviewed on other assignments who might have an interest in your published material. They'll be flattered that you remembered their interest in the subject. See, too, that your favorite librarian, researcher, or professor gets a copy. In other words, spread the news of your writing widely, as if you were announcing the birth of your first child.

One writer, new in town, had form letters of introduction copied on his letterhead, with an explanation of the services he was prepared to perform for local businesses. He sent these by mail to a list of prospective clients. He added a note about the best time to contact him, but also suggested he'd call shortly thereafter for an appointment.

Add all sorts of organizations to your list of possible promotional outlets. As you think about how organizations in your vicinity might be useful in your promotional scheme, remember that you don't have to actually belong to them to reap benefits. On occasion you can attend seminars by other professionals as a guest of a member or as an interested spectator. You'll be doing so primarily to let it be known you're a local writer with this or that current project in the works. Discreetly dropping such mentions into the general information hopper can be a quite efficient way of getting new assignments. One thinks first of such groups of professionals as public relations people and anyone even remotely involved with the publishing process (printing, editing, designing, or advertising). But your promotion campaign needn't stop there. Groups such as the local Kiwanis or Rotary or Knights of Columbus, organizations of management trainees or medical secretaries, and the like are possibilities, too. Any of these organizations may be very happy to help a published writer in any way they can. (Certainly meetings of those groups in publishing, public relations, or advertising will be fertile ground for discovering possible writing jobs in the corporate world, such as company histories, speeches, and conference presentations. If you haven't time to attend a particular meeting of interest to you, you can still ask a friendly member of the organization to keep her eyes and ears open for any leads to such jobs.)

Even if you consider yourself apolitical you may still discover it's worth your time to make the acquaintance, either in person or by mail, of your city and state officials. Under the quite legitimate guise of keeping them informed about their constituents you can, now and then, write them regarding current issues, enclosing copies, of course, of any pertinent or particularly interesting published material of yours. The same holds true for such executives as those at the Chamber of Commerce and the Better Business Bureau.

Regarding publicity for your books, there are ways you should think of helping the publisher's promotion department long before the book is out. Let's say you're about to publish a book on the joys of woodcrafting. Part of your plan should include making a list of the obvious places such a book might sell. Then add all of the other prospects, no matter how farfetched they might appear—church groups, clubs of retired persons, lumberyards, scout groups, junior high school shop teachers, and so on. Think in terms of target audiences (groups, trades, individuals, and geographic areas, for instance) when you devise your list. Keep asking yourself "Who would be interested?" until you have exhausted every last possibility. Send the list to your publisher, but don't stop there. You can do even more on your own. You can send a letter to some of these target audiences, announcing the arrival of your book as well as where and how to get it. (A letter directed to a friend or acquaintance within the group is even more discreet *if* you can count on that person to pass the information on in time to do some good.)

An example is the writer who appeared on local television to support a favorite cause. He received about a thousand letters from interested viewers. A year and a half later when he was about to publish a book on a closely related subject, he made certain that flyers went out to every one of the people who had written him earlier.

Whenever you try a promotional ploy—in person or by mail—take notes. Periodically pause and *measure the response* that particular tactic had. Did new contacts and firm assignments result from your efforts? How soon? Is there some way you might speed up the process?

Use business cards. Most people you meet aren't experts at remembering names. It's far more likely they'll remember yours if you hand them your card. This is especially true if your name is a tricky one to spell. A well-printed card on hand also spells "professional."

Much material that you receive comes with the senders' business cards attached. Slip these cards into a business-card file. This saves cluttering your Rolodex with names that you may not need for some time.

The more direct route

There are many times in your freelancing career when direct advertising is your best bet—when you need to promote your book, to search out freelancing jobs in your area, or to spread your network of researchers in faraway areas. You might want more public-speaking engagements. Other times you'll need to collect data on some esoteric subject. Or you'll be looking for a collaborator. Or perhaps you're considering getting away for a month to a writers' colony or other hideaway to concentrate completely on a novel. In all of these situations writers can turn to direct ads for success.

You'll save your budget a hefty blow if you weigh carefully any paid ads you take out. Be as on target as possible with the project and the audience the publication is reaching. Analyze the results carefully before repeating any ads.

Many publications take ads from writers. The best ones for many freelancers, however, are those newsletters targeted to the right audience. (PR Aids, mentioned earlier, is a good example.) This is especially true if these ads cost next to nothing. In my city the advertising community has its own publication. I was about to place a paid advertisement when, at a luncheon, I was introduced to the editor, who saved me the trouble. He "interviewed" me and ran a brief story in the news column in the next issue.

I also asked to be put on the mailing list of the publication. Overnight I was familiar with a whole new territory of freelance possibilities, from freelance commercial artists to ad jingle writers, to the best printers in town. See if your area has a similar publication and get on the mailing list.

You can send out your own news releases for occasions other than public speaking, too. If you've just published a series on the latest technology used by the fishing industry but don't think people in your area will ever see it, write a release, send it with a glossy photo to your local newspaper, your fraternity quarterly, your college monthly, or the newsletter put out by a trade organization your spouse belongs to. Don't overlook small weekly newspapers. The neighborhood "shopper" might also be interested in such a feature about what you've done.

Another kind of direct ad is a notice on a bulletin board in an office, library, specialty shop, or school. Use your research techniques to ask who might be interested and where these people or groups congregate. Then see if you can put up a notice on a wall they'll see when they walk in.

If you are a writer/photographer, try typing a list of themes your photographs fall into and shipping the list out to as many outlets as you can unearth, with a bio sheet and a covering sales letter attached. The obvious outlets are those listed in market directories, like *Writer's Market, Photographer's Market,* and *Working Press of the Nation.* But there are newsletters, such as H.T. Kellner's *Moneygram,* and many, many others. And don't forget those specialized groups (a church group, a charity organization, etc.) who might be interested in what you have for sale or know people who would be. Enclose a card or coupon they can mail back to you with their order.

Basic training

Developing your own public relations plan is an important ingredient in your total marketing mix. It helps expand your reach into other areas, reinforcing any advertising you've done. This sort of plan should be a well-developed part of your ongoing work as a freelancer. Public relations requires organization, discovering who your publics are, how you can be of benefit to them, and how you can best tell them about what you have to offer. Your own talent and enthusiasm and energy are the adhesives that will hold the plan together effectively. Take them and approach your brainstorming sessions with relish. You'll think of all the usual groups that might be approached (people on campuses, at schools, churches, art groups, service clubs, social service agencies, etc.), of course. But there are many others, such as government officials, Chambers of Commerce, social groups, study clubs, senior citizens, ethnic groups, professional organizations (legal, medical, academic), Friends of the Library, and so forth. After you've defined your opportunities, then mesh them with your objectives for your own unique strategy.

Basically, any thoughtful campaign you use to make your abilities known to a new market, or to remind an editor of your talents, will have three objectives: general good will, ongoing advertising/publicity about yourself and your skills, and new and better assignments.

Examine the situation as you would any of your assignments. *Analyze* what would best suit your objectives, *research* the markets in depth for overlooked areas and contacts, thoroughly *check* details and statistics involved before you make your pitch, *consider* your resources and how best to apply them. Naturally your objectives must be geared to the results you want and, perhaps the single most important factor, to the percentage of your budget allocated for promotion.

These are supplements, however, to your nuts-and-bolts correspondence with editors you want to remember you. Unfortunately, out of sight may be out of mind. It would be sad, indeed, if a busy editor overlooked you for an assignment just because your name and specialty hadn't come to his attention for a while.

Set some kind of simple schedule for reminding your contacts that you're still available. The following are some suggested items that can catch the editorial eye:

1. If work of yours has been praised in print (a good review of your book) or been otherwise praised by an authority (letters of thanks for your top-notch consulting or teaching job), send photocopies to other clients you'd like to have the information.

2. Occasionally photocopy and send out an article you've published to other editors simply for their amusement or edification. As I discovered, there's no telling when someone might want to reprint it.

3. Keep up-to-date background material about your work circulating everywhere. Never assume information about you gets to the right or helpful source without your guidance.

4. Whenever you try a promotional ploy, in person or by mail, take notes on the technique's effectiveness. Did new contacts or firm assignments result? How soon? Is there some way to speed up the process?

The gallant giveaways

Think about your specific qualities as a writer. What would best project your image in some silent, ever-present reminder to your clients? Incorporate it into your business gift at the end of the year to some special editor friends or clients.

What would you like to be representative of your work through the year—a desk calendar, a bookmark, a pen with your name on it? Author Alan Levy, knowing how difficult it is for a writer to get some things done behind the Iron Curtain, had special ballpoint pens made for gifts. Closed doors suddenly opened. Another writer liked a pencillike pocket flashlight he was given as a door prize. He had some imprinted with his name and telephone number and gave them to some of his clients to celebrate National Do-Nothing Day. They remembered him with assignments.

One writer/photographer saw an ad in a national coin magazine—a reproduction of a Viking ship on an old coin. He had some of these inexpensive but handsome items attached to a paperweight with his name and phone number on it and sent them to his favorite editors.

A travel writer knew a craftsman who could inexpensively reproduce various items from her world travels into almost anything. From time to time she commissions felt bookmarks, picture frames, desk boxes, etc., and sees that the editors and publishers she knows get a unique reminder of her work each year.

Another author had a felt banner made with his own clever slogan reproduced by some art students and sent some to his favorite clients.

Yet another writer described his promotion this way: "A gold pendant advertised by a well-known company and mentioned in a news release had an interesting little history behind it. I had something similar (and far less expensive) made for my own little public relations campaign around Christmas. Then I saw some exotic recipes in a newsletter. I typed them up and mailed them out as presents to a special editor who I happen to know loves to cook." A wine/food assignment eventually came unsolicited from that editor. "Though it had not been my specialty up until then, I discovered I loved good food and figured I could handle the job."

Would an editor with an extensive library like a system for keeping tabs on the books he lends? There are packets of cards available for such purposes. They have places for notations of the date and name of the borrower and a bookmark that goes with the borrowed book noting from whom it was borrowed. If you decide to give such a gift to a client, have your name printed unobtrusively on the cards if you wish.

Just as there are ideas all around for articles and books, there are obviously all manner of ideas for publicity about your freelancing business. Watch for them everywhere. Allocate some of your time to develop them in your special way. Make notes on possible angles, amusing tactics, or catchy jingles and slogans. Many of the ideas can be reinterpreted so they won't require expensive chunks of your budget. Two last thoughts: Remember, variety and humor are useful keys that unlock all sorts of doors. Also, whatever direction you choose to follow, be sure it reflects good taste. If your advertising is clever and helpful and reminds the recipient of your talents, you've achieved your promotional goal.

Chapter 9
Expanding
Your
Territories

■■

Three keys

Expanding a freelancing operation into new regions makes me think about the Mona Lisa, some feisty Irish and Scots, and an ancient Chinese custom. Let me explain.

When the Mona Lisa was stolen from the Louvre there was a well-publicized empty space on the wall for two years. During that time more people entered the gallery to stare at the *blank space* than had, in the twelve years previous, come to look at the masterpiece itself. That's hype!

Advertising campaigns from "Ask a man who owns one" to "Does she or doesn't she?" (and fortunately beyond) have relied upon slogans. The word *slogan* came from war cries. The Gaelic *sluagh*, meaning army, and *gairm* (a shout) evolved into *slogan*.

The etymology of the word *bamboozle* is more clouded by controversy. One explanation has it, however, that it came to us from an ancient Chinese custom of punishing swindlers by whacking them on the hands and backs with bamboo poles.

Hang on to these three ideas as you plot your trek through even more of the freelance jungle: (1) A certain amount of hype is needed to make one's voice heard in the ever more crowded marketplace. (2) You need a "battle cry" to hang your writing efforts on (for yourself, not necessarily for public consumption). (3) *Don't* go so far as to bamboozle anyone.

What you want to do is strategically employ the methods and techniques that professionals have repeatedly relied on to gain results. They should be familiar by now. They include doing your research in advance; being aware of time limitations and deadlines; testing market reaction to any novel experiment before putting it into force; remaining flexible but keeping control of the situation; providing a handle—a catchy title, for example—so others will more easily remember you and your ideas; and using the self-confidence all of these give you to present a relaxed, unharried professional appearance.

Expanding your territories requires another look at yourself and your business operation for weak areas that need to be eliminated. Ask yourself these questions:

1. Have you learned all you need to know to present yourself in the most professional manner? Look at related areas that might help. Tap any and all sources to facilitate becoming a generalist about your own business.

2. Have you kept current with the changes in your industry? What problems do others—printers, bookstore owners, publishers, editors, commercial artists—face every day?

3. Have you studied the competition as fully as you ought? By noticing how others accomplish what they do, you can acquire some of their techniques to upgrade your business practices.

4. Have you paid attention to current legislation that's bound to affect future business decisions in the industry? To do so you must read newspapers, news magazines, organization newsletters, the *Congressional Record,* etc., and maintain open lines to important contacts who know about or may be able to influence that legislation (top-notch newspaper reporters, editors, elected officials, influential business persons, etc.).

5. Have you joined business associations and taken part in community affairs? Sought out seminars and public appearances of experts in your field?

6. Have you observed outstanding people in other fields and attempted to discover by what means they leaped forward in their careers? (Bold changes of direction? Timely innovations? Carefully conceived publicity campaigns?) Here again, the brainstorming procedure can hurry you along in areas you're unfamiliar with. Take time to lunch with friends in other businesses and quiz them intelligently.

7. Have you set performance goals and stayed with them?

8. Have you honestly evaluated the work you've done?

9. Have you trained yourself to troubleshoot problems?

10. Have you learned to delegate and practiced motivating others to cooperate with you?

These pump-priming techniques are exercises you'll want to return to repeatedly throughout a long and happy freelance career. But the one I want to reemphasize (because too many successful freelancers fail to recognize its importance) is number 10. You learn to wear so many hats as you're creating your business that you may discover you've been too slow to delegate small tasks to others, thereby slowing down your production and profit. When your business reaches a point where you can afford to hire help, and you need it, do so. You can't afford not to.

Developing your list of prospects

Top-notch salesmen start out by developing a list of prospects. They glean names from whatever source they can, building a list of people to contact. They sort through it to find the best-sounding prospects so they'll save time and money by avoiding blind alleys. They make their initial contacts, then review what happened, noting all reactions. They use these notes for follow-ups. They are constantly looking to expand their market.

Many freelancers tackle the first step, making a partial list, but they fail on the remaining ones. They're not good salesmen. Creative burnout and procrastination, their bugaboos when they're trying to write, plague them too when they're attempting to sell—perhaps even more so then. If you wish to expand your business intelligently, don't let this happen to you. Remind yourself that freelancing, at times, may be nearly 50 percent selling and 50 percent writing.

Creatively juggling such a plan in freelancing is possible if you are realistic about the market. Remember that where there is plenty of competition, you have to stand out from the crowd, like that blank wall that once held the Mona Lisa. Your material and your presentation of it have to offer the editor or other client the best and more of it than others are prepared to provide. But the next step is *developing* your prospect list. This requires you to learn the market possibilities so well, gleaning the best of them and concentrating on realizing their full potential, that the market seems to evolve by itself.

Go back to your original markets. If you're working well with them, you should be negotiating for higher pay. If you have a better idea for them, why not have it put on a regular basis? A column or contributing editorship, even if this is only a title, is a start.

A.F. "Arky" Gonzales, Jr., found it was quite easy to work his way onto the masthead of American publications as their "European Editor." In a *Writer's Yearbook* article he said, "The titles don't immediately pay off in a salary, but they do give a writer a certain cachet and visibility. . . . The ultimate goal, of course, is to write so many articles for these few key publications that you eventually slip yourself into a staff position with a salary, expense account, and an office budget."

Gonzales admittedly had a distinct advantage—he was living abroad and convinced the periodicals they needed European coverage. But no matter where you live, you can put his go-getter sales approach to work.

To expand your territories, ask yourself:

■ Have you exhausted the possibilities with one market? If you have, would their competitors be interested in your work? Can you get them to put you on contract?

■ What outlets have you ignored because you were too busy, disorganized, or timid to try? (Now that you've established sufficient credits, isn't it time to be slightly more adventurous? You tried them once long ago and they rejected you? Remember the musical chairs game. The editor has probably moved elsewhere by now. Even if she hasn't, try again. Editors are human; they change their minds. They're under constant pressure to upgrade their operations. Your idea might be the very thing they've been looking for.)

■ Have you been writing articles when you should have been putting together book proposals? Are you ready to write one? Or do you want to start out by collaborating?

■ Are you querying as many new markets with enough ideas to meet your financial goal by the end of the year? Don't worry about getting more acceptances than you think you can handle—remember the attrition rate on assignments. With a rosier financial picture you can employ help or purchase better equipment. Think of that gothic novelist who lies back and dictates to a platoon of secretaries. She turns out books at the rate of twenty a year.

■ What general promotion techniques have you been ignoring? Couldn't you make yourself better known among editors and readers?

■ Should you write that novel that's been fermenting in your mind for so long?

With answers to these questions, you lay out a course for the months ahead, steering clear of unproductive paths as you move into new territory.

Some freelancers, however, make fine plans and work long and hard to climb halfway up the ladder—then something dismal happens. They freeze or become hesitant, unwilling to risk the tenuous gains they've made with a particular editor, afraid that too bold a move, a move made too soon, will backfire. They continue in stagnant patterns, regularly turning out good material but reaping the same income each year, never really getting ahead. Stay alert for the times when your career might take off. When you feel their approach, don't hesitate too long. You may lose more from hesitation than you have gained with all the patient work piled up to your credit over many years. The only salvation in those dilemmas is to trust those moments when your intuition (and market realities) tell you the time is ripe to leap—and then *leap*.

Tapping the markets in progression

The beginner must try to place his work in almost any publication, even though some of them strike the accomplished professional as very limited, nonpaying markets. These first markets include church publications, fillers for local newspapers, features for weekly newspapers, or even student publications. Rate of pay and circulation don't usually matter much to the novice. The point is to get published.

But, for the advanced beginner, the easy-access markets have been your turf long enough. You've paid your dues and sharpened your writing skills. The novice work has brought you expanded assignments and small but welcome checks.

The next step is to assess your financial foundation and potential. If easy, though insufficient, income sources have to keep meat on your table while you experiment elsewhere, you should be sure that you can rely on them for steady assignments (even if your editor moves to Tahiti) and that you can shorten the time required to complete them, squeezing the bread-and-butter work into the first week or ten days of every month.

There's one more consideration: Are you psychologically prepared to face these writing chores regularly—every thirty days if that's necessary? Conversely, can you quickly switch over to even more demanding but business-expanding assignments?

Your progress might look like this: Your base is a combination of feature articles for a variety of newspapers in your region and brief but interesting local travel stories. You've checked with your editors and lined up a solid four months of work for them. Your next step is to dig into those clipping files you started long ago, which you haven't given much thought. You've tried a couple of ideas from them on *Yankee, Kiwanis,* and *Off Duty,* but you didn't hit pay dirt, and figured those markets weren't for you. Now's the time to go back and scan those periodicals again (and at least twenty similar ones) to discover what they've been publishing since you queried them. Find anything new or revealing in their tables of contents? How do their published articles differ from your proposals? (They're giving their readers lots of solid tips like "where to purchase," "how to make," "what's the latest hobby trend," while your suggestions were more generalized?) Can any of your queries be revamped with a couple of hours at the library so you, too, can help the reader? Perhaps you've misread or misinterpreted the writer's guidelines, or possibly the editorial direction has been altered while you weren't watching. If your queries simply can't be reworked (and few, if any, can't), look at your clipping folder to see what can be offered to your higher-paying markets. Set yourself a timetable to get out twenty-five new queries within two weeks to the markets you've picked. (Yes, twenty-five.) Work as furiously as you can on this—as heatedly as when you attempted to perfect that first feature story for the *Pawtucket Times* or the *Daily Iowan*.

Pull out all the stops. Besides referring to your dictionary and thesaurus, reach for other books to sharpen your techniques. By this, I mean, look at writing you admire, be it fiction or nonfiction. Take a graph and copy it closely. Then rewrite it, using the general form and outline of the thought but supplying your own words. This is an exercise that has its merits all through your writing career. But it may offer its most help right now, at this crucial point in your writing and freelancing adventure.

A new plateau

Let's say you've reached the plateau at which you can count on selling a variety of short articles to regional or trade magazines. You have succeeded—but not yet at the level you want. You still long to write travel articles for the likes of *Travel & Leisure* and the *New York Times* travel section (or, *Reader's Digest* and *National Geographic*).

No one can promise you'll be able to make that enormous leap into top-paying markets. But all the writers who have bolstered their credits by good work in the lesser markets have put themselves in the running for a shot at the top. This isn't a one-time phenomenon but a process that works over and over on each rung up the ladder. They have learned how to formulate queries and to come through with excitement and precision in well-turned products so that top editors take them seriously.

The same gradual approach pays off for fiction writers. Perhaps you've been successfully writing short stories and have placed some of these in literary magazines or the alternative press. If your ambition is to write a novel, these initial publications will help in the difficult task of placing your first manuscript. Fiction editors may already be aware of your talents, since part of their job is to keep up with the fiction that's being published in the quarterlies. This is excellent support for your decision to get on with the big book.

Though most publishers will expect to see the complete manuscript of a first novel, if you've had encouragement from the fiction editor of a publishing house you may be able to get a contract on the basis of a few chapters plus an outline of the rest. (See Chapters 11 and 12 for other ideas on dealing with editors, and how agents can help in contract negotiations.)

Judith Appelbaum and Nancy Evans, authors of *How to Get Happily Published*, have some excellent suggestions on a variation of the stepping-stone theory used to pick a book publisher, which they call the "Affection Approach." Basically it hinges on the proposition that "an editor's excitement about a work may be more important than sales forecasts in determining publishability." They quote Richard Marek, former editor-in-chief of Dial Press, who says, "I judge mostly by an editor's enthusiasm."

Appelbaum and Evans suggest four ways to find the most promising editorial partner: (1) Compile a data bank of cards listing editor's names and as much information about that editor as you can glean. (2) Investigate personal publishing (editors who, though they may work for large publishing houses such as Random House or Doubleday, publish books under their own imprint). (3) Discover an editor who might be just right for you by following your own passion for a book or books which this editor helped get into print. (4) Advertise for a publisher/editor through a *Publishers Weekly* ad or the "Publishers Wanted" section of the newsletter published by COSMEP (Committee of Small Magazine Editors and Publishers). (See the Resources chapter.)

Explorations into the territory before you may lead to frustrations. Sometimes you'll be ahead of your time with an idea or concept. We all know people such as artists or writers who suffer from being out of step, occasionally, in this manner. They sometimes appear foolish because they forecast what others can't yet envision. Or their style of expression is too avant-garde for all but the most fearsome publisher to toy with. In *How to Get Happily Published* the authors cite this instance of a faulty editorial decision regarding a nonfiction work. John Fischer, former head of trade books at Harper & Brothers, reports, "I hate to remember the time when James R. Newman first told me his scheme for a history of mathematics. . . . He wanted to gather all the basic documents of mathematical thought and arrange them into an anthology which would trace the development of the science in the words of the masters themselves. . . . I told him it was impossible. Nobody would buy it." The book was eventually published in four volumes by Simon & Schuster. By the time Fischer reported his error in his column "Easy

Chair" in *Harper's* magazine, it had sold "over 120,000 sets, in addition to those distributed by two book clubs."

This is not to suggest that all of your rejected projects will come to such a wondrous end. Some ideas are ahead of their time. Some are simply no good at all. And some, though fine concepts, will, for other reasons—problems steming from your side of the fence and problems coming from the world of publishing in general—never see the light of day. There is a fine line between all of these, and no one should claim otherwise. Still, with a strong belief in your idea and a good deal of perseverance coupled with patience, you may find that it eventually pays off handsomely. So, if you cannot find an immediate market for your venturesome new work, put it away in a file marked "So What Happened?" Mark your calendar or tickler file for a reexamination of the material in a year or two. You might well discover it is on target then. Or if it's *still* ahead of its time, hope for an editor who is more farsighted than his colleagues. Trends in the making are of interest to the thoughtful editor, if not to all. There's even a new magazine devoted to the idea, called *Next*.

To reach out for higher plateaus in your freelance effort, you'll want to consider all of these possibilities just mentioned. Other than negotiating for a lot as a special correspondent, or adding photographs to your package (discussed at the end of this chapter), or reexamining your ideas to see if they were ahead of their time when first presented, a writer's course through the freelancing ranks might look like this: He writes for newspapers, then moves to the pulps and small-circulation magazines. Eventually he publishes in periodicals paying from $300 to $500; he moves on from that level to payments of $750 to $1,200 or $1,500 per article. All of the time, of course, he is developing his writing techniques and discipline to be prepared for the bigger jobs. Then, a shift to writing nonfiction books or writing a syndicated column might be the next step. Or he may turn to lecturing and teaching writing, or he might decide to negotiate a screen adaptation of his novel. The point of transition from one level to the other can be a synthesis of several of his already utilized talents, a revival of earlier ideas, or an entirely new venture altogether.

Richard Marek, addressing the members of the American Society of Journalists and Authors, said, "This is a profession of lies, and I hope some day the lying will stop." He was referring to the exaggerated claims some editors make to snag a particular author or book for their publishing houses, as well as the problems in communication between editors and authors, editors and their production departments, editors and publishing house sales departments, etc.

You as an author can hardly be expected to do much about that. But you can stave off deadbeats you run across, both at periodicals and book publishing houses. Remember, the more knowledgeable you are of the problems in the marketplace, the better prepared you'll be to deal realistically with them. Attempt to build a steady scaffold of techniques that will help you scale the outer barriers of publishing. Once over them and inside the outer walls you'll discover fallible, charming, imperfect, interesting human beings. They are, more often than you might suspect, sympathetic and helpful to the skilled and determined freelancer. Many of them, with little effort, will even become your good and loyal friends.

Blue-pencil blues

Writers relatively new to the business sometimes consider an editor's cutting or rewriting of their prose a loss. Sometimes it is. Many times it isn't. Rarely have I met an editor worth her salt who wasn't more help than hindrance. I don't believe a writer exists who can't occasionally profit from that editorial blue pencil. On the other hand, there are some periodicals where as a general rule copy is almost totally rewritten in-house to fit the peculiar, well-recognized style of the magazine. If you object to your work being fitted into their prose style, perhaps you should be marketing your work elsewhere. (And then there are the amusing moments in the rewrite business. One writer got an assignment from a highly stylized woman's magazine. She overdid it, though, and wrote her article in the ultimate version of that magazine's journalese. She received a note from the editor later which read, "You really outdid us this time. This is great caricature, but for heaven's sake, you know I can't send this upstairs!" The writer, more contrite the second time around, rewrote the piece.)

To proceed farther faster in your business, practice diligently to be your own best editor. When I spoke about giving even a minor market or brief assignment your best shot, I meant it. At each turn of the freelance road you should be attempting to make every article, play, poem, brochure, or book your very best to date. To do so you'll need, on occasion, to revise your material. The first thought, the first word pounced on, the first sketchy outlines are seldom going to be able to withstand the final analysis. Human beings aren't organized to spout forth in perfection, every syllable or arrangement of phrase a gem. Those who seem to be so gifted have generally spent many years silently developing and editing their unspoken observations. Actually sitting in the editorial chair can help you edit your own work. I know writers who have taken on brief stints at editing jobs primarily for that purpose. Having reached a point in their own creative efforts where they've been stymied, they took a breather from freelancing. They claim the process jarred open their eyes and sharpened their editorial skills immeasurably.

Short of taking an editing job to sharpen your skills, try some exercises. With your 3,000-word article or story in front of you, imagine you are required to edit it to fit a magazine page that only allows you 1,500 words. (If you were in the editor's chair, that might be just what would be required.) Longtime freelancer Theodore Irwin, who has had to do this for stories such as his "In Most Babies: Brain Damage Can Be Prevented" published in *Look*, says, "You've got to be extremely terse and pack a lot of essential information into a few words." (For an example of how Irwin managed, see *Writing the Magazine Article: From Idea to Printed Page.*)

If you still need help, get an editorially talented, hard-nosed friend, sibling, or spouse to criticize your work from time to time. Your prose will improve, and so will your ability to undergo the editorial blue pencil without getting the blues.

Revamp and retrench if necessary

Many times it doesn't make sense to continue in a given direction. If you've tried valiantly to make a go at a specialty but discovered you've hardly made headway, reconsider. Retrenchment may be what's in order, before you get in over your head financially or otherwise.

Early in my writing career this lesson was fortunately brought home to me in the nick of time. One of my short stories was accepted for publication by a small, literary magazine, but the editor held up publication until the autumn issue so it would have the best positioning and chance at a prestigious prize. This was heady news to a neophyte and for weeks I glowed with the already accomplished fact. Unfortunately, the magazine was published in Portugal and the autumn issue, for some reason, was held up at the border until long past the award deadline. Naturally, I was nonplussed at the outcome. And, although my retrenchment was mostly mental—I hadn't, thank heavens, spent any unearned prize money—it was devastating. Yet, it was probably one of the best lessons a beginning writer could have had. Moral? Try to wait to count the chickens until they're cackling merrily around the barnyard.

Revamping your operation requires getting and staying in touch with every available contact. It also means keeping a watchful eye out for new ones. One writer told me, "If I have a week when no new leads come in, I work backward. If I've corresponded with an editor previously and received encouraging words but no assignments, I'll drop him a short note, saying something like 'Hey, I wrote a few months ago. Remember me? Any new stories you're contemplating farming out? If so, can I help?'" Of course, the man is a fairly well-known professional who can afford such informality occasionally. But the idea of reminding editors that you're still available to take on assignments is a good one.

Revamping may mean reminding yourself of the availability of certain helpers that you may have put off referring to. What about *PR Aids*? Recall Washington Researchers? Or any of the other helpers in the Resources chapter?

Revamping may mean facing up to the trying but necessary chore of asking for a raise. Experts in this area suggest you prepare for the eventuality as you go along. First, keep a special file containing notes on all the meaningful projects you have completed for one employer. These will help substantiate your request for more money. Some kind editors will bestow these increases without nudging from you, but you certainly can't count on it. (Keeping track of just why you deserve a higher rate has an added advantage. The freelancer, possibly working with a sense of timidity that isolation brings on, may need the psychological boost.) Second, if you do something exceptionally well (possibly saving the client a good deal of money), don't wait long before you apply for that raise. Finally, if you want to remain on good terms, leave yourself a graceful way out if the first request for an increase is negative. Don't burn bridges unless you intend to do so.

Revamping, of course, may also mean developing another specialty. Bone up on what is happening, where others have moved, the direction of your target market a couple of years hence. When you read something like the following, ask how you can incorporate it into your plans.

"Issues that a short while ago were obvious have become very,

very complex and puzzling," John Mack Carter, editor-in-chief of *Good Housekeeping,* told a Women in Communications conference. He was referring to many subjects, including Southeast Asian problems, racism, sexism, consumerism, the environment, violence on television, and freedom of the press. "Suddenly, a curious thing happened. The guy in the black hat showed up decked out in a white hat. You just don't know who the enemy is anymore. The press can no longer say, 'We are just journalists; we just report the news.' Everyone knows we do make the news and we make it through that personal, subjective journalism we introduced a few years back."

Take heed of such words by a leader in the publishing industry. Have you kept abreast of these profound changes in the global picture? And have the global messages filtered down to your locality yet? Some of the subjects you will dig up as a freelancer are covered heavily elsewhere but may need your input in publications close to home.

If you're pushing your skills into a new area, it's bound to make others a little suspicious now and then, even if *you* know you're competent to handle the new situation. Remind yourself this new arena is one in which you're going to have to sell harder than before. Be totally prepared.

If you manage to get a big assignment every now and then, that should clue you that you *can* get more. If you are at a point where some editors trust you to deliver, you're halfway home. Assuming it takes three queries to land one hot assignment, prepare yourself for the strikeouts and keep after the home runs. Your self-confidence will grow with practice. Proposing and selling ideas, whether in person or on paper, will eventually become second nature to you. You'll even look forward to the challenge of areas you haven't tapped yet. Success, no matter how slight, whets the appetite as nothing else can.

A few last thoughts:

Don't be turned off too quickly from a field that seems foreign to you. Even specialized publications for engineers will often run a more general piece, say, about travel. They also look for material that relates to the personal lives of the engineers—how they can cope with rising costs, make their marriages work, or develop more up-to-the-minute, creative thinking techniques.

If you're changing specialties, you may have to go back a step or two until you've proved yourself. But move ahead quickly once you've paid your dues. Be alert to any chance for pointing out to clients that you're now as qualified as anyone else. Investigate the possibility of reviewing books in your new field—this offers further visibility. You will be deluged with material about upcoming publications in your new specialty, and you'll add to your personal specialty library (a break for your budget).

For some people, the best way to insure increased sales to higher-paying markets is to find a temporary partner. There are multitudinous ways to collaborate. Even a short-term arrangement might help as you face the uncertainty of a new area. And again, there's bartering. Might you convince someone in public relations to trade her expertise for your editing skills, for example?

Is it possible you could publish something in your area of expertise yourself—a booklet to be sold by direct mail or, once printed in a small edition, sold to a company to use as a good-will handout to their employees? Such tactics immediately give you a track record in your new field. Then build on the sale by offering similar projects to other outlets.

Remember the Mona Lisa and face the facts. Advertising—subtle or otherwise—is one of the primary sales tools of business. Use the *concepts* of advertising to improve your situation. And if you aren't adept yourself, ask a friend to help.

Multiple submission

Once taboo, multiple submission has become a moderately common practice in publishing today for certain kinds of articles, for some book proposals, and for finished book manuscripts. But there is a very big *if* involved. The submission is accepted *if* the recipients know that others are receiving the same material at the same time. Trouble lurks dangerously close for any freelancer who doesn't keep everything aboveboard.

A writer new to the field of publishing (but not to the techniques behind sales) naturally assumed the quickest and best way to reach potential customers was a sort of blitz to let possible clients compete for a given product. She prepared her material and had it photocopied several times. Shortly after sending the envelopes she received letters from all but one of the editors. All of the letters conveyed considerable interest in her project. What she felt saved her was the fact that one editor called instead of writing—by the time the letters from the others arrived, a contract from the editor who had acted quickly was on her desk as well. Of course, she still had to respond to the others, but the fait accompli of the contract gave her the confidence to handle the editors with considerable aplomb. She now realizes, a bit belatedly, she might have made bitter enemies of the others by her method and says she wouldn't do it the same way again.

On the other hand, Chet Cunningham reported in an article in *Writer's Digest* that he submits multiple book proposals—as a standard procedure—to six editors at a time:

> Multiple submissions are simply good merchandising. You send out a partial [book], say, to Avon. Avon says no thanks, but it takes two months. If you got two-month service from six different publishers, one at a time, with your original, it would take you a year to cover all six. By sending out six partials at once you can cover the same publishers in two months, and get your product to 18 publishers in only six months! This is especially important if you have a subject that is topical or tied in with the news. In a year the idea might be so out of date the book would not be worth publishing.

More and more, agents of writers with salable book proposals or manuscripts routinely offer the material to several editors at once. But they announce they are considering other offers when they do so. They don't, as a rule, use the term *multiple submission,* though, since some editors still resent the idea. Other terms, such as "We're exploring this idea with several publications," are apparently more acceptable.

The manuscript auction, formerly held only for the biggest names among authors, is increasingly in use as well. When an agent submits the material to several clients at the same time, he announces in the cover letter (or follow-up phone call) that there is a deadline for acceptance or rejection. If there is a floor—an amount below which an offer will be disregarded—this, too, is announced up front. The best offer (advance money and terms of the contract) will be accepted.

As for sending articles or queries to several competing periodicals at a time, only the bravest of the professionals submit their material to more than one top-paying slick simultaneously. The editors of these publications *usually* reply quickly enough, so it isn't actually necessary to do this, and it isn't worth taking the risk of alienating them. If they've spent time considering an idea *unaware* that their competition has a chance at it too, you'll earn their animosity. Don't do it. Multiple submission works best with sales of one-time rights to non-competing markets, as with spin-offs.

Spin-offs

Spin-offs—making your material work in a number of ways—are a way of making your money earn money. Professionals all do it, quite legitimately. You either send the same article to many markets (such as newspapers in Atlanta, Boston, Chicago, San Francisco, and Des Moines, marking the upper right-hand corner of the manuscript "one-time rights in your market only"), or rework research material and perhaps the beginning and end of an article and sell the re-vamped piece elsewhere, labeling it "one-time" or "second rights." Many markets will buy second rights quite happily. (See *Writer's Market* for editors' requirements on rights.) It's one way writers have of raising the income on certain material without much if any added effort. (A market that pays only five cents a word *might* be acceptable to a freelancer's budget if he knows he has five or ten more just like it where he's likely to sell the same article.)

Julian Block sells the same magazine material to a number of controlled-circulation magazines. He sends it out with a form letter. He doesn't bother to query, since he knows the market and figures his subject (taxes) is of universal interest. His material for duplicate markets goes out in large packets. Those magazines that pick it up send him regular checks. (And after he has a certain amount of success with one magazine, he proposes a series of articles or a column.)

Not only can you write spin-off material, you can sell reprints of what you've published to specialized markets on occasion, or gain additional revenue if a publication sells a large number of reprints of your material. For instance, an article on photography which used specialized materials manufactured by a specific corporation might be proffered in bulk to that company for its employees' bene-fit. Some large companies have racks for such free literature for their employees. Or perhaps you've written on stress management and the article, reprinted separately, would be interesting to corpo-rate managers who want to see that their management trainees around the globe have a copy. (See also Robin Perry's method of increasing his readership later in this chapter.) Of course, there are times when the magazine itself furthers the word about your work. One hundred thousand copies of Tom Mahoney's piece "A Seat Belt Could Save Your Life" (printed by *Reader's Digest*) were ordered by the American Safety Equipment Corporation and sent to fifty indus-trial firms and automotive companies for distribution to company personnel.

These spin-off manuevers do two things—they add a little more revenue to the coffers, and they spread the word about your expertise at the same time.

Norman Lobsenz, speaking to ASJA colleagues, says, "Cultivate your sources very carefully. Take time to rework the same ones." An example he gives: One of his articles involved the ten questions marriage counselors were asked most. Because he had cultivated his sources over a period of years, he could quickly contact them with a request for material. They sent him all he needed in the next mail. "Essentially they did all the work. Of course, a specialty helps. With a backlog of material at hand, most of your research is already done.

"Tell a major magazine what you're going to be doing," he reminds professionals. "If they are interested, they'll even come up with the angle that suits them best. Then, tell secondary magazines you've done it and ask are they interested?"

Marvin Grosswirth, a prolific writer, speaking to an ASJA writers' conference, said, "Two essentials for spin-offs: I figure I have to have at least 90 percent of the research material already in hand. I have to be a fast writer. I never spend more than two days on it. If it takes more time than that, I'm losing money. I try to see that the major outlets pay for all the research and phoning that I may need by over-researching at the beginning. That way the cost doesn't come out of my pocket later if I need 'a little more' for the spin-offs."

Photography

An important way to expand your coverage of the freelance territory is to add photography to the talents you can offer a client. Books such as the *Amateur Photographer's Handbook* and others (see the Resources chapter) will give you as much as you need to know about photography for your freelance needs. While top magazines hire their own freelance photographers or have them on staff, secondary markets may expect the writer to supply photographs with a story or come up with ideas on how to obtain stock photos.

Photos you supply should be 8x10 black-and-white glossies or 35mm color slides, never color prints. Send black-and-white contact sheets for the editor to choose which photos he wants, to save yourself, and him, money. Some magazines even want their stringers and correspondents to ship them the exposed roll of film so it can be processed on the magazine's premises. The editor will tell you if this is the procedure, and how to ship them. Noted travel-and-recreation specialist Pete Czura told Curtis Casewit in *Freelance Writing: Advice From the Pros,* "The ability to obtain good, usable color shots will turn on an editor. . . . Today, especially in the field I work in, most of the editors are aware of the importance of quality color photography. If there was one piece of advice I'd offer a beginning writer, it's to learn how to use a camera and shoot pix with some imagination. Shots with different angles, shots with different lenses, shots with impact are the ones editors like."

If you aren't about to become a photographer, by all means consider an informal or formal hookup with a good freelance photographer. You can do this on a one-time basis, on a local-story basis only, or as a regular team. Many married couples who are freelancers have worked out such an arrangement. They may both be writers and photographers and take turns with which part is handled by which partner for each assignment. Naturally, they double or even triple their income by covering so many bases.

Writer's Market and *Photographer's Market,* as well as the editorial guide sheets from specific periodicals, will tell you how much a client is paying for photographs. With an investment of from $100 to around $250 and a few months' practice, you'll be able to make this a part of your business.

Additional thoughts on expansion techniques

■ When the same bland renewal notice for a magazine subscription arrives in the mail, you don't give it a second look. If you want to renew an editor's interest in your material or build up assignments on a higher level than in the past, think about your presentation. How well does it sell your ideas? Is your timing and the sequence of ideas logical? Is the market holding you back or are you holding yourself back through fear, inexpertise, or timidity?

■ One writer had an idea you might want to try: She designed an inexpensive one-page "brochure," 8½x11 inches, printed sideways and folded in thirds. Inside were photos she'd taken and teaser quotes from her writing.

■ Remember, some top-notch freelancers spend as much as three or four hours a day on the phone—keeping in touch with publishers, editors, agents, clients.

■ Robin Perry used copies of his book on photography as premiums—gift books to corporate executives which they then gave their employees. He made money from the sales and added to his local reputation. The author had, naturally, signed each copy, which gave them added appeal.

■ Let's say you're working in a public-information job for a college. You place an article in the local Sunday supplement, but rules at your school don't allow you to accept remuneration. That shouldn't stop you from keeping the editor honest nor from gaining some advantageous prestige. Ask him to contribute the money you would have received to some worthy charity. By arranging such payment you also please other freelancers because you don't undercut those who *have* to be paid for their work if they want to eat regularly.

■ If you have a book about to be published, you might want to try to write a short piece on a related subject and submit it to the op-ed page of your local paper. That gives greater visibility and subtle promotion for your book.

■ Grants, contests, awards, and other financial aids are possible expansion tools you might want to explore from time to time.

Old Chief One-Feather knew it well. As he told author Marilyn Holmes, "If you don't have a target, you'll miss it every time."

Chapter 10
The
Money
Migraine

■■■

Fighting an occupational disease

Twenty minutes prior to the onset of a migraine headache, many sufferers experience a phenomenon called the aura, during which they have visual disturbances that may include seeing colors, flashing lights, monsters, and apparitions. Lewis Carroll, a migraine victim, put his apparitions to good use by featuring them as characters in *Alice in Wonderland.*

Some monsters appear to the freelancer during the old money migraine common to our occupation. Three of the most familiar ones are the grinchy late or nonpaying client, the gobbler who wants all rights in perpetuity, and the nearsighted ne'er-do-well who's unreasonable about paying legitimate expenses. If they've shown up in your business, read on. We all experience the money migraine from time to time, whether we're just starting out or are fairly advanced in this business. Some of the reasons were mentioned in Chapter 1—the nature of the business itself and the nature of the person who generally goes into freelancing. The money migraine is not *only* due to most freelancers' inexperience in money management, but it's often an area where improvement is possible. Thomas Paine put it this way: "Those who expect to reap the blessings of freedom must undergo the fatigue of supporting it." He wasn't talking about freelance writers, but he might as well have been.

It's a truism that some people are too busy trying to make money to save it and some are too busy saving it to make it. But when you tell me you can't take the time to pay attention to the financial details of your business, I simply have to ask, can you afford not to?

Anyone who promises to solve all of the freelancer's money problems is suspect. But while there's no sure answer, some things help—a hardheaded attitude, some scheming, and lots of ingenuity. Fortunately, these are some of a freelancer's strongest attributes. When you're feeling weak-kneed about certain aspects of the world in which freelancing has placed you, especially that peculiar province of bankers, lawyers, accountants, publishers, and business people, the first and last thing you need to do is remind yourself that *you are in business,* too. What applies to their fiscal security applies to yours as well.

Staying ahead of cash-flow problems

The following are some tips writers have used to keep their bank balances healthy:

■ Keep a cash reserve to cover the slow months. Use it only for this purpose and replenish it as soon as possible.

■ Synchronize accounts receivable with accounts payable as much as you can by your early planning method (see the section on budgeting in Chapter 13).

■ Apply for credit with suppliers. If you are on friendly terms, ask to pay on a periodic basis, if need be, especially if you have established a good credit rating. Explain that your income arrives in spurts instead of on a regular weekly, biweekly, or monthly basis if this is the case. Some suppliers may be willing to bill you on a two-, three-, or four-month basis—allowing you a discount if you pay early. Talk this over with them, explaining it saves them billing and postage costs.

■ Slash expenses to the bone. You can only cut corners so far. But a close analysis of your budget may uncover frills that you *can* do without briefly without hurting your professional stance.

■ Apply for a short-term bank loan for your business. If a commercial loan doesn't seem feasible, check credit unions of organizations you, your spouse, or other family member may belong to.

■ Join forces, thereby sharing some of your expenses. (If you can't contribute this month, perhaps your partner can.)

■ Take a temporary part-time job.

■ Apply for a grant. (See the Resources chapter; see also the section on augmenting your freelance income in this chapter.)

Spotting dead ends and deadbeats

You shouldn't need much help with this after twelve to eighteen months of freelancing. But in case some of you have been lucky enough to get this far without having to wait for acceptance letters and/or payment checks, I'll mention the more common problems:

1. An editor says he'll send a reply to your query tomorrow, but it never arrives.
2. The editor disappears or moves on to an entirely different kind of publication.
3. The periodical folds precipitously.
4. Amnesia overtakes everyone, from the postman who supposedly accepted your manuscript for shipping, to the mailroom person at the publication, to the slush pile reader. (Some writers, let it be said, are also at fault. They forget to enclose an SASE, or they put

inadequate postage on the return envelope, or their scrawl is illegible on the package, etc.)

5. Your article is accepted; you're jubilant. You open the galleys, correct and return them on deadline. Next editorial move? The article is killed through no fault of yours. Even then you have to wait an unduly long time for the kill fee. Needless to say, the article's timeliness has been its undoing—the poor thing is *dead*.

Can you spot these disaster areas beforehand? In many cases, yes. Some professionals I know, for instance, refuse to do more than send a query to a new publication, carefully noting what the results are. There is always a shakedown period at a publication. You don't want to get caught in the fallout.

Magazines that pay on publication are notorious in freelance writers' circles for creating problems. Many times "pay on publication" means "several months or more *after* publication" (if then). While the most important issue for a beginner may be publication at all costs, for the professional freelancer it never is. Avoid these markets entirely (except for spin-off material), or your budget and nerves won't stand the strain.

One tactic writers must sometimes use is to wait the required time for an answer from a publisher or editor, then send a registered letter advising they're withdrawing their manuscript (or query). They have to go to the trouble of retyping it, of course, but they are then free to submit it elsewhere.

Another way to head off deadbeats is to be sure, if you've accepted an assignment by phone, to immediately follow the conversation with a letter of assignment, detailing the article topic, length, agreed-upon rates, delivery date, and expenses to be paid.

Collection tactics

Bill collecting is time-consuming, frustrating, detracting to your fund of creative energy, and necessary. Unfortunately, it's getting more necessary every day. Even markets one assumed would always pay on time become dilatory on occasion.

One writer I know got so frustrated about a foot-dragging client that he wrote across his third invoice "10 percent discount for *immediate* payment." He got the full payment in the next week's mail. That's a lesson in psychology we might all heed.

Timely billing is the first step toward timely payment. Send your bill *with your manuscript*. Make certain your invoice has your Social Security number on it, and your terms: on receipt, or whatever other arrangement you and the editor have made. State on the bill exactly how you want the check made out—Joe Blow, or Blow Bylines, Inc. (If you're incorporated, of course you'll use your employee identification number rather than your personal Social Security number.) Bills for any out-of-pocket expenses should be clearly listed, with a photocopy of receipts attached if your editor requires them. Proper invoicing and recordkeeping can forestall some problems before they arise. Keep copies of all unpaid invoices in a tickler file. Review it regularly. (For a sample invoice, see fig. 10-1.)

Second billing. This can go out with a pleasant letter of reminder and perhaps a touch of humor. Jog the editor's memory if a few weeks have gone by without payment. Editors *are* busy and often overworked and understaffed. It *may* be lost on the desk or in the accounting department. If you receive no answer within ten days after this, however, maybe you're being ignored.

A more hardheaded letter, reminding the editor that you met your obligations and you request that he meet his, is now in order. Perhaps a phone call at this point will speed matters up. Some writers call collect: even if the calls are not accepted, the message is getting across.

Charge interest on unpaid accounts over thirty, sixty, or ninety days, just as you are charged if you're delinquent in your payments elsewhere. You may not receive the additional amounts, but again, you're getting a businesslike message across.

What can you do if all else fails? Let *Writer's Digest* or your colleagues in your professional organization know. Alert others to the problems with the delinquent client. Offer to negotiate a settlement, or ask a lawyer to write a letter doing so. Sometimes when a client's back is against the wall, it is the better part of valor to allow him to save face. Finally, you can threaten to go to small claims court. Most clients will settle at this point. If not, then you can go ahead and actually take them to court.

If you continue to work for a slow-paying market, at least request expense money up front in future transactions. That way you've covered your out-of-pocket expenses and forced some commitment on the client's part. *If* your relationship with a client has been good and you believe there truly was a mix-up, simply ask for an advance against expenses next time around. (And try to negotiate for billing long-distance calls directly to the client.)

Beginning freelancers often say it hadn't occurred to them to bill for their out-of-pocket expenses while performing an assignment.

```
                        (Your Letterhead)

(Social Security
or Employee I.D. No.)
                                    Date:_____
To:_____
   _____
   _____


For Services Rendered:
   Story:_____
         _____
   Delivered:_____

   Photos:_____
          _____
   Delivered:_____

   Expenses:_____
            _____
            _____
            _____
   Other fees:_____
   Taxes:_____
   Total:_____
   Terms:_____(on receipt)___
   Send check to:
```

Fig. 10-1. *Sample invoice.*

But their rate of pay drops dramatically if they have to deduct these costs from their fee. They may refrain from asking because they're afraid of offending the editor and losing the assignment. In truth, most editors *expect* to have to pay reasonable expenses.

So bill the editor. He might just surprise you. And certainly if you're negotiating for a higher fee after several assignments, refer to your expenses so far. Use that figure for ammunition, as well as anything else you can think of—current rate of inflation, your superior record as a freelancer (always on time with assignments, etc.). Or cite the statistics recently released by the research department of the National Endowment for the Arts. They've found writers to be among the lowest-paid groups in the nation; take away technical, medical, and science writers, and those statistics are even worse!

Augmenting your freelance income

Basically there are three avenues to pursue to keep your financial picture sunny: diligence in negotiating the best freelance deals, scouting for sources of augmenting that income from time to time, and adding secondary sources of income to the overall financial setup.

The prime ingredient in the discovery of funds to supplement income is your own *ingenuity*. People in other businesses have advantages you don't. They can, like the publisher of the magazine you write for, apply to numerous people to raise capital: customers, suppliers, insurance companies, banks, employees, other companies, venture-capital firms, investment bankers, and governments. If your business is a sole proprietorship or partnership, you don't have those options. The ability to get credit depends on your personal reputation. Third parties cannot invest in the business without incurring responsibilities for business debts as well. That usually means you have to rely on relatives or very close, good friends.

If you are borrowing from a bank, the Small Business Administration, or other lending institution, personal guarantees by you (and any partner) will probably be required. However, if you have recently left a full-time job, would that former boss be of any help? If not for a loan, then, perhaps, as one who might recommend you for a grant?

The pros and cons of public funding of writers are as numerous as the writers who do or do not get the grants. I have known some writers who wrote less and less the more they skipped from one grant to another. Certainly most will admit that it's easier to get a second and a third grant after you've got that first one. But does the grant really help you write?

For many writers, the chore of getting the grant in the first place may be more than it's worth. If, however, you want to try, check the information in the Resources chapter, and don't overlook small local possibilities. Your friendly librarian, again, is a likely guide to sources of such local funds.

Trying for *prizes*, on the other hand, may not be such a bad idea. If you have a novel on the back burner or if you write in a specialized field (science, medicine, psychology, etc.), you may qualify for annual prizes given by a variety of organizations, some of which come with a cash award, no strings attached (see the Resources chapter).

Many prizes, even if they don't carry a cash award, will eventually help line your pockets, since the prestige of winning can be a feather in your cap and portfolio. So if you think you have a chance, take the time to fill out the forms and send in the required material.

I've spoken about partnerships in Chapters 4 and 8. But another sort of sharing actually brings in rent: Any extra property or equipment that you use only part-time might be a source of revenue. Photographic equipment, including a darkroom setup, drawing table, light table, and so forth, might be just the item someone around the corner from you is looking to use rather than buy. The same goes for *any* item you possess. Post notices everywhere. It takes careful arranging, of course, to set up such a plan and it can't be spelled out in general terms, but if you look around you may find you have that other source of income, no matter how small, that would help relieve the strain on your business budget.

If none of the preceding sources are any help to you and you refuse to contemplate marriage just so you can have a spouse to support your writing business over the rough spots, consider the following suggestions for secondary sources of income.

Consulting

This sideline, like Joseph's coat, is of many colors and contrasts. James Kobak turned his into a full-time business when he saw that publishers were in great need of his business acumen. When a large Eastern university wanted to update their media department they contacted Richard Pinney, a freelance journalist, artist, and media expert. They called him in to make a study and lay out preliminary plans for them. And many successful writers find letters in their mailboxes asking them to read and judge manuscripts for contests—for a fee, of course.

If you have published in a special area, you might think about some institutions which could use your expertise. It's probably more graceful for all concerned if you have a friend mention your name, but it's not necessary. As in applying for any kind of assignment or position, advance preparation is the key. Summarize the current problems faced by your potential client as you see them, then briefly propose some alternatives. When writing them up, you should be careful to give enough of the idea of your plan without adding the trump card too soon. You want them to hire you to provide the final keys to the solution.

Sales techniques that have succeeded down through the centuries should be remembered whenever you're trying to talk someone into something. Remember, people resent having other people's ideas forced on them. New ideas will often bring on an instinctive reaction of resentment if not presented in the proper way. Try to bring up your idea in such a way the other person may think it was his own idea to begin with. At the very least, don't appear too anxious to have your idea accepted. In pointing out the benefits precede them with "Have you ever considered this?"

A writer I know who was experienced at fund raising for charity groups just happened to be talking to the mayor of her city, which was a large one with many fiscal problems. Almost jokingly she suggested she knew how he could turn some of those financial problems around with an old, tried-and-true fund-raising gimmick. The novelty of the idea, or rather the novelty of trying it on such a grand scale, appealed to the mayor and she had herself a consulting job. Since it was her idea, he reasoned, she would be best to oversee the mammoth project.

Another writer who successfully put consulting into his business picture was a man who had developed a large network of contacts in a wide variety of fields through his freelancing and former work as a reporter for a newspaper. He wanted, however, to become a consultant to a university president. He didn't just want to handle press releases or print the in-house employee newsletter. His talents inclined him to think he could write speeches for the president, get him press coverage others could not, and come up with money-saving magic for the entire university system. He listed the numerous categories he'd researched in depth for his published work. He also listed the kinds of conferences he attended regularly and the broad base they gave him for uncovering the best of the new ideas being put into practice elsewhere. He knew he had considerably more to offer than most people who had worked and built careers from one position to the next in tight formation. With this security blanket tucked in his briefcase, he approached the president directly. He and his samples landed the job. Now he works as a consultant one week per month and keeps the freedom of his freelancing schedule.

Teaching

Teaching is a traditional financial base for writers. It is often the first route freelancers explore, for good reasons. Time is usually flexible. The proximity of good libraries and educated companionship is stimulating. The ivory tower can beckon invitingly after several years of scratching out a living elsewhere. The chase after editors, the haggling for peanuts, the worrying over the landlord's preference for cash over art—all are debilitating.

What's waiting for you, if you decide to pursue this possibility? Aside from the aforementioned benefits, there are a few problems as well, mainly stiff competition in a tight job market, especially for full-time faculty positions. If you want that kind of security, in most cases you'll need at least one advanced degree (M.A., Ph.D., M.F.A.). Without it, you'll face an uphill struggle. A long list of excellent publishing credits and some fast talking will certainly help. So can your sex. Women are currently in high demand since employing them helps many colleges comply with equal opportunity laws. Furthermore, today's female students often seem more eager to study with successful women writers than with their male peers.

For writers looking for part-time employment, the liveliest areas are currently community colleges and continuing-education departments at universities.

Most writers gravitate toward teaching the obvious—writing, journalism, or literature. But it's possible to devise your own course based on a specialty of yours, especially if you're heading toward community colleges or continuing education departments. A writer who is an expert on money management could offer a beginners' section on budgeting and finances. A photojournalist could teach portrait photography and/or photojournalism tricks to the amateur photographer. A medical/science writer might come up with a fascinating topic that, handled with a broad brush, would appeal to everyone from the young college student who is interested in science but doesn't want to major in it to the retiree who has always wanted to get some background in the sciences. Travel writers have given courses for the armchair traveler. Tax experts teach ways to beat tax trauma. And, Edith Lynn Hornik-Beer, who publishes her work in the *New York Times* among other periodicals, teaches a course, "Specialized Writing for the Non-Writer" at the New York Botanical Garden.

By combining your own expertise with someone else's, you may be able to teach part-time even without opening traditional academic doors. Speak to the administration of your nearby academic institutions. Don't forget the business colleges and schools. Find out first what they are looking for before you approach them with your own suggestions. Ask the public relations person what courses the students applying to the continuing-education departments request most often. Plan your strategy carefully.

When you go, be prepared with an outstanding résumé. Remember: Academics will be impressed that *you have published.* They have faced the publish-or-perish syndrome for years. The simple fact that you have managed to get your words in print can be a big plus for you. The students themselves tend to yawn over texts and courses taught by people who haven't been in the thick of things. The fact that you're going to give the students as much opportunity as possible to talk with you, a successful writer, about how you do things, what your frustrations are, how joyful it is to be your own boss and see your name in print, will be a big sales incentive. Some of the other faculty or administrators may even visit your classes to learn how you do it.

Fig. 10-2 is a sample of a presentation for a writing course—it's one that was successful for me. There are no rules; it's up to you to make your own. But it is advisable to give your interviewer a general outline of your intent in the suggested course, a breakdown for the segments of time for which you will be paid, and an idea of your sources (your own syllabus or published texts, etc.).

Performing

Writers have learned to perform before audiences as a means to increase their income (through lecturing) and to help sell their books (through the guest spots on radio and TV shows). The advantage of lecturing is that you can integrate it into a varied freelance life. And

Course: <u>Writing & Selling Nonfiction--From Idea to Printed Page</u>
Summary of intent: A sixteen-week workshop in freelance writing concentrating on magazine article and feature writing. At
least eight written assignments on subjects ranging from humor,
profile, and historical to travel, seasonal, and round-up.
Classroom and written critiques. Study of markets. Effort:
to extend the students' knowledge of periodicals where they
might sell their prose, help them to learn preparation of
professional manuscripts, and increase their experience in
interviewing, researching, organizing, writing, and editing.

1. <u>The Short Happy (?) Life of the Freelance Writer</u>
    Analysis of article slants; general organizing tech-
    niques; comments on discipline; Q & A.
    Assignment: short profile (writer as own subject)

2. <u>I'm O.K., but You're Not Jonathan Livingston Seagull</u>
    The search for a salable subject; fitting subject to
    approach; Q & A.
    Assignment: analysis of three different kinds of
    published periodical articles

3. <u>Can Sarah Lawrence Find Happiness with the Marquis de
    Sade?</u>
    Market analysis--who wants what and why?
    Assignment: short seasonal

4. <u>Have Guts, Will Tangle</u>
    Research techniques examined--where to start, when to
    stop, which kind for which purpose?
    Assignment: short historical (using research techniques)

5. <u>To the Rescue of That Alien Jingle</u>
    The query; short and longer outlines examined.
    Discussion of magazine editors' lingo; Q & A.
    Assignment: three selling queries with outlines
    attached for three separate markets (the slicks, a
    regional, a trade)

6. <u>Better than a Slap in the Belly with a Wet Fish</u>
    What happens after you receive a "go ahead on spec"?

Fig. 10-2. *Sample course proposal.*

In-depth research, systematizing the material, preliminary drafts; Q & A.
Assignment: how-to piece

7. Lady Chatterley, Where Are You?
The problems with interviews explained; notes vs. tape
recorders and other problems; the follow-up.
Assignment: in-class interview and man-in-the-street
techniques (class divided)

8. Charades and Miracles
The lead--where is it? Q & A.

9. Do-It-Yourself Monster Job
Substance and style in writing; organizational questions.
Assignment: as-told-to article

10. Procrastination Makes Perfect
Rewriting techniques explored in depth; measurements.
Assignment: revision of article previously submitted

11. Blood May Be Quicker than Water
Semiotic techniques for improving creativity; Q & A.
Assignment: notebook pages on advertising, etc.

12. Never Work without Ulterior Motives
The selling title; making errors pay; anecdotes.
Assignment: the round-up

13. Those Magical Words: All Expenses Paid
Discussion of travel writing, stringing, spin-offs, etc.
Assignment: travel article with photographs

14. Don't Call Me Ingrid
Humor writing--who wants it? What makes it so diffi-
cult? Q & A.
Assignment: humor piece

15. The Great Agent in the Sky, the Carabinieri--and You
Agents; the writer and the law; Q & A.
Assignment: profile of a local celebrity

16. Final Examination (one hour)

Text: Instructor's syllabus
References: See attached list.

Fig. 10-2. *(cont.)*

the more you lecture, the better known you become and the more you can sell your books or other writing. The more your work sells, the higher a lecture fee you can demand. It's a very happy merry-go-round.

Here are some suggestions on lecturing from the editors of *Coda,* the newsletter of Poets & Writers, Inc.:

> Start locally: neighborhood libraries, Y's, churches, senior citizen centers. Don't forget junior and community colleges or local hospitals. Always send the prospective sponsor a sample of your work. To find new sponsors, consult the *Sponsors List* from Poets & Writers, Inc. [see the Resources chapter], which includes 505 reading/workshop sponsors nationwide. Get in touch with your state arts council. Start early. The better-paying series book writers a year in advance. Ask for the room you want and be specific (lighting, seating arrangement, podium, etc.). Ask about the audience. What kind and how many are expected? Help promote your reading by any means you can. Keep it short and be as dramatic as possible. Make the audience laugh. Make sure your books are available for sale. Get paid.

When you lecture on your special subject or give a reading of your short fiction or poetry, you are nurturing your writing, getting input from an audience, and receiving no small amount of ego stroking. It will amaze you how it will help build your confidence in your work.

Editing

Freelance editing can provide a lucrative sideline for highly energetic writers. A woman I know gave up a full-time editing position in New York when she moved to the suburbs to write. As she was building her own portfolio of clips, however, she continued to take on jobs for her old company. Eventually, her contacts turned up several other publishing companies that needed material edited, which they'd send her on a freelance basis.

How do you get such editing jobs on a freelance basis if you don't have publishing-house experience? In most cases, again, *you* have to find *them,* not the other way around.

First, become acquainted with the different kinds of editing publishing requires: copyediting, content editing, acquisitions editing. Basically, the copyeditor is the one who checks every detail in the manuscript for grammatical and factual error, seeing that it conforms to whatever style is considered best by the publishing house and that it is consistent throughout in the use of type and so forth. The content editor may also pencil edit but is primarily concerned with clarifying ambiguous passages, suggesting rearrangements of material so the manuscript reads better, and dealing with other conceptual matters. This is the person whose mind is focused on the book as a totality. The acquisitions editor is most important to the publisher as an idea person. She scans literally hundreds of newspapers, magazines, competitors' catalogs, and the like for ideas for books and for possible new authors to add to the publisher's list. In very large publishing houses content editing and acquisitions editing are totally separated. Smaller firms have editors who handle both. Although it is more usual to get freelance jobs either copyediting or content editing, there are occasions when an acquisitions editor will take on a part-time assistant. According to a fine editor of my acquaintance, "having a sense of mission" may be the most important sales tool you have to convince a publisher of your worth. "Persistence is the next in importance," says another freelance editor. "I'd written to the company but got a response like, 'How would you like an eighteen-month temporary job at very low pay?' 'No thanks,' I said, 'but I am a freelancer. If any jobs come up that you'd like me to tackle, I'll be happy to come in and talk about them.' I repeatedly reminded them of my availability until I finally got a call. I did a big research job for them. Since then, I've been given a variety of jobs for the same company on a freelance basis. The main point to remember besides persistence is take any assignment offered you to get a foot in the door. If you do a bang-up job on it, you're sure to get other assignments."

If you want to try your hand at such jobs, show lots of enthusiasm, and let the client know what kind of editing and/or researching you do best. Keep after them until they hire you. Then give it your all.

Even a small-scale editing job can be parlayed into a worthwhile item on your résumé. You might want to check with the local weekly newspaper to see if the overworked managing editor has any entry-level jobs you might handle, even on a now-and-then basis. Does your library publish a magazine or informational pamphlet? If so, does the editor need help? Wherever you find such publications, you have an opportunity to start your editing career, paid or unpaid, although you may not be called "editor" for a long time to come.

One freelancer eventually added "editor" to her résumé by approaching a creative writing teacher at a community college. She offered to help correct student assignments for free, with a catch: If the work was satisfactory she'd like a letter of recommendation ("To Whom It May Concern") regarding her editing skills.

That "I'll help you for free" approach was also the way I discovered an expert researcher in my neighborhood, or rather, she discovered me. She wanted to add experience working with a publishing writer to her résumé, which was already heavy with library training. I couldn't have been happier to take her on.

Corporate freelancing

The assumption that writing and editing brochures or corporate reports isn't as "creative" or exciting as book or magazine writing is common among students I've had. Which is, all things considered, a shame. Many of those students aren't ever going to see their byline in a national slick, either because of the competition or their limited desire to compete. But they could make a good living using their skill with words if they'd consider these other markets.

Corporate writing jobs are out there. If you want, you can get assignments to write company brochures, annual reports, company histories, audiovisual scripts, material for trade shows, seminar guidance manuals, and the like, as well as writing jobs at a medical school or university (news notes for communications between faculty and administration, special pamphlets and flyers for intrafaculty communications, as well as news releases.) Check with your librarian, who will often have a great deal of information about your community's business leaders and can offer possible names for your mailing list. Telephone public relations representatives or the local arts council for additional names for your list. Spread the word that you're available for freelance assignments in any way that seems reasonable in your community.

Apply directly to the department that might be interested in your skills. Also try to get to know someone personally there—PR person, dean, professor. (Of course, you can approach the personnel office. This is the standard procedure. But because it is less direct, chances of connecting with the right person in the right department are slimmer.)

Ways to get the word out that you are available for corporate assignments (other than the direct one mentioned above) are several. If you are interviewing a business executive for an article or book, you might want to mention during that interview that you are also available to his company for freelance assignments. In outlining your abilities, describe briefly the most outstanding jobs you've handled for other companies or organizations. If this is your first stab at a business-writing assignment, mention your best writing credits, detailing the work that was required to accomplish them.

When you are published in your local outlets, be sure the squib about you says that you freelance for corporations or universities or whatever. Some writers drop hints until they become the subject of a feature story in their college alumni magazine, local weekly paper, or church bulletin. Although this method doesn't guarantee that the right corporate people will find out about you, at least it gives you something tangible to duplicate and mail to company presidents with a cover letter offering your services.

Have you ever considered doing a communications survey among various clients in your community? Large or small, all businesses have communications problems from time to time—employee to boss, boss to employee, department to department, company to the outside world. With studious library research, as well as through personal contacts with business people in your town or city, you can discover which companies most need your help. (The editor of the advertising community's magazine might be someone to tap discreetly for information on this subject. Check also with a member of the IABC—International Association of Business Communicators—if you know any personally.)

Fig. 10-3 shows a partial sample of questions a writer devised in an effort to comprehend some of the executive reasoning behind each company's corporate communications program. Once he had the answers he was prepared to suggest ways in which each could streamline and upgrade communication efforts. He also compared the answers from the several regional firms he was working for with those of similar companies he was familiar with elsewhere. With some, a monthly newsletter turned out to be the most effective communications vehicle; for others, periodic company-wide memos and a series of bulletin boards was the better method. As a communications specialist, working on a freelance basis, he managed to convince the executives that his method of a broader survey than any in-house worker had access to made him their best bet for communications analysis.

Heading into corporate communications on a freelance basis takes considerable cunning and a fine sense of two things: the nuances of the English language and an ability to persuade. The writer

Company_____

Executive_____

Title_____

Address_____   Telephone_____

        _____

        _____

_____

1. Which applies to your company's communications package?

   a. written communications objectives

   b. written communications policies

   c. written job descriptions

   d. administrative guidelines for communications staff

   e. outside consulting firm regularly used

   f. program formally and periodically evaluated

2. Communications program

   a. one-person staff

   b. new communications program

   c. communications program undergone major budget cut or
      increase

3. Audience

   a. community leaders

   b. customers, dealers, educators, students, handicapped,
      management, minorities, retirees, stockholders,
      financial analysts, union workers, etc.

Fig. 10-3. *Sample corporate communications survey.*

of any company publication has to get to the point quickly with lots of punch. The time you'll spend poring over those glossy annual reports and brochures from the Fortune 500 in your library to prepare for your stint will be money in the bank. You can also learn more about corporate business by finding a friendly in-house editor and questioning him closely. His guidance can be invaluable.

Public relations

Another potential sideline gold mine is public relations in its many forms. There's probably not a company, organization, or agency extant that doesn't need more of the good news about them fed to the public on which they rely.

What do you write for these outlets? Well, there are press releases, new-product releases, jingles for radio and television advertising, speeches for their executives, flyers, trade-show banners and other paraphernalia, slide/tape shows, and many others you'll discover yourself. You need to be gregarious and outgoing, and it helps to have a specialty. A woman I know was the local whiz on all aspects of fund raising for nonprofit organizations, having spent many years helping out for free before she decided she ought to be paid and paid well for her efforts. Another, whose sense of humor was irrepressible, found she could apply it to humorous jingle writing instead of just amusing her teenagers.

Even with only a generalized knowledge or expertise in one area, you're still not out of the ball game. Very small companies, who can't afford a big agency's help, worry about their image as much as large ones. Since they can't afford to spend a lot of money on image building, you'll have to settle for small fees, but you can take on two or three such clients and have a steady income, *if* you're careful to keep track of the time you spend for each. Don't let your enthusiasm overcome you to the point where you're giving far too much time to a client whose payments are minimal. (But *do* give him a fair shake. He may eventually become your biggest booster.)

Points in your favor when you try small-company publicity:

1. You give them individualized attention they might not get from a large agency.
2. You charge far less than an agency.
3. You're a small entrepreneur yourself, so you're aware of possible image problems.

4. Your specialist's background may offer contacts, if not techniques, that are helpful shortcuts which an agency's personnel simply cannot provide. Especially true because you are probably already dealing with the local media. (See fig. 10-4 for a sample publicity release schedule.)

5. If you have other skills (in photography, art, or design) you can also supply these at a far lower cost than they might have to pay an agency with high overhead.

Before you negotiate with possible clients, make sure you have a firm list in mind (or better, on paper) of those shortcuts you've developed. Make your sales pitch as professional as possible, since that will be one thing the client will be listening for—how well do you sell yourself? It may be his only measure of your ability to sell his product or service.

Newsletters

Developing and publishing newsletters is a thriving business. Over 5,000 are currently published, and new ones start every day. This offers a lucrative sideline for freelancers. You can add to your profits by dispensing specialized information you're privy to through a newsletter. Readers of newsletters buy specialized, timely information without the pressures of advertisers' hype.

Some thriving newsletters have been started on a shoestring. Others began when a shrewd freelancer with a great idea got a bank loan and put his idea to work. And newsletters don't have to be long to be profitable. Some are only two manuscript pages in length. Subscribers hungry for the specialized information they provide pay anywhere from $20 to $50 or more for the service. Some highly specialized, informative newsletters (usually providing great money-saving or investment tips) have made their owners rich almost overnight—a year's subsription sold for $100 to $500, with anxious subscribers happily reenlisting early. Why? Because busy people in high places need up-to-date information and don't have time to fish around or research it themselves. Their insider's newsletter comes to their desks like clockwork. In a matter of a few minutes' scanning, they gain vital, fresh information necessary for their work, their investment planning. or other special interests.

Some enterprising freelancers have combined their talents by setting themselves up as consultants in a specialty, drawing fees from

PUBLICITY RELEASE LIST FOR ___							
PUBLICATIONS	CONTACT:	Date:					
Newport Daily News	JSL						
Providence Bulletin	PM						
Journal	JW						
Barrington Times							
Westerly Sun	NJ						
Pawtuxet Valley Times	?						
Pawtucket Times	BL						
Cranston Mirror	?						
Woonsocket Call	cK						
Coventry Townsman	?						
East Side/West Side	HT						

Fig. 10-4. *Sample publicity-release log.*

companies and organizations on an individual project basis, and also offering a newsletter to an even wider variety of clients who for one reason or another couldn't or didn't take advantage of the on-the-spot consultancy.

One of the quickest routes to learning more about the newsletter business is through the International Entrepreneurs Association (IEA), which offers an in-depth analysis of the industry. See if your library has this lengthy report and use it as a start-up operation manual. It will tell you if the newsletter business is right for you, as well as steps to take to start. It give you checklists to test your topic, alerts you if your price is too low or too high, details expense variables related to subscriber-acquisition advertising, lists tricks for extra subscription revenue, suggests a market consultation source, and much more (see the Resources chapter).

Mail-order business

Some freelancers have found this to be an ideal second-income source. It fits the flexibility and independence pattern you've achieved as a freelancer. But there are sad stories of great losses suffered by people too anxious to cash in on the mail-order craze; so do your homework and proceed with caution. Generally, writers opt to sell books and related informational tools, but it isn't necessary to stick with these.

Mail-order sales in the U.S. topped $21.5 billion in 1977, an increase of 12.2 percent over the preceding year. Because of the phenomenal growth, book publishers are scrambling onto the bandwagon in a big way. Of the thirteen industry segments using mail order, an industry report showed, books and magazine subscriptions were third and fourth in dollar volume, behind only ready-to-wear and insurance. Among other reasons for the growth of this field is the fact that more women are in the work force every day and they, the elderly, and busy executives of all sorts find mail-order shopping both timesaving and convenient.

In researching this subject I talked with a man with an astounding success story. He's more entrepreneur than writer, but he has had phenomenal success so far in the mail-order business. He sells a variety of how-to books and grossed "in the high six figures" during his third year in operation. He offered these clues to his success: Keep your costs at rock bottom, keep your hand in all aspects of your business, and learn to write the convincing ad, without overselling your product.

If this field interests you, look into the companies that sell their success stories with useful tips (see the Resources chapter). Also, speak to as many people as you can who have tried mail order at one time or another. You'd be surprised how many have. You've probably not known about it, though, because if they've failed, they don't advertise the fact around the neighborhood.

Here are some clues to start with:

■ Test your inexpensive ad first, before putting out any other money on your idea. And then test again. Your total expense for this will run to only a few dollars if you're smart.

■ There are stringent rules about the mail-order business. Check your state and IRS rulings, the SBA, or ask an accountant or lawyer. They can lead you to an information source.

■ Much information on writing a selling ad can also be purchased for a relatively small amount. Successful ads all include the most pertinent techniques you, as a writer, have been aiming for in writing your leads and queries. They use key selling words, economy of language, and correct punctuation.

For the cost of some of these information booklets containing salesmen's techniques and mail-order miracles, the writer can get a quick course. (He might otherwise spend thousands of dollars and considerable time on a school or college course.) Some of these booklets can also be found in your own library, where you don't have to spend a penny for them.

Although there are, of course, some variations in the psychology of sales, depending on your source, your instructor, or the philosophy of economics presented in any one approach, there are some you'll discover are repeated by otherwise wildly divergent practitioners. The point here is, even if you don't want to go into the mail-order book business yourself, you can apply the techniques these successful business persons use in your sales pitches to periodical or book publishers and your other clients.

Other sidelines

Anyone who has ever driven along Sunset Boulevard through Hollywood and Beverly Hills has seen the map peddlers. Usually working out of the back of a car, they set up a card table and sell maps of the homes of movie stars. Michael Chellel, an aspiring actor (but he could well have been a freelance writer), developed a new twist on that old idea, and it paid off. He decided to put the superstars of yesteryear to work by creating a map of their tombs and burial sites. His reasoning: More tourists would rather gaze at Clark Gable's gravestone than at Sylvester Stallone's driveway.

Or take your cue from the English Department at the University of Arkansas at Little Rock. They developed a sort of hotline for participle danglers—a telephone service that offers help for people who need to improve their grammar and punctuation. They deal with the most common errors of written English. Now that's an idea worth considerable expansion.

If you can spare the time or can employ a part-time helper, you might want to set up a simple telephone-answering service for people who don't have an answering machine. That doesn't mean you have to be interrupted by calls all the time. You could arrange to monitor calls every three or four hours or have your helper alert you to the most important calls.

Two other ways writers can find outside income to help support their freelancing without being tied to a full-time job are the mail room and the friendly reminder service. The mail room is a private post office, which also offers such services as mail forwarding, telephone message service, typing, bookkeeping, filing and minor office tasks. The friendly reminder service is just that. Busy people who tend to forget important dates are reminded by mail one week in advance of the time they want to remember. The former service would require more money up front to insure mail privacy for the clients. Both of these ideas could be set to motion best, perhaps, with an outside office. But even if they simply paid the utility bills or a fraction of the office rent without tying up your time, they could be a phenomenal advantage.

Consider a filler service for your regular clients, which is basically a clipping service.

And how about:

A company that provides discount office supplies most needed by writers.

A tutoring service in the area of your expertise.

Helping another writer, professor, or anthologist clip, copyedit, or research.

Arts and book reviewing.

Ghostwriting. (This can be anything from brief contributions to a busy columnist's regular work to ghosting reports or books.)

Jokes, jingles, one-liners for a wide variety of markets.

Commercial reports, reference material writing, instruction materials, résumés.

Your hourly rate

For every freelancer starting out, the problem of what to charge for what kind of job is uppermost in his mind. Should I try for the top? Should I ask less? What will I lose if I do? There are ways to figure your costs, your needs, and therefore what you must have to profit. You can figure this out ahead of time for various kinds of jobs and then test them against going rates for similar jobs and salaried positions in your town.

You must first consider how long it will take you to do a certain kind of job. Research time, travel to the library, parking fees, photocopying costs—all should be counted. Rewrite time comes next. (No one, not even Nabokov or Tolstoy, got away from this one.) How much real time is involved? Time spent soliciting assignments and potential contacts comes next. Most writers I've known are only able to guess at this one, though they probably should be more exact. When it comes time to prepare tax papers you must be (see Chapter 13), so why not now?

There are also the hidden costs of completing an assignment. These are the ones we tend to forget. The range is huge, but let me name a few to jog your memory: pencils, pens, paper, postage, staples and other supplies, photocopies, bus fare or gas for your car, tapes for your tape recorder, insurance or service for your typewriter, overhead costs for your office. To figure your hourly rate, add up all your costs and divide by the time it takes to complete an assignment. If your total is $150 and you can do the job in ten hours, your rate is $15 per hour.

Negotiating

In any marketplace there are ranges of standard fees and specific payments an individual business person arranges. The difference is often quite large. Much of it depends on the skill of the negotiator.

The best advice for pricing your wares is to find out what the going rate is in your area. Research this soundly before you approach your possible client. Use your library, your contacts, the competition's advertising or public relations agency—any person or method you can think of to gather this data.Then have a good idea of how much work and time any job you're contemplating will require. Figure what your time is worth to come up with an acceptable rate. Remember: Most people underestimate the time involved in a new job or underestimate what the traffic will bear for top-notch results. Once burned, they quickly raise their rates. (A guide to average going rates for a variety of writing tasks can be found in *Writer's Market.*)

The fee you end up with depends, of course, on your ability to do the work, your track record, your locale, and *your salesmanship.* When all else fails, gulp, name a figure, and see what happens. If you don't get the job, you might want to lower your quoted price, but don't do it on the spot. Say you'll think the problem over and see how you might be able to accommodate them. Then get back to the client with your "alternative."

Whatever the problems, you can negotiate and bargain with someone else if you remember a few of these tips:

1. Sell yourself on the idea first.

2. Get to the right person before you start your negotiation. There's no point wasting your time talking to someone who is in no position to talk money matters.

3. Know why you deserve what you're asking for. Your TIP sheet (see fig. 7-1) and hourly rate schedule and backup data in your accomplishments will help here.

4. Negotiate from physical as well as moral strength. Be rested and your confidence will come across as a plus the other person can't ignore.

5. Win points at the start of the interview with the right approach. Remember, you want the idea to appear to be the client's; you're just calling his attention to it.

6. Think big. You can always come back down the scale but never up after you've received one agreement.

7. Keep some ammunition in reserve. Be prepared to counter a negative reply with an irresistible alternate plan.

8. Sell from the client's point of view. He wants to make money, save money, reach more readers with his message. Offer to help him.

9. Build in your future negotiating success now. Let the client appear to be getting the better end of the deal. He'll be happy to talk with you again.

10. Know salesmen's techniques for handling the "your price is too high" objection. Never retreat when the prospect objects to your price. Be prepared to explain why your price is a *bargain.*

Chapter 11
The
Professional
Stance

■■

Book contracts

Salesmanship and a strong salable property are the prime assets when the time comes to negotiate a book contract. But these alone are not enough. Since your chance of making a profit from a book and using it as a stepping-stone in your career depends so much on the provisions of the contract you sign for it, you must be knowledgeable and aware of the nuances and ramifications of book publishing agreements. This is true whether the book in question is your first or whether you've been through the mill before.

Realize that the publishing world, particularly book publishing, has changed dramatically in the past few years and goes on changing. Conglomerates have increasingly swallowed up distinguished, older, independent companies. Few family-owned firms remain untouched by this phenomenon. (The exceptions, of course, are the small publishing houses which have sprung up in the last decade, otherwise known as small presses.) Then, too, libel suits are on the rise (see Chapter 14). This does not mean necessarily that more libel is being committed. But the bandwagon of people willing to bring libel actions is increasingly overloaded. Both phenomena—conglomerates and libel suits—are causing publishers to take harder and harder looks at their bottom lines. And this is bringing grief to book authors stumbling in the shifting sands. Publishers are revising their contracts to garner every business advantage from changing laws and distribution practices. The revisions may appear slight to an inexperienced eye or to someone who has been out of touch with marketing methods for a while.

In the next chapter we'll examine more fully the relation of author to agent. For now, suffice it to say that a good agent will be abreast of developments in the book industry and can't be misled or bluffed into signing away rights that may appear negligible to you. Further, the agent's experience prepares her to comprehend the legal nuances of contract language and to assess their relevance to your particular book. The agent will probably know which amendments to standard contracts will be most acceptable to any given publisher—amendments that enhance your options and safeguard your chances to share in any profits from the book.

In signing a contract you may put yourself under the risk of legal obligations or even legal punishment. The guidance of an experienced agent can save you from being either too frightened by such prospects or too reckless. A negotiating publisher may take advantage of an author intimidated by the mystifying threats built into contractual language, whereas most agents have learned to see the risks in perspective and resist intimidation. Many editors prefer to deal with agents, since this saves them the time and anguish of explaining the terminology to a novice.

While an agent's value to a writer is nowhere greater than in contract negotiation, that is not at all to suggest you must or should leave it all to the agent. Even if you have the best agent in the world, it is still advantageous to you to learn all you can about contracts—by talking to other writers, by reading the books listed in the Resources section, by consulting lawyers when appropriate. A good agent will always expect to be a middleman between you and the publisher, following your wishes and instructions. You should therefore know what you can reasonably try for and how your wishes can be expressed in the language of contracts.

To put the written contract in proper perspective, remember it is almost always a formalization of an agreement which has been worked out in several less formal steps. Before the contract is drawn up, the author or agent and the editor will agree on several points— the kind of book to be delivered (or revisions to be undertaken on a complete manuscript), the date of delivery, and the amount of the advance, along with other relevant special considerations (inclusion of charts or photos, whether the author will pay for permissions in case of a textbook, arrangements for collaboration between experts and author, etc.).

Since such particulars obviously vary from book to book, they can't be printed in the standard contract form each publishing house provides (see Appendix). Blank spaces are left in the printed form. Previously negotiated details will be typed in the blanks of the contract presented to you for signature. Since all of the standard contract except for these typed insertions appears in printed form, the novice might assume other provisions are nonnegotiable or need not be negotiated. This is not the case, and you must remember that in the standard printed form almost all of the monetary and legal advantages lie with the publisher. Lines and passages of the standard contract can, of course, be struck out by agreement between you and the publisher. Amendments made for your benefit can be typed in or added at the end before you bring yourself to sign the document. In fact, there's seldom a situation in which an author or agent can't get some provisions, at least, deleted or amended to give the author the break he deserves.

Are you, then, going to haggle over every word and phrase in the contract before you sign? No one in her right mind would recommend that. Beginners particularly must be aware that they lack the bargaining power to induce a publisher to give them the ideal contract the first time out. Even experienced agents know to shoot for the best terms that can *reasonably* be expected, taking care not to sour the publisher-author relationship. It doesn't hurt to remember the publisher is also taking some risk in issuing your work. Your role is to bargain firmly but tactfully and reasonably.

All decent contracts contain some provision for the *reversion of rights* to the author. The specifications should include reversion of all rights when the book has been out of print for some time, and, in case of publisher's default, the reversion of particular rights on an agreed schedule. It may be contracted that subsidiary rights will revert to the author in a year or eighteen months after book publication if the publisher has failed to sell any of them in that time. When the rights revert to you, of course, you will get 100 percent of any money they bring in.

Many standard contracts give the publisher an option on your next book, but before you rush to sign an agreement containing such a clause, think about your long-term future and perhaps do a little negotiating to get these terms readjusted so they are a little more favorable to you. You can ask that the clause be stricken completely if you are leery of tying yourself to a particular publishing house. Consider, too, that while the clause obliges you to submit subsequent work to that publisher, it lays no obligation on him to publish what you produce. So negotiate for provisions that (1) the option will be picked up or voided by the publisher on the basis of an idea or outline submitted rather than a complete manuscript; or (2) the contract for the next book provides for a specific increase in advance money; or (3) the publisher must exercise the option at a time mutually convenient rather than at his exclusive convenience; or (4) the option may be voided by particular enumerated circumstances.

Advances

The advance, spelled out by your contract, is the money a publisher pays for the time and effort put into the writing of a book. Traditionally the advance has been conceived of as a loan made by the publisher to the author to keep him alive and producing until the royalties begin to come in—at which time the publisher will recoup his loan by withholding the amount of the advance from the author's share of royalties. It should also reflect the prospective sales. The better the prospects for a bestseller, the bigger the advance should be, obviously.

In the case of many books, where the royalties do not amount to as much as the sum advanced, the advance serves in effect as an outright purchase price by the publisher. So it is elementary prudence to dicker for an advance which represents either a fair return for your labor as a writer or the best return you can reasonably expect. Negotiating your advance from strength requires a few tips from people in general sales. Point out, for example, that the publisher is going to get a far better product if the writer is free from money worries and can concentrate on production.

Some publishers will tell you their offer of an advance is small because they expect to invest heavily in promoting the book and that, therefore, you will be money ahead in the long run if the contract promises larger than usual royalties to make up for the skimpy front money. In such cases make sure that the contract specifies the amount the publisher is required to lay out for promotion.

If the contract does not provide reasonable protection against it, the publisher may try to recover all or part of an advance he has paid to you when, for any reason, he chooses not to issue a book. This is clearly unfair if you have kept your part of the bargain faithfully. So, at the minimum, make sure that the language of the contract shelters you against recovery attempts. If you deliver your work on time in the form and content specified, you have every right to the advance money. In practice, publishers are often willing to grant extensions of deadline beyond the date specified in the contract without penalty to the author, but you can expect this of them only when it is to their advantage. So safeguard your advance by making sure the contractual deadline gives ample time for you to meet all the obligations you have undertaken.

An advance isn't all you'll want in the way of financing your project. You should think, too, about possible perks. You noted when you wrote your book proposal what it would take to complete the job. Will there be extra costs for travel, extensive research, artwork, photographs, charts, computer printouts, periodicals, books, long-distance interviews, photocopying, researchers, or secretarial help? The publisher will expect you to cover most of these expenses. It's up to you to ask him for help. If you live near your publisher and will need office space while you're in the city, ask if there's an office available for you at the publishing house. Can you photocopy material on the office machine? Will the editor send you books you need that she has on hand? Ask for anything that would help. It can't hurt to try. But ask early. Realize there are limitations. Give your editor time to justify the expenses or other arrangements within the publishing house's hierarchy. Some publishers regularly agree to such arrangements with authors, others seldom if ever. (Some even have their own photographers who can be sent out on assignment for you if that's necessary.) And keep in mind that it's sometimes easier for an editor to justify such expenses as these than a more sizable advance, especially for a new author.

Royalties

Besides the amount of the advance and the conditions governing it, you'll be negotiating for the royalties your book can be expected to earn. Royalties are basically a percentage of the retail price of books actually sold by the publisher. These percentages are also usually typed into the blank space of the standard contract, since they reflect a special agreement between author and publisher and may vary to compensate for other features of the contract.

At present, the prevailing escalating royalty schedule for adult hardcover books is:

10 percent for the first 5,000 copies sold, escalating to
12½ percent for the next 5,000, and then to
15 percent for all copies sold thereafter.

The traditional practice was to compute these royalty rates and the author's earnings from the list price of all copies sold. Thus, if sales totaled 3,500 copies at $10 list price, the author's royalty earnings would be $3,500. Current complexities of distribution have led to some publishers' disposing of many copies at less than list price through chains of bookstores and other outlets. As a consequence, some standard contracts now provide that the author's royalties will be computed on net proceeds from the sale of the book rather than the number of copies sold. Such contracts are not necessarily disadvantageous to the author, but you should be wary of them. The larger volume of sales made possible by wholesale deals *may* more than compensate for a smaller earning per copy. The important thing is to read carefully and fully understand what your contract actually provides, and negotiate from that basis without illusions or misunderstandings about what you have agreed to. Faced with the very considerable range of royalty arrangements in the current market, each of us must balance our notion of the book's potential against the mathematical equations. It's a good idea to do a little pencil work while you negotiate. Compute what you would earn in various hypothetical cases if your royalty was based on list price, weigh that against earnings on net in the same cases, then decide from that what you want to try for in contract negotiations. To help you, you can ask the editor to give you realistic figures based on the sales department's projections.

If you're contracting with a paperback house, the royalty rate may range from 5 to 20 percent, with 10 percent a very common figure. Escalation rates are also less standardized than for hardcover publishers and therefore permit and require more negotiation. Do not assume that because marketing techniques are different with paperbacks, escalation clauses are negligible. While a paperback publisher may count on selling what he can of his first print run (from 100,000 to 250,000 copies) and then dropping the book from his list, it not infrequently happens that, even after a number of years, he may reissue the book with another relatively large printing. You deserve a greater share of the profits from the reissued book and should have it provided for in the original contract.

Textbook publishers are way ahead of trade-book publishers in accurately forecasting sales. They base negotiation and contracts on previous experience with relatively stable school markets, so there's apt to be less flexibility (and risk) in dealing with them. It's also easier to predict what you'll make for your work, so the whole process of contracting goes forward at a quieter pitch.

It's easier to predict, that is, if you and your editor take the time to do a little pencil work while you're considering the contract. Textbooks have a relatively fixed market, depending on the subject and the number and kind of schools in which they may be used. The competition from comparable texts is at least relatively easier to identify than in the case of books intended for the general market. A textbook publisher usually plans to market his books over a period of years. Taking these factors into consideration and using simple mathematics, you can work out the potential advantages of various royalty arrangements which might be acceptable to your publisher. Obviously, a text with a chance for a nice share of the national high school market for ten years of projected usefulness will call for different royalty arrangements than one which will be used only by special students or scholars for thirty years. A typical, widely used college text in literature, published in paperback, pays a royalty of 8 percent of 80 percent of list price on copies sold. But this can hardly be taken as a significant example, and any group of typical figures would be less useful to you than common sense and basic arithmetic.

Subsidiary rights

The potential sales of a book are your real leverage when it comes to negotiating a contract. Never omit from your calculation the income that may be generated by resale of all or part of your book. Even when the advance and royalty schedule agreed on are better than you'd dared hope, keep your negotiation aggressive—suggest to the editor that he make up for your concessions by giving you a better deal on subsidiary rights.

Subsidiary rights specified in the contract determine, among other things, your share of any money resulting from a resale of the book to a paperback reprint house or a book club. A standard contract will usually provide for a fifty-fifty split between hardcover publisher and author. But the amendments you're looking for may change the contract to provide the author with an increased percentage if the resale exceeds a certain dollar figure—55 percent for a sale over $50,000, for example, or 60 percent for a sale over $100,000. You may not expect such a bonanza, but neither may your publisher. So nail down your chance at the lion's share.

Every writer dreams of a big sale to the movies or for TV dramatization. In moments of realism most of us understand that such possibilities are remote, hardly more so for nonfiction than for the vast majority of novels and stories. Because the odds are so great in most cases, neither the publisher nor the author may be motivated to fierce bargaining about the division of the spoils should there be a miraculous stroke of luck. Yet, however conservative a writer may be in his expectations, it would be foolish to exclude such eventualities from the negotiation in any case. Standard contracts are usually printed with blank spaces in which the agreed-on movie or TV percentage split will be entered. It is by no means rare for a publisher to yield 100 percent of all movie rights to the author without much fuss or to retain only 10 percent against the author's 90 percent. But circumstances alter cases. Everything depends on the particular book. If there is *any* reason to suppose that filmmakers might now or later be interested in the fruits of your labor, then your contractual share of film rights ought to be a matter of strong contention by you or your agent.

Since *options* for possible film use are considerably more common than outright sales, a good contract will spell out not only the percent division of proceeds from this source but whether you or your publisher will have the right to make the contracts with the potential buyers.

The same principles ought to prevail in the disposition of rights to reprint in foreign countries. If you or your agent have nothing better to go on, make an educated guess about the potential market for your work in the countries not covered by the basic contract. Ask for anything up to 100 percent of all foreign sales (knowing this will not always be attainable), and be sure the contract specifies who will have authority to contract with foreign publishers.

Other subsidiary rights include permission to use all or part of your text in magazines and newspapers. *First serial rights* refers to publication in such outlets before the book appears, *second serial rights* to reprint after book publication. Your contract ought to retain for you 100 percent of first serial rights, except when your publisher has arranged for their sale. In such case he may have a legitimate claim for as much as 10 percent, the standard fee for agenting. Most contracts grant the author only 50 percent of the sale price for second serial rights. But when the author's track record or expertise contribute substantially to the prospect of such sale, the contract should be amended to provide an escalating percentage for the writer as sales multiply.

While it is of first importance to see that your share of profits from any reprint of your book material is protected in the contract, that isn't the end of the story. Those clauses turn into money in the bank only when the rights are actually sold. Who is going to sell them?

Publishers handle the disposition of subsidiary sales through departments set up to manage that part of their business. They especially consider resale for paperback reprint their prerogative, and some may even resent the interference of an author or literary agent in the course of their transactions. You may or may not be informed of the attempts your publisher has made to find secondary markets. If you are lucky enough to be told (and if you trust him to have made the big pitch for you in all cases), you still may have avenues he has not deigned to explore. It's important not to duplicate the publisher's efforts to get a chunk of your book in *Esquire* or to sell the whole thing to one of the major reprint houses, even if you have contacts there and believe your publisher is halfhearted in his sales efforts. (He may be pushing someone else's book harder than yours.)

When it's clear that the publisher has drawn a complete blank, *then* go into high gear on your own. If your book has drawn heavily

Author
c/o Agent
New York, New York

Dear Author/Agent:

This is to confirm our understanding relating to an 0000-
word excerpt from (the "Work") _Title, author (fiction)_ .

    1. You hereby sell us, and we purchase from you, exclu-
sive world wide *first English language periodical serial
rights to publish the Work in __magazine__ and its affiliated magazines and the right to publish the Work in any
book or periodical anthology or similar publication of
__magazine__ or its affiliated magazines.

    2. In order to induce us to make this purchase, you
hereby represent and warrant to us that:
    (a) You are the sole author or publisher, and owner,
of the Work; and have the power and authority to make this
sale;
    (b) The Work is original, and does not infringe upon
any statutory or common law copyright, proprietary right or
any other right whatsoever;
    (c) The statements made in the Work are true;
    (d) The Work has not heretofore been published or
used in any medium for any purpose;
    (e) You have not heretofore granted first English
language periodical serial rights to any other person;
    (f) The Work is an excerpt from a book to be pub-
lished in no event before 120 days from this date.

    3. We agree to pay you a fee of $_____.

Fig. 11-1. *Sample first-serial-rights agreement.*

4. You shall indemnify and hold us harmless from any loss, damage and expense (including reasonable attorney's fees) that we may suffer or incur by reason of the breach (or alleged breach) of any of the foregoing representations or warranties.

5. You agree not to grant to any third party any periodical rights to the Work or to the book from which the Work is excerpted which would cause publication in any other periodical on or before 30 days after the book publication date. You shall notify us from time to time **the projected book publication date.

6. We have the right to edit or otherwise change the Work. You agree to make such changes in the Work as we may from time to time reasonably request prior to publication. ***We are under no obligation to publish the Work in our magazine or otherwise apply the Work to any specific purpose. If we publish the Work, we shall give you authorship credit in the usual manner. You hereby agree to our using your name, pseudonym, photograph or other likeness in connection with the advertisement and promotion of the Work, or any adaptation or version thereof.

7. This Agreement constitutes our entire agreement with respect to the Work, and supersedes any prior agreements. It may not be modified without the prior written consent of each of us.

Author/Agent/Publisher Signature   Magazine Signature

*for the United States, Canada, the United Kingdom and non-exclusive first serial in all countries in which magazine is incidentally distributed.

**the publication date 120 days prior to

***Subject to author's approval, not to be unreasonably withheld.

Fig. 11-1. (cont.)

on the expertise you've acquired in the course of writing shorter pieces, chances are you have a network of markets and potential markets for this kind of material, so when your book is in print (or under contract) you're in a good position to knock again at the familiar doors. Though the publisher has failed to make a book-club sale, don't concede the game. *Literary Market Place* has an extensive listing of book clubs. Among these may be one that your personal experience and expertise tell you would be open to your work, though the publisher never even considered it.

Let's assume your book has received some good reviews or has been circulated by a book club with their usual advertising. Collect and copy all the good notices as they appear and package them to promote your efforts at resale to magazines or newspapers. One author I know went to the expense of printing up a small brochure of quotes from the reviews of her book and mailed it along with query letters to a broad range of regional publications. It brought an extraordinary number of requests from editors to see a copy of the book, and a good number of reprint sales followed. It's probably uneconomical to mail off copies of your book on a scattershot basis to editors who *might* be interested. Try to elicit an expression of interest first, then mark the section of the book you think particularly suited to the needs of the publication and fire away.

Disposing of subsidiary rights yourself will impress everyone connected with the sale of your book, from the publisher on down to the owner of the bookstore on the corner. It's an elegant form of advertising.

Reading the royalty statement

If you find publishers' contracts confusing, you'll develop a love-hate relationship with royalty statements, which must be ranked high among the creations of the accountant's art. Nevertheless, knowing how they work is essential to keeping a clear view of how your book is doing and how you stand financially.

Semiannual statements are fairly standard, although there are publishers who send statements only once a year, a devastating practice as far as an author is concerned. Not only that—what royalty statements usually don't tell you is what you want to know: how many books have been printed, how many are still in inventory. It's sometimes quite difficult to get this information from your editor. And if some of the sales have been made within the month prior to the date of the statement, they will not appear on it for another six months. The deferred-payment practice (keeping an author's royalties in the publishing house's coffers long after the returns are in) is all too prevalent. This "lag," as it's referred to in publishing circles, is costly to the writer and profitable for the publisher. He's using your money free of charge for at least six months and in some cases much longer than that. The lag is generally blamed on the accounting process, a relatively flimsy excuse in the computer age. (Of course, the machines can't do anything without being told by people. But that's begging the question a bit.)

Another reason for this lag is the need to allow for any returns. Books normally are sold to bookstores for a discount and are returnable for the full amount paid. These returns can come in at any time and the publisher is obliged to credit the bookstore's account. Commonly the first royalty statement on any given book will show few or no returns because the book is still out on bookstore shelves, and all copies out on consignment may be reported on the royalty form as sales. Thus the author may be misled into believing that his royalties are accumulating faster than, in fact, they are. On subsequent royalty statements the publisher will report the returns and deduct these from royalty earnings or the sale of subsidiary rights. (This, too, is changing. Some publishers now offer an even larger discount to the bookstore, but on a nonrefundable basis. On the face of it this would seem a great advantage to the author as well as publisher. Not all authors agree, however. One recent book that received fabulous reviews in one particular area of the country, and that could have been expected to sell like hotcakes, was never even ordered by most of the area's bookstores because of the publisher's "no-return" policy.)

There will also be notations on the royalty statement regarding other kinds of sales, if any, including paperback, book clubs, mail order, and exports. All are priced individually, with different percentages of royalties due the author for each category. Increases in mail-order sales are attractive to publishers, especially if the royalties for them are lower. The writer may well lose a considerable portion of income from her books if she allows the publisher to keep royalties in these categories at the bare minimum.

Ideally, a royalty report should reveal current data on all the publisher's operations in which the author has a financial interest as provided by contract. It should separately report gross sales, net sales, and returns and indicate whether the returns are of copies entitled to the full royalty rate or ones that have been offered at some discount. It should reveal the number of copies in print and the number printed during the period of the report. If the publisher has withheld money as a reserve against possible returns, the amount of reserve should be indicated. In the event of a change in list price of the book, data covering number of books sold at each price should be forthcoming. There should be a summary of the sales royalty statements the trade publisher has received from book clubs, mass-market paperback editions, and foreign publishers, since the author's rightful share of such proceeds in many cases will depend on sales volume in each of these categories.

Unfortunately, at present many publishing houses do not issue royalty statements that fully meet these conditions. (A typical royalty statement is shown in fig. 11-2.) And as with other outmoded bookkeeping practices, the lag permits some sleight-of-hand manipulation or at least delay in money due the author. Many royalty statement forms currently in use do not provide the author with a clear and reliable picture of his interest in his property.

The Authors Guild and other writers' organizations have long lobbied for more forthright royalty statements. You can supplement their effort by requesting of your publisher information omitted from your royalty statement.

Pushing for more timely accounting and payment will take plenty of effort on your part. Strangely, you may even have to lobby with your agent at this point, even though his money is also being held up! Agents seldom like to rock the boat that's keeping them afloat.

You have a legal right to ask to see the publisher's account books if you're convinced the royalty statement is incorrect. But this can be a very costly, time-consuming business. If you think you have an airtight case, discuss it with your agent, lawyer, or accountant. Sometimes if a writer is ready to go through with such an examination, or if an agent gently but firmly announces he has *proof* of wrongdoing, a check will be forthcoming.

Caution: You aren't going to endear yourself to the publisher if you insist on bringing in a CPA to check his books. Prepare yourself for it.

When you're trying to get money from a publisher who has accepted your manuscript and refused to pay for it, as happens with article publication in particular, there are ways to force his hand. You can take him to small claims court (depending on the amount due). Or if you're dealing with a publisher in another state, check to see if your state has a "long arm" statute. If it does, the publisher, though a nonresident, may be subject to the jurisdiction of your state's courts, because he's doing business with you. Ask a lawyer if

```
STOKE & BYWATER, Inc.
PUBLISHERS
In account with       (name of agent)
Author     Henderson Paul
Title      MAKING DO                          $10.95
───────────────────────────────────────────────────────────
Sales for six months ending 9/30/81
    5,000   copies sold at royalty of   10%      $ 5,475.00
      210   copies sold at royalty of   12½%     $   287.44
    1,200   copies sold at royalty of    7%      $   920.80
            copies mail order at
                royalty of               5%      $   (none)
      311   copies, special and
                export sales at royalty of
                10% net receipts of $2,799       $   279.90
Other earnings
    Reprint              $ 5,000.00
    First serialization  $   333.33
    Second serialization $   (none)
    Foreign publication  $   (none)
    Newspaper syndication $  (none)
    Book club            $ 3,500.00              $ 8,833.33
                         *Earnings for period    $15,796.47
Deductions
    Advances             $10,000.00
    Expenses             $    65.80
    Purchases of books   $   438.00
    Debit balance, prior
      report             $    (none)             $10,503.80
                         Balance due             $ 5,292.67
                         Unearned balance
                         (to be applied to
                          next statement)        $    (none)

*The above royalty is subject to adjustment when number
of copies returned by booksellers is determined.
```

Fig. 11-2. *Sample book royalty statement.*

the recalcitrant can be forced to pay. If so, it's a matter of serving the publisher with the proper legal papers. Freelancers who do so report the publishers' attorneys rather quickly offer to settle out of court.

Copyrights and work-for-hire

The new copyright law, effective January 1, 1978, specifies that the moment you've written something, you hold the copyright to it. It sets up a single standard for coverage of material, whether published or unpublished, that effectively keeps control of the work in the hands of the author until such time as he sells the copyright, leases it, or gives it away.

Under the new law, works by a single author are protected from the time they're created for the life of the author plus fifty years. For works created by two or more authors, the copyright lasts for the life of the last survivor plus fifty years. If you create something using a pseudonym, copyright is in effect for a hundred years after the work was created or seventy-five years after it's published, whichever is shorter. But if you identify yourself to the Copyright Office as the creator before the time has expired, the regular life-plus-fifty years rule becomes effective.

Prior to this law, copyrights were treated differently and were protected for a different length of time—twenty-eight years after publication date, at which time they had to be renewed by the copyright holder or they became public property. For those of you holding such earlier copyrights, I highly recommend pausing to make a list of these and the dates when renewal can be effected. Indicate the dates on a calendar, attached as a codicil to your will or given in letter form to your financial adviser for safekeeping. Once such copyrights lapse, there is *nothing* you or your heirs can do to retrieve them.

There are other regulations, of course, too numerous to mention here. To find out all about the copyright law write to the Copyright Office, Library of Congress, Washington, DC 20559 and ask for their free kit. And check the Resources chapter for books which give fuller explanations.

Work-for-hire is another matter. When you sell "all rights" to your article to a periodical, you are giving up the copyright. When you sign a "work-for-hire" clause, you are, in effect, doing the same thing. Don't sign them. If you do, you forfeit any further income from that material. The periodical (or book publisher) holds the copyright thereafter. Work-for-hire copyrights, like those for pseudonymous or anonymous works, are good for a hundred years after the creation or seventy-five years after publication.

Norman Schreiber, a well-known nonfiction writer, said in *Writer's Digest*, "For companies, copyright ownership is an asset that's as transferable as real estate, machinery, and bank accounts. If publishers consider this important enough to have, so should we."

By understanding the new copyright law and its effect on your status as a writer, you'll be able to bargain better in all spheres of the publishing arena in the future.

Schreiber goes on to point out some useful hints in negotiating and upgrading your status as well as making more money:

> In those pre-1978 days a magazine enforced its policy simply by announcing it. No signed agreements were necessary for a magazine to keep the copyright to any contribution. This bred the notion that the magazines were entitled to be the original owners of copyright.
>
> The new law specifies that the writers should be the owners of copyright. It protects us from unwarranted infringement of our work. What the law does is provide a situation from which negotiations can begin.

Schreiber points out you should not write "First North American Rights" in the upper right-hand corner, as most professionals used to do. Instead write "© 198   [your name]" on the cover or first page.

If you get a work-for-hire notice, reply that you don't sign them "as a matter of policy." Explain your position to the editor. He may not be aware of the ramifications of the new law and how it affects your pocketbook or that of your heirs.

If you do accede to such a contract, insist on a good deal more money for anything you write. And ask for all the perks the regular staff of the periodical receive—medical benefits, travel and expense money, etc. Be absolutely outrageous in your demands, since, as you'll tell them, all rights in perpetuity must mean a great deal to them if they've gone to the trouble to print up such a form and to demand them.

Chapter 12
Agents, Book Packagers, and Other Helpers

■■

What agents can do

What is the function of an agent? A good one knows which publishing houses are in the market for what sort of book or project. They know which publisher will release which rights and what the probable bottom line on other negotiations will be. They know and like to deal with certain editors. You might hear, "Don't expect more than a $15,000 advance on this one." Or, "Without good connections to your celebrity, I don't think they'll buy this idea at all." Or sometimes, "I think this is a real winner. I can think of three houses right off the bat that'll offer good money. It's perfect for an auction."

And then, of course, you may hear nothing for a long period of time. Good agents' telephones are seldom silent. These busy people are in constant touch with those who buy ideas, books, movies, scripts for TV miniseries, book excerpts, and subsidiary rights, as well as with their clients, the writers who call to ask, "What's up?"

"They call me for tea and sympathy, money, and plot discussions. I'm a good friend who can also be objective," says agent Scott Meredith, who says he put in an answering service on his home line after a Thanksgiving dinner was interrupted by forty-one calls. "I'm part salesman, part lawyer, part literary critic, and part father-confessor. I get calls from clients who are broke and can't pay their bills, from clients who are drunk or who have been arrested for beating their wives. One writer called from a neighbor's to tell me his house was on fire and all his manuscripts were burning. Why did he call me? Because he wanted to talk to someone who would be sympathetic . . . and I was."

A writer gains a certain amount of prestige by having an agent, as many a beginning writer has discovered. Agent Frieda Fishbein told the editors of *Writer's Market* that was because agents save editors time and money. "Editors know that agents, if they are competent, weed out the hopeless material. Material from agents is usually given preference in being read earlier than material that comes in 'cold.'" And, of course, there is a growing tendency in publishing houses to refuse to read anything at all that comes in unsolicited.

Agents negotiate book contracts and subsidiary rights, both foreign and domestic. These include sales to book clubs, special sales (for example, premiums), movie and television options, syndication and reprint rights, and so on. Depending on the arrangement you make, your agent may handle all of your works, only your books, or only certain kinds of books. Some agents will tell you at the beginning what they will want to deal with and what they won't. If they don't, ask. You may want to give an agent only certain kinds of writing (your novels, for example) and sell the others yourself. Some writers feel the advantage of a large literary agency lies in the specialists who negotiate what writers sometimes call "the West Coast rights" (i.e., anything to do with film or television). But most good agents who have been in the business any length of time will have some sort of representation in this highly specialized area.

It's a rare agent these days who will handle magazine articles or short stories. If he does, it is usually because that author is making him enough money on book sales. (Sometimes it's not the writer who thrusts the job of negotiating an article sale upon an unsuspecting agent. On a couple of occasions when I was about to negotiate an article fee, the editor stopped me, saying, "Do you have an agent?" When I said yes, she replied, "Well, I should be talking to him then." She did, and the agent negotiated the final fee, as surprised as I was by this turn of events. It doesn't happen often, though.)

Agents also help negotiate solutions to conflicts between you and your publisher. They push for timely payment of advances and royalties. They keep accurate records of your sales. Some agents are also lawyers, or have lawyers in their company, and can review alleged abuses by a publisher, alert a writer to possible problems stemming from something he is about to publish, and act as a knowledgeable go-between for the writer. Some agents act as middleman by finding the right author to write a book on an idea an editor or publisher has. (See the section on packagers later in this chapter.)

Do you need an agent? Two answers: yes, and no. Nearly a third of the literary works published are sold by writers without agents. You can, if you're fortunate and a good salesman, place your book with a publisher without an agent, though this is becoming more of a rarity, especially for writers living outside the main publishing centers. Once a publisher says "Yes, we want to publish your book," many writers feel they're much better off letting an agent or literary lawyer handle the contract negotiations. Publishers have been known to send out outrageous contracts to unwary writers operating without the usual middleman. They may try to buy all rights for very little, if any, cash advance. A writer can also lose a considerable amount of money by not having the subsidiary rights and other clauses in the fine print of a publisher's contract negotiated by an expert.

According to some writers, a lawyer with literary expertise is the best of all possible worlds. For others, an agent who is also a lawyer is that miracle. If a writer only occasionally produces a book, he might choose to engage a lawyer, whether an expert in literary matters or not, to draw up his contract. He would be paying the lawyer a one-time fee, as opposed to an agent's 10-percent fee on all money he makes from the book. Besides, in such an instance he may have trouble getting an agent to handle his now-and-then literary output. But most writers use agents instead of lawyers, unless they're making very large sums from royalties or have particularly complicated legal problems with their publishers or others.

Other writers, having been burned by their dealings with agents or literary lawyers (or both), prefer to sell their own wares. They do a good deal of spadework first to learn as much about the hustling of books and book proposals as possible. Some have succeeded in getting good contracts, sizable advances, and at least as good a deal on subsidiary rights as their colleagues with agents. These writers, though, spend a large part (50 to 80 percent) of their time pushing, selling, and pitching their ideas instead of actually writing.

It's for that very reason—promotion—that many writers rely on an agent. It's worth the 10 percent. "It's okay to be your own agent some of the time," says an author I know. "But what happens when you've got three simultaneous deadlines and a heavy cold? And your part-time typist has just bopped off on her honeymoon, and the part of your manuscript you thought would be back from the copyeditor by now isn't? It's always *then* the publisher's promotion department wants information, the advance money hasn't come through and has to be wheedled out of them, or your book subject is suddenly big news because of something that happened halfway around the globe and your book's potential sales have jumped dramatically. That's when I'm awfully glad I've got a hotshot agent to go to bat for me."

Writers who do want to operate without agents still occasionally need advice on contracts for books or articles. One of the best ways to get this advice is to join an established writers' organization that offers such help: the Authors Guild, the American Society of Journalists and Authors, the Writers Union of Canada, etc. Remember, too, that it's easier to negotiate if you've stayed current with trade publications such as *Publishers Weekly* and *Folio*. In these trade publications you'll discover what the going rates are for material similar to yours, what problems have arisen related to negotiating subsidiary rights, and the like.

Certainly if you think the subject of your book is a natural for Hollywood, look for an agent—either a regular literary agent or a Hollywood specialist—to handle it. Ordinarily an agent's expertise will bring the author a larger advance and better sales of other rights. He will also protect the author's interests when it comes to who might write the film script, and so on.

Some agents specialize in handling lecture tours or publicity and promotion. But generally they're only interested in the very well known and highly promotable authors. Writers have, on occasion, concluded that they needed help arranging tours, getting media coverage, changing their public image, or preparing for the electronic age in other ways. But this is an expense that only the few writers near the pinnacle of success can normally afford.

Another consideration: Many editors prefer to deal with agents rather than writers, especially at the contract-negotiating stage. They can usually rely on the agent's knowledge of contractual nuances, which is a timesaving, and therefore money-saving, factor. (If, however, you wish to be your own agent, see the information on contracts in Chapter 11.)

Looking for an agent— the needle in the haystack?

There is a chick and egg problem in finding an agent that's, if you'll pardon the pun, hard to unscramble. If you haven't published, you can't get an agent. If you can't get an agent, it's almost impossible to get a book published.

One of the more amusing ways for a writer to find an agent was used by Colleen McCullough. She described it when I interviewed her for a *Writer's Digest* profile.

> I'd been going the beginner's route, sending the manuscript [of her first novel, *Tim*] out unsolicited, unagented, waiting for months for a printed rejection slip. The parcel would come back completely untouched. . . .I decided I'd be an old lady before I published my first book. I knew I had to get an agent but couldn't since I hadn't published anything. I tried phoning to get one but it was no use. OK, I thought, I'll write one a letter. If I'm as good as I think I am—if I'm a *writer*—I should be able to persuade an agent to at least read my manuscript simply by writing one a persuasive letter.
>
> Still, I didn't know which one to send the letter to. Then one day I was making a cake—out of tuna fish—for a friend on a diet. I *hate* fish. The smell of fish was *all* through the house. The list of agents was on the table. I looked down and the name

Frieda Fishbein popped out. I sat right down and wrote the world's most persuasive letter and sent it off. Frieda wrote back saying, "If the manuscript is half as entertaining as the letter, I'll read it."

Most agents, however, insist that they only accept new clients on recommendation from other authors, editors, or people they know in the publishing business. It used to be, too, that a legitimate agent seldom if ever charged a "reading" fee to an unknown. But that, like many other things in publishing, seems to be changing. If you come across an agent who requires a reading fee, attempt to negotiate. Ask that the fee be dropped or later credited to your account if she accepts you as a client. Or look for another agent without a reading fee. A writer with a good track record of published material in periodicals of repute who has a top-notch book idea shouldn't have too much trouble finding an agent who will work on a straight commission basis. The problem, then, becomes finding the right agent for you.

Other ways to find agents include asking published writers, editors, publishers, and agents themselves (who are often the faculty of writers' conferences and seminars), writing to a publishing company where an editor you admire works to see if any suggestions are forthcoming, getting the pamphlet *The Literary Agent* from the Society of Authors' Representatives, and checking the listings of agents in *Literary Market Place, Writer's Market,* and other such volumes. (See the Resources chapter.)

The best preparation for finding an agent is to get something published first. Then when you write asking for names of agents, include some clips of your work as a preliminary sales tool, just as you've done in many other situations. You can't expect a stranger to know who you are or what you've accomplished unless you show him. (A demonstration is always better than a lecture.) If you supply an SASE you'll usually get a quicker reply.

You can also write directly to a publisher proposing your book. If the publisher is interested in your potential book or in you as an author, you'll hear from him. Then it will be time, if you want one, to get an agent to help with the contractual negotiations.

Why are agents so hard for the novice to find? The answer is obvious. If they are established and competent, they're already handling the work of numerous selling writers. That's a time-consuming business. They're understandably reluctant to take on new talent— writers who might require considerable coaching and patience before their books are ready to sell. Although there are exceptions, generally the better established the agent, the more reluctant she is to start out with an unknown.

Before you look for one, though, remind yourself what you're looking for. Trust is the key word between author and agent. You need to find one with whom you see eye to eye. Then, you must give her your trust. She should be working for you and your interests. If she isn't, then the relationship isn't worth the effort for either of you. Remember, though, that an agent, if she's any good, should be a sound business person. That's what you hire her for. She may, therefore, be rather blunt about the chances for your book proposal or manuscript. She knows pretty well what the market is accepting and what it is not. But no agent is infallible. If the one you've found doesn't see any hope for your idea, that doesn't mean there is none. You must make up your own mind whether to stay with the agent and drop the project, or drop the agent. Since good pairing of author and agent is important, it pays to shop around until you find the one that is right for you.

Young and hungry: is she your best bet?

A struggling author back in the fifties had a good track record. She'd sold many short stories, two novels, articles in the slick magazines. When she gave her agent her third novel, however, she sensed he wasn't very enthusiastic. She worried whether it was the book or the agent that was off base. After much soul-searching, she moved on to a new agency. Twenty years later she's certain she made the correct choice. Her agent now buoys her up when she has doubts. And the agent continues to sell the books, getting sizable advances for them each time. "I went with her when she was young and hungry," the author says. "She worked like crazy for my books from the outset. I think it's made a big difference in my entire career."

Moral No.1: You have to decide for yourself whether a small, new agency or a large, old, established one is right for you.

Moral No.2: Most agents take on a new client for the long haul. They need to see that you have "more than one book in you" before they invest their time and effort presenting your work to editors.

(I've had several agents myself. I found one through a friend, one through a fortuitous accident, one through a newspaper ad, and one by the word-of-mouth process so prevalent in publishing circles. Each in his fashion helped me and each was quite different in his approach toward the writer and toward publishers. Two of those agents were with large agencies and two were independents with that lean look that can sometimes be such an advantage.)

You should also search for an agent who will do the most for you in the long run, someone who understands who you are and what you're capable of, someone who will even, from time to time, nudge you when you need it and who, when it's necessary, is gentle but firm in delivering criticism. She should know the market well enough so that she doesn't waste everyone's time submitting material blindly to the wrong houses or editors. She should be able to accurately read the potential for a manuscript or book proposal, then pitch it to the right publisher. And the most important point of all: If you employ an agent, you'll want her to know how to hustle in the publishing world and negotiate the very best advances and contracts for you. That is, after all, why you employ her.

Agents' fees

Generally, an agent charges a flat 10 percent of your earnings on any material he handles for you. On subsidiary sales, where there is a subagent involved, your agent's fee will be 15 to 20 percent (10 percent for your agent, 5 to 10 percent for the subagent). Although it's true some agents have been demanding, and receiving, 15 percent on a writer's earnings, the consensus among the professional writers I know, as well as the fee suggested by the ASJA, remains 10 percent. When an agent asks for 15 percent, most writers change agents or become their own agents. If an agent isn't earning enough to keep his fee at 10 percent, it's reasoned, either he isn't a good enough salesman to get a higher advance for his client, or he doesn't have much of a stable of good writers and isn't much of a business person. The agent should be taking the bigger nick out of the publisher's, not the writer's, income.

Other fees an agent may charge to his client include: (1) the costs of photocopying a manuscript for multiple submission; (2) 10 percent of any money accruing from his efforts to get a recalcitrant periodical publisher to cough up long-overdue payments; (3) insurance for an original manuscript; (4) fees for copyright registration; and (5) long-distance phone calls (especially if these should happen to be overseas). Regarding the second item above, the wise writer usually exhausts all avenues before putting the matter in the hands of her already harried agent.

It used to be that contracts between writers and agents were uncommon. That, too, is changing. Some agents have written agreements with their writers. Georges Borchardt is one. He outlines in a letter how he works and the commission he takes (10 percent on U.S. sales, 15 percent on British sales, 20 percent on translations). He asks writers to commit themselves to an exclusive contract—all of their work is to be sold through him.

Donald MacCampbell is an agent who originally had contracts with his authors. "Later, when I discarded contracts and began working on a gentlemen's-agreement basis," he says. "I began receiving these unwanted efforts (short stories, articles, poetry) from time to time until I was obliged to set a minimum commission of $250 on anything I sold." Naturally, since most short pieces don't bring in enough money to warrant paying that kind of fee, the writers got the message and stopped sending such material to him.

How to keep an agent happy

With or without a written contract between you and your agent, it's easier for everyone if you discuss as fully as possible at the outset just what is expected of each of you. All of the suggestions mentioned in earlier chapters about dealing with sources of information and promotion will help in conducting your relationship with your agent. Remember, agents are human and, if they're successful, very busy.

To keep your relationship on an even keel, you might want to talk about the following details before either of you commits yourself:

1. How much of a commission does the agent take on various kinds of sales?
2. Which material will he market; which will you?
3. What will subagents' fees be?
4. Will he deduct any expenses from your earnings?
5. How much and how often will you be told about submissions?
6. How much input does he want from you?
7. Does he handle auctions, lecture tours, other promotional aspects of your business?
8. Does he expect commissions on sales you make yourself?
9. Is this an exclusive contract?
10. What rights will he handle?
11. If the agency is a large one, does he want your various questions

channeled directly to someone else when necessary?

12. What records will he automatically keep for you? Which should you keep yourself?

13. Will he put your name up for other projects he hears about, and do you want him to?

14. What information do you want kept confidential?

15. How can you end the relationship? What obligations remain if it is terminated?

When to change agents

If you feel your agent is not spending enough time on your projects, or for any other reason is not the right person to be representing you, it's only fair to you both to look for another. (You will have remaining ties, however, covering any works that were negotiated by him. So it's best to keep relations as smooth as possible.)

And agents drop authors on occasion. A few years ago Candida Donadio had over two hundred clients. She finally decided she couldn't handle that many properly, and she cut back. As she told Poets & Writers, Inc., "What happened was, those who were dissatisfied—thought I wasn't hustling enough for them, wasn't tough enough—tended to leave anyway. It's a fluid business, and I find that things usually come to a natural conclusion."

Deciding whether and when to change agents is as difficult for some writers as deciding whether or not to divorce. That's probably because agents, as Scott Meredith noted, do much more for a writer than negotiate contracts. In many cases they do become a partner as close as a spouse, at least in financial matters. To make the break, the Authors Guild suggests a simple letter from writer to agent "suggesting it's better for both parties concerned to part company."

Packagers, lawyers, specialists

Book packagers, new on the publishing scene, combine the roles of agent and book producer. The packager finds a writer for an editor's pet project and/or a publisher for a writer's manuscript. But his role as middleman doesn't stop there. He shepherds the manuscript through the production process before he hands over the entire thing to the publisher for promotion and distribution. (In the case mentioned earlier where an agent hears about an editor's idea for a book and finds a writer for the project, the agent is only partly playing packager, since he does not handle the production of the physical book.)

How this process often works: The manuscript is sent by the writer to the packager, who checks it over to see if it follows the proposed outline. He then forwards it to the editor. When it has been approved by the editor it's sent back to the packager, who oversees all the details of production—copyediting, interior design of the book, typesetting, paste-up. He sends one copy of the page proofs to the editor and one to the author, keeping the actual pasted-up boards himself. The author corrects the page proofs and sends them back to the packager. When all materials are ready, he forwards the negatives to the editor. The book jacket design and sales promotion efforts are usually handled by the publisher.

Depending on the packager's contract, the author may work for a flat fee, share royalties with the packager, or negotiate other terms. (Some writers report packagers have asked them to sign contracts splitting proceeds with the packager on a fifty-fifty basis. This seldom makes business sense for a publishable writer.)

However, if you think you'd like to try this method, the best way to call attention to your availability is to get the word out in publishing circles. Packagers are listed in *Literary Market Place* (LMP) under "Consulting & Editorial Services." Also keep a watch out for the ads book packagers place, or place one yourself.

Collaboration

In considering the helpers available to a writer, let's not overlook the obvious—another writer. Writers, agents, and editors all feel strongly one way or another about collaboration, depending on whether their own experiences with collaborators have been positive or negative. There are cases where collaboration works perfectly and others where it's one disaster after another. Consider what may lie ahead *before* you get involved. A collaboration between friends can ruin a friendship. Or it can be the stimulating experience that keeps both of you working at top form.

The advantages are obvious: a pooling of resources, contacts, efforts. However, you also pool the proceeds. Draw up a contract specifying who will do what kind of work, how moneys are to be divided, and so on.

This agreement should be a well-thought-out document that is legally binding. If it is a long-term agreement, it should be discussed with a third party (accountant, lawyer, agent) so any negative elements will be ironed out prior to signing. Include a buy-out or phase-out clause in case there is a change of heart by one or both partners.

A collaborative writing effort means two people agree beforehand what kind of contribution each will make to a given work. The problems aren't the same as those involved in ghostwriting for a non-writer—a doctor, for instance—who wants to have her thoughts or discoveries published. But a number of problems do exist, even though the partners themselves may have no inherent disagreement. Each is bound to react differently, for instance, to what an agent or editor or publisher tells him, how the book looks, what sort of publicity it gets, and so forth.

An example of a collaboration that works is the one between Judi Kesselman-Turkel and Franklynn Peterson, who explained their method thus to the members of the ASJA:

> One of us will write the first draft and do all the research. Then the other will edit the first draft, asking for clarification or amplification where needed, making suggestions, cleaning up the language, and typing the second draft. That way, we find that by the time we send our completed manuscript to the publisher, there's little for the copyeditor to do. Because the "uninvolved" partner approaches the manuscript cold, we know that if (s)he understands technicalities and is entertained, the book does what we've set out to do. Our writing has improved since we've joined forces, because we hold one another to high standards.

Before you make any final decision about collaborating, be certain you've evaluated your own most important needs. If your analysis shows that two heads are better than one, go to it. There are numerous potential writing partners who will heartily agree.

Chapter 13
Keeping Book
on
Keeping Books

■■■

Setting up a system

Bookkeeping is an off-putting subject to many writers. This is unfortunate, since it is an essential tool no one should try to do without. You can overcome the notion that it's just a drag on your creative prowess by giving yourself an occasional pep talk. Simply remind yourself that by keeping good records on a regular basis, you're putting yourself in the driver's seat. Otherwise, in spite of all else you might accomplish, you'll be allowing forces other than yourself to run your business. For one thing, whether your freelance operation shows real profit or not will be evident in well-documented books; any losses won't overwhelm you, since they will appear in time for you to make needed alterations in your work habits or list of clients. On the slightly more positive side, if your income is growing, you might be edging toward a higher income-tax bracket. By noting this possibility early, you'll be in a better position to make the decisions that will save money and offset your tax liability (see Chapter 14). All told, the IRS is far less likely to quibble with you about your tax return if you can demonstrate that you are careful about keeping books.

Keeping control of the financial end of your business, then, will be, according to your temperament and approach, a relative cinch or a constant headache. But it doesn't have to be the latter. Much depends on how you lay out your initial plans and how willing you are to diligently record the necessary information. Whatever system of keeping track you choose, you'll want it to be simple to use, easy to understand, reliable, accurate, consistent, and designed to provide information on a timely basis. (There are no specific accounting systems required by the government. What *is* essential to the IRS, though, is that you *keep track.*)

Most beginners will not need more than a simple record book using a single-entry system of recording expenses and income. For others, a more complicated ledger book might be in order. What you choose will depend, in part, on the size of your business and your expertise at keeping books (or willingness to learn). But you'd be wise to choose a system that allows for expansion as your business grows. For one thing, there's the psychological boost it will give you. You're stating emphatically that you're preparing for the day when you're no longer an unknown but a well-paid freelancer. Then, too, freelancing *is* an unusual business, full of pleasant surprises, and when your business suddenly takes that jolly turn and you're making more money and have more clients than you ever truly imagined you would, you will need a bookkeeping system that can handle it.

Checks and balances

First of all, get a separate checking account for your business. It immediately demonstrates to clients and the government that you're seriously in business. It is also far simpler to keep track of business expenses when they are separated from your personal ones. Shop around, though, for the most attractive banking advantages before you open your account. While banks offer certain perks for personal accounts—free checking with minimum balance, overdraft protection, and even interest—not all of them will do so for a business account. What type of checkbook you choose doesn't matter so much as how well and how regularly you keep it in balance. If you're just starting out freelancing, you may want to use only the checkbook as your primary tool for bookkeeping for a while until you're certain you are going to continue freelancing. If that's the case, remember that you will be simplifying your bookkeeping chores only if you religiously record every withdrawal and explanation about the expense and every deposit with the necessary information to back it up—not just the amount but the date and client or payee.

Hints on balancing the checkbook: When your bank statement arrives each month, balance it by noting any outstanding checks, by check number and amount, any deposits made but not yet recorded when the statement arrived, and any bank fees deducted or interest received for the month. Correct any mathematical errors in your checkbook and note that the checkbook amount is in balance with the bank statement as of a certain date and check number. Each month when the outstanding checks from the previous month turn up, cross out the notation on them and transfer the amount and check number of any that have not yet been cashed to the new month's statement. Devise a way of noting on the check stubs that they're either cashed or still outstanding. For instance, make an X or slash mark on the stub to flag your attention, signaling the check has been cashed by the bank. If you discover that your balance and the bank's don't agree, take your canceled checks, checkbook, and current bank statement to the bank and ask for help. The sooner you catch any gross errors concerning the way you are attempting to balance your checkbook, the better off you'll be. Then, armed with the advice from your banker on a better method, tackle the job the next month with more care.

Bookkeeping simplified

If you're definitely in business as a freelancer, a better, though still relatively simple, form of bookkeeping is the account book or journal. It's called a single-entry system because records of income and expenses are shown on the same page (although separated into different columns). Whenever you receive income or pay for expenses, either by check or by cash, an entry should be made on the journal page. At the end of the month add up the totals for each column, leaving several lines blank before beginning to record the next month's figures. (You may need this space to make comments or adjustments at the end of the year. Besides, the clearer the distinctions are between entries for various months' figures, the easier it is to read. For a sample of this system, see fig. 13-1.)

At the end of the year (or six months if you prefer), set aside a page to record in summary form the transactions for the previous pages. This is a simplified form of a balance sheet, giving you a clear view of your entire year's totals at a glance.

Regarding the balancing procedure: Be certain you verify the figures in your journal with the actual canceled checks each month, not just the notations in the checkbook. If there is any discrepancy between these figures, you must naturally go by the one on the canceled check. Correct any errors at this time, whether it's a figure or notation regarding income or expense. You'll be doing this for three reasons: for taxes and client billing purposes, for help later with your budget, and for bookkeeping practice.

To simplify your bookkeeping chores, try to pay as much as you can by check. If you must pay by cash for minor expenditures—small amounts of photocopying and the like—write a check to petty cash. Let's say your petty cash needs for a month amount to roughly $15. Each month draw a check for that figure marked petty cash. Keep the cash in an envelope with a few blank petty cash slips. When you spend some, mark the petty cash blank with the amount, date, and reason for the expense. Or set up a small notebook to record these items specifically for your petty cash expenditures. When all of this cash has been spent, draw another $15 check to petty cash.

For larger amounts you need to withdraw from the business account for your own income, draw a check to yourself with your own name on it instead of the word "cash."

A slightly more complex journal system might be your best bet if your business demands it and you're more willing to take the time

			RECEIPTS			PAID	
MAR	2	PERIODICALS				5	75
"	3	GAS (WICI) MEETING, BOSTON				10	—
"	3	DUES (WICI)				35	—
"	4	POSTAGE				15	—
"	10	REAM PAPER				8	31
"	12	UNITED PRESS	100	—			
"	14	CHICAGO TRIBUNE (TRAVEL PIECE)	150	—			
"	18	OFFICE SUPPLIES LTD.				22	80
"	15	BELL TELE. COMPANY				14	38
"	20	J. MERCURIO, RESEARCHER				28	—
"	23	YANKEE MAGAZINE	400	—			
"	28	PSYCHOLOGY TODAY	500	—			
"	30	ATHENAEUM PUBLISHING COMPANY	3,600	—			
		BALANCE RECEIPTS	4,750	—			
		EXPENSES				139	24
		BALANCE FORWARDED	4,610	76			

Fig. 13-1. Sample page from a single-entry account book.

monthly to spell out the financial details. It is more work, but it can save headaches at the end of the year when you must compute your taxes. The advantage of expandability mentioned earlier is another plus. With dividers between a number of sections, you can keep track of other items you may need to know about without scrambling through files repeatedly. (Sample pages from this sort of journal are shown in fig. 13-2.)

You'll probably want to consult an accountant before you choose a particular method of keeping the more complicated journal (since you'll be using his services at tax time and he may have a favorite plan for keeping such a cash-disbursements journal), but you can try to keep one yourself if you wish. Look at the examples in this chapter. Check books at the library if necessary. Or see if you can locate a student of accounting to help you set up the pages correctly. Some of the following section headings will help:

Monthly journal sheet. This shows all income and expenses for a month. The difference between these sheets and the simple journal is the room this page allows for recording in separate columns what the expense was or what sort of income was received—advances, royalties, rent, dividends, commissions, etc. The separation of a variety of transactions into several columns allows you to balance them separately at the bottom of the page. By balancing figures across the page and vertically you have a more finely examined set of figures less susceptible to errors of simple arithmetic, as well. Of course, these entries, too, should be verified at the end of the month, both against the figures in the bank statement and against the actual canceled checks. The end-of-the-month balances can be carried on to the next month's page, but it is usually better to simplify things and to not keep such a running balance. That way, if the figures on one page are incorrect they can be changed without upsetting all of the others.

Yearly balance sheet. This is a one-page summary of the twelve monthly journal sheets. Using the final totals for each column, you transfer them into twelve monthly columns. These pages may be balanced quarterly, semiannually or annually; as with the simpler journal form, the main advantage is that they provide a year's picture of income and expenses at a glance. With several sheets comprising each year's balance put side by side, you can quickly ascertain not only if you're making a profit or falling behind but why either might be so.

Profit and loss statement. This will be done monthly (if you're making big bucks) or yearly (for everyone else). It's a means of

APRIL 1981

	Date	CK #		CASH		RECEIPTS		COMMISSIONS	FEES	SUBS	AUTO	MAILING &	
				DEPOSIT	PAID	ROYALTIES/ ADVANCES	OTHER	PAID	DUES			SHIPPING	SUPPLIES
1	APR 1	276	FINEST TRAVEL, INC.	-	196 -			X8604 250 - 1000 -					
2	APR 2	-	DANDY AGENCY	8750 -	-								
3	APR 3	277	TEXACO, INC.		122 -						122 -		
4	APR 5	278	CASH (PETTY)		25 -					4 25			8 23
5	APR 7	279	NAT'L OFFICE SUPPLY		52 80								52 80
6	APR 7	280	POSTMASTER		17 84							17 84	
7	APR 10	-	DANDY AGENCY	5400 -		6000 -		600 -					
8	APR 11	281	COLOR CODES LTD.		28 50								
9	APR 12	-	MEDNET INC.	250 -			250 -						
10	APR 14	282	INTERNAL REVENUE S.		1934 -								
11	APR 17	283	CASH (PETTY)		25 -								9 -
12	APR 17	284	SALLY HENDRICKS		30 -								
13	APR 19	285	LOU BROWN + CO.		40 -								
14	APR 20	286	STEIN, GREENE ATT'YS		150 -								
15	APR 21	-	McCALL'S	1500 -		1500 -							
16	APR 26	-	LOS ANGELES TIMES	150 -		150 -							
17	APR 26	287	WJCI		35 -				35 -				
18	APR 30	288	T.C. ADAMS		400 -								
19	APR 30	-	BANK INTEREST	7 84			7 84						
20	APR 30	289	N.W. BELL CO.		157 50								
21	APR 30	290	GREY BOOKSTORE		27 95								
22													
23			TOTAL	16057 84	3201 59	17450 -	257 84	1850 -	35 -	4 25	122 -	17 84	70 03
24													

Fig. 13-2. Sample pages from a cash-disbursements journal.

	EQUIPMENT	FURNISHINGS	XEROX PRINTG PHOTO	MAINTENANCE	RESEARCH OFFICE HELP	TELEPHONE	LIBRARY	TRAVEL	ENTERTAINMNT	OFFICE RENT	GENERAL ACCOUNT	AMOUNT
1								156 —				
2												
3												
4							12 52					
5												
6												
7												
8			28 50									
9												
10											PROD.INC.TAX 1954 —	
11									16 —			
12					30 —							
13				40 —								
14										150 —		
15												
16												
17												
18											SALARY APR. 400 —	
19												
20						157 50						
21							27 95					
22												
23	—	—	28 50	40 —	30 —	157 50	40 47	136 —	16 —	150 —		2354 —
24												

Fig. 13-2. (cont.)

spelling out the above information from the balance sheets. Usually freelancers can do one quite a bit more simply than other types of businesses can. But practice drawing one up at the end of your year. You never know when you might need one. If you're anticipating taking out a loan, the lending institution or private business person you may be soliciting will undoubtedly require one. The same might hold true if you are applying for a grant. And you may be glad you have one—it helps demonstrate you are a reliable business person— if you are ever faced with a legal matter.

A record of furniture, fixtures, and equipment in a separate section of the same journal is an added convenience when, at tax time (or perhaps during any problems dealing with an insurance company), you need to see quickly what has been purchased, from whom, when, and for how much. With all of this together you can then also record by which means of depreciation you are operating— another bit of information the IRS requires of businesses.

This journal can also hold information about payments to your retirement fund (see Chapter 14), your savings account, insurance payments, dividends received, receipts from medical and disability insurance, details on payroll and subcontracts, accounts receivable and payable, loans, leases, etc. Only your own particular situation and your and your accountant's preference will dictate what is or is not included. Generally, freelancers don't have to be concerned about most of these details but, if and when they do, the same journal is expandable to include them and you have, as near as is possible, a complete financial accounting of your situation in one handy book. Perhaps the only item other businesses record in this sort of journal is inventory, and for freelancers it is probably simpler to keep an inventory record in a separate log.

Operational tips

■ No matter which of the three bookkeeping systems (simple checkbook, single-entry journal, or the more complicated cash-disbursements journal) you choose, you will also need to have a method of filing backup receipts. You should have something— receipt, invoice, canceled check or petty cash ticket—for *every* expense notation. Make sure before filing these that they indicate all of the important information (date paid, amount paid, to whom paid, check number or cash payment). Keep these receipts for business expenses filed separately from any personal expenses.

■ All funds received or disbursed from your freelancing business should pass through your business checkbook. Your monthly bank statement should be balanced against your receipts/disbursements journal sheets, as well as verifying your checkbook balance.

■ Record all cash receipts in the proper column by category. (If you're receiving a salary or regular commissions from someone as well as freelancing, you can keep the data in the same book, but keep the receipts in a separate column. If you regularly receive rent or other such moneys from another source, separate those receipts also.)

■ Record gross receipts, commissions deducted, and net receipts at the same time for more ease in figuring your taxes.

■ Be accurate when you spread the figures across the page. They need to balance both horizontally and vertically.

■ Balance each page *monthly*.

■ Record the balances on the balance sheet *monthly*.

■ An adding machine or calculator with a printout tape for your permanent records is a decided advantage in balancing your books; it is also helpful as proof of balances during any tax audit. As you balance each page of your journal you can staple the tape to it or file it with the backup material (receipts, invoices, petty cash tickets, etc.). The cost of the adding machine or calculator is a deductible business expense.

This is what your system should tell you:

Weekly:

1. Accounts receivable (so you can take action on slow payers).
2. Accounts payable (so you can take advantage of discounts).
3. Payroll (if any).

Monthly:

1. General ledger and journal entries posted and balanced.
2. Profit and loss statement tallied (at least within fifteen days after end of month. From this you can act quickly to adjust items, reduce expenditures, correct faulty buying procedures, etc.).
3. Bank statement reconciled.
4. Petty-cash accounts balanced and filed.
5. Tax matters attended to, if necessary.
6. Accounts receivable "aged" (i.e., rebill slow payers).
7. Inventory journal reviewed; material updated and recycled to new markets.

Additional hints:

To keep on top of income (receivables), don't be penny wise and pound foolish. Keep track of the amounts due you, when you can expect to receive them, and from whom. Send out invoices regularly. Regarding expenses (disbursements), ask for discounts from suppliers. Ask yourself if you're paying too much interest on outstanding balances.

Be careful to record in a journal, daybook, or other device the name of anyone entertained, the business association or project involved, and any other explanations that will be necessary at tax time. Details of business travel should also be recorded. For both entertainment and travel expenses be sure you have verification or backup data filed away properly.

Prepare for the inevitable (taxes), by checking to see if you need to make quarterly estimates and payments. Even if you don't, you should be able to roughly estimate for yourself the tax bite that will come due eventually. Be aware that if you employ part-time help, or form a partnership or small corporation, you'll be required by law to keep more extensive records. Since there are other regulations as well and some of these change periodically, you'd be wise to use an accountant or lawyer to help prepare any necessary papers.

Review all facets of your financial status regularly. Stay abreast, too, of changing conditions in the overall economy. This will help your own approach to your markets by giving you data on which to make sound business decisions.

If you need another reason for keeping clear account books, remember that if you're traveling extensively on assignments or are temporarily disabled or ill, your accountant can readily take over your financial recordkeeping without the hassle of sifting through the folders of receipts and expenses you might otherwise be relying on.

Poor accounting methods can affect you in two ways: they give you the idea you have more money than you actually do, or they leave you worrying needlessly. (Just remember, the borrowing-from-Peter-to-pay-Paul principle eventually backfires; relying on it too often can spell economic woes no one needs.) Since proper bookkeeping is crucial to your efforts to profit from your work, be careful you don't conceal weaknesses or distort your actual financial picture. The results of this hard work will be a sense of well-being as well as the pleasant prospect of financial health at each step along the way to more and more income.

Recordkeeping and inventory control

When you were first contemplating freelancing, you considered your assets and liabilities. This time it will be necessary to attempt to fill in dollar amounts (actual and fair market value estimates). Admittedly this is not easy, since some of the assets are difficult to place a value on. In such cases, the best one can do is make an educated guess. Try realistically not to over- or undervalue these items. In a situation where you can get input from experts—insurance agents, accountants, bankers—it might be worth your while to do so. Even if you cannot put a figure beside a category, at least note the category and some descriptive information about it so your log will be as complete as possible. (Again, accessible backup material, perhaps including photographs of especially valuable items, should be on file.) For recordkeeping purposes your inventory log will record information on items already mentioned (your library, copyrights, etc.).

You'll also want to log projects already completed and available for sale or resale. Note, too, ideas you're currently contemplating expanding into queries to clients. A simple ring binder for sheets listing these, perhaps a page per month, is all that's required. Do keep it simple. Its purpose is to give you current information *quickly*. You'll need to achieve a reasonable amount of turnover of your inventory; otherwise you've tied up time, effort, and money in projects that aren't paying off. If you also mark on the sheet a section for assignments received, date completed, date paid, etc., you have all the information you need to remind you where resale possibilities exist, where to offer your material, and where (because of competition between periodicals or other clients) you must *not* offer the material. (See sample inventory control sheet, fig. 13-3.)

Assets:

1. Memberships in professional organizations (include tangential organizations).
2. Library, photograph and slide library, copyrights.
3. Inventory of unpublished articles.
4. Research files, clippings, etc.
5. Collections (antiques, fine art, etc., if owned by company, partnership, or corporation).
6. Furnishings and equipment (same as 5 above).
7. Automobile (same as 5 above).

Name/Client	Initial contact	Job/Query	Work stage	Work stage	Accept/Date	Paid/Date
McKinney/McCalls	ASJA mtg. 7/2	Double Trouble	7/15-initial intvs. 7/17-back-p calls			
Ostermann/Marathon	thru ELC 7/25	North Sea Rigs	8/2 intvs+res. complete	11/20-final/draft fini	acc. 11/30	
tr.ed/BH&G	mail query 6/6	Newport Xmas	spin-off re-write 7/12	——	acc. 7/19	
ProJo Meras	tele. query 5/8	European series (6)	6/18-part 1 drafted 6/20-parts 2,3 drfth.	7/5-pts. 1-3 fini 7/29-pts. 4-6 drfth.	1-3 acc. 7/10 4-6 acc. 8/8	7/14 8/12
RDigest	ASJA 5/9 conf.	First Person (Cape)	8/10-1st draft 8/5			
RDigest/Europe	office call 6/12	Romanian Monsters	6/17-research library 6/30-intvs	7/1-tapes transd.		
RDigest/Europe	office call 7/20	LGedda/genetics	7/22-research contacts made			
Dallas T-H MCarlton	tele. query 7/21	NYC iron facades	8/1-draft			
MedNetWks	call to me 7/10	Emerg. Medicine	8/4-intvs.			
People/Wingo	staff lede	McGuirl & Co.	field intvs-7/18 tape transd-7/10	story filed-7/11 cd'l work-7/5,16	——	8/5

Fig. 13-3. Sample inventory control sheet.

8. Investments.
9. Savings.
10. Commissions and fees receivable.
11. Other.

Liabilities:

1. Office rent or mortgage on building.
2. Regular monthly bills (utilities, salaries, etc.).
3. Debts to suppliers, etc.
4. Assignments pending.
5. Commissions due agent, etc.
6. Other.

This sort of recording of assets and liabilities actually need only be done at the outset of your financial recording. Once it is, a simple update every year is all that's required to keep you and any financial adviser informed.

Depreciation

As a small-business entrepreneur you will probably use what is called a straight-line depreciation of your fixed assets based on the expected life of the items. (Fixed assets are those pieces of business furnishings and equipment in use for a year or longer, such as automobile, tools, equipment, furniture, and fixtures.) Buildings are also fixed assets, but normally the depreciation on them would be smaller because of a longer estimated life—say twenty years. Fig. 13-4 is a sample depreciation schedule for building and equipment.

The freelancer described in this sample depreciation schedule has made enough from sales of her books to build an addition to her home for her office ($20,000) and put in a word processor ($8,000), which took the place of her typewriter. She no longer needs a secretary, which, she says, has streamlined her operation and eventually saved her money as well as helped her make it. The other equipment included new files, desk and desk chair, shelves, lamps, and so forth, for her new office. If you are working on a more stringent budget, you will still save at tax time if you carefully log all business equipment you have, its original cost, where you purchased it, and its estimated life value.

The IRS claims that no asset may be depreciated below a reasonable salvage value under any method used in computing deprecia-

Item	Date Purch.	Cost	Est. Life	Yearly Deprec.	Accum. Prior Deprec.	This Year's Deprec.	Total Accum. Deprec.
Office	Jan.77	$20,000	20 yr.	5%	$2,000	$1,000	$3,000
Word Proc'r	Jan.78	8,000	10 yr.	10%	800	800	1,600
Other Equip.	July78	4,000	10 yr.	10%	400	400	800
Total		$32,000			$3,200	$2,200	$5,400

Fig. 13-4. *Sample depreciation schedule—building and equipment.*

tion. How does one determine salvage value? The amount of salvage value is the least amount a person can get away with that is reasonable to that particular asset.

You can receive more help in figuring depreciation and other costs for free from your local SBA office. Also check to see if they have on file the names of retired businessmen who act as free consultants to people interested in starting up a business. While your business is obviously quite different from most they'll be asked about, there are some problems you share in common which they can help with.

The complete strategist does more than break even

Businesses need to know their break-even point. This figure gives you a sense of how much you must make under certain conditions to cover your cost of operating with no loss (and no profit). It is, as freelancer James B. Kobak so aptly puts it, not really a place to *stop*, though. Breaking even, even in these times, just isn't good enough.

But a break-even analysis will allow you to consider the changes possible in one or more of the factors involved in your business—changes which might increase your profits or stop the drain on resources. To figure a break-even point, separate fixed costs (rent, etc.) from variables.

The break-even point is defined as that point where revenue equals cost. Expenses must be separated into fixed and variable costs. Fixed costs are those costs that remain constant over a short period of time. Variable costs are those costs that change proportionately to any changes in the volume of business. An example of fixed and variable costs as they relate to net income plus a break-even formula are shown in fig. 13-5.

The break-even formula may be expanded as follows: Dividing variable costs by sales revenue gives the part (.65) of each sales dollar that is required to cover variable costs. This is known as the variable cost percentage. The contribution of each sales dollar to cover fixed costs and profit is .35, otherwise known as the profit-volume ratio. Since profit is zero at break-even, the division of the total fixed cost by the profit-volume ratio gives the dollar amount of sales required to cover all fixed costs.

Taxes and deductions

Although the IRS requires no specific accounting systems for businesses, the details it asks for do add up. You'll want careful records of income, expenses, deductions (travel, entertainment, and business gifts especially), receipts for equipment purchased, depreciation schedules, assignments of ownership, and a number of other things. As the IRS puts it, "These records must be accurate and accessible." Accountants who know about tax liability for small businesses suggest freelancers get away from receipts-in-a-shoebox as quickly as possible for that very reason. Too many problems arise for those who don't attempt to keep books in an acceptable fashion.

When can you toss out the records, as far as the IRS is concerned? In general you can ditch them three years after a given taxable year's due date for the tax return, or the date filed, whichever is *later*. The major exception is if someone has omitted over 25 percent of gross income or filed a false or fraudulent return. In that case he's asked to keep them forever, presumably adjacent to his jail cell. These dates, however, are minimums. Many records should be kept longer: for example, cash books, depreciation schedules, general ledgers, financial journals, financial statements, and audit reports. Some records to keep for six to seven years: accounts payable and receivable, canceled checks, inventory schedules, payroll records, sales vouchers, and invoice details. Oh, yes, and copies of your tax returns—forever! (Remember that if you use your safe-deposit box to store tax returns, the cost for rental of the box is tax-deductible.)

Regarding any problems with the IRS, the law is firm: The burden of proof is on the *taxpayer*.

	Fixed	Variable
Sales		$100,000
Cost	Fixed	Variable
Direct material, supplies		$10,000
Labor (Payroll or outside services)		20,000
Overhead (Electricity, property taxes, heat, insurance, etc.)	$ 8,000	30,000
Administrative expenses (Office, supplies, telephone, etc.)	20,000	5,000
	$28,000	$65,000 +28,000
Total cost		$93,000
Net income		$ 7,000

Break-Even Formula

Break-Even Sales = Fixed Costs + Variable Costs and Profit

$$B.E.S. = F.C. + \frac{V.C.}{S} (B.E.S.) + 0$$

$$B.E.S. = 28,000 + \frac{65,000}{100,000} (B.E.S.) + C$$

$$B.E.S. = 28,000 + .65 \ B.E.S.$$

$$.35 \ B.E.S. = 28,000$$

$$B.E.S. = 80,000$$

Fig. 13-5. *Sample breakdown of fixed and variable costs, and the break-even formula.*

You can deduct all of the obvious expenses involved with your writing business up to 100 percent of your gross earned income from writing, but no more than that. By obvious expenses I'm referring to supplies, equipment, postage, copying costs, magazine subscriptions, books, professional memberships, travel, business entertainment, professional help, and so on. *Keep those receipts.*

Expenses connected with a home office are deductible, but the space must be used *solely* for your writing business, and you must be employed primarily as a writer. No other use of the same space is permissible. If you use one room of an eight-room house for your office, you will figure one-eighth of your rent (or mortgage payment) plus one-eighth of your utility bills, etc. Part-time writers are still in limbo, since the IRS has not yet ruled on the matter of a home office for moonlighters. *Keep receipts.*

Automobile and mileage expenses are deductible as well, if you use your car for your business. It pays to figure out your actual costs and compare them to the standard mileage deduction to see which way of calculating your expenses gives you the largest deduction. *Keep receipts.*

You may deduct for depreciation of your office equipment and any related tools you use (like cameras) a certain amount each year of its useful life (see Depreciation, above). You may also deduct for purchases of necessary equipment or depreciable assets in the year in which you bought them, under the Investment Tax Credit clause—10 percent of its useful life if that useful life is seven years or more. This does not apply to real estate, however.

Engage an accountant to help prepare your tax return. The fee you pay him is deductible, and his expertise in tax matters will reap dividends for your business. Even if you are good at figures, you can't expect to know all the details of the ever-changing tax laws. Keeping the books is time-consuming enough. You need to spend your time on writing and making money for the business. Let your expert handle the details of tax filing for you, if you possibly can.

Interestingly, the term *accountant* is misunderstood by many people, even in the business community. The well-rounded accountant is not the figure-checker wearing a green eyeshade of years past, but a capable management consultant. Accountants are moneymakers for the small-business person. They acquire an intimate knowledge of his business and personal financial situation, so they can lead him (already overburdened with the details of trying to make his business successful) through the financial paths he must follow to succeed.

One of the secrets of successful management is knowing where to turn for the best service. What should you be looking for when you are searching for an accountant (i.e., financial adviser)? Look for someone who can provide financial planning, capital raising, and competent, complete financial services.

If you still want to go it alone, in spite of all that experts advise to the contrary, at least get copies of IRS publications for your business library. Read them well before you approach the filing of your tax form. They will help you prepare your papers more efficiently. You'll get the most return on your money invested in bookkeeping tactics. Then be certain you put the figures together and file in plenty of time. Treat the April 15 deadline each year as you would any other; start way in advance, do your research well, check and recheck your figures.

A tax-related question that often comes up in freelance circles is: Should I incorporate? The answer to this question is complicated and requires professional advice based on a knowledge of your individual circumstances. The following are some generalized reasons for incorporation that may or may not apply to your situation. A person will incorporate to limit liabilities to creditors. (The liabilities to creditors will be thus limited to the assets of the corporation in any legal settlement. Creditors can not turn to the stockholders of a corporation in settlement of any claims.) Also, when a person has a partnership (Schedule C) and the net earnings from the business have placed the partners in or near a 50-percent tax bracket, they are usually advised to incorporate, thereby limiting the amount of taxation. The maximum tax on self-earned income is 50 percent. By incorporating, one is allowed the added tax deduction of a pension plan and a profit-sharing plan which will substantially decrease taxable income while building a future retirement account for existing stockholders and employees who qualify. A 50-percent tax bracket varies depending on filing status.

Are Keogh plans necessary for freelancers? All experts agree these are a must for anyone freelancing if his net income from his operation has cleared $5,000 or more in any taxable year.

State and local laws differ widely not only on taxes but on other regulations regarding business transactions, so check yours. Better yet, use your financial adviser for this purpose. He knows what you should be doing and when and can remind you in time.

Budgeting

Someone once asked me if I'd recommend that freelancers read up on budgeting, since, after all, they're supposed to be people for whom learning from research is part of the job. While I hate to budget, and advising someone to make a study of budgeting seems unduly harsh, I don't see how I can do otherwise. At least try your hand at filling out a budget sheet for a few months. Make the proper tallies to see *where* you might be going wrong. (If you're always coming out in the red, it's *somewhat* easier to change the patterns once you're faced with the actual figures.)

One of the best ways to start budgeting is to faithfully record the details on a special page for the purpose. After you've recorded these for a month or two, you'll have a better idea of what sums to enter in your budget for the month. At the end of the year, add them up and divide by 12, putting the resulting figure in the proper slot (even though you may pay some sums quarterly, semiannually, or annually). With an accurate monthly record, you'll be able to more easily adopt countermeasures if your receipts aren't tallying with your expenditures.

A budget sheet faithfully kept will show clearly where problems lie (see fig. 13-6). Are expenses in one category heavier than you imagined? Is disaster looming around the corner if you continue to work for a specific market? Where and how can you cut down? Do you have to negotiate for a higher fee from your best client? Should you aim for more sales volume? Do you need to consider a part-time job? Are you paying too much rent for your office? Are you billing properly? Has your inventory of stories and ideas been turned over quickly enough?

Obviously, this budget sheet, too, needs to be balanced monthly. Be sure you carry over the figures on the following month's sheet where indicated. To accurately record figures on this sheet, you'll have to tally up those petty-cash slips you've collected.

Count in the current inflation rate when you're setting up your future budget pages, saving yourself from too many unpleasant surprises when new costs arise.

Wise counselors advise couples (both of whom are working) to live on one salary if they possibly can, using the other's income for future goals: business investments, vacations, luxuries, etc. This is pretty difficult to do in today's economy, but in some cases it might be possible. If this is your situation, it might be worth a try—something to aim for.

		MONTH:		YEAR TO DATE	
		PLAN	ACTUAL	PLAN	ACTUAL
1	INCOME	10,000	9,578	10,000	9,578
2	Royalties (textbook)	2,500	2,400	9,350	9,000
3	Roy., advances (other)	400	400	1,600	1,600
4	Salary-contrib. editor	—			
5	Miscellaneous				
6	UNCONTROLLABLE EXPENSES	(1,000)	(958)	(1,000)	(958)
7	NET INCOME	11,900	11,420	14,950	14,220
8	REGULAR EXPENSES				
9	Rent	150	150	600	600
10	Fees & Dues	40	40	160	40
11	Subscriptions	9	10	32	34
12	Automobile	25	23	100	98
13	Mailing & Shipping	16	19	64	63
14	Supplies	22	15	88	83
15	Furnishings	6	—	24	—
16	Equipment	8	13	32	13
17	Xerox, Printing, Photo	12	17	48	62
18	Research, Office help	25	25	100	100
19	Maintenance	20	20	80	80
20	Telephone	45	57	180	197
21	Library	10	18	40	56
22	Travel	22	—	88	62
23	Entertainment	25	24	100	80
24	Business gifts	5	—	20	20
25	Miscellaneous	15	—	60	—
26	BALANCE	454	431	1,816	1,588
27	PROFIT (OR LOSS)	11,446	10,989	13,134	12,632

Fig. 13-6. *Sample budget sheet. The first two columns show details for one month; the second two columns show figures for the first four months of the business year. Figures in parentheses are debits.*

Ask a friendly accountant to look over your budget to see whether you're being realistic about requirements, if you think you need help. He can also guide you to data you'll need for borrowing, business organization, and tax requirements at the same time.

Final tips

■ Recognize that you have the power to succeed if you acknowledge economic realities.
■ Anticipate and control expenses.
■ Measure your success periodically with a review of the total picture.
■ Define attainable goals and set aside savings regularly, no matter how small the amount. The method becomes habit-forming.
■ Use experts for guidance.
■ Use reserve funds as a financial defense, and invest intelligently.
■ Devise a financial strategy that works. Keep accurate track of your finances with good bookkeeping principles. The time spent on them will improve your position and give you more time to write, which is the core of your business and your pleasure.

Chapter 14
Looking to Your Future

■■■

Putting your money to work

The preceding chapters concentrated on many tactics and maneuvers to help you enrich yourself and make your business grow. Now, after all your work, it's high time to concoct a solid plan that puts your money to work. If you're like a lot of people, this may be the most difficult task of all, but it can and should be done. So pencils and papers ready! What you'll need is a well-thought-out scheme to set aside funds for your future. Notice, I didn't say retirement. Seldom, if ever, do serious writers actually retire, though admittedly they may slow down when the need to keep such a hectic pace diminishes. But the pace diminishes comfortably if, and only if, they've been prudent and foresighted enough to tuck away some money for the future.

Familiar truism: "Them that has—gets." So look first at how the rich get so much for their money. They invest in antiques rather than just buying furniture. They get along with fewer but better items, figuring the price of anything worthwhile is bound to go up in the future. If they have money to invest, they put it to work in areas in which they have expertise. They often invest in their own companies by gobbling up stock rather than taking salary increases. They borrow wisely—from banks, against insurance policies, or on their own homes, rather than in areas where interest is much higher. They shop around for the best bank to put their money in.

Simple enough clues, but ones that writers, often too busy trying to make money, overlook.

Think once again about the start-up plan for your business discussed in Chapter 2. You had to devise a figure, your basic reserve, which was the amount you'd need to live on and do business with for a certain period of time—six months, for example. You more than likely put it in a savings account, or perhaps in a special business checking account so you could write checks against it when necessary. Most people feel they need that sense of security an account in a commercial or savings bank offers. They are familiar with the convenience such institutions offer their customers as well. Both are good reasons to keep a certain amount of your money in either a checking or savings account. However, with interest rates shifting often and radically, even many of those conservative individuals have sought a better return on their savings. At the very least, do as the rich do and shop around for the better-paying banking institution before you open your account. If you have access to larger sums even for a brief time, you might want to look into other places to stash the bulk of your savings. Ask your accountant for advice.

Before you see any experts, however, be sure you've asked yourself the following questions regarding three crucial factors:

Liquidity requirements. How fast might you need cash? Could you wait a week, a month, a year? (If you have your emergency savings account up to the point where it should be, you could wait longer. The less cash you have readily available, the more liquidity you require.)

Chance of premature need. What if you commit your funds for six months but need them back in four months? If you withdraw them prematurely there may be a penalty and, very probably, additional bank handling fees.

Safety factor. Does taking even the slightest monetary risk bother you? This is not an idle question. Only you can know the psychological implications that getting too far out on a financial limb has for you. If risk taking bothers you too much, you'll want to avoid any but the most secure investments, either the most secure *class* of investments (e.g., savings accounts) or most secure *type* of investment in each class (e.g., within stocks, it would be the blue chips).

For that big windfall—a sudden bestseller or its equivalent—you should discuss with your accountant as soon as possible how to protect as much of your profit as possible. Income averaging, or spreading the income over a period of years to lower the tax bite, is one method quite often favored by writers in such situations. But it isn't the only alternative. Your accountant will advise you on the best path.

Here are some general tips to use in devising your financial plan over the long stretch:

1. Develop a credit rating and keep it first-class.
2. Keep enough money in your bank account to see you through several months' expenses at the minimum.
3. Consider letting your spouse own the insurance policy on your life, and vice versa. (Discuss this fully with your accountant or legal expert, though. There are problems you should be aware of.)
4. Make properly drawn wills, paying close attention to copyrights.
5. Keep careful records of any money that has been used to purchase property.
6. Shop around when you want a lawyer—their fees differ widely, and you may not even need one.

Regarding point number 6 above, I'll admit that finding the proper lawyer for your particular set of circumstances is a challenge. As with your other major business decisions, you should do some research first. If you wait to do this part of your homework until you are in a bind, you're apt to leap blindly and be unhappy with the consequences. (Study carefully *Law and the Writer* and other books listed in the Resources chapter.) The recent Supreme Court ruling allowing lawyers to advertise hasn't yet, at least in Rhode Island where I live, seemed to alleviate the writer's problem of finding legal experts specializing in literary law. In the meantime, check your local library's business department for a copy of the *Martindale-Hubbell Law Directory* as a guide to tracking down the right lawyer.

The blueprint

Your first step in planning your financial future is to arm yourself with as much detailed personal financial data as possible. You'll want a clear picture of your net worth. A ledger sheet (see Chapter 13) listing both household and business possessions, contracts, annuities, insurance policies, Social Security payments and benefits, and so on, is very helpful. With this data at hand, your accountant or other financial adviser will be in a better position to help you make decisions about where to put your money to best prepare for the future. For your basic reserve you should probably start with a savings account, a retirement plan (into which you may put tax-deferred dollars), and insurance policies (life, medical, disability). After that, you'll be able to consider speculating, if there's anything left over.

The savings-account part of the basic reserve can be in a commercial bank, a savings bank, or a credit union (if you have access to one). The main consideration is liquidity (that is, availability on short notice—within a day or two) and the amount of interest your money is earning. Most experts suggest that the balance in your basic reserve account should be kept at the minimum required to support yourself for approximately six months to one year. This is essentially an emergency fund, something to fall back on in case of illness, disability, loss of big accounts, and the like. (See the section on basic reserve later in this chapter.)

Whatever vehicle you choose (savings account, money-market fund, bonds, cash-reserve management account, etc.), there are three requirements: your money should be safe, it should be earning more money (through interest), and it should be liquid.

The Keogh nest egg

The Self-Employed Individuals Tax Retirement Act (the Keogh Act) was enacted in 1962. Its primary purpose was to allow the self-employed person to defer tax payments on certain moneys, which are legally and properly put into a special retirement fund. Naturally, there are very specific regulations surrounding the manner in which you set these funds aside without incurring a tax liability. A Keogh Plan (or the alternative IRA, or Individual Retirement Account, meant for people employed by companies and who are part-time freelancers) is one of the best ways a freelancer has of saving for the future. Any writer who's qualified and not taking advantage of this is losing money every year.

More than one writer has been burned by not looking carefully into the details—picky little time-consuming realities but very necessary to your financial health. Just tucking money away in a sock, mattress, or savings certificate and calling it your retirement plan will not suffice. The government regulations are firm, so handle your Keogh Plan with care. You must set up a legal plan with a financial institution acceptable to the IRS.

As Grace W. Weinstein, a writer who did start a Keogh Plan, describes in *Law and the Writer:*

> The Keogh Plan provides that you, as your own employer . . . may set aside in an Internal Revenue Service-approved fund, up to 15 percent of your net earned income each year, to a maximum of $7,500. Alternatively, under a more complex and little-known provision of the 1974 law, you can establish a "defined benefit" plan under which you stipulate the amount of monthly pension you want to receive, subject to a formula based on current age and income, and contribute whatever amounts are necessary to provide that income.

The Keogh Plan is a fine way for you to watch out for yourself. It allows you to contribute according to your income. The minimum is established at 100 percent of earned income or $750, whichever is less. With a hard look *in advance* at probable earnings for the coming year and with a well-established production schedule, writers can stash at least that minimum away. It's wise, if you can do it, to take it off the top at the first of the year. This way you know you've protected some of your earnings from the tax bite and put aside something for your future. Another method is to tuck bits and pieces away monthly in a savings account and convert the lump sum to the Keogh Plan later. If you do it that way, though, be certain you convert it before the legal deadline. (The IRS says you can now make adjustments regarding your Keogh payments up to April 15 of the following calendar year.)

There are penalties for premature withdrawals from the plan, of course. If you make a withdrawal before you reach fifty-nine and a half years (except in a case of complete disability or death), a penalty tax of 10 percent of the amount in your plan is included in your taxable income for the year. There is a "rollover" clause, however, that allows you to reinvest any amounts withdrawn into another such account within sixty days after receipt of the moneys without the need to pay taxes on the amount so distributed. For instance, if you put your Keogh moneys into a mutual fund and it performed poorly, you could then withdraw it and reinvest within the time limit in another acceptable vehicle without a penalty.

Another benefit is that if there are years when you shift from freelance life to a full-time job or have been unlucky about making money from freelancing, you don't need to make any contributions to keep your Keogh Plan in force. The money you've socked away continues to earn interest and is sheltered from taxation until you withdraw it. (See fig. 14-1 for three examples of Keogh plans.)

Over the years these tax savings compound considerably depending on what vehicle you choose to put them in. The many variables of an individual's tax status change over the years, as do the tax laws. Says Weinstein:

	Writer 1	Writer 2	Writer 3
*Taxable Income	$15,000	$30,000	$50,000
Maximum contribution	$ 2,250	$ 4,500	$ 7,500
Deduction	$ 2,250	$ 4,500	$ 7,500
Tax bracket	25%	36%	50%
Tax savings	$ 562.50	$ 1,620	$ 3,750

*No allowance for interest, W-2, and other income; writing income only. No personal deductions.

Fig. 14-1. *Three examples of Keogh plans.*

When you calculate your income tax each year, you also calculate the amount you can deposit in your retirement fund. *Advance contributions may be made on an estimated basis, as long as you come out even at the end; excess contributions will no longer disqualify the plan, but they are subject to a 6-percent excise tax.* New legislation makes life a little easier: instead of having to calculate net income precisely before the end of the year, never quite knowing whether an anticipated check will actually arrive on time, *you now have until the date you file your tax return for the tax year.* [Italics mine.] Your Keogh contributions for 1978, in other words, may be made right up to April 15, 1979, with the allowable deduction taken on your 1978 return. Of course, the earlier you make your contribution (or part of your contribution), the sooner it will start to earn tax-sheltered interest.

The Keogh Plan can be established through a number of investment vehicles, and through a sometimes confusing array of financial institutions—banks, life insurance companies, mutual funds. Consult with your accountant before making this step. One writer I know didn't, and a clerk at the bank who failed to ask the proper questions filled out and filed the forms incorrectly. It was a terrible tangle he never did get straightened out.

If you are in a position where you have accumulated enough money and would like to protect more than $7,500 a year (the Keogh maximum), you will want to consult with your accountant or legal adviser about various other tax shelters, such as the defined-benefit pension plan mentioned earlier. Under this plan, instead of putting aside a fixed percentage of income you decide on a figure needed for your retirement and put away enough money each year to reach that goal—obviously something many freelancers can't afford to do. For older people, however, with some accumulated edge (from a good track record and more or less steady freelance income), the advantages of a Keogh-plus plan increase. Also, this added-benefits plan appeals to two-income families in which one income comes from self-employment. For those of you contemplating incorporation, the tax-shelter benefits of a corporate pension plan are somewhat different. Get advice from your legal counsel or accountant or both.

There is considerable difference among Keogh plans and the yields they offer, the benefits provided, the fees charged. It pays to shop around. Examine the complete plans and read the fine print on the prospectus. If you don't understand it all, ask for clarification on each point. Compare the total earnings over a period of, say, twenty years rather than just the percentage of interest paid. Sometimes the difference between advertised rates and true yield can be substantial.

An insurance company, for instance, might claim to give you a high yield for your savings dollar. If you looked closely, however, you would find they are quoting figures on net investment—that is, after sales commissions and other administrative expenses have been deducted.

Points to remember about Keogh plans:

■ The main thing you're looking for in any tax shelter is the opportunity to convert part of your tax bill into profits or earnings. You can do this by: (1) deferring payment of taxes until a more convenient time (when you might be making less money and are therefore in a lower tax bracket); (2) taking advantage of special deductions or lower tax rates; (3) turning current deductions into future assets.

■ Changes in the law make your retirement fund easier to handle now than in previous years. If you accidentally contribute more money than you're allowed, you may now withdraw the excess without more trouble. You don't have a 10-percent penalty on withdrawal of it as in previous years.

■ You can take your contribution to Keogh Plans "off the top"— that is, you deduct these contributions after your business expenses, but before you start adding up your other deductions, such as dependent exemptions or mortgage interest payments, etc. Thus the taxes you defer are the fattest, the dollars at the highest rate.

■ You can be covered by a Keogh Plan while you are also covered by a corporate pension plan—for example, if you're a freelancer who also teaches or works in a corporation and moonlights. The rules say that the money in your Keogh must be made by self-earnings for personal service, though.

■ All dividends, interest earned, and capital gains are sheltered from current taxes. There is no distinction in such a plan between long- and short-term gains. If your plan involves investments in the often volatile stock market, you don't have to key your market strategy to the calendar, since taxes are not immediate. There is no federal taxation on these investments until the funds are withdrawn, though depending on which state you live in, the moneys may or may not be protected from state taxes.

■ If you choose a Keogh Plan that does not involve an insurance policy, you will have to decide on a trustee (the law requires that this be a bank or savings institution). You can then decide how they are to invest your moneys—stocks, bonds, mutual funds, real estate, a simple savings account, or some combination of these.

■ If you hire helpers—secretaries, typists, researchers, and the like—you are required by law to have a plan for them as well (and contribute to it) if you have one for yourself and if your employees work more than twenty hours a week, or a thousand hours over a twelve-month period. Check with your financial adviser or the SBA for regulations regarding your employees' plan and the contributions you must make.

Tax savings from Keogh Plans continue during retirement, which may be on or after age fifty-nine and a half but no later than seventy and a half years. If you wish, you can withdraw all of the moneys and perhaps qualify for five-year income averaging, which mitigates the effect of receiving a large amount of income in one year if previous years' incomes have been substantially lower. Or you can draw on your Keogh over your life expectancy during retirement years, when your income may be lower.

Social Security benefits

The government regulations on Social Security payments and benefits are complicated. But the freelance writer should become acquainted with them and keep track of his contributions throughout the lifetime of his business. Full-time self-employed freelancers are required to contribute according to their earnings. (Many writers feel that the Social Security regulations are unjust, since they tax the self-employed at a rate higher than the one used for people who are employed by others. But the self-employed writer receives consideration others do not [see below]).

What you must pay into Social Security depends on your gross and net earnings from each year of writing, as well as the amount of time you spend doing the work. If you are earning only a bare minimum or are not writing continually, this will not apply to you, even though you may be receiving royalties from a lone book done earlier.

Since there are borderline cases—you may consider yourself a full-time writer although you aren't earning a living from it yet and are subsisting on a small retainer of some sort or your parents' or spouse's largesse—it's best to check the law itself. Talk to your financial adviser, check the books mentioned in the Resources chapter or with your local Social Security office for a copy of the law. If you *are* writing continually and have net earnings of $400 a year or more, you are required to contribute to your Social Security plan just as if you were employed by someone else. Here is an additional clause you might want to consider: If your net earnings aren't $400 but your gross is $600 or more, you can pay into your Social Security account *if* your net earnings were at least $400 in two out of three previous years. You can't use this method more than five times. Since there are other qualifications as well, check first to see if you qualify for this option. In some ways Social Security helps freelancers more than it does people not self-employed, so learn what you have coming as a result of paying your share.

As a self-employed person, you pay only on your *net* earnings, while others pay on their gross salary. And you may include moneys earned from related work as well—on any of those jobs suggested throughout this book as solutions to your cash-flow problems: consulting, teaching, lecturing, research for others, and so on. (Note: In a situation where you're considered in someone's employ and have earned income from full- or part-time employment as well as from your freelancing, your Social Security payments will be based on the earnings from that employment first and freelancing second.) Since each freelancer's situation is an individual matter—teaching writing on a part-time basis, lecturing elsewhere, and freelance writing, for instance—there's no way to generalize about the eventual payout. Your accountant or tax adviser should be consulted regarding your own case.

Depending on how you look at it, here's some good news and some bad news: Social Security taxes are on the rise. The wage base, that portion of earnings covered by Social Security, was increased on January 1, 1981, to $29,900 (from the previous figure of $17,700). The tax rate for self-employed persons is 8.10 percent. And it's scheduled to increase automatically each year thereafter. These changes may be reflected in any corporate retirement plans in which you might be participating if you're moonlighting. Check these periodically with your accountant to see how they affect you.

You don't get the benefits from Social Security, of course, until you reach "insured status." That's when you've made enough payments over a certain amount of time, figured in quarters. As a freelancer, you again have an advantage, as you do not have to receive a certain amount of your income during any one quarter. If you net $400 or more during the calendar year (or over the longer period mentioned above), you qualify. (However, if you stop freelancing for too long you could lose your "insured status.") For these and other reasons already mentioned, it's advisable to stay current with the ramifications of Social Security regulations.

On your long-range calendar, note a specific time to review your Social Security status. Send them a postcard every two or three years requesting an update on your accumulated earnings. (There is a prepared card for this purpose which you can pick up at the local office.) You must request this information yourself, not your spouse or secretary. Don't procrastinate. Corrections cannot be made after three years, three months, and fifteen days from the calendar year in which you earned the money.

Your net-worth ledger sheet should reflect these figures. You might also want to include the benefit amounts Social Security offers other than retirement pay: disability, Medicare, and survivor benefits.

Freelancers have an added advantage when it comes to Social Security and earnings after retirement. Normally a retired person can earn no more than $250 a month (or $3,000 in one year) without a reduction in his Social Security payments. Under Social Security rules, royalties attributable to a copyright obtained before the taxable year in which a beneficiary attains age 65 shall be excluded from gross income from self-employment for deduction purposes provided that the property to which the copyright relates was created by the beneficiary's own personal efforts. Royalties attributable to a copyright obtained in or after the taxable year in which a beneficiary attains age 65 shall be included in gross income from self-employment for deduction purposes.

Some pointers on Social Security:

■ You must *apply* for benefits. At that time the exact amount of your monthly cash benefit is determined.

■ You may elect to retire at age sixty-two instead of sixty-five. If you retire before sixty-five, however, your benefits are reduced to take account of the longer period of time over which you will receive payments.

■ If you continue to work past sixty-five, you get a special credit. This "bonus" (1 percent a year or 1/12 of 1 percent a month) is added to your retirement benefit for the time you worked and did not get benefits from age sixty-five to seventy-two.

Insurance

Many workers' total financial plans include a life insurance policy. Freelancers, of course, may also elect this option. If they do, they need to consider three things before deciding which kind—term or cash-value—they wish to purchase: the reasons for buying life insurance; an estimate of present and future needs; and the amount they can afford to spend.

It's been my experience that one usually doesn't have to look for an insurance agent from whom to purchase life insurance. Opportunities to consider all sorts of companies and their plans present themselves constantly, both at the door and through the mail. If you have let it be known around town that you are setting up a freelance business, you, too, I'm certain, will be inundated with solicitations to purchase life insurance.

There are two basic types of policy. *Term,* or *temporary,* life insurance provides protection for only a specific period of time (say, during the years a family has dependent children to provide for), accumulates no cash value, and has premiums that are raised whenever the current protection period expires and the policy is renewed. *Cash-value,* or *permanent,* life insurance provides level benefits, accumulates cash value, and generally has premiums that are constant over your entire lifetime. Term insurance was designed to cover a temporary need—for example, the unpaid balance of a major purchase, mortgage coverage, or a risky financial venture. It provides maximum protection at the lowest cost, when you're figuring the short run. Term policies generally come in five-year multiples, but you can purchase a term policy for as little as one year. Cash-value life insurance policies vary considerably. Most feature level death benefits throughout the life of the insurees (these remain the same under all conditions) and level premium payments. You pay the same amount each year whether you're twenty-five or sixty. The cash value is always available as policy loans or collateral for loans at a relatively low interest rate.

You'll also want to consider the length of time you'll need income in the event of the death of the insured, and the amount of income per month needed for that period.

Deduct from that total figure any other moneys that will be available—for example, Social Security benefits, annuities, royalties, moneys from other investments.

Determine whether you need or want to leave a lump-sum as well as a monthly-income benefit. If this is too much for your budget, you might want to purchase a decreasing-term policy and wait to buy a whole-life policy until you have more income.

If you've recently purchased insurance and want to add an additional decreasing-term policy, try to get a reduced rate by applying for a rider attachment to the first policy. The company saves by selling two policies at once and should pass at least some of those savings on to you.

Just because a policy pays dividends doesn't mean it is your best bet, by the way. You are paying a higher premium to receive those dividends, and those dividends are often less than you could earn if you bought a term policy and invested the difference.

Some other points to remember:

■ The payment period may differ from policy to policy. On a twenty-year policy one company might require you to pay over the entire period, another only a portion of that time. ·

■ You'll be looking for convertibility without additional medical examinations (the opportunity to convert a term policy to cash-value policy during the term period without the requirement of proof of insurability).

■ You'll want the option for your beneficiary to draw the money out in a lump sum as well as just on a monthly basis.

■ If you put your money in a savings account you can get it at any time without a penalty. Withdrawing the cash value of an insurance policy is a different matter. You either surrender the policy or borrow against the cash value as collateral. (At going interest rates, however, the low interest rate charged for borrowing against your policy might be one of your best bets if you do need to borrow.) But, of course, the cash value of many policies (and therefore the amount you can borrow) is quite low in the early years, which might be when you most need the money.

■ Interest paid on a savings account is taxable income at the end of the year. Accrued income in an insurance policy isn't taxable until the policy is surrendered. The issue here is that though the money isn't taxable, you can be getting less than you'd net after taxes from a higher-interest investment. However, advice as to which path is best for you should come from your financial adviser, who knows you and your circumstances.

Research the various possibilities before even discussing them with an insurance broker. Then get figures and policy descriptions from more than one agent and compare them carefully. After you purchase a policy take the trouble to spell out the details of the benefits, dates of premium payments, etc., in the ledger where you've recorded the other elements of your financial picture. This saves having to read through the fine print each time you want to be reminded of what insurance liabilities and benefits you have.

Statistics show that one should consider disability insurance before life insurance. The key element in the disability insurance premium is the waiting period. The longer the waiting period before benefits begin, the lower the premium. The second element is the definition of disability. Look for a policy that pays when you're "unable to perform duties of your or similar occupation." Otherwise, you may not receive the money you thought you would unless you become totally incapacitated.

For disability, medical, or dental insurance, an individual is usually at a decided disadvantage. He's obliged to pay higher premiums than he would be if he acquired the insurance through a group. Many freelancers receive coverage under a spouse's or family's group policy through a spouse's place of business. Others join groups through professional writers' organizations. And still others have found they can negotiate much more reasonable coverage on an individual basis by thoroughly researching the possibilities through their own insurance agent in their own locality.

Libel insurance

The number of libel cases and the cost of libel insurance are definitely on the increase. "Litigation in all areas has increased in the past few years," Larry Worrall, assistant vice-president, Employers Reinsurance Corp., one of the largest libel insurers, told *Folio* magazine. Libel suits against magazines are rising, as are those against book publishers. Part of the reason for the rise is the increase in investigative journalism as well as recent changes in the laws that formerly protected members of the press. And the Supreme Court has left more decisions on libel cases to the individual states to determine.

The problem is that in most cases part if not all of the costs involved in settling a libel suit are passed on from publisher to writer. And the costs are far too high for the freelancer's budget to absorb.

"You may never have been sued for libel. You may never have even thought of being sued," says Michael S. Lasky in *Law and the Writer.*" But *it can come from anywhere at any time from anyone.*" [Italics mine.]

In brief, Lasky reports that if any of the following three elements is missing, there is no libel:

Defamation—Generally defined as injury to reputation, it must apply to an identifiable person and it must be published.

Identification—Unless the plaintiff can prove that the defamatory meaning actually applies to that individual, there is no libel. A third party must understand that the reference is to the plaintiff whether by nickname, pseudonym, or circumstance.

Publication—Printing, posting, or circulating are the first steps in publication of a libel; someone reading the message is the second step. Most courts subscribe to what is called the *single publication rule*. This means an entire edition of a newspaper or magazine is treated as a single instance of publication rather than every single copy constituting a separate case of libel.

According to John Hohenberg, author of *The Professional Journalist*, the following definition has been used in the Columbia Graduate School of Journalism (and its undergraduate predecessor) for more than sixty years as a criterion by which a libelous publication may be recognized:

Libel is defamation expressed in writing, printing, or other visible form. . . .

Any printed or written words are defamatory which impute to the plaintiff that he has been guilty of any crime, fraud, dishonesty, immorality, vice, or dishonorable conduct, or has been accused or suspected of any such misconduct; or which suggest that the plaintiff is suffering from any infectious disorder; or which have a tendency to injure him in his office, profession, calling, or trade. And so, too, are all words which hold the plaintiff up to contempt, hatred, scorn, or ridicule, and which, by thus engendering an evil opinion of him in the minds of right-thinking men, tend to deprive him of friendly intercourse and society. *Odgers on Libel and Slander.*

Hohenberg also cites the New York state definition of libel (Section 1340 of the New York Penal Code) as follows:

A malicious publication by writing, printing, picture, effigy, sign, or otherwise than by mere speech, which exposes any living person or the memory of any person deceased, to hatred, contempt, ridicule, or obloquy, or which has a tendency to injure any person, corporation, or association of persons, in his or their business or occupation, is a libel.

The freelancer's disadvantages mount because, while he often bears most of the burden, he has less opportunity to purchase libel insurance at a reasonable rate. Says Lasky:

> Firms such as Employers Reinsurance Corporation of Kansas City, Missouri, offer libel insurance to publishers but rarely to freelance writers . . . [their] minimum premium on a libel insurance policy for a book ranges from $500 to $2,500, but those premiums may be increased to recognize unusual libel or copyright infringement exposures. The premium is payable one time only. For accounting purposes, the policy is issued for a one-year period, but the book is actually covered as long as it is not revised or supplemented and until the statute of limitations, which runs from one to three years in various states, has expired."

The top writers' organizations are constantly looking into ways freelancers can obtain reasonable libel insurance. Where all this will end is anyone's guess. But it will pay you to keep as informed as possible.

Some writers report they have managed to get libel coverage by purchasing an umbrella clause on their homeowner's insurance policy. Others, in a position to incorporate, have found that they, like a publisher, can get this coverage for premiums as low as several hundred dollars a year.

Some other tips from lawyers, professional writers, and editors:

■ Get written releases from institutions, minors' legal guardians, and anyone mentioned in any sensitive story you may be writing.
■ Discuss the story with a libel lawyer before you investigate or write it.
■ Double-check any photographs of criminals or people under indictment.
■ Be careful with any sensitive story but especially those involving professionals or alluding to bankruptcy.

The final test might be the easiest for anyone to answer: How would you feel if this were being written about you?

Chapter 15
On
Your
Own

■■■

The case for syndication

Once you've written something, it's a joy to think you can get paid for it again and again. Syndication is one of the most lucrative ways to secure that pleasure. As proof, look at Erma Bombeck, Sylvia Porter, Art Buchwald, Charles M. Schulz, and Jack Anderson.

Syndicates are essentially agents in that they don't generate the material in-house: they promote and sell an author's or artist's material to the newspaper and magazine market. Naturally there's a contractual arrangement. The usual split between a syndicate and author is fifty-fifty on all moneys received, less the expense of producing the camera-ready material. A syndicate might start by offering a package of several new columns by different authors to a long list of outlets. As an added incentive they'd probably set a low rate for the newest material, say $10 for each column. If a particular feature takes off, runs for several months, and proves popular with readers, the syndicate would then try to negotiate the prices upward. In other words, it can take quite a while to earn the big money—if ever. So even if your material is accepted by a national syndicate, hold off spending the money until you have it.

Landing a spot with a large, national syndicate is a long shot. The competition is tough. Over ten thousand freelancers a year submit feature ideas to one of the large syndicates. Over three thousand features, other than cartoons, are already syndicated to daily and weekly newspapers on such subjects as medicine, travel, business, self-help, astrology, politics, and humor. To get an idea of the competition, scan the lists in *Editor & Publisher Year Book, Working Press of the Nation,* and other directories at your library.

The alternative is self-syndication. "The prospects of self-syndication are good if you are prepared to work *very hard,*" says one often-published travel writer. Much depends on how much money you're aiming for and how many outlets you need to make syndication pay for your efforts.

A self-syndication success story

When some sixty syndicates turned down a liberated-girl cartoon feature by Ricky Kane, she didn't get mad—she got a better idea. Kane remembered a children's word game in which a clue phrase (singing bird with a beard) is countered with a short, rhyming, synonymous expression (hairy canary). With more rigid rules—the rhyming words must have the same number of syllables (Alcoholics Anonymous: Sobriety Society)—she developed a feature called "Wordy Gurdy." She took samples to the *Washington Star* Syndicate, and they bought it.

The *Philadelphia Inquirer* and six other newspapers signed up for "Wordy Gurdy," and Kane seemed on her way to success. She offered a $10 prize to readers sending in the best word rhymes, and was soon swamped with thousands of letters. "It was visible proof that people liked the feature," she recalls. Even so, the *Inquirer* dropped "Wordy Gurdy" for another feature. Soon afterward the *Washington Star* Syndicate canceled as well.

The same day she received notice of the cancellation, Kane stuffed all the reader mail she could carry into a large pillowcase and marched into the office of the president of United Feature Syndicate. "There!" she said. "Look at this!" She dumped the letters in the middle of his floor and went into a five-minute sales pitch. Result? "Wordy Gurdy" got a new syndicated home.

"Reader participation was the gold key," says Kane. "Readers loved the game. They were addicted to it. Teachers were using it as an assignment for students. People were staying up late nights trying to be original so they could get the prize and their names in the paper." But the mail on the president's carpet was the clincher.

Fortunately, the deal was struck on the spot. Fortunate for United Feature Syndicate, that is, for when an editor of the *Dallas Morning News* learned that "Wordy Gurdy" was being dropped by the *Washington Star* Syndicate, he sent word to Field Newspaper Syndicate— and Kane arrived home with her pillowcase of mail to find a message from Field: they wanted "Wordy Gurdy," too.

Making your own breaks

Your own efforts at syndication will receive a large boost as well if you can show an editor that your material will draw a good reader response.

Dennis Cleary decided to self-syndicate two weekly columns, "Men of Independence" (historical coverage of the American Revolution) and "Trivia Trips" (every subject under the American sun), after he "got tired of receiving mimeographed rejection notices from national syndicate offices."

"Have something to say," he advises, "and get it in print. Getting it in print makes you humble *quick,* especially if you haven't perfected your style and content."

Another reason for self-syndication is the joy of it: "Every single column should be fun or have at least one memorable line in it. People read for pleasure," says columnist Michael Novak, "and regular readers have a high appreciation for the art of writing. Practicing the art is to join with one's readers in the common pleasure."

Marilyn Holmes, former manager of the Capitol News Service, Denver, handled syndication differently from both Cleary and Novak. Noting that Colorado dailies were cutting back on reporters sent to cover the capitol, she stepped in and offered a supplement to the wire services with personalized material for each city and its legislators. She added a section on capitol news for a number of Colorado weeklies that couldn't use the features or hard news she offered the dailies.

While much of the material is of value to all the papers, she personalized the first two or three paragraphs for each area and sent the stories out on a telecopier. (When she started out, however, she was shipping them by bus to the client newspapers.) "The one thing that they all bought was the voting records of the city or town's legislators," she says. "And because of the physical features of the state, certain counties needed different kinds of information on agriculture, ski reports, tourist tips, water-quality control, air pollution, insurance data, etc."

Newspapers are not the only outlet for your syndicated material. "If your idea would fit into a trade magazine, for instance, it's possible to line up a number of these for your cartoon or column, if they're not in competition with each other," says Julian Block, who sold his tax tips to multiple markets for years.

The occasional article or column can be syndicated in much the same manner as a daily or weekly feature. The writer arranges to supply a number of newspapers with material on a timely basis—more or less regularly, depending on the agreement with the client. This method works well when the writer is stationed in a fascinating or newsworthy place. John Dornberg, in Munich, wrote regularly for the *Paris Herald Tribune;* Anne Perryman covered Southeast Asia and Africa; and Arky Gonzalez and Alan Levy self-syndicated their stories from all over Europe this way. Many travel writers find this is a profitable approach.

A realistic approach

Here is a potpourri of tips from syndicate editors, newspaper editors who buy syndicated material, and self-syndicators. Before you bundle samples of your comic strip or column off to newspapers or magazines for consideration, listen to these suggestions:

Know your competition. Study the market *very well* before you begin. If an editor already has "Pogo" or "Peanuts" or Erma Bombeck, he doesn't want another. (One editor recently tried to break this pattern. He had been running one popular feature, but agreed to replace it with a similar—and competing—one. The experiment lasted one month. He was deluged with complaint mail from readers, which forced him to drop the second feature and restore the original.) Come up with a truly *original* idea. Or at least ask, Does my material fill a gap in today's journalism?

Test any idea you come up with on friends and family (near and far). Then see if any editor you know will help by running your feature free with a reader-response gimmick built in. (This way the editor gets a chance to test his audience-response setup as well.) Don't think just of large metropolitan dailies for your testing. Consider small weeklies, shoppers, agency newsletters, the library's giveaway paper, local radio and TV—any outlet that will help you judge an audience's reaction to your idea.

Some additional hints:

1. Get your material published locally first. Then move on to a regional market if you can. Try to self-syndicate even if you want to move into the larger national syndicates. You'll learn your trade.

2. Sell by personalized mail, with a follow-up by telephone if any interest is expressed.

3. Approach a less busy associate or assistant editor in person. Give him enough material to show you can deliver high-quality material over a long period of time.

4. If you sign a contract, see if you can get a guarantee for a certain length of time.

5. *Study the market all over again* if you don't sell the first time around. You may be off target with your idea or wrong in your timing. Don't expect success overnight. Even "Peanuts" took a while to become established.

There are basically two ways to sell your material—by mail and in person. Those who swear by the former advise, "*Sell by mail.* Large mass mailings, though, will waste your time and money. Instead, focus on a dozen outlets at a time, personalize your cover letter and package, and target it well. If you don't get a reply, write again—a short, personal query." And the advocates of the personal approach: *"Sell in person.* If you take the time to get out and around your region, you can meet the editors personally, even though your visit is brief. Be businesslike; be prepared to answer questions. And ask a few, too. Then you won't be just another name on a letterhead." And of course a combination of the two approaches is a possibility worth considering.

While it's true that a few years ago the newsprint squeeze wreaked havoc on the syndicate business, both in newspapers and periodicals, today there is more hope for would-be syndicators. Imaginative editors who need to compete creatively with the electronic media for their audience are changing or enlarging their formats. They're constantly searching for that fresh idea that will recapture former readers and attract new ones. It's up to you to cash in on that need. Watch what they're up to. Think ahead to discover what they might be looking for. Research your markets, over and over, as thoroughly as you can. It will save you time, effort, and money in the long run.

What's in it for you

Writers with big syndicates can earn $10,000 to $20,000 in the early years, very gradually working up toward six-figure income if their features take off. But the self-syndicated writer usually can't expect such money, since his promotional efforts can only partly compete with those of the large syndicates.

For instance, self-syndicated writers absorb all costs of duplicating and mailing their material to the individual outlets. Because of this, smart writers determine first how much income they require, then make arrangements to publish with a specific number of newspapers or other outlets (trade magazines, for instance). They supply the material on a weekly, biweekly, or monthly basis. Such a self-syndication plan is similar to convincing an editor to put you on a "stringer" or retainer basis.

Producing camera-ready material can be expensive. In many instances, however, it's the *only* way outlets buying material will accept your work. Prices vary according to geography and demand, so before offering to send your column this way, see what photo-typesetting will cost in your area. Figure what a sample mailing to, say, fifty target outlets would set you back—add up the costs of camera-ready copy, packaging, and postage. Remember that newspapers pay for your work based on *their* circulation. Small dailies and weeklies can't pay much, so you'll need to build a volume business if this is your only kind of outlet.

Don't be greedy—keep your prices competitive. Two to ten dollars for all your work may seem an infinitesimal amount, but bear in mind that those figures will multiply.

The money you can make varies enormously. For weeklies, your starting pay might be fifty cents to a dollar. Tops would be around $7.50. Daily newspapers might start you at $5 to $10 or perhaps $25. An arrangement with a large-circulation paper where you offered a regular column a certain number of weeks a year could bring you as much as $50 or more each time your material appeared, but this is rare. Payment depends on a number of factors, including your skill at negotiating, the outlet's standard fees, and how much the editor wants your work.

One-shots, such as travel articles, are paid for on a variable scale, too. You can get as little as $15 and as much as $150 for the same article, pictures included. Unfortunately, only trial and error will tell you which end of the spectrum you can expect.

Three last tips from those who've self-syndicated their material for a good number of years: Save huge amounts of postage when you're just starting out by contacting local newspapers first and building up a following. Count on submitting to five times as many outlets as you will actually sell. The hardest part is getting editors to look at what you have for sale.

What makes a self-publisher run?

Out on the publishing plains—on the frontier of self-publishing—sites for homesteading are more wide-open than ever. Basically, what is required are a strong belief in one's own work, perseverance, some organizational skills, patience, and a degree of know-how—about writing and placing ads, about printer's language, and about dealing with retail outlets that sell books, either as a primary or secondary business.

In modern times, "self-publishing" has come to mean "vanity publishing" in the minds of many. And there *are* companies who will gladly take thousands of your dollars to print your book. Period. Usually they run come-on ads in magazines for writers, as well as in the national and local press. In your local paper's want-ad section your're apt to see an announcement stating that a "nationally known publisher will be in town to interview writers" on such-and-such a date. Stay away. No one will say it can't work—but usually it doesn't. The chances of your book, so printed, reaching much of an audience at all are slim. In most cases it will end up collecting dust in your attic—if you still have one after putting up the cash to have it published.

But true self-publishing is something else. It is a booming business. These days more books than ever are being self-published—fiction, nonfiction, poetry, art, design, crafts, guides, etc. Some are amateurish in their production. But others are quite professional—and as good as any commercially published book. They, like any book brought out by a large publishing concern with a list of hundreds, can bomb, or they can break the bank. As a self-publisher, the author *is* the publisher—as well as the designer, salesman, distributor, and publicity agent—of his book. Fortunately, he also collects *all* the money from any sales of his volume.

How do you start out if you're going to make a profit? First, with a sound, well-researched idea for a book (appealing to a wide audience), a garage or basement space for storage of the finished product before it's sold, some part-time help for packing, shipping, typing, and so forth. It is also wise, they say, to have a post office box (more businesslike), and if you can negotiate it, a credit arrangement with a printer. Next, you want critics, experts, etc., to endorse your book so your advertising will have credibility.

There are certainly many reasons successful self-publishers give for continuing in the business. They'll cite the ghosts of Blake, Poe, Whitman, and, more recently, books like *How to Be Your Own Best Friend, Winning Through Intimidation,* and the *Whole Earth Catalog* series.

"Self-publishing is an affirmation of your belief in your own best bit, because no publisher will care quite as much about your work as you do," says Patricia O'Toole, a freelancer from Los Angeles, who collaborated with Irene Gresick on a book about self-publishing.

Len Fulton, dean of the self-publishers, started seventeen years ago. He puts out five small-press trade publications (the annual *International Directory of Little Magazines and Small Presses* and the monthly *Small Press Review* among them). Says Fulton, "When you're paying for the typesetting yourself, you begin to see that certain words, phrases, and clevernesses—some of the things you thought were ingenious—are not so ingenious, not so necessary to the book. There's a fiscal pressure on you that causes you to be a *very tough editor.* [Italics mine.] Everybody ought to do it at least once."

Ways to start up: romantic and classic

Novelist Dorothy Bryant falls into the romantic mold of self-publisher. Bryant decided to self-publish her second work, *The Comforter*. In spite of the fact that she had *no* experience and no opportunity to get advice from knowledgeable sources, she managed to sell over three thousand books in five years, mostly by word of mouth among her friends and admirers. There was no formal advertising, no radio or TV shows, few bookstore sales. Yet she realized $3,200 on her $1,800 investment. That's about 15.5 percent annually, which is a better return than many savings vehicles provide. Of course, if none of them had sold, she would have been out $1,800.

If your book is so great that once people get hold of it they can't *help* but push it for you, Bryant's route might work for you, too.

A more classic plan is that of Phil Philcox, publisher of *The Logo Design Book*—published under the name Phil Adams). Philcox developed a mini-course in graphics design, primarily on logos. As a former commercial artist, he saw the need for such a book. He approached traditional big publishers, who offered him no advance and only a 12-percent royalty. Says Philcox, "The mathematics didn't work out: I was permanently hunchbacked from working over the drawing board for twelve months, with both hands stuffy-fingered from typing, and my possible income was $18,950, *if* we sold five thousand copies!" His point, of course, was that a year out of his life for only a *possible* income of $18,000 or $19,000 wasn't enough incentive. It seemed too iffy. He was certain there was a ready market for his idea.

Feeling readers who applied the techniques outlined in the book would earn $50 to $100 the first time they tried them, he bravely put a $50 price tag on the cover and decided to publish it himself.

Philcox did indeed know his territory. His commercial-art background helped him reach a specialized audience: he put together a professional presentation and approached the editors of periodicals in the field. He offered one copy of the book, one 5x7 black-and-white photo of the author, one camera-ready book review, three camera-ready ads with order coupons, miscellaneous sales literature, including a brochure, and a cover letter offering them 50 percent of the cover price for each copy sold if they'd run the ad over their address.

By the time I heard his story, he'd sold 1,300 copies to net $48,275 and reported he'd barely touched the total market he envisioned for his book. "I've found the best way for me to sell books is to share the profits with someone of lesser talent and more influence. There are people out there with some money (for printing expenses) and some influence (for getting free ads in magazines) who want to leap on the publishing bandwagon if they're going to make money," he said.

Dee Pattee's paperback volume was put together when the Olympics were coming to Munich. Dee, who'd helped many people learn the ins and outs of Munich quickly through her job as a tour guide, saw her book through the printing stage herself. Now revised and in its second edition, it's a Munich visitor's prize.

Such city guides, state guides, guides to everything from parks and fishing spots to film-star graves, and many other kinds of books have appeared because they had an angel—their author—who believed in them enough to self-publish them.

One writer began her publishing venture when she remembered the slogan, "I can get it for you wholesale." She started a central clearinghouse in her area of all the great bargain outlets and published a book of tips on good buys in her region. She learned by doing, asking questions of everyone along the way, clipping newspaper ads, checking out all the directories she could find. She collected names of people who could lead her and called on manufacturers and all the outlet stores and discount hideaways she could uncover. Working out of an office in her car, she did the legwork for hundreds of people who didn't have the time or energy for it.

Her first 48-page catalog had over a hundred listings. By now, a few years later, the volume has grown to a 150-page volume with more than 700 listings. Her out-of-pocket expenses for the first run came to around fifty cents a booklet. Why her success? She wrote a light, breezy, amusing book that offered good bargains, thereby giving her readers two of their basic requirements—entertainment and economy. Her market strategy: She went to bookstores in her area. She hired someone else to supply grocery stores, drugstores, newsstands, and other outlets (including the discount houses themselves). She sent out a press release that captured the fancy of a feature editor at her city newspaper. From there the booklet virtually sold itself.

A familiar but important refrain: Reseach the project first. Look for financial pitfalls. Your budget should be scrutinized continually, especially on your first time out. You need to be certain you don't overextend your bank account. Next, get acquainted with several printers in your area. Get their specification sheets and discuss approximate costs with them. When you do, have a firm idea of the length of your book, trim size, kind of cover, and the details regarding any artwork. You'll also want to discuss paper stock and the number of copies you'll require in the print run. (The more copies printed at one time, the lower your costs per copy will be.) After you have your printer's figures, get an accountant's advice. And read all the volumes on self-publishing you can find in your library.

Since experiences along these paths vary widely according to your area, up-front money, publishing expertise, the idea behind the publication, and general management, it's best to talk or write to a successful small publisher in your region who is doing what you would like to do. I'm not suggesting you go straight to the person who would be your biggest competition if you did start, though some people do. (Or they'll work for a while in someone else's operation, learn the ropes, then skip off to start on their own.) First find a going concern in a neighboring state. Talk to the proprietors about the business on the local level. This gives you a chance to investigate possible problems in your neighborhood before you face them yourself.

Discuss printers and other details with them. They'll already know which ones are overpriced, what specialized outlets exist for your promotional campaign, and how to handle numerous details of the self-publishing business in your area.

As an alternative, ask commercial artists, designers, and people in public relations or advertising for this specialized information. See if they can recommend the titles of production and design books you should read.

Seminars and workshops on many of the aspects of self-publishing are beginning to appear all over the country. Some give you the hands-on experience you may need before venturing into the field. Look for notice of them in *Publishers Weekly, Folio,* and other trade publications, as well as in your local press.

Search for up-front funding (investors, savings, loans, grants, etc.). Can you get someone to invest in your work for a percentage of the proceeds? Talk to a shrewd business person. Tell him about the successes of other self-publishers.

Advertising and promotion will require you to pound pavements or to invest in some direct-mail advertising. Fulfillment (filling book orders) is the other side of the coin. It can be almost as pleasurable as banking the cash—but someone has to *spend time doing it.*

If you're going to succeed at self-publishing, *it's up to you.* As self-publisher, you maintain control of all elements of manufacture, promotion, and distribution of your book. The amount of money you have to spend on the project and your expertise (or the experts you borrow or hire) may even produce a product superior to that of an established publishing house.

If you're going to self-publish, you'll have to be prepared to do yourself or supervise:

Content editing, copyediting
Book and jacket design (text, heads, artwork)
Layout, paste-up, typeface selection, paper selection
Typesetting
Printing, binding
Calculating press run, pricing
Publicizing, promoting
Sales: wholesale, retail, bookstores, libraries, subsidiary rights,
    direct-mail, advertising, personal appearances, etc.

Can you make a dollar out of fifteen cents?

One of the most successful entrepreneurs I know asks himself that question often. It is a refrain that he uses to stimulate his creative juices and to remind himself that there's always another way to skin a cat, if he can only discover what it is. Over the years he's taught himself to do just that. So have legions of self-publishers. Many of them have found the quickest way for them to do it is to master the art of "wheedling and dealing."

In fact, according to Patricia O'Toole, "Mastery of the art of whee-dling is essential for all but the affluent self-publisher. The more that can be begged or borrowed, traded or stolen, the less forbidding the task. No matter how despicable the practice seems, wheedling is necessary. After a little wincing, it comes naturally. Most writers have mastered Librarian Pestering. It's a matter of applying these principles to all your publishing needs." Or you can barter. O'Toole suggests you try trading your writing skills for use of an IBM Com-poser or other word processor that sets type. "Now's the time to make peace with Cousin Norman, the business whiz," she advises. "It boils down to this: Ask for everybody's help. The worst you'll get is a boot print on your seat. At best, those you ask will think enough of your work to lend assistance or advice."

Other self-publishing paths

Publishing your own magazine or newspaper is another do-it-yourself activity that writers are increasingly investigating. One of their role models must be the now-familiar story of DeWitt Wallace, founder of *Reader's Digest*. As a voracious young reader Wallace kept a file of magazine articles that particularly interested him. Finally, believing there was a market for his idea of reprinting already published work cut and edited heavily to his liking and unable to interest publishers in his sample magazine, he borrowed $1,800 and brought out his own magazine. The first print run was for 5,000 copies. Of course it has grown now to sales worldwide in the many millions of copies a month to become one of the biggest success stories in magazine publication.

If you think you've got a better idea, as Wallace did, are brave enough to put your money and efforts where your mouth is, your start-up will be a process similar to that for book publishing. Many of the same rules apply. The success you achieve will depend, in part, on your writing ability, your organizational expertise, the competition, the amount of money you've arranged up front, your target audience, and your system of distribution.

Folio magazine reported that Jim Crockett turned a small-time quarterly into a million-dollar operation. "In the process he has turned down ads that *Playboy* would be glad to run, severely limited editorial white space and graphics, used no advertising salespeople, and produced a monthly magazine with a staff of three." Crazy? No—he simply knows his readers and how to reach them. His magazine is called *Guitar Player*. The readers rely on the magazine for technical data in their field. The first year he put out four issues, thirty-odd pages each. It grossed $20,000. It's now a monthly. Crockett's background: journalism and music.

It's also possible to self-publish newsletters. The process works approximately the same way. You put up the money, and mail the newsletter to people on your list (friends, names you've garnered from free or purchased lists, lists you've managed to put together yourself). Eventually, you may have a valuable specialized list which you can sell to others.

G. Douglas Hafely, Jr., edits and publishes *CA$H Newsletter*, which has been in circulation for over two years. Betty Yarmon's PR newsletter *PR Aids*, the *Freelancer's Newsletter*, and the *Newsletter on Newsletters* were started when someone saw a real need, got to work, and filled the gap.

The range and variety is almost endless, it seems, in the field of self-publication. The small-town weekly newspaper, the big-city "underground" or "alternative" paper, the publishing co-op (a group of writers pooling resources)—all are popular routes today for writers with an urge to publish.

Some writers continue to self-publish their books or magazines even after they discover they can get them published through existing channels. Their reasoning: Why not, when we can reach an even wider, well-targeted audience and make more money this way?

If you decide to get involved in self-publishing, you'll discover a congenial group of nonconformists ahead of you. They even have their own annual conventions, which are reported in *Publishers Weekly,* with the agreements and frictions between them quoted as attentively as if they were already "establishment." Len Fulton, seeing the problems resulting from small publishers' beginning to act like large ones, cautioned the American Association of Independent Presses to "stay modest, essential, non-glorified; build up mailing lists and share information and services."

Thanks to their diversification and strong sense of independence, quite a few self-publishers these days *are* learning, like my entrepreneur friend, how to make a dollar out of fifteen cents.

Chapter 16
Miscellaneous Tips

■■■

The following are valuable hints gathered from writers throughout the world.

Article ideas are around you all the time. Most busy freelancers find that as they get on a regular schedule of researching and querying markets they uncover an abundance of ideas and places to offer them. Their problem, on the contrary, is to keep the workable ideas in perspective and to discard or file for later use those ideas that aren't right for them or aren't ripe yet.

Still, would-be freelancers find it difficult to recognize the right idea or angle and are always asking published writers, "Where do you get your ideas?" Look first at what constitutes a good idea for an article: a subject and a specific angle on that subject. (Instead of deciding to write on "inflation," a professional would propose a feature on how one family in Middletown, Ohio, is coping with rising costs to, say, *McCall's* or *Good Housekeeping.*) Also, an article idea will sell more quickly if it is important and timely, taking into consideration basic human drives (sexual gratification, maternal love, self-preservation, acquisitiveness, etc.). These selling ideas, which are of vital interest to readers, should also offer something extra—new details on an old story, added insight into an age-old problem.

Since ideas are everywhere, you should be looking for them wherever you go—at conventions and professional meetings, as well as doing business, cashing your checks, sitting at the laundromat, traveling to a relative's, having a medical checkup, or fighting with your lover. But observing isn't enough. Once an idea has clicked in your mind, jot a note to yourself so that you're clearly reminded of it when you are next at the typewriter. Otherwise the clever notion will disappear with yesterday's newspaper or in the heat of today's frantic schedule. And as soon as possible, draft a query about your idea and the angle you'd follow—a couple of brief but very specific paragraphs will suffice at this point—and list at least six possible markets for the story. Then list ten to a dozen possible spin-off markets. With this plan, you have already conquered the vagueness that surrounds most beginners' writing wishes, and have committed yourself to a professionally conceived follow-through.

From the above you can conclude that **getting ideas is only the start.** Organizing your thoughts and insights is an essential next step. In fact, it should perhaps be the *first* step. For that, even professional writers who are blocked may well want to try a couple of fundamental exercises: *reading as a writer* and *creative listmaking.*

Everybody knows that we learn to write by reading. But while we admit that we read to pick up ideas on style (as well as subject matter), to upgrade our vocabularies, or to sharpen our use of language, we seldom take the trouble to analyze *in detail* exactly how an admired book or article is put together. Yet such detailed and exhaustive analysis can be as useful for professionals as for beginners.

Detailed analysis consists of conscientiously noting every aspect of a paragraph or a page. What is the pattern of phrases, sentences, and punctuation? Which words have been chosen and placed in what grammatical order to get the passage started? How have related words and syntactical patterns been added to deepen, move, and qualify the opening statement? How has the author managed the economy of structure to get the most expression into the minimum number of words, while still maintaining clarity? How are the transitions effected so that the piece remains unified though it may range over diverse material?

Many of these questions can be answered in your head if you simply take the time to concentrate on what you are reading instead of skimming or skipping along in pursuit of the main idea. But they are answered better, and the answers are more apt to stick in your mind, if you mark the passage with underlinings or a highlighter, or with highlighters of different colors, each color indicating a different aspect of the piece you are analyzing (pink for direct quotes, yellow for indirect, green for transition words and time modifiers, blue for synonyms that stem from the key words in the topic sentence or paragraph, etc.). Such marking enables you to review the *structure* of the passage at a glance.

When you have gone this far, it is common sense to continue your study by imitating the structure you have marked out in a paragraph or page of your own. In a useful exercise of imitation you will try to recreate not only the paragraph and sentence patterns but the tone and sparkle resulting from the author's choice of words. The least such an exercise can do is make you more keenly aware of how many different considerations must be taken into account and fitted together by the craftsman in words.

After you've conscientiously and thoroughly performed such exercises a few times, you will find that in most of your reading you are more aware of style and structure than before, and that your reading is more useful to you as a writer.

Creative listmaking has already been suggested in many of the foregoing chapters, but here I'd like to suggest the most creative use of this tool that has yet come to my attention, a use actually taught in a college course in creative writing. The idea is this: Lists become sentences. To make a list is one fine way of processing words and ideas as a preliminary to the construction of rich, densely loaded sentences. Someone who is told "List things on which you depend" jots down

Organization
Orderliness
Fingernails
Mirrors
Black coffee
The American Heritage Dictionary
My driver's license
My purple Flair pen
Brown paper bags

The amusing and far from useless sentence that might come from her list: Brown paper bags, organization, orderliness, my driver's license, mirrors, black coffee, fingernails, and my purple Flair pen do not fail me when everything else lets me down.

John Ruskin may well have started with lists of adjectives, arranged in sequences that display some jolts of incongruity, when he set about writing the following:

> In a community regulated only by laws of demand and supply . . . the persons who become rich are, generally speaking, industrious, resolute, proud, covetous, prompt, methodical, sensible, unimaginative, insensitive, and ignorant. The persons who remain poor are the entirely foolish, the entirely wise, the idle, the reckless, the humble, the thoughtful, the dull, the imaginative, the sensitive, the well-informed, the improvident, the irregularly and impulsively wicked, the clumsy knave, the open thief, and the entirely merciful, just and godly person. [Italics mine.]

Major and minor markets are all hungry for your material—if, that is, you can write well and you practice analyzing their needs before you submit your material to them. It doesn't matter whether you're willing to give up the idea of fame or recognition for solid cash or are aiming for both by focusing on one or two top markets. Alan R. Blackburn did the former successfully and wrote of his numerous sales to the hidden markets (business annual reports, speeches, fund-raising brochures) in *Writer's Digest.* Jerome E. Kelley, on the other hand, took a hard look at the *Reader's Digest* First Person Award Story. Writes Kelley, "I read it carefully and noticed something that had escaped my attention during the many years I had read the publication. The structure of the piece seemed, to me at least, to be startlingly simple—almost too simple! On a scratch pad I outlined it as follows: A problem exists, the problem intensifies, the problem is solved."

So remember the watchword for matching your talents to the markets for freelance profit: analyze, analyze, analyze.

Once the writer has the article idea, a common next step is **the search for the title.** Here are some of Mort Weisinger's tips to trigger creative titles, from an article in *The Writer.*

Use arresting superlatives to establish that your material or subject is unique. Editors and readers find them hard to resist ("I've Got the World's Most Mysterious Disease"; "He's First Florist of the Land"; "Meet the Highest IQ in America"; "World's Most Charming Business").

Ask a question in your title ("Who is Tokyo Rose?"; "Should You Fight a Traffic Ticket?").

Use captions and the active voice ("Listen! Mark Twain Speaking!"; "The Man Who Takes Wooden Nickels").

Try negative titles to grab attention ("What You Don't Know About Beauty Contests"; "Men—Don't Be Ashamed to Cry").

Use numbers ("Ten Tested Tips for Staying Thin"; "The Man of a Thousand Faces").

Try puns if you're clever ("Big Name Hunter"; "Astrology— Hit or Myth?").

Subsidizing your writing efforts (early on or during lean times) can include MaryAnne Raphael's trick. Laid up with a temporary infirmity so she couldn't go to her full-time job, Ms. Raphael used the time to write several chapters of a book and a book proposal. Then she approached some businessmen and asked if they'd like to invest in her novel. They did. She completed the manuscript and was able to start in full-time on a writing career.

Even while still in college or while learning more about the art of writing longer works, some writers make rather good money from their incidental writing efforts. Mike Porter is one. He told *The Writer,* "If someone had suggested four short years ago that at this stage in my life I would be earning over a hundred dollars a month as a semiprofessional comedy writer, I would have sworn they were ready for the little men in the white suits." Nevertheless, he now provides a monthly comedy service to some twenty-five radio personalities—broadcasters in major cities around the country. Says Porter, "My basic premise is simple: disc jockeys thrive on high ratings. Humor, when used effectively, has proven to be an excellent method to boost the listening audience. Since my clients rely on comedy daily on the air, they burn up copious amounts of material in the process." Porter supplies some of that badly needed material—for a fee of approximately eight dollars an hour.

Getting organized, according to Donna Goldfein, author of *Every Woman's Guide to Time Management,* is a major portion of the freelance start-up. "As the athlete in training is coached to regularly pace his/her time, it is equally important to pace one's writing schedule. Create a rhythm of daily doing the things you dislike first, and treat yourself to an *award* time immediately following the completion of the task. This habit will result in better control of your time and less pressure from attempting to complete too much at deadline." Says writer Goldfein, "Place these reminders near your work area: DO IT NOW; FIRST THINGS FIRST."

Your tendency to procrastinate can be offset if you type an invoice immediately upon receiving an assignment and tack it over your typewriter. Those dollar signs will catch your eye every time you gaze up or start to go away from your desk.

Pen names, pseudonyms. There are few reasons for these rather archaic tools for writers. Yet often the question of whether to use one is primary in the minds of would-be writers. Arky Gonzales's reply to the question is three questions of his own: Are you a spy? Are you an ex-con? Have you embezzled money from a bank and want to tell others your success story? If you answer yes to any of the above, then by all means use a pseudonym. Otherwise, why bother? There are cases where women write under men's names and vice versa for legitimate reasons. Some writers who moonlight in genre fiction and erotica use them to protect their mainstream careers. And sometimes when a professional has two articles coming out in the same issue of a periodical the editor will request that one of them carry a pseudonym. But in general, a pen name isn't worth the trouble.

Recycling your mail. One freelancer I know applies a creative approach to her mail and In basket to get new ideas and new assignments. "Every now and then I discover my thinking has become too channeled," she says. "It usually happens when my checkbook reports I'm running too close to the line. Instead of panicking and doing a quick low-level assignment just to fill the till, I take a deep breath. I sit back and analyze my situation. People have suggested I'm wasting valuable time. I don't think so. Actually, this is when I've taken my quantum leaps forward. I take the day's mail and try to think how to pair things to make them pay off. Here's how it works: One day I receive an invitation to a conference for technical writers. I haven't any idea how I got on *their* mailing list. I'm not a technical writer. But I think about the conference and the possible connections the subjects to be discussed *might* have to areas I am interested in. I list them. In the same mail are a few of the magazines I subscribe to: *Ladies' Home Journal, Psychology Today,* a business journal, and *National Geographic.* How could any of the ideas on my list be turned into articles for these magazines? I ask. I concentrate first on the highest-paying ones. I make a conscious effort to go for publications in markets I haven't 'hit' yet. If no ideas jell, I try to include another piece of mail—the White House newsletter, for instance—to see if a sparkling idea—something no one else would have thought of—comes to me. There are all sorts of ways to do this. The primary point is that one must consciously attempt to unblock the blocking mechanism. This creative control over the subconscious data that comes to us all gets the juices going in a manner most people only realize haphazardly. Since I'm living on my ideas, I can't afford to leave them all to chance."

The book proposal. Writers usually attempt to give enough information about their idea in any proposal so an editor can decide if the finished book will be a salable commodity. Writers well-known to an editor need not go into such depth or detail as someone who has not published a book before. Generally speaking, though, most editors will want to see a detailed table of contents describing the various sections of the book and showing the order in which it will unfold. A preface or even a letter describing the need for such a book, the target audience, and the scope of the market is also of vital importance. If there are already other books on the market dealing with some of the same material your book will cover, it's wise to do some sleuthing. Examine these books—or at least their tables of contents—closely so that your note on audience and marketing will demonstrate how your book will either give this same audience considerably more than those others or will gain the attention of yet another segment of a wider audience than they were attempting to attract. (Don't pretend that those other books don't exist. That will only demonstrate your ignorance. The editors you will propose your volume to will undoubtedly know about what is already in the marketplace. That's their job.) After you have researched your field enough to write the above material, it's time to sit down and write several chapters of the book itself. These need not be the first three in the book, but that is generally a good way to start. This writing—on spec, of course—is necessary for the editor to judge several things about you as a writer. Essentially, she must see that you can write well, that you have enough enthusiasm for your idea to carry you through the writing of a book-length manuscript, and that you've researched in considerable depth already—enough to know your material and the manner in which you'll get the rest of it. If there are to be any unusual elements in your book's format (lots of illustrations or photographs or unusual type needs, for instance), these should be spelled out in the manuscript segment that you present, along with a solid explanation of the need for them. Once you have this material arranged and typed manuscript-style, with a covering page (title of book and your name), you can put it in a box (the kind that typing paper comes in) or a plastic report cover with removable plastic binding. Write a cover letter to the editor you've chosen and mail the proposal with sufficient postage for its return if it is rejected. Or, with proposal ready, approach a literary agent, again with return postage in your package.

Promoting your book. Franklynn Peterson and Judi Kesselman-Turkel see it this way: "An author who won't don peddler's clothes over her artist's smock will have to kiss a lot of toads before she finds that prince of a publisher who will promote her book even half as much as she's entitled to." What to do? Promote it yourself, of course. Help the publisher promote it, too. "During negotiations, you can test how much promotional effort your editor has in mind," say these two authors, who have published numerous books. They continue:

> Ask for a clause that spells out how much money the publisher will commit to publicizing your book. You could be shocked; the editor might agree to it. More than likely you'll be turned down, but to ease the blow, your editor just might quote a projected publicity figure or two. Ask him to follow up by sending you a letter with those figures. Again, you'll probably be turned down. But at each frustrating stage of negotiations,

you'll be clarifying in your own mind what to expect from your publisher—and with luck you might start your editor thinking promotionally.

Surviving the book tour can be problematic unless you learn early to rely on a few essential rules. It doesn't matter if you are a veteran traveler or not; the strenuous city-a-day tour (four to six interviews in each city) is both exhilarating and physically exhausting. Take your cues from those who have been there. Even the freelancer traveling to speak to potential clients for a syndicated column or other project might do well to listen to these tips, offered by Nancy Winters in a *Travel and Leisure* article: Rely on a simplified wardrobe for travel and appearances. Keep unpacking to a minimum. Pack your favorite food and drink in small amounts to carry with you and indulge in while waiting in airports or hotel lobbies. Call before each appointment to check time, address, and other details. Have an official count on items being carried and check this each time you embark from your hotel, car, plane, or bus. Bring an extra pair of glasses if you wear them (and vials of necessary medication, etc.). Prepare for extremes of weather with at least one item for very cold and one for very warm weather in your suitcase.

"Keeping an inner balance is essential," says Winters. "Ongoing projects helped, and Gahan [her husband and coauthor] alternated between studying hieroglyphics in preparation for a trip up the Nile and reading Nero Wolfe while I needlepointed a ladybug pillow for our house in the country. To orient us and keep the whole thing from turning into one long hotel suite, I skimmed tourist guides to each city as well as the Yellow Pages."

Networking. Once your name begins to appear on everything from commercial mailing lists to bylined articles in the local weekly, this part of your freelance business will grow more rapidly than you ever imagined. I once received a letter from a total stranger which read, in part, "Do you need the address of the South American Explorers Club in Lima, Peru? Do you need a commercial photographer in Panama for pictures to go with a story? Maybe some accurate captioning by a writer of the pictures you took while on a visit to this country? I'm trying to set up a network for myself. I'm doing a bit of personal advertising in order to make use of my own contacts." The writer was obviously a resourceful type. I was delighted to have his name to add to my card file of potential helpers.

Finding an office—the bare-bones beginnings. Space is often at a premium for writers. This is especially true for the writer who lives in a tiny cubicle of an apartment. One writer's office became a reality when she noticed a sketch in a magazine. It was offering suggestions for decorating a children's room, but she saw the potential in the artist's line drawing, took it to a friend with carpentry skills, and a few days later was sitting in her new office. The "room" was tiny, true, but it served her needs while she could only afford an apartment. All the office consisted of was a loft over her couch—one long ledge with a ladder to reach it. The project wouldn't have worked without the high ceilings of the old Victorian house where her apartment was situated. But the idea is still valuable, for instance, if you are looking for more space for book, magazine or file storage.

Writers have also obtained needed storage space by sharing some of the new storage vaults with others. Several companies will rent you a five-by-five foot unit for about $12 monthly. These are usually unheated, and users must provide their own insurance (a floater policy addition to your existing insurance), but it offers easy access for either short- or long-term storage needs. If you can't see using one of these, you might want to "rent" space in a friend's barn, garage, or basement.

If you need to get away from your own environment in order to write that novel or history of the bald ouakari, some writers have gotten a rent-free vacation in an exotic locale by using a vacation-exchange club and moving into someone else's digs while the owners moved into theirs.

Loss protection. Not all losses freelancers might face come from nonpaying clients or from failing to negotiate higher rates with existing markets. Some of the common ones all people face, such as burglary, can be especially devastating for the freelancer who has an office in his home. He's put in, let's say, at least a thousand dollars' worth of equipment, works himself hard, yet has to be out of the office to conduct interviews and do research. While he's gone, he gets ripped off. He's lost more than personal items of luxury—he's sustained a business loss that might not be covered by insurance. (And even if it is, he is inconvenienced, and his production schedule may suffer.) To prepare for such eventualities, consider what this writer did. He had a longstanding habit of keeping a careful daily log of what went on, and the habit paid off. "I got so I jotted a note about everything of importance that happened each day in my daybook. When a repairman came to fix the typewriter, it was noted, with time in and time out. When another one showed up to fix the TV or the plumbing, in went the notation. It didn't take any time and it was a welcome diversion from the novel I was writing. But, once when I happened to be out of town for a weekend, my house (and home office) were burglarized. I looked back in the day book to see when the last strangers might have been in the place. I wanted to know who had access, who might have noticed I had expensive equipment sitting around. There were several notes immediately preceding the break-in. The police were happy to have such an accurate record. They nabbed the guy and I got my equipment back."

His daybook was a certain kind of insurance. Another kind available (though not yet in all fifty states) is provided by the Federal Crime Insurance Program, PO Box 41033, Washington, DC 20014, toll-free telephone 800-638-8780. For approximately twenty-five cents a day you can have ten thousand dollars of theft coverage, and no matter how many times you've been ripped off the coverage cannot be canceled. They offer residential and commercial coverage. For small-business persons with their offices in their homes there are certain requirements that have to be met, such as a dead-bolt on the door between business and residential premises.

Research technique. Leon Taylor writes, "Begin clipping the back page [of a newspaper] first: Therein lie those nuggets of stories that the dailies bypass in their rush to press. Often they are tailor-made for a magazine article or even a book. Thomas Thompson was intrigued by a Texas murder item one day, and decided to follow up. He followed it straight into a bestseller, *Blood and Money.*"

Collaboration on a formal or informal arrangement for a low-cost clipping service. These busy snippers are your friends, family colleagues, and others who have been alerted to a particular subject you're researching. Some tips if you want others to help you in this way: Be very specific about what you are looking for. Tell them your deadline, or better yet, give them an earlier deadline. Offer to pay them a small fee to cover postage if you think it's appropriate and would be gratefully received. And offer to reciprocate if the members of your clipping service are busy writers, too.

Part-time and one-time writers discover their own ways to put books together. Raymond Petteruto knew the restaurant business, but he wasn't a workaday writer. When people kept seeking his advice about the restaurant business, though, he saw the need for a down-to-earth manual. Since he wasn't basically a writer he knew he'd need a method to help him. He gathered twenty-four boxes, one for each chapter he had decided on, and began putting into those boxes facts, tips, and other things a novice entrepreneur should know before launching himself into the restaurant business. "My guide was the question, What would I need to know, from zero on, if I were to try and create a small restaurant? By the time his two dozen boxes were filled, he knew he had enough for a selling booklet. He laid it out logically from that zero point on, until all of the information had been included.

Another small subsidy possibility if you are just getting started in the freelance field might be in your own backyard. Families have histories and personal stories which are told and retold through the years, but which are seldom written down. Snapshot albums and home movies have generally taken their place. But an enterprising freelancer with a knack for listening and writing can help people put their memories down on paper in a permanent style to pass on to their heirs. These make fine gifts for some of the elders in a family— grandparents or uncles who "don't know what to give the children" for special occasions. Try to guide the history for maximum enjoyment of the later readers. Think in terms of important memories (for example, the journey out west on a Conestoga) passed along haphazardly from generation to generation, particularly intriguing hobbies, growing up on a farm, details of early school days, choosing a spouse, the children's first amusing tricks as toddlers, and so on. Otherwise a long, rambling, and not very interesting monologue might be the outcome. (If you take on such a project, be prepared for the grapevine to broadcast the information about your talents. You may find you have more of these projects than you can reasonably handle.)

Greeting cards have come a long way since 1843, when Joseph Calcutt Horsley, a British artist and member of the Royal Academy, printed up a thousand copies of his Christmas card. From that first hand-colored sepia drawing with a simple sentiment sprang an industry that the National Association of Greeting Card Publishers estimates sells more than seven billion items each year, for an annual income of $1.8 billion. The manufacturers have discovered there's money in individuality. Now colorful graphics, old-movie photos, cartoon characters, and interesting animals decorate the pithy message, the perfectly friendly insult, and other realistic sentiments of today's card senders.

Even if you don't have any talent as an artist, you can use the ideas garnered from a study of card display racks to improve your communications with your clients. If you have amusing photographs you can have them duplicated to send out with bills or as postcards. Or you can ask an art student to do a simple line drawing of your idea for similar impact. (An artist and a writer who shared office space and occasionally clients did this with some success. A late-paying commercial client paid up and sent a note asking for more cards for his own use. Without meaning to, these two suddenly had a sideline business of cards with clever drawings and two or three pointed remarks to attract attention.)

Taking on a corporate client is sometimes unnerving, even to the pro who has been writing magazine articles successfully. Here are a few questions to ask if you wish to consider working for one, either by contributing to an existing company periodical or by offering to produce one for them.

1. What is the purpose of the publication—its goals, uses, function within the company or outside?

2. Who will the audience be? How much persuasion or effort is needed to gain the audience's attention? How interested will the audience be in specific details of the business or knowledgeable about the general field?

3. What format and end product are desired by the client (size, number of pages, number of copies, how to be distributed, how often, etc.)?

4. What restrictions are there, both on time and finances (deadline, responsibilities of editor/designer and client, printing and overall budgets, where printed, purchasing and payment policies, government or industrial restrictions, client preferences and taboos)?

5. What materials to be used will be provided by client—graphics, photos, logos, charts (number and details of these provisions, status on delivery to printer, etc.)?

"Think serial rights even before you've written your book," say many successful authors and their agents. When you are conceptualizing the project and outlining it, consider how parts of it might be of interest to a periodical. Those who conceive of their work originally with serial rights in mind have a helpful head start on their own marketing plan, and one more selling point for their project proposal in the first place. (Some writers right at the beginning make a list of possible magazines and other outlets—syndicates, newspapers, international outlets—that would be interested in this or that segment of their book, if it is properly handled.) A story within a story is an obvious natural. So, too, is one particular aspect—say, "How to Foil Home Burglaries" in a volume on crime in America. With a few words or paragraphs written as a lead and an appropriate ending tacked on, if necessary, these passages become lucrative spin-off material to the market-savvy writer. This can hold true for writers of fiction as well as nonfiction, although it is often much more difficult to pull cohesive sections from fiction that stand on their own merits in a shortened version.

Travel writing appeals to the would-be writer because of the seeming glamour surrounding world-journeys-for-pay. Getting started in it isn't all that difficult for the hustling writer, since there are always weeklies with a few inches available now and then for an instructive and amusing piece on travel (though seldom with much money to pay for it). Problems abound, however, if you want to make money in this overcrowded field.

If you can afford to travel on your own or are planning a trip and want to try your hand at this form of freelancing, there are some things to do before you go. Talk with several editors (in person, by phone, or by letter) regarding your plans, places you'll be visiting, people you'd consider interviewing, and so forth. You can sometimes get a noncommittal letter of introduction from them or, more rarely but possibly, a general letter of "assignment." This letter doesn't actually commit them to publishing any of your writing, but it helps open some doors, especially in foreign countries. At the least it should help establish that you are a working writer looking for good material. If you cannot get such a letter (beginners seldom can), then take with you some backup material (résumé, copies of your articles or other published prose) to present when strangers ask who you are and why you're asking all those questions. Letters of assignment have helped me travel alone through Europe on a shoestring without too much confusion. They helped me hitch a ride on a ferry that had already put up the gangplank and was heading out into the Mediterranean. They helped me considerably behind the Iron Curtain when valuable photos were about to be seized. They got me into many museums and private libraries for my research. They've made me numerous friends. I even think they're the reason I once danced with a top government official at a dinner party. But most of all, they kept me company and reminded me I could be courageous at home, when need be, so I could be equally tenacious abroad. Whether you are traveling on assignment or are specializing in travel writing, any time you write long, descriptive letters, ask the recipients to save them and return them to you unless you've typed them and saved a carbon or Xerox for your files. Much of this material is worth its cost to your budget since it is part of the record of your live research. The impressions you record on the spot, the amusing anecdotes and overheard conversations are useful when you are ready to write the travel article.

One man who had freelanced for years and had contacts all over the globe saved the envelopes with foreign stamps addressed to him, not just the stamps. His collection is worth a considerable hunk of money and is part of his estate, as are the letters from various famous dignitaries and infamous characters he's crossed paths with in his globetrotting.

Getting a loan and establishing credit as a self-employed individual sometimes seems to be an impossible task. Here are a few tips that Richard F. Walsh, assistant treasurer and manager of the Reliance Cooperative Bank, Cambridge, Massachusetts, offered to an East Coast freelancers' organization.

> If you are of legal age and have a steady income, you most likely qualify; but verifying your income is of utmost importance. A self-employed person can accomplish this by presenting to the lender copies of tax returns for the prior three years. A review of these tax returns gives the loan officer an overview of the applicant's earnings history over this period, even if income fluctuated from year to year. If you have a past credit history, including loans or credit-card activity, a complete listing will also be helpful to the loan officers. If you're just starting out on your own, or if you've been in business only a short time, you may have to secure a coborrower. If the coborrower is used and the loan is paid on time, the applicant will earn a good credit rating for maintaining the contract. The initial loan should be kept for a minimum of one year and made for a reasonable amount, so you can prove you're able to meet your obligations.

Even after you substantiate the fact that you are a good credit risk, however, each additional application for a loan will be examined individually by the bank. But since freelancers occasionally need loans to see them through dry periods (especially at the outset of their careers), it's a good idea to establish your credit rating early and be sure that if you take out a loan, you maintain the regular payment schedule.

Getting an agent to handle your work can be similar to obtaining a bank loan, notes Elyse M. Rogers, freelance writer of fiction and nonfiction. "When one is a poor credit risk and really needs the money, no bank will lend any. On the other hand, when an applicant is successful and has a reputation for making money, the same bank will lavish greenbacks on this person who doesn't need it." So, whether you have an agent, want to find one, or simply want to get more clients to work for, look at Rogers's tips.

There are many facets to a good business relationship, but I think they can be summed up by saying: Be professional. The ten points to achieving this status are:

1. Be polite. Relax with some small talk first.
2. Be confident. Learn the fine line between cockiness and confidence and observe it at all times.
3. Be competent. Show samples of your best work. Deliver on time.
4. Be realistic. Don't overbook assignments when you find you're starting to get them regularly. Plan ahead what you can and cannot take on.
5. Be truthful. If it's not your type of work, admit it. If you already have too much to do, tell the client.
6. Be available. Help the client out of a crisis if you can.
7. Be cheerful and optimistic. Life is traumatic and publishing is a business fraught with problems. Your attitude can be a helpful tool everyone will appreciate.
8. Be aggressive. There are many competitors out there. You'll be forgotten if you don't remind clients now and then you're still in business.
9. Be a hard worker. All the above attributes won't help you finally if you aren't willing to work incredibly hard without constant reminders.
10. Be patient. No one starts at the top. This last will facilitate your rise up the ladder.

How not to get a grant. These suggestions come from an overburdened grants officer at a state council for the arts: Prepare your grant application with a two-inch purple felt-tip marker on apricot paper. Leave at least one-third of the questions blank. Don't cooperate with anyone in a similar area while planning the application materials. Don't tell the others what you hope to do. Then all of you with the same idea will be able to sit around and commiserate with each other when none of you gets the grant. The budget is one of the most important parts of your application, but you can "guesstimate" figures and no one will mind. Make sure you ask for about 400 percent more than you need. That will impress the decision makers, all right. After you've applied, be sure you call the grants officer and tie him up on the phone a long time, way before he's had an opportunity to consider your grant request or, probably, any others.

Problem solving. If you're really having trouble unraveling the current snarl in your work or finding it impossible to come to a good decision about which way to turn, ask a friend or two to sit down with you and hold a brainstorming session. Try the ideas on for size. It helps if you or someone else writes them down. You'll finally take one path, but keeping your notes from the session may remind you of other alternatives you may want to consider later. Such creative approaches eventually do build your business. If on the contrary you sit in the quiet of your room with little or no personal contact with editors or the day-by-day nitty-gritty of the publishing world and wonder why stacks of rejection slips grow higher, get out for a while. See what is going on that you've been missing. Take a walk, call and visit a client. Exercise for fifteen minutes before you approach your typewriter again. And set a goal for yourself of deciphering your knottiest creative problem refreshed.

Types of writers. A brief thought from an editor's point of view: Writers fall into three categories. There is the serious professional. Then there are the crybaby ("I'm not being paid enough; I don't have enough time; I can't make your deadline; you didn't tell me you wanted all *that*") and the b.s. master (the kind who is "the greatest," at least in his mind—he promises everything, but he seldom delivers).

Writer/photographer tips. If you are preparing to shoot photos, ask the client some questions before you even pick up your camera: What is the purpose of the photo? When, where, and how can you get it? Who are the principals involved? How will the photos be used in the layout? Do you want horizontal or vertical shots? What is the company's philosophy on such issues as equal opportunity, safety-violation problems, and other details that could prevent the photo from being used in a company publication?

Other tips include: Shoot anything interesting while on assignment, not only the photo that is necessary for it. Get people into your pictures but avoid obviously posed shots. Take more than just one or two shots of each subject or situation. Film is relatively cheap, especially if you bulk-load it yourself. Supply detailed caption information with each photo. Keep track of photos you shoot in an effective filing system. Read up on the legal aspects of photography, particularly concerning model releases and invasion of privacy. In some extraordinary circumstances a poor photo is better than none at all.

The hazards of the writing business are well described by Hayes

Jacobs in *Writing and Selling Non-Fiction.* They include loneliness, the predators looking to use published writers for their own gains, fatigue, the lure of cheap commercialism, and the perils of success.

Others come and go, like this year's problem with book distribution or another year's emphasis on the publishers' practice of book dumping, brought about by new legislation in Washington. The working writer must live with it all and continue to write. Fortunately, he is in an occupation where he can help not only himself but others he's concerned about. In Ronald Gross's article for *Writer's Digest,* "Writing for Social Change," he reminds us all, "I've discovered how a writer can do well by doing good." Citing his experience as a professional, Gross says, "A piece last year, for an education journal which can't pay, won a distinguished-achievement award from the Educational Press Association, which led to other assignments for good fees." How do you get the knack of writing for movements advocating social change and still pay the rent?

> The how-to consists of several parts. Chief among them are a special interest or commitment that's strong enough to enable you to develop expertise and creative judgment in a field; some strategies and techniques . . . and, of course, the usual "little bit of luck" that no freelancer can survive without.
>
> The point is: the work is there to be done. The unfinished business of building a better America needs writers as much as it needs the labor and the caring of every other kind of worker. . . . The freelance writer is in an exceptional position to look hard at any institution or aspect of our society, ask tough questions, and inform people about the facts and issues that will shape our future.

With those words in mind and the numerous tricks from this volume up your sleeve, you're well on your way to succeeding as a freelance writer, whether or not you make a grand slam with many bestsellers or have work published bimonthly in the highest-paying periodicals in the land. Best of all, you've taken on the big order of working for yourself instead of dully returning to the nine-to-five job for someone else and, in the process, you've discovered how you can contribute to the well-being of humanity at large.

Appendix
Book
Contract

■■■

The following is an actual book contract. Contracts differ widely in content, language, and form. For more detailed information consult The Writer's Legal Guide by Tad Crawford (Hawthorn Books, 1977), Law and the Writer (Writer's Digest Books, 1978), or any of the other sources listed in the Resources section. Comments are in brackets.

Dear

This letter is our contract with you. It sets down the terms of our agreement to publish your book, currently entitled

1. You grant to us during the term of the United States copyright, and during any renewal or extension thereof, the exclusive right to publish and sell, including the right to permit others to publish and sell, your work in book form in the English language throughout the world including the United States of America, its territories and possessions, the Dominion of Canada and the Republic of the Philippines, and non-exclusive in all territories outside of the British Empire and Commonwealth. [*Although first-book authors may have difficulty keeping some of the world rights, most seasoned pros or their agents market British and foreign rights separately.*]

2. You shall deliver to us at your expense no later than
                                    two typed copies of your work in final form including photographs, illustrations, charts, index and other necessary material, all complete and ready for the printer and accompanied by all necessary permissions, licenses, releases and consents. The work will be no less than   words nor more than   words. [*While the publisher will want the author to provide everything, some of these are negotiable.*]
        If you do not so deliver your work to us in form and substance satisfactory to us in our judgment (which shall be final), by the date specified or at another date agreed to by us in writing (such time to be deemed of the essence), we may terminate this agreement by notice to you, and you shall then repay all amounts which we have advanced to you; such termination if not caused by circumstances beyond your

control shall be without prejudice to any other remedies we may have for breach of contract. [*A volatile clause with good arguments on both sides; however, a writer who has honestly and professionally met the requirements specified in his contract should not be asked to return an advance. Writers with track records sometimes agree to return it only if the rejected manuscript is subsequently sold to another publisher.*]

We shall send you proof sheets of the work which you agree to read, revise, correct and return promptly. You agree to pay the cost of alterations in type or in plates required by you (other than those due to printer's errors) in excess of 10% of the cost of composition. We will present the corrected proofs for inspection at your request. [*Ten percent is a pretty typical allowance for AAs.*]

3. We shall publish your work at our expense in manner and style and at a price we believe appropriate. Publication shall be within one year of our acceptance of the final copy, but our failure to publish within such period shall not be a breach of our agreement if the delay is caused by circumstances beyond our control. [*Try to get this paragraph altered to limit the publisher to any delay beyond an agreed-upon length of time—say eighteen months—beyond which all rights and moneys revert to the author without penalty.*]

4. You and we shall take such steps as are necessary on our respective parts to secure and preserve a valid United States copyright in your work in your name. You shall (though you also authorize us to do so on your behalf and in your name) take such steps as are necessary to record our interest in the copyright, if we shall so desire, or to renew or extend the copyright if this agreement is then in effect. If we deem it desirable we may take such steps in your name as may be necessary to obtain a copyright in other countries. We shall publish your work in the United States in a way that complies with the provisions of the Universal Copyright Convention. [*See that the copyright paragraph requires the publisher to register a claim for copyright in the author's name and that all copies of the work and any portions published by any subsequent licensee are printed with the proper copyright notice.*]

5. You represent and warrant to us, and to those to whom we may license or grant rights hereunder, that you are the sole author and/or owner of your work and that it has not previously been published in book form; that it is original, is not in the public domain, and does not infringe upon or violate any personal or property rights of others; that it contains nothing scandalous, libelous, in violation of any right of privacy, or contrary to law; and that you have all necessary permissions, licenses, releases and consents and the full power to enter into this agreement and to grant us the rights herein provided for. [*Try to have the phrase "and to my knowledge" inserted before "does not infringe upon or violate . . ."*]

6. A. You agree to indemnify and hold us harmless against any loss, damage, liability or expense (including counsel fees reasonably incurred) arising out of any claim, action or proceeding asserted or instituted on any ground which, if established, would be a breach of any of the warranties made by you in this agreement. We shall promptly notify you of any such claim, action or proceeding and shall have the right at your expense and through counsel of our choice to defend it. If we believe that the settlement of any such matter is desirable, we shall confer with you. If, within such time as the situation may allow, you do not consent to the proposed settlement, you shall upon notice by us immediately undertake to continue the defense and shall furnish us with security in such form and amount as shall under all

the circumstances be in our opinion adequate. If you fail to assume the defense and to furnish such security, we shall have the right at your expense to settle such matter upon terms we think advisable or to continue the defense thereof. If, however, it is finally determined by judgment or by abandonment or settlement of such claim, action or proceeding without liability to us that no breach of the warranties in question has occurred, we shall bear one half of all the expenses incurred in this connection.

B. If in our opinion your work contains material which may be libelous or otherwise involve us in litigation, we shall not be required to publish the work. Without limiting the foregoing, you shall, if we request it, make such changes in your work as we shall deem necessary, but failure on our part to require or recommend any changes in your work shall in no way affect your obligations under subparagraph A of this paragraph 6.

[*Paragraph 6 is reasonably liberal as contracts go. Established writers attempt to have the wording changed to read "against any final judgment (after all appeals have been taken)" and limiting the author's liability to a "percentage of the sum to him under this agreement."*]

   7. We shall pay to you:

A. On each copy of the trade edition sold by us except as provided in the following subparagraphs, a royalty of

[*Be certain to note that royalties are on retail and not net. If you must settle for a contract on net, find out how the net is calculated.*]

B. On copies of the trade edition sold by us, at a discount of 50% or more (but less than 70%) from the publisher's retail price through channels outside of the ordinary wholesale and retail trade (other than remainders as described in paragraph H), a royalty of 10% of the amount we receive.

C. On copies of the trade edition sold by us, at a discount of 70% or more from the publisher's retail price (other than remainders as described in paragraph H), whether through normal trade channels or otherwise, a royalty of 10% of the amount we receive after deducting all manufacturing costs.

D. On copies of the trade edition sold by us for export (except as provided in paragraph J), a royalty of 15% of the amount we receive.

E. On copies of a textbook edition sold by us under our own imprint, a royalty of 10% of the publisher's retail price of such edition.

F. On copies of a hardcover reprint edition issued by us at a price lower than the regular trade edition, a royalty of 10% of the publisher's retail price of such reprint edition.

G. On copies of a paperback edition issued by us, a royalty of 7½% of the publisher's retail price of such paperback edition except on copies sold at a discount greater than 50% the royalty shall be 4% of the publisher's retail price.

[*B. through G.: These are negotiable. For further information see* Law and the Writer *and* The Writer's Legal Guide.]

H. On copies sold at a remainder price (any sale at or below manufacturing cost, whether through normal trade channels or otherwise, being deemed a remainder sale for purposes of this clause), no royalty shall be paid; however, prior to remaindering your work under this clause, we shall make reasonable effort to notify you and afford you the opportunity to purchase all or part of such overstock at the remainder price. [*Try to establish a time limit before which the publisher may not sell the book at remainder prices.*]

I. On copies sold directly to the consumer through mail-order coupon advertising, or direct-by-mail circularization, a royalty of 5% of the amount we receive. [*This is a standard for direct-mail sales.*]

J. On copies, bound or in sheets, sold for export at discounts of 60% or more, a royalty of 10% of the amount we receive.

K. On copies sold from a reprinting of 2,000 copies or less made after the initial publication of your work, one-half of the applicable royalties under the foregoing clauses. [*This is to allow the publisher to keep your book in print.*]

L. On copies furnished without charge or for review, advertising, sample, promotion or other similar purposes, no royalty.

All sales subject to royalties under any of the provisions of this paragraph 7 shall be computed net of returns.

8. We may publish or permit others to publish or broadcast without charge and without royalty such selections from your work for publicity purposes as may, in our opinion, benefit the sale of your work. We shall also be authorized to license publication of your work without charge and without royalty in Braille or by any other method primarily designed for the physically handicapped. [*Add, if you can, the statement that the publisher should limit summaries to 7,500 words and see that all necessary actions to protect the copyright are taken.*]

9. You grant to us the exclusive right on your behalf to license, sell or otherwise dispose of the following rights in your work: publication or sale of your work by book clubs; publication of a reprint edition of your work by another publisher; condensations; serializations in magazines or newspapers (whether in one or more installments and whether before or after book publication); dramatic, motion picture (including but not by way of limitation, film strips based on the story and film strips or motion picture photographed directly from the book), phonograph, and radio, television, cable or other broadcasting rights and electronic, mechanical, visual or other reproduction rights; publication of your work in the British Commonwealth; publication of your work in foreign languages; publication of your work and selections therefrom in anthologies, compilations and digests; picturized book versions, microprint and microfilm versions.

In the case of each of the rights specified in this paragraph 9, the net proceeds of its disposition (after all commissions, foreign taxes and other charges) shall be shared equally between us except that as to British Commonwealth and foreign translation rights the division of net proceeds shall be 80% to you and 20% to us, and except that as to first serial, dramatic, motion picture, phonograph, radio, television, cable and other broadcast uses the division of net proceeds shall be 90% to you and 10% to us.

[*Various rights in paragraph 9 may be negotiated; what the publisher gives up here, however, he will expect to get back on other points—say in the amount of advance or the percentages in paragraph 7. Publishers are somewhat more likely to part with broadcast rights, provided that you have not written a blockbuster novel.*]

10. If the copyright of your work is infringed during the term of this agreement, then, upon notice to that effect by either of us, we shall confer with regard to the infringement, and if no mutually satisfactory arrangement is arrived at for joint action within seven days thereafter, either one of us shall have the right to bring an action or proceeding to enjoin the infringement, and for damages. If we proceed jointly, the expenses and recoveries, if any, shall be shared equally, and if we do not agree to proceed jointly, either of us shall have the right to go forward with an action or proceeding, bearing all the expenses and retaining any recovery. If we proceed alone, you shall permit the action to be brought in your name and shall take all steps necessary, including the execution of such documents as may be required, to enable us to proceed. [*Let this stand.*]

11. On publication of your work we shall deliver to you ten copies without charge and you shall have the right to purchase further copies at a discount of 40% from the publisher's retail price. [*Even for your first book contract where you may win no other concessions, at least ask here for twenty free copies.*]

12. You have advised us that

is acting as your representative in connection with your work. All sums which may be due you under this agreement shall be paid to your representative, and such payment shall be a full and complete discharge to us. A copy of any notice required by this agreement to be given to you shall be sent to your representative. [*This is a standard paragraph indicating that an agent is representing you and all moneys will be sent to the agent for disbursement to you.*]

13. A. We shall following publication render to you on March thirty-first and September thirtieth of each year semi-annual statements of account as of the preceding December thirty-first and June thirtieth. Each statement shall be accompanied by payment of all sums due thereon. In reporting sales we may withhold a reasonable reserve for future returns. If in any six-month period the total payments due are less than $50.00, we may defer the rendering of statements and payments until such time as the sum of $50.00 or more shall be due. [*This clause is reasonable but could be improved by requiring publisher to specifically account for the number of copies printed, bound, and given away and the number of salable copies on hand.*]

B. The amounts paid to you hereunder during any one calendar year (despite anything to the contrary in paragraph 13A) shall not exceed $. If in any one calendar year the sums accruing to you from this agreement shall exceed this amount, you shall be paid the excess amount only in the succeeding calendar year or years, provided that the total amount to be paid in any succeeding year shall not exceed said annual maximum. [*Strike this clause unless you're making so much money you want to defer income until a later tax year.*]

C. You may, upon written request, examine our books of account insofar as they relate to your work.

14. A. In case we fail to keep your work in print (and for all purposes of this paragraph the work shall be considered to be in print if it is on sale by us in any edition or if it is on sale in any edition licensed by us during the term of this agreement) and you make written request of us to keep it in print, we shall, within sixty days after the receipt of your request, notify you in writing whether or not we intend to do so, and if we elect to do so, we shall have six months thereafter in which to comply. If we fail to comply (unless the failure is due to circumstances beyond our control), or if we do not desire to keep your work in print, then this agreement shall terminate and all of the rights granted to us shall revert to you subject to subparagraph C of this paragraph.

B. In case of such termination you shall have the right for thirty days thereafter on prior written notice to us to purchase the plates, if any, of your work at one third of their manufacturing cost, including composition, and any remaining copies or sheets of your work at the manufacturing cost. If you fail to do so, we may dispose of all of them as we see fit, subject to the provisions of paragraph 7 of this agreement.

C. Nothing contained herein shall affect our right to sell remaining copies of your work on hand at the date of termination of this agreement, nor shall such termination affect any license or other grant of rights, options or contracts made to or with third parties by either of us prior to the termination date, or the rights of either of us in the proceeds of such agreements, nor our rights under paragraphs 5 and 6 of this agreement.

[*Let paragraph 14 stand.*]

15. You agree that the work covered by this agreement shall be your next published book. [*This paragraph is negotiable for seasoned pros only.*]

16. You hereby grant us the option to publish in book form, on fair and reasonable terms to be arranged, your next work. We shall be entitled to a period of two months after the submission to us by you of the completed manuscript within which to notify you of our decision. If within that time we notify you of our desire to publish the manuscript, we shall thereupon negotiate with you with respect to the terms for such publication. If the parties are unable in good faith to arrive at a mutually satisfactory agreement for such publication, you shall be free to submit the manuscript elsewhere, provided, however, that you shall not enter into a contract with another publisher for the publication of such manuscript unless the terms of such contract are more favorable to you than those offered by us. [*If you grant the publisher option on your next work, try to change this paragraph to require him to make his decision on a reasonably detailed proposal rather than a completed manuscript, unless it is a work of fiction. Also make certain it doesn't bind you to the terms of the present agreement.*]

17. You shall execute and deliver to us whatever documents and assignments of copyright or other papers as may be necessary in our opinion to fulfill the terms and intent of this agreement. [*Let stand.*]

18. In order to keep the work up to date you shall, if called upon by us, revise it for new editions while this agreement is in effect and shall supply any new matter that may be needful to that end. In the event you neglect or are unable by reason of death or otherwise to revise the work, or supply new matter in a form satisfactory to us, we may procure some other person to edit or revise the work, or supply new matter, and may deduct the expense thereof (including royalties to such other person) from the royalties payable to you, and in such revised edition may describe such person as editor or co-author. If revisions require resetting of more than 50 per cent of the work, and if the royalty rate provided in paragraph 7 is on a rising scale, the rate on the new edition shall begin at the original rate provided for the first edition. [*Two things to be aware of here: (1) that control of the revision rests with the author or in case of death his literary executor, and (2) that if the revisions are major, requiring substantial rewriting, the possibility of negotiating a new advance is left open.*]

19. If we are adjudicated a bankrupt by a court of competent jurisdiction or if we make an assignment for the benefit of creditors, then this agreement shall terminate and all of the rights granted by you hereunder shall revert to you and the provisions of subparagraphs B and C of paragraph 14 shall be applicable. [*Let stand.*]

20. Any rights in your work not specifically granted to us hereunder are reserved to you. You agree, however, not to exercise or dispose of any of your reserved
rights (or to participate in the writing or publication of any other work) in such a way
as to affect adversely the value of any of the rights granted to us under this agreement.
You agree to notify us promptly of the disposition of any right which is reserved to
you. [*Seasoned professionals can usually get all but the first sentence deleted.*]

21. Except for loss or damage due to our own negligence, we shall not be
responsible for loss of or damage to any of your property, including the manuscript of
your work, and our liability for any such loss or damage shall in no event exceed the
amount payable to us under any insurance carried by us covering such loss. [*Let
stand.*]

22. This agreement shall be deemed made in, and shall be in all respects
interpreted, construed and governed by the laws of, the State of New York, and the
parties agree to litigate any controversy, claim or dispute arising out of or in connection with this agreement or the breach thereof solely in Supreme Court of the State of
New York, New York County, which the parties agree shall have exclusive jurisdiction to which the parties hereby submit. [*Let stand.*]

23. Any notice called for in this agreement shall be sent by mail to you or to us
at the address set forth above. Either of us may designate a different address by notice
given in the same manner. [*Let stand.*]

24. The waiver of a breach of, or of a default under, any of the terms of this
agreement shall not be construed a waiver of any subsequent breach or default. No
waiver or modification of this agreement shall be valid unless in writing and signed
by the party to be charged. [*Let stand.*]

25. This agreement shall inure to the benefit of and be binding upon you, your
heirs, personal representatives and assigns and upon us, our successors and assigns.
[*Let stand.*]

If the foregoing correctly states your understanding of our agreement, please sign the
enclosed copy of this letter where indicated below and return it to us, whereupon it
will constitute a binding agreement between us.

Very truly yours,

By _____

Publishers, Inc.

Accepted and Agreed to: _____

Date _____

Citizenship _____

Glossary

Writing, Editing, and Production Terms

■■■

AA author's alteration. Changes in proof made by author.

acetate transparent plastic sheet placed over mechanical (q.v.) on which color separation can be indicated or directions to plate-maker given.

advance moneys paid to book author prior to publication. When this sum has been equaled in royalties (q.v.) from the book's sale, the advance has been "paid back" and the author will begin receiving royalties.

agent author's representative. Normally handles submissions and contract negotiations for a set percentage.

align to line up; to place letters or words on the same horizontal or vertical line.

alternate spellings two equally correct and accepted ways to spell the same word. Example: *ax* and *axe*.

anecdote brief story used to illustrate a particular point.

aperture a camera's lens opening. The diameter of the opening is controlled by an expandable diaphragm.

ASA American Standards Association. These letters plus a number indicate the emulsion speed of film. This designation system is now standard with all American and many European film manufacturers.

as-told-to (noun) a nonfiction article or book for which there are essentially two bylines; one of them is usually that of a celebrity. Example: "My Story" by Sophia Loren as told to Alan Levy.

assignment a definite commission given a writer by an editor to do a specific piece of writing.

auction competitive bidding for a book manuscript or proposal following simultaneous submissions to several publishers. Usually the publishers are given a minimum bid (floor) and a date by which to respond.

backgrounder   information relayed to or interview given to members of the press (by politicians, for example) for background purposes only, not for publication.

backlighting   illuminating the side of the subject opposite the camera. This technique produces a halo effect around the edges of the subject.

backlist   all titles in a publisher's catalog that are still in print.

back matter   everything after the last text page of a book (appendixes, glossaries, bibliography, index). Also called *end matter.*

beat   the area (geographical or by subject matter) to which a writer is assigned, or in which he has special competence.

bleed   area of plate or print that extends ("bleeds off") beyond the edge to be trimmed. Applies mostly to photographs or areas of color.

blues (short for *blueprints)*   final proofs before a book or magazine is offset-printed.

blurb   laudatory summary of a book, used on book jacket.

boldface (noun and verb)   dark, heavy type; to mark or set something in boldface type.

bracketing exposures   a method of insuring good exposure by taking three different pictures of the same subject: one at the meter reading, one a step above it, and one a step below. A useful system when the accuracy of the meter or amount of available light is in doubt.

bristol board   good grade of thin cardboard or pasteboard with smooth finish with many uses for artists and designers.

bulletin   one in a series of factual reports issued irregularly.

bullets   large boldface dots set next to paragraphs or items in a list for emphasis.

camera-ready copy   text and illustrations in final form to be photographed by printer's camera.

caps   capital letters.

caption   identifying heading above table, illustration, or photograph in a book.

cast off   to estimate the number of typeset pages that will result from a given manuscript.

clear for 10   to indent the first nine numbers in a list so they will align with the following two-digit numbers.

compositor   typesetter.

confirmation letter   letter of agreement between a client and the writer spelling out terms of the writing assignment, deadline, rate and date of payment, etc. Can be initiated by either party. See also *letter of assignment.*

consumer magazine   general-interest magazine aimed at the mass market.

contrasty   describes prints with dark shadows and bright white highlights. Caused by underexposure or overdevelopment of the negative, or by using paper or film with the wrong contrast.

contributing editor   an out-of-the-office, regular or occasional staff writer/editor who is often paid a regular stipend or retainer, but may be paid only for contributions actually published.

copy   any piece of writing intended for print or broadcast.

copyediting   checking copy for fact, spelling, grammar, punctuation, and consistency of style before it goes to typesetter.

copyright   legal term detailing ownership of creative material (e.g., short story, magazine article, song, play, poem). Copyrights are granted by national governments.

copywriting   the writing of short items needed in the composition of a publication—captions, explanatory notes, filler.

cover letter   the letter that accompanies a manuscript and explains the nature of the submission and any conditions arising from the author's dealings with the publisher.

credentials   writer's identification papers, used to establish credibility with subjects to be interviewed or with editors. Can also refer to press cards and the like.

credits   list of writer's published material. Writer's *portfolio* consists of samples of work.

crop   to trim away part of a print or other artwork.

data processing   the sorting and presentation of data, usually by computer, from any field to make it available for use.

deadline   the date on which a manuscript must be in the hands of the publisher.

deadwood   superfluous verbiage in a manuscript; useless information in your files.

delete   to take out in typesetting or to cross out in manuscript.

dodging   shading a segment of the negative during the printing process to block out or otherwise alter the exposure of areas of the print.

downtime   the time during which printing equipment is not in use or is operating at a low level. Also, time spent waiting for materials, instructions, etc., during which printing is held up.

dry mounting   a method of adhering photos to backboard by the use of a special wax-coated paper, heat, and pressure.

dummy   a mock-up of a printed piece showing how the various parts will be arranged.

editor's query a question to the author about points in a manuscript that are unclear or insufficiently developed.

ellipsis three dots (...) that indicate an omission, often used when shortening quoted matter.

em dash a dash as wide as the letter M in the type being used. In manuscript it is represented by two hyphens.

en dash a dash half as wide as an em dash, most frequently used in place of the word *to*.

end matter see *back matter*.

exposé sensational revelation of hidden elements in a situation of public importance or in the life of a celebrity.

extract (noun) long quotation set off from main text by smaller type, by narrower measure, or by space above and below (or a combination of these techniques).

face any style of type.

fair use the limited use of quotations from previously copyrighted material, in a manner not considered a violation of copyright, and not requiring permission.

figure (or *fig.*) illustration.

fillers short bits of information, or entertaining writing, sometimes humorous, used by editors to fill small blank spots in pages of a periodical.

flush left/right type set to the extreme left/right margin.

FOB (front of the book) designation used by periodical editors for articles to be placed in the opening pages of the magazine.

folio page number.

font all the type (letters and signs) in one size of one typeface.

freelancers (or *free lances*) writers, photographers, artists, or editors who are self-employed; that is, not on the regular payroll of a publication.

front-list books books published within the last two seasons. The term is used when calculating discounts and returns to and by bookstore owners. Usual rate of returns is higher on front-list books than on backlist books.

front matter everything before page one (title page, foreword, acknowledgments, dedication, contents page). Front-matter pages are usually numbered with lowercase roman numerals.

full-returns policy publisher's agreement with bookstores and wholesalers that they may return any unsold volumes for a full credit within a prescribed period of time after publication. The policy is considered necessary to entice booksellers into taking the risk or ordering and stocking books, such as novels, they wouldn't otherwise order, or would order in smaller quantities.

gag a comic idea that may be put to use in a variety of ways. The gag idea need not be submitted in final form.

galleys (or *galley proofs; proofs*) long sheets of typeset copy used by editors and writers for last-minute revisions and checked by proofreaders for errors made by the compositor.

gang printing printing of several jobs on the same sheet, to be cut later.

ghosting a condition in which the printed image is faint, caused by faulty distribution of ink on rollers.

ghostwriting writing intended to be published as the work of another, on which the actual author's name will not appear.

glossy (noun) photograph printed on shiny (glossy) paper.

gray scale a logarithmic scale of gradations of gray from white to black, used to measure tonal range and contrast of copy to be photographed.

halftone a photomechanical reproduction process in which tone differences are obtained by the relative size and density of tiny dots produced by photographing the original through a fine screen.

head type set apart from main text to describe what follows, such as chapter head, subhead, running head.

house publishing company.

how-to articles and books devoted to explanations of how the reader can accomplish or make something.

imprint to print a person's or a firm's name and address on a previously printed piece by running it through another printing press.

in-flights periodicals commissioned or published by airline companies, usually distributed without cost to passengers.

in-house publications periodicals published by and generally, though not always, read only by employees of a company or corporation.

International Reply Coupon a form which may be purchased from a post office, used in lieu of return postage from foreign countries.

itals italics; italic type.

jacket paper cover on a hardback book.

justify to set a line of type to a specified width.

kill to delete.

kill fee a certain percentage of the total agreed-upon fee, which is paid when for any reason the completed and approved article is not published. Also called *salvage fee*.

layout the hand-drawn preliminary plan of the basic elements of a design (sizes and kinds of type, illustrations, spacing) shown in their proper positions prior to paste-up.

lead   the beginning of a nonfiction article; beginning of a book. A lead ought to catch the interest of the reader and generally indicate to him what he can expect from the rest of the work.

leaders   series of dots "leading" the reader's eyes along a line from one word to another; often used in tables.

leading (pronounced *ledding*)   space between lines of type.

legend   identifying words below table, photograph, or art.

letter of assignment   an editor's written confirmation of an assignment, which legally serves in lieu of a formal contract.

letterspace   to put extra space between letters.

light table   a table with a translucent surface and a light source below on which slides can be spread for viewing.

list (noun)   new books published by a particular house. Most houses issue two lists annually, in the fall and the spring.

logo (short for *logotype*)   the distinctive type treatment of a company name or trademark.

lowercase   uncapitalized letters.

manuscript preparation   putting a piece of writing in a form convenient for the editorial process. Includes typing, spacing, punctuation, legible corrections.

market research   survey of the likelihood that some type of material or publication will be bought.

mass market   the reading public at large, not subdivided by considerations of special interest, education, or taste.

measure (noun)   width of a full line of type.

mechanicals   pasted-down corrected type, plus artwork, ready to be photographed for offset printing. Sometimes referred to as *boards*.

middle matter   text.

moonlighting   work done in addition to one's main occupation. Often done after working hours or at night.

ms.   abbreviation for manuscript.

New Journalism   nonfiction writing that relies heavily on fiction techniques.

network   a group of editorial contacts, researchers, collaborators, authorities useful to the writer.

nonreproducible blue pen   marker whose ink does not photograph, used on camera-ready copy.

North American Serial Rights   notation on manuscript that signifies material is being sold or purchased solely for publication in North America. Writer retains the right to publish the material in other countries.

on spec   on speculation. An article written on spec is one that has not been assigned by the editor, who has no obligation to buy the finished work.

op-ed   opposite the editorial page. Usually a page of comment by members of the readership and syndicated columnists; style is often more similar to that of a feature than an editorial.

outline   the skeletal plan of an article, book, or other project.

overhead   all the expenses of office, travel, time, research, and special equipment involved in a freelancer's business.

overlay   sheet of acetate (q.v.) or tissue paper placed over artwork to protect it, to indicate instructions to the printer, and/or to show the breakdown for color separation.

overrun   a printing of a quantity in excess of what is ordered or what is actually required.

over the transom   unsolicited, as material sent to a periodical or book publisher blind, i.e., without benefit of an agent.

packaging   the preparation and manufacture by an independent entrepreneur of a book which is to be distributed by an established publisher.

page proofs   paginated reproduction of type circulated before a publication or book is printed; used for checking purposes.

page rate   fixed rate of pay used by some periodicals, based on each page of material as it appears in print.

parens   parentheses.

paste-up   the process of positioning and affixing copy onto a stiff backing in preparation for being photographed.

PE   printer's error. Notation made by proofreader to distinguish between typesetting errors and editorial changes.

permissions   written permission to use quoted or copyrighted material; a note printed with the material indicating it is being used with permission of the copyright owner.

photojournalism   the practice of telling a story through a series of pictures. May or may not accompany a manuscript on the same subject.

photomontage   a composite photograph which can be made in several ways by combining exposures, negatives, or prints.

point   measure of type height, approximately 1/72 inch.

press release   information or announcement sent by public relations firm (or freelance PR writer) to newspapers and other outlets, designed to draw publicity.

primary source   a person who has firsthand knowledge of the facts. Also, documents directly bearing on the issue under consideration.

proofs (noun)   See galleys.

proofreader's marks   standardized set of symbols used in correcting galleys before sending them back to the typesetter.

proportional scale wheel   a two-part circular gauge used to determine proper percentages in reduction and enlargement of artwork.

public domain   previously printed material not protected by copyright. The source should be acknowledged when used, but need not be paid for.

purple prose   overblown language.

Q&A   question and answer. A form of interview in which the material is simply divided between the questions and the answers, preceded by an explanation of who the Q and A stand for.

query   a brief, informative inquiry from freelancer to editor to ascertain if the proposed material might be usable in his magazine.

ragged right   unaligned right-hand margin.

reference library   a special section maintained by most public libraries, filled with reference books—encyclopedias of various kinds, almanacs, biographical dictionaries, books of statistics, etc.

regional publications   magazines devoted to the special interests or needs of people living in one part of the country. Requirements of such publications provide a market distinct from national magazines.

register mark   a symbol, usually an X in a circle, used on copy for positioning prior to photographing.

remainders   unsold copies of books marked down below original cost. The author usually receives an announcement if his book is to be remaindered and is given an opportunity to purchase them at discount; he may also ask to purchase the printing plates back from the publisher at this time.

reporting times   in a large project to be completed in stages, dates by which the author will give the editor a progress report. Also refers to the time it takes an editor to report acceptance or rejection of a manuscript or query.

reserve-for-returns clause   paragraph in a publisher's contract that permits withholding payments to authors until the returns from bookstores have been calculated or until the return period has expired.

rough draft   the first versions of any written material, to be revised and polished before publication.

round-up   article form in which several persons' answers to the same question are given.

royalties   percentage of moneys from sales of a book paid to the author, as specified in the book contract.

run in (verb)   to merge a paragraph with the preceding or following one.

running foot   words at the bottom of a page accompanying the folio.

running head   words at the top of a page accompanying the folio.

SASE   self-addressed, stamped envelope. Sent with unsolicited matter (ms., questionnaire, etc.) to facilitate reply.

secondary source   a person who has opinions or hearsay evidence on the subject under consideration. Also, critical articles or opinion, as distinct from firsthand knowledge.

self-mailer   a printed piece designed to be mailed without an envelope.

serialization   printing or broadcasting a piece in consecutive installments.

sidebar   a short, related feature that accompanies a longer piece and is set off by means of a box, and often by special type treatment or tinted paper.

slant   the angle of specific approach to any given material. May be a treatment that appeals to special interests of the intended readers.

slug (noun)   full line of type. Also, an identifying word or phrase at the top of each manuscript page.

slug (verb)   to check subsequent proofs against galleys by comparing each line of type.

slush pile   the accumulation of unsolicited manuscripts in a publishing company's office.

spin-off   article formed from research and writing leftovers.

staff writer   a writer on the regular payroll of a periodical or newspaper.

stet   literally, "let it stand" (Latin). An instruction to the typesetter to ignore any markings or changes and to keep the original wording.

stock files   collections of photographs or color transparencies (q.v.) kept by a photographer for all-purpose use; a photographer's inventory of photographs.

stringer   writer who does occasional work for a newspaper or periodical often as a correspondent from a certain location. The term came into being because such writers were paid by the column inch and the editor "strung" their copy together to measure it and determine their pay.

style sheet   instructions on punctuation, capitalization, and other typographical matters provided to writers by some major publishers to insure correctness and uniformity.

subsidiary rights   all rights not sold to the publisher in the initial contract. Can include movie, TV, and paperback for books and second serial and world for magazine articles.

syndicates   editorial companies that sell the work of columnists and other regular contributors to numerous outlets in this country and abroad.

syndication   the multiple distribution of an author's work through various publishing channels.

tearsheets   literally, pages torn from a periodical or newspaper. Some publications reprint individual articles separately and will supply these "tearsheets" to the author or to a particular readership.

technical writing   the translation into clear and interesting language of the special knowledge possessed by technicians in a particular field. The writer need not be a technician to perform this service.

tickler   a reminder file (to tickle the memory), often calibrated to days of the week or month.

TIP (time in progress) sheet   a record of days and hours spent on an assignment, useful in computing hourly rates to be charged to a publication. Also called *time log*.

TK   "to come." Designates written or photographic material not available at the time of manuscript submission, to be supplied later by author.

title(s)   book(s) on publisher's list. Also, specific name of a book.

tonality   the tonal gradation of a photograph.

trade books   general fiction and nonfiction (as opposed to textbooks and reference works).

transparencies   positive colored photographs on transparent film, also referred to as *slides*.

underscore   underline.

uppercase   capital letters.

variant spelling   a secondary way to spell a word, usually less accepted. Example: *wooly* is a variant of *woolly*.

vignette   to make a photograph, regulating the light so the edges of the photographed subject fade into background, leaving no clear boundaries.

widow   a short line ending a paragraph at the top of a page. Also, a short line at the end of any paragraph.

Resources

■■

The Resources that follow are divided into four main sections. The first three—Writing Aids, Marketing Aids, and The Publishing Business—include books, magazines, courses, and organizations that are of general interest. The final section consists of chapter-by-chapter listings directly related to the topics covered in the individual chapters. I welcome your comments, additions, and criticisms of the Resources, and of the book as a whole. Write to me c/o Writer's Digest Books, 9933 Alliance Rd., Cincinnati OH 45242. Note: Many of the books listed may be available through your library if they are not in your local bookstore. And you may find yourself on the mailing lists of related companies and organizations once you write for brochures or catalogs from one.

Writing aids

The Art of Readable Writing. Rudolf Flesch (New York: Macmillan, 1962). This volume has something for everyone—the novice and the veteran, the student and the teacher, no matter what kind of writing he may be or wish to be involved with. Includes an excellent readability formula, tips on blue penciling your work, and a brief list of other books the author recommends.

The Careful Writer: A Modern Guide to English Usage. Theodore M. Bernstein (New York: Atheneum, 1965). By the former Assistant Managing Editor of the *New York Times* and author of *Watch Your Language,* this helpful compilation of used and misused words should be on every writer's shelf.

Dictionary of American Slang. Compiled by Harold Wentworth and Stuart Berg Flexner (New York: Thomas Y. Crowell, 1975). Fascinating reading by itself, this book and others of the genre (*if* handled with care) can be enormously helpful in polishing your writing and lifting it out of the ordinary. Excellent bibliography.

The Elements of Style. William Strunk, Jr., and E.B. White (New York: Macmillan, 1978). A classic in the field. Thoroughly reliable and so well written that it is a pleasure to read.

On Writing Well: An Informal Guide to Writing Nonfiction. William Zinsser (New York: Harper & Row, 1976). An informal and highly readable book with good information on self-editing, interviewing, travel writing, etc.

Simple and Direct: A Rhetoric for Writers. Jacques Barzun (New York: Harper & Row, 1975). An absolutely reliable guide by a master teacher and stylist. Useful for practitioners at all levels of development.

Strictly Speaking. Edwin Newman (New York: Warner Books, 1975). A classic by the witty television personality and journalist. Every lover of the language would do well to read this.

Writers at Work: The Paris Review Interviews. George Plimpton, ed. (New York: Viking Press. Continuing series). One of the classics of our time. The interviews are, for one thing, very well designed, and their content is rich with the meditations of many of the greatest contemporary writers.

A Writer's Capital. Louis Auchincloss (Minneapolis: University of Minnesota Press, 1974). This versatile and experienced novelist adds a generous sprinkling of personal insights to his meditations on the joys and sorrows of his craft. Reminds us that writing involves the whole of one's life.

The Writer's Craft. John Hersey (New York: Random House, 1973). A fine collection of writers speaking on their own behalf on such subjects as the writing process, the writer's life, writing and survival, and the writing method.

The Writer's Voice: Conversations with Contemporary Writers. Conducted by John Graham, edited by George Garrett (New York: William Morrow, 1973). A collection of conversational interviews with a group of working writers about their craft and art. Highly readable and enlightening.

Writing: Craft and Art. William L. Rivers (Englewood Cliffs, N.J.: Prentice-Hall, 1975). Excellent and copious examples are linked and supported by a first-rate explanatory text. Students and more advanced practitioners will find it reliable.

Writing the News: Print Journalism in the Electronic Age. Walter Fox (New York: Hastings House, 1977). As the title explains, Fox deals with today's journalism which is so influenced by electronic technology. A good, brief primer for the novice in nearly any area of newspaper or magazine journalism.

Writing courses

Center for Research in Writing, PO Box 2317, Providence RI 02906. A.D. Van Nostrand, a professor of English at Brown University, has devised a system for teaching writing called "functional writing," based on the premise that the writer should organize his material for the reader and not for himself. Students are taught to compose within the frame of reader expectations. The Center publishes two texts and a correspondence course. Write for further information.

National University Extension Association, 1 Dupont Circle, Suite 360, Washington DC 20036. The association publishes a number of directories of continuing-education courses at various colleges and correspondence schools.

University of Iowa, Writers Workshop and Translation Workshop, Iowa City IA 52242. One of the best places to study with well-known writers and translators. Sponsors an annual competition ($1,000 prize and publication) for best volume of short fiction. Write for requirements. *The Iowa Writers' Workshop: Origins, Emergence, and Growth,* by Stephen Wilbers, University of Iowa Press, is a fascinating look at the history of this long-acknowledged first-rate literary outpost.

University of Southern California, Professional Writing Program, Administration 356, Los Angeles CA 90007. James P. White, Director. An intensive two-year course leading to a Master of Professional Writing (MPW) degree. Classes in writing novels, nonfiction books, stage and screen plays, television scripts, and magazine articles. One of the few programs offered by a large university that deals with how to market material.

Marketing aids

Folio: The Magazine for Magazine Management, 125 Elm St., New Canaan CT 06840. If you want to understand the editorial process and changes in the field, this rather specialized magazine will help. It is read by the people who truly shape magazine publishing.

Freelancer's Newsletter, Dept. A, 307 Westlake Dr., Austin TX 78746. Offers listings of freelance opportunities, new magazine names, addresses and editorial policies, etc. Subscriptions are $39 a year (22 issues).

Literary Market Place (LMP) (New York: R.R. Bowker, annual). Considered the bible of the industry, this directory has names of publishers, agents, editorial services, a variety of reference books, etc. Whether you're looking for a publisher for your book manuscript, companies that sell lists (for those interested in direct marketing and self-publishing), or public relations executives and literary agents, this is the place to turn to first. There are also listings of courses for the book trade and writing conferences. And if you want to get work in freelance editing or with certain corporate accounts, you can get your name on the lists of editors and writers available.

Magazine Industry Market Place (New York: R.R. Bowker, annual). A wealth of information in one volume: leading periodicals, newsletters, writers and photographers, mailing-list houses, etc. Does for the magazine industry what LMP does for the book industry.

Publishers Weekly, 1180 Avenue of the Americas, New York NY 10036. A venerable and highly respected publication which year in and year out deals authoritatively with what's going on in the world of book publishing. Less attention is paid to periodicals, though you will find some space devoted to new magazine markets. Many professional freelancers consider it must reading.

Working Press of the Nation. Joseph F. Roberts, Jr., ed. (Burlington, Iowa: National Research Bureau, Inc. Annual). Five-volume directory (newspapers, magazines, television and radio, feature writers, photographers and syndicates, and internal publications) you can use to find more markets for your writing. Most larger libraries keep this one.

The Writer, 8 Arlington St., Boston MA 02116. An old reliable magazine which takes a middle line in dealing with writers' problems and marketing opportunities. *The Writer* also publishes a number of books on writing and marketing valuable to the practicing writer.

Writer's Digest, 9933 Alliance Rd., Cincinnati OH 45242. This monthly magazine balances timely advice on marketing with brisk pointers on the art of writing and regularly features in-depth interviews with writing stars. The magazine also offers a variety of services to writers. Write for further information on these.

Writer's Market. John Brady and P.J. Schemenaur, eds. (Cincinnati: Writer's Digest Books. Annual). An annually updated listing of over 4,000 markets with information about what editors do and do not want, rates of pay, etc.

Professional organizations

American Society of Journalists and Authors, 1501 Broadway, Suite 1907, New York NY 10036. This group's purpose is "to elevate the professional and economic position of nonfiction writers, provide a forum for discussion of common problems among writers and editors, and promote a code of ethics for writers and editors." Publishes a monthly newsletter, a membership directory, and books about nonfiction writing.

The Authors Guild, 234 W. 44th St., New York NY 10036. This highly professional and reliable group of writers is an asset to us all in dealing with publishers and problems of the trade. Its publication provides timely and relevant seminars, surveys, and newsletters. Membership depends on a showing of professional achievement. Before gaining membership, try to borrow copies of the Guild's *Bulletin* for tips about problems and opportunities.

Poets & Writers, Inc., 201 W. 54th St., New York NY 10019. This publicly supported organization provides numerous channels of communication among writers and between writers and the community at large. The twin publications *A Directory of American Fiction Writers* and *A Directory of American Poets* will list you when you've made a solid beginning in your career. Writers who depend on lecturing for part of their income find this a distinct benefit. The organization newsletter *Coda* will keep you posted on trends, competitions, activities of other writers.

The publishing business

The Bantam Story. Clarence Petersen (New York: Bantam Books, 1970). Good historical reading on a big change in publishing—the paperback revolution—that may be prelude to what is happening now in the world of print.

Editors on Editing. Gerald Gross, ed. (New York: Grosset & Dunlap). A chatty and forthright compendium of comments from twenty-five editors on various aspects of their experience.

The Memoirs of a Publisher. F.N. Doubleday (Garden City, N.Y.: Doubleday, 1972). For anyone interested in writing or working in the world of American publishing, this and other books like it are must reading to get a historical perspective, and much more. Great cocktail party and editorial luncheon anecdotes.

On Writing, Editing, and Publishing. Jacques Barzun (Chicago: University of Chicago Press, 1971). Another of Barzun's excellent contributions to practitioners in these fields. Don't fail to read this one.

Publishers on Publishing. Gerald Gross, ed. (New York: Grosset & Dunlap, 1961). This anthology will give you a lively idea of the kinds of people you'll be encountering when you deal with publishers—their experiences, prejudices, and expectations. It's also first-rate entertainment.

Publishing courses

Association of American Publishers, 1 Park Ave., New York NY 10016. Puts out a particularly useful directory of courses in book publishing for the novice looking for guidance to classes available as preparation for a career in publishing. All the courses are fully described. Information on regional location and tuition costs.

Emerson College, 148 Beacon St., Boston MA 02116. Professional writing and publishing career-oriented graduate program. Guidance in strategies for success in fiction writing, nonfiction writing, film and broadcast writing, book publishing, magazine editing and publishing, advertising and public relations.

The George Washington University, Washington DC 20006. The College of General Studies offers a Continuing Education for Women Center emphasizing a publication specialist program. Comprehensive and time-intensive study of the communications field.

Radcliffe Course in Publishing Procedures, Harvard Summer School, 10 Garden St., Cambridge MA 02138. An excellent and completely professional program structured as a six-week summer course. Guest-lecturing editors and publishers on the scene give students contact with those in a position to hire them.

University of Denver Publishing Institute, The Dean, Graduate School of Librarianship, Denver CO 80208. One of the most respected short courses (four weeks) in the field. Write for information.

Introduction

Service Corps of Retired Executives (SCORE). For all the problems of establishing and operating a small business, this volunteer group of experienced people offers tips and a practical point of view. Check with your library or phone book to find a nearby office of the Corps.

Small Business Administration, 1441 L St., NW, Washington DC 20416. Your business problems as a freelancer are not unique. The SBA can guide you to solutions as relevant in your field as in any other. There are field offices in many major cities, and the main office in Washington provides a number of free publications, including the basic one, *Starting and Managing a Small Business*.

Chapter 1

American Society of Journalists and Authors Directory, 1501 Broadway, Suite 1907, New York NY 10036. Listings of top-notch writers publishing in the nonfiction field today, alphabetically, geographically, and by specialties. A source for names of possible collaborators, editors, teachers of writing, etc. The ASJA has a Dial-a-Writer service for even quicker contacts: 212/586-7136.

HELP: The Useful Almanac. Arthur E. Rowse, ed. (Washington: Consumer News, 1978). Consumer facts, such as the ten biggest rip-offs, foods that kill, avoiding deceptions in all sorts of businesses, etc.

Journal of the Fictive Life. Howard Nemerov (New Brunswick, N.J.:

Rutgers University Press, 1965). One of the best books available dealing with the conflicts and solutions of the writer's mind, by a renowned poet, fiction writer, and critic.

The New Fiction: Interviews with Innovative American Writers. Joe David Bellamy (Urbana: University of Illinois Press, 1974). Deals more with the reasons for new forms of fiction than with the mechanics of doing them. Interviews with Tom Wolfe and Jerzy Kosinski, among others. Discussions range from the blurring of fiction and nonfiction to the death of the novel.

The Order of Fiction. Edward A. Bloom (Indianapolis: Odyssey Press, 1964). Introduction worthy of considerable study for those who would write fiction and those who would read it with as broad an understanding as possible. Fine glossary of fiction terms.

Reporting for the Print Media: A Workbook. Fred Fedler (New York: Harcourt Brace Jovanovich, 1973). Good set of exercises for the beginning reporter.

Reporting Today: The Newswriter's Handbook. M.L. Stein (New York: Cornerstone Library, 1979). For the journalist, student, or reporter needing refresher points. Deals with news gathering, features, interviews, laws.

Writing Fiction. 2nd ed. R.V. Cassill (Englewood Cliffs, N.J.: Prentice-Hall, 1975). A basic primer by an author who has long been a successful teacher. The essence of the recommended method is to learn to write by "reading as a writer"—analyzing the stories of the best practitioners. Includes comment on useful exercises and keeping notebooks.

Chapter 2

Community Journalism: A Way of Life. Bruce M. Kennedy (Ames: Iowa State University Press, 1973). An entertainingly written survey which combines reliable information with illuminating anecdotes about this aspect of the trade.

The Craft of Interviewing. John Brady. See listings for Chapter 7.

Directory of Publishing Opportunities (Chicago: Marquis Academic Media, 1975). Academic and special-interest periodicals are often not listed in popular marketing guides. This volume lists 2,600 such possible outlets, arranged according to field of interest.

How You Can Make $20,000 a Year Writing, No Matter Where You Live. Nancy Edmonds Hanson (Cincinnati: Writer's Digest Books, 1980). Good chapters on easy-access markets, magazine writing for the nonmetropolitan, and how to put it all together. Entertainingly written.

Newswriting and Reporting. James M. Neal and Suzanne S. Brown (Ames: Iowa State University Press, 1976). A step-by-step guide to writing simple polished news stories. Suggested assignments are given at the end of each chapter.

Rooms with No View. Ethel Strainchamps, ed. Compiled by the Media Women's Association (New York: Harper & Row, 1974). Deals with women's fights for equality in publishing, television, newspapers, etc., but is an interesting look inside publishing for others as well.

The Writer's Handbook: What to Write, How to Write, Where to Sell. A.S. Burack, ed. (Boston: The Writer, Inc., 1980). This collection of pieces by writers, editors, and agents is loaded with information both useful and entertaining. It also lists a large variety of markets.

Writing Mysteries for Young People. Joan Lowery Nixon (Boston: The Writer, Inc., 1977). It's always worthwhile listening to an author who draws on successful personal experience. Here Nixon takes you all the way through the writing process from the generation of the idea to the preparation of a final manuscript for submission. She's analyzed it all, including vocabularies suitable for various age groups.

Writing without Teachers. Peter Elbow (New York: Oxford University Press, 1975). The exercises leading up to the formation of successful and marketable stories are heavily emphasized in this encouraging book for writers finding their way.

Chapter 3

Alternatives in Print: Catalog of Social Change Publications (San Francisco: New Glide Publications, annual). For those in search of market possibilities for short or longer writing about "activist" issues and counterculture and Third World concerns, this is a helpful listing of publications.

Ayer Directory of Publications (Philadelphia: Ayer Press, annual).

Annotated lists of magazines, newspapers, trade publications, community throwaways, campus weeklies—no corporate or college magazines. For special interests.

A Complete Guide to Marketing Magazine Articles. Duane Newcomb (Cincinnati: Writer's Digest Books, 1975). How to get salable magazine article ideas, and develop and pretest them.

How to Get Happily Published: A Complete and Candid Guide. Judith Appelbaum and Nancy Evans (New York: Harper & Row, 1978). This volume breezes happily through all sorts of publishing knots with aplomb, and offers well-researched information on many elements in the freelance life; especially interesting is the section on self-publishing and the resources allied to it.

How to Write Plots That Sell. F.A. Rockwell (Chicago: Contemporary Books, 1975). How to take existing stories and update them, keeping their appeal and turning them into cash. Details various sources of plots: Bible, news, folk tales, literature, quotations, etc.

Mechanical Bride. Marshall McLuhan (New York: Vanguard, 1951). A tough look at advertising and hype, this is a classic you shouldn't miss.

The Mediamatic Calendar of Special Editorial Issues. (Media/ Distribution Services, Inc., 423 W. 55th St., New York NY 10019). Deals with subjects to be covered by consumer, trade, technical, and professional journals with the editorial closing dates. Gives you many months' warning of what you should be querying editors about. Published three times a year.

Standard Periodical Directory (New York: Osbridge Publishing Co., annual). Basic statistical information on some 2,500 U.S. and Canadian periodicals.

The TV Scriptwriter's Handbook. Alfred Brenner (Cincinnati: Writer's Digest Books, 1980). Written by someone who's been there, this is an informative guide through the maze of television scriptwriting, dealing with story treatments, scene building, dialogue, and much more.

Ulrich's International Periodicals Directory (New York: R.R. Bowker, published biennially). Looking for foreign markets? This guide, indexed by subject matter, lists 62,000 periodicals around the globe.

Writing and Selling Non-Fiction. Hayes B. Jacobs (Cincinnati:

Writer's Digest Books, 1975). Hayes Jacobs has a rich store of experience as a freelance writer and as a teacher to share with you. His presentation is sprightly and clear.

Other helps

Gale Research Company, Book Tower, Detroit MI 48226. Gale Research publishes a number of comprehensive directories available in most large libraries. Some examples: *Encyclopedia of Associations, Research Centers Directory,* and *The Directory of Directories* are useful tools for nonfiction writers, and their *Contemporary Authors* series gives brief biographical sketches of authors with current books in print.

Magazine Publishers Association, 575 Lexington Ave., New York NY 10022. Their collection of displays and information on various aspects of the publishing business is open to the public. Worth visiting when you are in New York.

National Writers Club, 1450 S. Havana, Suite 620, Aurora CO 80012. A national nonprofit representative organization of freelance writers. Publishes a newsletter and other helps.

Women in Communications, Inc., PO Box 9561, Austin TX 78766. Despite its title, this is not a group of women exclusively. Large national organization of people in many segments of the communications field. Contests, programs, networking, lobbying are among the activities they provide.

Chapter 4

By Design: A Graphics Sourcebook of Materials, Equipment and Services. Jon Goodchild and Bill Henkin (New York: Quick Fox, 1979). A thorough, informative guide; includes tips on lighting and furniture.

Office Encyclopedia. N.H. and S.K. Mager, eds. (New York: Pocket Books, 1975). Includes information on office English, office procedures, business practices, punctuation, dealing with printers, computation, office machines, postal regulations.

Oxford Guide to Filing Efficiency. See listings for Chapter 6.

Reader's Digest Index. Reader's Digest Association, Pleasantville

NY 10570. The contents of monthly *Reader's Digest* magazines, indexed to help you research a wide range of topics. These indexes are free on request to professional writers. Helpful shortcut to keep on your library shelves.

A Treasury of Tips for Writers. Marvin Weisbord, ed. (Cincinnati: Writer's Digest Books, 1965). Collection of half-page to one-page tips on interviews, writing, researching, and business practices by eighty-five practicing writers, all members of the ASJA.

Other helps

Goldsmith Bros., 141 E. 25th St., New York NY 10010. One of many suppliers you can order office supplies from in bulk. Write for free catalog.

The Machinery Dealers National Association, Box 19128, Washington, DC 20036. This organization has a free list of surplus and salvage dealers all over the country. While much of the equipment these dealers handle will not be of help (mostly industrial) from time to time you might discover just the item you're looking for at a fraction of the cost you'd have to pay for it new.

Publisher's Central Bureau, 1 Champion Ave., Avenel NJ 07131. Books at discount.

Stationers, Inc., 601 E. Main St., Richmond VA 23219. Carries a special Reporter's Notebook (No. 801), which is similar to a steno notebook (spiral binding, hard pasteboard covers), but because of its size (4x8) it is much handier for writers taking notes on the run.

Sprint Telephone Service, S.P. Communications, 1 Adrian Ct., PO Box 974, Burlingame CA 94010. Helps save money on your long-distance calls. If you think you could use this service, contact them and they'll mail all the details. Three separate basic services, minimum usage charge, etc. If you use long distance a lot in your business, it can save you a bundle. Not available yet in all states.

Support Services Alliance. See listings for Chapter 14.

Chapter 5

Breaking into Print: How to Get Your Work Published. Philip J. Gearing and Evelyn V. Brunson (Englewood Cliffs, N.J.: Prentice-

Hall, 1977). The authors take you step by step through all the phases of your occupation. A comprehensive index makes it easy to mine for specialized information.

Choices: Coping Creatively with Personal Change. Frederic F. Flach, M.D. (Philadelphia: J. B. Lippincott Co., 1977). Worth a look in the process of examining who you are, what you want to do, whether it's time for a change.

Every Woman's Guide to Time Management: A Personalized System of Controlling Time. Donna Goldfein (Les Femmes Publishing, 231 Adrian Rd., Millbrae CA 94030). Particularly useful to the novice who must write at home part-time; helps you organize the office and come to grips with time management.

Freelance Writing: Advice from the Pros. Curtis Casewit (New York: MacMillan, 1974). Top writers give inside advice on all markets open to the freelancer—from small-town newspapers to big-time publishers. Ideas, outlines, money matters, interviewing, subsidiary rights.

Getting Things Done: The ABC's of Time Management. Edwin C. Bliss (New York: Scribner's, 1976). How to accomplish everything you want to through time planning and organizing of your priorities.

Magazine Writing: The Inside Angle. Art Spikol (Cincinnati: Writer's Digest Books, 1979). A top magazine editor tells what editors want. Many bits of information and anecdotes. How to psych yourself up to sell something, how and when to break the rules, plus technical advice in writing, how to use camera and tape recorder, avoid libel suits, etc. Humorously written.

Writing and Selling a Nonfiction Book. Max Gunther (Boston: The Writer, Inc., 1973). A fundamentally reliable treatise by a veteran freelancer; a pleasure to read.

Writing the Modern Magazine Article. Rev. ed. Max Gunther (Boston: The Writer, Inc., 1977). Includes three articles reprinted in full with structural notes as guides to writing comparable pieces.

Other helps

A job-sharing network may offer novice or intermediate writers just what they need to subsidize their early writing efforts. For more details see *Savvy* magazine, March 1981, for a list of communities which already have established such networks. Or work out details with another worker and an employer yourself. The idea is simple: two people, working on alternate days, share the same job and share the benefits and compensation as well as the free time left to write.

Writers' conferences, colonies. Each summer there are a number of conferences staffed by established professionals and attended by aspiring writers in need of a boost. These conferences are held in various regions. To find a convenient location and programs and instructors you want, consult the May issue of *The Writer* (8 Arlington St., Boston MA 02116) and *Writer's Digest* (9933 Alliance Rd., Cincinnati OH 45242) and the spring issue of the Newsletter of the Associated Writing Programs (Old Dominion University, Norfolk VA 23508) and *Coda* (Poets & Writers, Inc., 201 W. 54th St., New York NY 10019).

Chapter 6

Chases' Calendar of Annual Events. William D. Chase (Apple Tree Press, PO Box 1012, Flint MI 48501, annual). Good for finding unusual upcoming events to cover.

Oxford Guide to Filing Efficiency (Oxford Pendaflex Corp., 6251 Ragio Ave., Buena Park CA 90620). A pamphlet usually supplied with Pendaflex files when purchased. See if your local business-supply company has one or a similar description of filing tips, or write the company.

Writer's Digest Diary is available by mail. To order the 1982 edition, send $12.95 plus $1.25 postage to Writer's Digest Books, 9933 Alliance Rd., Cincinnati OH 45242. Specify #2662. Similar executive desk diaries can be sought out at your local office-supply store.

Other helps

Len Hartnett Archival Products, 300 N. Quidnessett Rd., North Kingston RI 02852. Where artists, photographers, and museum curators head for their supplies and filing systems for their photos and artwork. Not cheap, but definitely the best around and worth every penny.

Chapter 7

The Art of Cross-Examination. Francis L. Wellman (New York:

Macmillan, 1962). First published in 1903 and revised several times, it is a classic that deals with "the rarest, the most useful, and the most difficult to be acquired of all the accomplishments of the advocate." Essential reading for serious reporters and interviewers who are after the truth.

The Basic Guide to Research Sources. Robert O'Brien and Joanne Soderman, eds. (New York: New American Library, 1975). Techniques of researching from the ground up; problems researchers face and how to solve them; lists of general reference titles and special sources as well as what you can expect from them.

Confidential Information Sources: Public & Private. John M. Carroll (Los Angeles: Security World Books, 1975). If you want to know what hidden facts are on file and where to find them, this is an unusual guide.

The Craft of Interviewing, John Brady (Cincinnati: Writer's Digest Books, 1976). Highly readable introduction to interviewing and researching for the interview. Brady tells you how to handle difficult situations with celebrities and much more.

Facts on File: Weekly World News Digest with Cumulative Index (Facts on File, 119 W. 57th St., New York NY 10019). Major news events of past years made easily accessible. Good summaries of world and national events. Extremely handy for general research.

Finding Facts: Interviewing, Observing, Using Reference Sources. William Rivers (Englewood Cliffs, N.J.: Prentice-Hall, 1975). Cogent examination of effective techniques and some of the hazards in getting at the truth by research. Loaded with illustrative examples.

Finding Facts Fast. Alden Todd (Berkeley: Ten Speed Press, 1975). One of the most useful and reliable aids for the writer who must constantly extend research into various fields. Tips on how to evaluate data as well as dig it up.

Future Facts. Stephen Rosen (New York: Simon and Schuster, 1976). A very useful and fascinating volume one can use as a first step in the reference process or as a stimulating guide in the process of finding article ideas or approaches to same.

Guide to American Directories. 10th ed. Bernard Klein, ed. (Coral Gables, Fla.: B. Klein Publications, 1980). Imaginative use of this guide may help you locate new marketing possibilities.

Guide to Reference Books. 9th ed. Eugene P. Sheehy, ed. (Chicago:

American Library Association, 1976). Always a good starting point. More than 10,000 titles are listed here, and the book is indexed by author, subject, title. Look for it at your library.

How to Reach Anyone Who's Anyone. Michael Levine (Los Angeles: Price, Stern, Sloan, 1979). While its title promises somewhat more than the book delivers, it is a help in locating well-known and semi-well-known people in various areas; at the very least, you discover the names of their agents and public relations reps. Saves trips to the library in many cases.

How to Win in a Job Interview. Jason Robertson (Englewood Cliffs, N.J.: Prentice-Hall, 1978). Written by a director of personnel of a Fortune 500 company using a pseudonym, this one tells you how to develop your own interview techniques to control any interview. By seeing the situation from the other side any freelancer might well use these hints to move forward and to negotiate many job situations.

Investigative Reporting and Editing. Paul N. Williams (Englewood Cliffs, N.J.: Prentice-Hall, 1978). A veteran journalist gives hundreds of techniques for getting the stories no one else can.

The Journalistic Interview. Rev. ed. Hugh C. Sherwood (New York: Harper & Row, 1972). Covers all phases of the interview: techniques, different interviews for different kinds of people, the interviewer's role. Also includes some very amusing stories of unusual interviews and how they were obtained.

The Modern Researcher. 3rd ed. Jacques Barzun and Henry F. Graff (New York: Harcourt Brace Jovanovich, 1977). The focus is on historical research, but the methods described and the comment on evaluation of material compiled will help in research of any kind.

Murderers and Other Friendly People. Denis Brian (New York: McGraw-Hill, 1973). Despite its unusual title, this book is valuable in describing the "public and private worlds of interviewers"; it offers many familiar names: A.E. Hotchner, Malcolm Cowley, Rex Reed, Truman Capote, Gay Talese, Alex Haley, and Studs Terkel, among others. Strangely, no women interviewers. Worth studying, however.

The New Muckrakers: An Inside look at America's Investigative Reporters. Leonard Downie, Jr. (New York: New American Library, 1978). Written by the metropolitan editor of the *Washington Post,* this book gives descriptions of such reporters as Jack Anderson, Bob

Woodward, and Carl Bernstein, and explores somewhat the controversies surrounding their tactics and careers.

Newsletter on Newsletters. See listings for Chapter 10.

PR Aids, 221 Park Ave. South, New York, NY 10003. Editor: Betty Yarmon. A newsletter for public relations executives around the country. Deals with all aspects of the field. If you're seeking an authority on a specific subject or have other specific research needs, you can place a free notice in *PR Aids;* you may be surprised how quickly help appears.

Publishers' Trade List Annual (New York: R.R. Bowker). For those who want to keep track of trends or analyze the special interests of particular publishing companies, these volumes can be extraordinarily useful. Consult them in your library or bookstore.

Readers' Guide to Periodical Literature (Bronx: H.W. Wilson Co.). Index of articles from general-circulation magazines. Extremely helpful in seeing what's already been written on a subject you might be researching; helps clarify your thinking on a subject you might be contemplating querying an editor about.

Reference Books: A Brief Guide. 8th ed. Marion V. Bell and Eleanor A. Swidan (Baltimore: Enoch Pratt Free Library, 1978). Head for this one when you go into a library reference room. It will steer you effectively to the best of the other reference books.

Reference Books in Paperback: An Annotated Guide. Bohdan S. Wynar, ed. (Littleton, Colo.: Libraries Unlimited, 1972). With this as a guide you can build your own library of reference books in paperback and save a considerable outlay of money in the process.

Research Centers Directory: A Guide to University-Related and Other Nonprofit Research Organizations. 6th rev. ed. Archie M. Palmer, ed. (Detroit: Gale Research Co., 1979). For certain research problems in fields where you are not at home, this directory can immensely speed the task of finding experts. Until you consult it, you may not realize how very many organizations in the U.S. carry on continuing research programs.

"Secrets of a Private Eye." Nicholas Pileggi. *New York* magazine, October 4, 1976. A lively report on what it's like to be a private investigator as well as some tips for the freelancer who is intent on digging up information the way the real pros do it.

Statistical Abstract of the United States. U.S. Bureau of the Census

(Washington: U.S. Government Printing Office, annual). One volume designed to lead you on to more detailed treatments of particular subject matter in other reference works. But it will also supply all the information you may need for some research requirements. Pretty heavy going sometimes, but worth it.

Statistics Sources. 6th ed. Paul Wasserman and Jacqueline O'Brien, eds. (Detroit: Gale Research Co., 1980). Another basic primer with detailed reference material you will refer to often.

Subject Directory of Special Libraries and Information Centers. 5th rev. ed. Margaret L. and Harold C. Young, eds. (Detroit: Gale Research Co., 1979). No matter how esoteric the subject you are researching, there's probably a private library somewhere in which you can find the specialized material you need. The index of this five-volume directory may provide the necessary first step in unearthing such material.

Subject Guide to Books in Print (New York: R.R. Bowker, annual). This excellent and thorough reference is used by most bookstores and libraries. Consult it when you want to know the titles available in your field of interest.

Super Talk. Digby Diehl (Garden City, N.Y.: Doubleday, 1974). Interviews with stars of all kinds; should give the novice some ideas about what sorts of questions bring out the best answers.

U.S. Government Printing Office, Superintendent of Documents, Washington DC 20402. The GPO has everything from transcripts of hearings to how-to booklets. Ask to be put on their mailing list and they will send you mail-order catalogs and, if you request, a list of their bookstores around the country.

Washington Information Directory, Congressional Quarterly, Inc., 1414 22nd St., NW, Washington DC 20037. There's hardly a richer source of information than the federal government with its multitudinous bureaus. Finding your way through the maze is the problem—and that's where this volume is invaluable. Lists agencies, committees, and many institutions which are based in Washington and processing governmental information.

A Writer's Diary. Virginia Woolf. Leonard Woolf, ed. (New York: Harcourt Brace Jovanovich, 1973). Like many other great writers, Woolf devoted some of her best efforts to journal entries. Not only is the book a valuable model, it addresses many of the problems of the writing craft with sensitivity and shrewd analysis.

Writer's Research Handbook. Keith M. Cottam and Robert W. Pelton (Totowa, N.J.: Barnes & Noble, 1978). Good bibliography of research materials and descriptions of each arranged by subject of interest.

The Writer's Resource Guide. William Brohaugh, ed. (Cincinnati: Writer's Digest Books, 1979). How to research, where to get information, what to expect of sources such as computer printouts, etc. Thorough compilation, interestingly written.

Other helps

Celebrity Service, Inc., 171 W. 57th St., New York NY 10019. A convenient source of the most current information on the whereabouts of celebrities; used by staff writers for newspapers and magazines and public relations executives. Also publishes *Celebrity Bulletin* daily, *The Contact Book,* and *Celebrity Register.* Some of these should be in your local library. The service is expensive but might be worth investing in if you write a great many celebrity stories or would want to share a subscription. Better yet, see if you can tap someone who already receives the information.

Multinewspapers, PO Box DE, Dana Point CA 92629. This company offers various subscription plans. You can get all kinds of English-language newspapers from around the world. Write them for their brochure and prices.

Out of Town Newspapers, Inc., Harvard Square, MBTA Kiosk, PO Box 151, Cambridge MA 02139. Another good source for all sorts of newspapers and periodicals you might not be able to get elsewhere.

Washington Researchers, 918 Sixteenth St., NW, Washington DC 20006. Even if you don't use their services, you might want to get their key-word telephone directory of the federal government.

World Association of Detectives, PO Box 5068, San Mateo CA 94402. Lots of uses for this organization, but primarily a source for general input, interviews, and discovering the name of a detective in your area whom you might want to watch work or query for simple research help.

Yellow Press, PO Box 14141, San Francisco CA 94114. An archival system and clipping bureau that has clips from many sources on many unusual and usual topics. A team of researchers and editors have compiled ten million newspaper pages, some quite rare. Check to see if your research topic is covered by their material, and if you can't get it elsewhere, this might be a good source.

For cheap national outlets for magazines and hard-to-find references, check with such companies as those listed below, and consult the fuller list in the current LMP:

Read-More Publications, Inc., 140 Cedar St., New York NY 10006; Research Services Corporation, 5280 Trail Lake Dr., Fort Worth TX 76133; F.W. Faxon Company, Inc., 15 Southwest Park, Westwood MA 05090.

Chapter 8

American Library Directory. Jaques Cattell Press, ed. (New York: R.R. Bowker, annual). Your local library will almost certainly have a copy of this directory. From it you can make up your own mailing list to suit your promotional or research purposes.

Another Look. Mary Townley (Reading, Mass.: Addison-Wesley, 1978). The teacher's handbook of this series is a truly epoch-making guide to those interested in the graphic aspect of bookmaking and visual thinking. It can open your eyes to what you actually see like no other text available.

The Complete Speaker's and Toastmaster's Library. Jacob M. Braude (Englewood Cliffs, N.J.: Prentice-Hall, 1965). This eight-volume set will give you plenty of preparation for a public-speaking engagement.

Creative Aggression: The Art of Assertive Living. George Bach and Herb Goldberg (New York: Avon, 1975).

Directory of College Stores. (Coral Springs, Fla.: B. Klein Publications, 1977). You can probably find a copy of this guide at the nearest university bookstore. Helpful in your publicity campaign as well as for any self-publishing efforts.

Dover Publications: A Catalog. (Dover Publications, 180 Varick St., New York NY 10014). This pictorial archive service is fairly unusual in that it offers a practical and useful catalog of novelty designs for book designers and small press or newsletter publishers. Multitude of drawings on variety of subjects which can be cut and pasted into a layout. Only charge is for the price of the book.

Fundamentals of Layout for Newspaper and Magazine Advertising, for Page Design of Publications and for Brochures. F.H. Wills (New York: Dover Publications, 1971). An excellent primer for those who want to learn all that goes into assembling periodical publications.

How to Write Better Résumés. Adele Lewis (Woodbury, N.Y.: Barrons Educational Series, 1977). All the things you need to consider when you are preparing or updating your career résumé.

Kellner's Moneygram. See listings for Chapter 9.

National Radio Publicity Directory. 9th ed. (New York: Peter Glenn Publications, 1980). Talk shows on local stations and national networks are listed here. Each is briefly described.

National Trade and Professional Associations of the United States and Canada and Labor Unions. 15th ed. Craig Colgate, Jr., ed. (Washington: Columbia Books, 1980). Handy information for the writer in search of sponsorship or PR opportunities. Annual.

Printing It: A Guide to Graphic Techniques for the Impecunious. Clifford Burke (Berkeley: Wingbow Press, 1974). Those who mean to handle any kind of production themselves will find this a near-perfect guide to the processes involved. Illustrations are well integrated with the text, and the commentary can save you money on several steps of the production process.

Production for the Graphic Designer. James Craig (New York: Watson-Guptill, 1974). An excellent guide for those interested in bringing out anything in print, especially those who need help with design elements, layout, etc.

Speak Out With Clout: All About Speeches and the News Media. Charles A. Boyle (Mercer Island, Wash.: The Writing Works, 1978). Fine preparation for a sometime career as a public speaker, by a speechwriter for corporation presidents, doctors, political leaders, and others. Entire sections on the Fourth Estate, writing news releases, handling news conferences, facing the TV camera; handy list of famous quotations. Everything you need to know about writing a speech, delivering it, getting someone to listen to it.

Speech Can Change Your Life. Dorothy Sarnoff (New York: Dell, 1972). Over two hundred ways to improve your total image both in speechmaking and in conversation. Helps take away nervousness and fear, helps you learn how to command an audience's attention, organize and rehearse your material and yourself, learn to speak dynamically without reading or memorizing. And much more.

Syndicated Columnists. Richard Weiner (New York: Public Relations Publishing Co., 1979). For promoting a book there's hardly anything better than a favorable mention in a widely read column. Weiner's book will indicate where you can get in touch with a columnist who might be responsive to your work.

Woman's Work Book. Karin Abarbanel and Gonnie Siegel (New York: Warner Books, 1981). Offers list of newsletters, magazines, and books regarding women and work rights, reentry problem solving, etc. Federal job information center contacts are among many other useful addresses.

Other helps

Bizzaro, Inc., PO Box 126, Annex Station, Providence RI 02901. A good place to get interesting, inexpensive rubber stamps to liven up your stationery, newsletter, etc.

National Association of College Stores, 528 E. Lorain St., Oberlin OH 44074. Puts out a directory of publishers which will be mailed to you on request.

Chapter 9

The Amateur Photographer's Handbook. 8th ed. Aaron Sussman (New York: Thomas Y. Crowell, 1973). A large, well-illustrated guide to all the angles.

The Art of Winning Foundation Grants. Howard Hillman and Karin Abarbanel (New York: Vanguard Press, 1975). This is not intended for *individuals* seeking grants, but the clearly stated program of defining a project and carrying through in a search for a sponsor may well be adapted to your needs.

Awards, Honors and Prizes: United States and Canada. Paul Wasserman, ed. (Detroit: Gale Research Co., 1978). All kinds of awards for writing are listed. Look for the programs that fit your circumstances.

Boss Lady. Jo Foxworth (New York: Thomas Y. Crowell, 1978). A lively read about the inside workings of the Madison Avenue ad agency business and one woman who made it her own turf.

The Chronicle of Higher Education, 1333 New Hampshire Ave.,

NW, Suite 500, Washington DC 20036. *The Chronicle* frequently lists books which lead the bestsellers on campuses throughout the country. Useful in forecasting trends of interest among young people and the whole reading public.

Directory of American Fiction Writers. (Poets & Writers, Inc., 201 W. 54th St., New York NY 10019). Some eight hundred practicing contemporaries are listed here, with addresses and phone numbers. Also listed are service groups and various reference sources.

A Directory of American Poets. (Poets & Writers, Inc., 201 W. 54th St., New York NY 10019). If you have published and want to be listed or want to find other writers, look here. Poets' names, addresses, and telephone numbers.

Editor & Publisher International Year Book. (Editor & Publisher, 575 Lexington Ave., New York NY 10022). If you need to correspond with departments of regional newspapers to market your work, this directory will provide names and relevant data. Also useful in planning book promotions and/or sale of serial rights.

Encyclopedia of Associations. 15th ed. Denise Akey, ed. (Detroit: Gale Research Co., 1980). Comprehensive directory of all sorts of organizations and sources of information many freelancers depend on. Gives a good idea of the purpose of each group and the printed information available from them.

Freelance Writing: Advice from the Pros. See listings for Chapter 5.

How to Get Happily Published. See listings for Chapter 3.

Kellner's Moneygram: A Market for Every Photo. Kellner's Photo Services, 1968 Rockville Dr., Baldwin NY 11510. A source of information about how to market your photos, find photo sources or photographers. For freelance photo-illustrators, editors, art directors, publishers, production managers, etc.

Life Library of Photography. (New York: Time-Life Books). This series on photography is informative to the unpracticed and practiced eye. Worthy of study in the local library at the very least.

Mediacracy: American Parties and Politics in the Communications Age. Kevin P. Phillips (Garden City, N.Y.: Doubleday, 1975). An interesting look at aspects of journalism's power in shaping American politics and policies.

Mom, the Flag & Apple Pie: Great American Writers on Great

American Things. Compiled by the editors of *Esquire* (Garden City, N.Y.: Doubleday, 1976). Russell Baker, Art Buchwald, Harry Crews, John Leonard, Edwin Newman, Jean Stafford, Tom Wolfe, and others treat the subjects humorously, irreverently, and fascinatingly. Highly readable and instructive at once. Good as models of the writing craft as well as for stimulating your own ideas for similar approaches to such universally interesting subjects.

The Overachievers, The Ultimate Businessmen: How to Find Them, Use Them, Be Them. Peter H. Engel (New York: Dial Press, 1976). A stimulating read, particularly if you're dealing with corporate types.

"The Partial Road to Complete Writing Success." Chet Cunningham. *Writer's Digest,* June 1979.

Photographer's Market. Robert D. Lutz, ed. (Cincinnati: Writer's Digest Books). An annual market directory that offers useful hints if you are adding photography to your freelance work.

Sell & Re-Sell Your Photos. Rohn Engh (Cincinnati: Writer's Digest Books, 1981). A thorough guide to marketing photo illustrations.

Writer's and Photographer's Guides (Clarence House, 1820 Union St., Suite 136, San Francisco CA 94123). This company publishes a series of guides, lists of writers and photographers, material for travel writers, etc.

Writing Book Reviews. John E. Drewry (Westport, Conn: Greenwood Press, 1974). A thorough and reliable guide to the art of reviewing; provides a list of questions the reviewer should ask of any book he examines.

Other helps

American Society of Magazine Photographers—The Society of Photographers in Communications, Inc., 205 Lexington Ave., New York NY 10016. Write for their excellent guide to practices in photography.

American Society of Picture Professionals, Inc., PO Box 5283, Grand Central Station, New York NY 10017. A rather loose organization of picture researchers who either work on retainer, on a staff basis, or as freelancers. If you have photos you'd like to place, it might be a good idea to get in touch with someone in this organization to let them know what is in your stock files and what your areas of expertise are. (Membership in the organization requires two years' experience in the field.)

Association of Media Producers, 1707 L St., NW, Suite 515, Washington DC 20036. Disseminates information, works to improve media products, etc. If you have a property that might serve as an audiovisual classroom aid, their membership directory will provide a number of possible outlets to be contacted.

CASE (Council for the Advancement and Support of Education), 11 Dupont Circle, Suite 400, Washington DC 20036. For those whose work will be of special interest to a particular college or to colleges throughout the country, this organization has a list of top alumni publications.

COSMEP (Committee of Small Magazine Editors and Publishers), PO Box 703, San Francisco CA 94101. The swelling number of literary magazines and small presses has led to the formation of this bustling organization devoted to the interests of all of them. It is useful to those who want to keep in touch with others committed to the same enterprise and to those who hope to pool their resources for distribution. The COSMEP newsletter will keep you abreast of developments in the field—opportunities and risks encountered by writers and publishers who go this route.

Crossroads Writers. Contact: A. Grimm Richardson, PSC Box 879, APO Miami 34005. This group meets annually to exchange information. Might be a good source if you need a contact in Central or South America for research or photo help.

P.E.N. American Center, 47 Fifth Ave., New York NY 10003. Offers efficient guides to sources of support money for those writers who merit assistance at some point in their careers. Writing programs and writers' colonies with financial aid are listed along with fellowships, contests, and awards.

Picture Division, Special Libraries Association, 235 Park Ave. South, New York NY 10003. Members receive free subscription to *Picturescope,* a quarterly with news of picture sources and collections, etc. Much of this information is difficult to turn up from other sources.

Second Chance Press, Sagaponack, NY 11962. This publisher isn't looking for what's new; instead, they want to publish what's been published before and has been relatively unsuccessful. "Our concept is to save really excellent books from oblivion," says publisher Martin Shepard. "While we might do an out-of-print book by a well-known author, what we are mostly looking for is the obscure book or the obscure writer."

Chapter 10

The Art of Negotiating. Gerard I. Nierenberg (New York: Cornerstone Library, 1971). Worth considering in a long-range study of the negotiating process in general. Psychology, general theory, and common sense about discovering what you want and how to prepare for negotiating for it.

The Complete Guide to Editorial Freelancing. 2nd ed. Carol L. O'Neill and Avima Ruder (New York: Barnes & Noble, 1979). For those who supplement their writing income by freelance editorial chores, this is a highly useful source of instruction. It explains the skills and resources required for proofreading, copyediting, manuscript reporting, translating, and indexing. Includes guidance on how to look for assignments.

Dollars in Your Mailbox: The Beginner's Guide to Selling Information by Mail (Green Tree Press, 10577 Temple Rd., Dunkirk NY 14048). A paperback that directs your attention to the most astute ways to get into the mail-order business.

Dunhill Marketing Guide to Mailing Lists (Dunhill International List Company, 2430 W. Oakland Park Blvd., Fort Lauderdale FL 33311). For those seeking pointers on how to manage direct-mail sales efforts.

Gadney's Guide to 1800 International Contests, Festivals and Grants (Festival Publications, Box 10180, Glendale CA 91209).

Games Mother Never Taught You: Corporate Gamesmanship for Women. Betty Lehan Harragan (New York: Warner Books, 1980). A somewhat limited view of the corporate world, yet it offers some information on negotiating and money manners that pays off. Worth a look. Also gives hints you can use in evaluating those corporate clients to see where they fit in the hierarchy of their business.

Grants and Awards Available to American Writers. John Morrone, ed. (New York: P.E.N. American Center, 1980). Many of the prizes listed are specialized and academic, but this directory is certainly worth consulting.

Headlines and Deadlines: A Manual for Copy Editors. 3rd ed. Robert E. Garst and Theodore M. Bernstein. (New York: Columbia University Press, 1961). A thoroughly professional guide for working editors. Tips on how to write a good lead, how to cut copy to the requirements of space, and how to compose headlines of maximum effectiveness.

"How the Pot Boiled and What Was in It." R.V. Cassill. *Book Week*, September 22, 1963. A brief description of how one writer kept the money migraine to a minimum back in the sixties; many tips are still useful today.

How to Read a Novel. Caroline Gordon (New York: Viking). One of the best volumes on the subject. Excellent guide for writing novels as well as reading them. Can be used by writer who plans to teach writing as well.

Instant Art for Direct Mail and Mail Order. Career Publishing Co., PO Box 19905, Dallas TX 75219. The various labels and decorations here can be easily adapted to your individual mailing tags.

Mail Order Moonlighting. Cecil C. Hoge, Sr. (Berkeley: Ten Speed Press, 1976). A guide to many directions in mail-order business; a history of some disasters and miracles so you can avoid the former and head for the latter.

A Manual of Style. 12th ed. (Chicago: University of Chicago Press, 1969). One of the most admired style books available. Gives specific, pertinent information on every stage of book production.

The MLA Style Sheet (Modern Language Association of America, 62 Fifth Ave., New York NY 10011). Highly regarded in academic circles and useful for any writer/editor.

Matrix, a publication of Women in Communications, Inc., PO Box 9561, Austin TX 78766. While only members receive this publication, it is possible to order tearsheets of articles you need if you cannot find a member of WICI to borrow them from. The WICI publications offer sound advice on many subjects: lobbying effectively, on being bank historian, self-publishing, etc. You might want to request reprints of "Will Writers Get a Better Break Under the New Copyright Law?" by Susan Wagner, Spring 1978, for instance.

Money Business: Grants and Awards for Creative Artists (The Artists Foundation, Inc., 100 Boylston St., Boston MA 02117).

National Directory of Grants and Aid to Individuals in the Arts (Washington International Arts Letter, WIAL, Box 9005, Washington DC 20003).

News Bureaus in the U.S. 5th ed. Richard Weiner (New York: Public

Relations Publishing Co., 1979). News bureaus listed by state with an index of newspapers, consortiums, etc.

Newsletter on Newsletters and *Newsletter Yearbook/Directory* (The Newsletter Clearinghouse, 44 W. Market St., Rhinebeck NY 12572). Stay up to date on who's publishing what kinds of newsletters with these two publications.

The New York Times Manual of Style and Usage. Lewis Jordan, ed. (New York: Quadrangle/Times Books, 1976). Alphabetically listed guide to thousands of the common stumbling blocks of writers, showing usage, spelling, capitalization, abbreviations.

"The (Not So) Hidden Assets of Annual Reports." *Money* magazine, April 1979. While this was written primarily for the would-be investor, there's much to be gained by a study of its approach if you're considering going after corporate clients.

101 Ways to Save Money on All Your Printing. Edmund J. Gross (North Hollywood: Halls of Ivy Press, 1971). An excellent book for the novice and a good refresher for others. Deals with details involved with printing flyers, brochures, booklets, etc.

Power: How to Get It, How to Use It. Michael Korda (New York: Ballantine Books, 1976). "All power is ritual and myth," Korda points out as he delineates the power of gossip, meetings, games of corporate weakness, and manners. An interesting book for the freelancer who wants to work for large or small corporations, negotiate for better terms with clients, or remind himself why he is freelancing in the first place.

Practical Guide to Newsletter Editing and Design. La Rae H. Wells (Ames: Iowa State University Press, 1976). For those who are seeking a no-frills handbook of essential instruction, this straightforward text is just the ticket. Thoroughly and clearly written.

Printing and Promotion Handbook: How to Plan, Produce and Use Printing, Advertising, and Direct Mail. 3rd ed. Daniel Melcher and Nancy Larrick (New York: McGraw-Hill, 1966). This book is designed like an encyclopedia. The format makes its excellent content easily accessible to the experienced professional and the novice.

Professional's Guide to Public Relations Services. 4th ed. Richard Weiner (New York: Public Relations Publishing Co., 1980). Weiner provides some of the most complete and up-to-date volumes in this field.

Publicity Forum: Advice from 22 Experts. Gary Wagner, ed. (New York: Public Relations Publishing Co., 1977). Everything about publicity from general to specific publicity, graphics, marketing by insiders.

The Publicity Process. David L. Lendt, ed. (Ames: Iowa State University Press, 1975). An excellent handbook for the beginner. Loaded with reliable tips on how to get the most for your publicity dollar.

Squad Helps Dog Bite Victim and Other Flubs from the Nation's Press. By editors of the *Columbia Journalism Review.* Compiled by Gloria Cooper. (Garden City, N.Y.: Doubleday, annual). Delightful pocket-size book that spotlights some of the major mistakes of the American press each year. Useful to demonstrate journalism's areas of stress for students and a nice reminder of the ways of getting ourselves in hot water when under pressure. (Not a bad gift idea for friends in the business who can take a friendly jab or two.)

Standard Rate and Data Service, Inc., 5201 Old Orchard Rd., Skokie IL 60077. Monthly guide to newspaper and magazine ad rates. Also includes editorial profile and circulation information for each title listed.

Strategies for the Harassed Bill Payer: The Bill Collector—and How to Cope with Him. George Belden (New York: Grosset & Dunlap). A glib and entertaining account by a working editor of the tricks used in the trade for deferring payments. Informative for those on either side of the editorial desk.

Thomas Register of American Manufacturers (Thomas Publishing Co., 1 Pennsylvania Plaza, New York NY 10001). These names and addresses may come in handy if your work could legitimately interest a sponsor. PR opportunities.

Winning Through Intimidation. Robert J. Ringer (New York: Fawcett Books, 1979). Some tips on how to do it yourself or at least protect yourself from others who attempt to intimidate you.

Word Abuse: How the Words We Use Use Us. Donna Woolfolk Cross (New York: Coward, McCann & Geoghegan, 1979). Amusing and informative tome on the misuse of the language, from the professional word abusers (people who devise unreadable matter such as insurance policies, for instance) to the art of the political bamboozlement, spoonerisms, and slogans.

Other helps

Associated Writing Programs, Old Dominion University, Norfolk VA 23508. The Associated Writing Programs is of particular value to those writers who have or hope to have college connections. The organization maintains a placement service for writers with qualifications for teaching at the college level. Publishes a listing of creative writing programs at undergraduate and graduate levels.

Association of Direct Marketing Agencies, 342 Madison Ave., Suite 1818, New York NY 10017. Disseminates information on direct marketing, public relations, multimedia.

The Foundation Center, 888 Seventh Ave., New York NY 10019 or 1001 Connecticut Ave., NW, Washington DC 20036. There are some 26,000 foundations in the country which offer various kinds of support to individuals and groups. The Foundation Center collects and disseminates information about them all. Write first for their publication *About Foundations: How to Find the Facts You Need to Get a Grant,* or visit their offices and library. Also useful: *Foundation Directory* and *Foundation Center Source Book.*

International Association of Business Communicators, 870 Market St., Suite 928, San Francisco CA 94102. The members are on staffs of corporations and companies, government agencies, nonprofit groups, etc., as the key people in charge of communications. Directory published by IABC is listed alphabetically (by member's name), geographically, and by industry. If you are looking for work with corporations, ask friends in business whether they are members of IABC; perhaps they can lead you in the right direction.

International Entrepreneurs Association, 2311 Pontius Ave., Los Angeles CA 90064. Write to see if they can provide you with free booklets or other information on various small business procedures and problems.

Residencies for Writers, Literature Program Office, National Endowment for the Arts, Washington DC 20505. 202/634-6044. The National Endowment for the Arts has added this form of grant-giving to help "emerging" writers. The localities chosen are, more often than not, away from the well-known hubs and involve such settings as libraries, hospitals, and writers' organizations. Over 150 grants were given in 1981 totaling over $500,000. Write for information and application.

State councils for the arts. Most states now have arts councils that can offer all sorts of help. For information on the one in your state, check with the library.

Chapter 11

The Copyright Book: A Practical Guide. William S. Strong (Cambridge: MIT Press). Clear and concise guide by a lawyer who specializes in copyright cases written for the layman, especially the creative one.

"The Copyright War between Editors and Writers." Norman Schreiber. *Writer's Digest,* January 1979.

"General Information on Copyright," Register of Copyrights, Library of Congress, Washington DC 20559. The basic necessary document to guide you in obtaining and renewing copyrights. The same office supplies additional information about handling complex or unusual copyright problems.

Large Type Books in Print (New York: R.R. Bowker. Annual). Large-type editions may turn out to be profitable subsidiary rights possibilities. Look here for potential markets.

Law and the Writer. Rev. ed. Kirk Polking and Leonard S. Meranus, eds. (Cincinnati: Writer's Digest Books, 1980). All the most common legal problems faced by freelance writers. Discussions of copyright, libel, invasion of privacy, various contracts and book rights, pornography, as well as taxes and retirement.

Literary Rights Contracts: A Handbook for Professionals. Richard Wincor (New York: Harcourt Brace Jovanovich). Written by a New York lawyer who also wrote *Contracts in Plain English.* Worth any freelancer's time and study.

The Media Law Dictionary. John Murray (Washington: University Press of America, 1978). A book for journalism teachers and journalists as well to keep close by. Deals with the First Amendment by definition and lists pertinent cases regarding it. If you don't keep it in your own library, then by all means be aware of it and see if your local library or newspaper's morgue has a copy you can check occasionally. Written by a professor of journalism, not a lawyer, it offers his solid background and lay knowledge and research into the field.

Other helps

American Library Association, 50 E. Huron St., Chicago IL 60611. What are libraries looking for and what are they being encouraged to buy? A shrewd examination of this organization's free catalog may enlighten you most valuably on such points.

Society of Children's Book Writers, PO Box 296, Los Angeles CA 90066. New markets; advice on contracts.

Chapter 12

Handbook of Everyday Law. Martin J. Ross (New York: Fawcett Books, 1977). A handy paperback that would be a useful addition to your personal library.

The Literary Agent. Society of Authors' Representatives, Inc., 40 E. 49th St., New York NY 10017. A pamphlet which not only provides a brisk explanation of the services an agent can offer, but also lists reliable practitioners and gives their business addresses. Particularly valuable to the beginner in search of an agent.

What Authors Should Know. Irwin Karp (New York: Harper & Row). The author offers legal advice for writers on copyrights, libel, invasion of privacy, etc.

What Happens in Book Publishing. 2nd ed. Chandler B. Grannis, ed. (New York: Columbia University Press, 1967). These essays were compiled to give a general picture of the book industry and its modes of operation. Provides good background reading to back up more current publications, like *Publishers Weekly,* for example.

The Writing Business. Donald MacCampbell (New York: Crown, 1980). By a literary agent in the business over thirty-five years. Divided into writing, agents, and publishing sections with hard information and interesting anecdotes about each. Manuscript preparation, contracts, etc.

Writing to Sell. 2nd ed. Scott Meredith (New York: Harper & Row, 1974). Meredith is a highly successful agent. If anyone knows all there is to know about contracts, he is the man.

Other helps

Volunteer Lawyers for the Arts, 36 W. 44th St., New York NY 10036. Offices throughout the country for free legal help.

Chapter 13

A Dictionary for Accountants. Eric L. Kohler (Englewood Cliffs, N.J.: Prentice-Hall). This book is periodically updated and gives a layman a guide to accounting language.

Dictionary of Accounting. Ralph Estes (Cambridge: MIT Press). Eliminates jargon and arcane or technical usages and gets directly to the point. Terms from finance, computer/data processing, and business. Helps you deal with those for whom this language is everyday speech.

Fear of Filing. Bill Holcomb and Ted Striggles. Volunteer Lawyers for the Arts, 36 W. 44th St., Suite 1110, New York NY 10036. No book will provide you all the information you need about the intricacies of your personal income tax situation, but this one makes a good beginning. May give you pointers you can pass on to your accountant.

How to Form Your Own Corporation Without a Lawyer for Under Fifty Dollars. Rev. ed. Ted Nicholas (Wilmington: Enterprise Publishing Co., 1980). Gives step-by-step directions for incorporating, plus forms to follow.

The Writer's Legal Guide. Tad Crawford (New York: E.P. Dutton, 1978). Good for all aspects of business and marketing details; excellent material on the new copyright law.

Other helps

Commerce Clearing House, Inc., 4025 W. Peterson Ave., Chicago IL 60646. For all the problems encountered by small businesses—from taxes to retirement plans—their free catalog offers information about available inexpensive guides.

Internal Revenue Service. Call your local IRS office to get the address of the regional center nearest you that will have pamphlets; most of them are free. They include: *Tax Guide for Small Businesses, Tax Withholding and Declaration of Estimated Tax,* and *Information on Self-Employment Tax.*

Chapter 14

Accounting, Finance and Taxation: A Basic Guide for Small Business. C. Richard Baker and Rick Stephen Hayes (Boston: CBI Publishing, 1980). Chapters on bookkeeping and how to incorporate; tips on tax strategies.

Encyclopedia of Practical Business (New York: Boardroom Books, 1980). A full-length study of many subjects the small-business person needs to comprehend to stay in business.

H. & R. Block Income Tax Workbook (New York: Macmillan. Annual). Written by a CPA with considerable authority, this lays out in simple terms the necessary steps one must take to do your tax work properly. In the examples of a small-business person it uses an artist rather than, say, a small retail store.

"How to Buy Life Insurance and Get Out of It Alive." John Dorfman. *Playboy,* March 1981. Fascinating reading since, as the article states, there's "one policy nobody seems to offer—the one that protects you from the hazards of insurance itself."

How to Pay Less Tax (Skokie, Ill.: Consumer Guide, 1980). Tips for the self-employed person.

How to Plan and Finance Your Business. William Osgood (Boston: CBI Publishing, 1980). Deals with all kinds of small businesses. Chapters on determining cash-flow policies, dealing with banks, and developing a financing plan are particularly relevant to free-lancers.

"If You Have a Part-Time Income from Self-Employment." Donald R. German. *Family Weekly,* October 15, 1978. A concise explanation of mini-Keogh plans. A little-known clause in the Keogh Plan doctrine allows people to set up a mini-Keogh with as little as the first $750 they earn from self-employment. If you're just starting out and not earning enough to stash away the amount for the regular Keogh, by all means consider this option.

Law and the Writer. See listings for Chapter 11.

The Professional Journalist. John Hohenberg (New York: Holt, Rinehart and Winston). A thorough study of the subject of journalism, for those who would practice and/or teach it, by a professor of Columbia University School of Journalism. See especially chapter on libel.

Where Have All the Wooly Mammoths Gone? Ted Frost (Engle-wood Cliffs, N.J.: Prentice-Hall, 1977). A superb small-business survival manual. Cities tax traps, tax shelters, etc., for the small business person. Also describes techniques to use to make people pay the money they owe you.

Other helps

Support Services Alliance, Inc., Crossroads Building, 2 Times Square, New York NY 10036. If you're self-employed or run a small business, this organization offers a variety of services you might want to check out, including leasing equipment, guaranteeing educational loans, group insurance, etc.

Chapter 15

American Odyssey: A Bookselling Travelogue. Len Fulton. (Paradise, Calif.: Dustbooks, 1975). Here's one person who took to the road to sell his own books to bookstores across the country. What he saw, heard, and learned adds up to an informative and entertaining saga.

Booklist, American Library Association, 50 E. Huron St., Chicago IL 60611. Favorable notice in this semimonthly magazine of book reviews will influence libraries' choice of what to buy. The reviews are significant indicators of trends in public interest and taste.

Bookmaking: The Illustrated Guide to Design, Production, Editing. Marshall Lee, ed. (New York: R.R. Bowker, 1980). Intended for laymen or beginners, this Bowker offering spells out the requirements for designing and producing a book.

Book Publishers Directory. 2nd ed. Elizabeth A. Geiser and Annie M. Brewer, eds. (Detroit: Gale Research Co., 1979). This publication concentrates on small presses, and includes special-interest and avant-garde publishers. Handily indexed by subject matter and geographical location.

Book Publishing: What It Is, What It Does. John P. Dessauer (New York: R.R. Bowker, 1974). An excellent introductory survey of the whole field of publishing. The nuts and bolts of the trade.

Bowker Catalog, R.R. Bowker, 1180 Avenue of the Americas, New

York NY 10036. Bowker specializes in books about book publishing; this catalog is an illuminating guide to what is available in this field.

Choice, Association of College and Research Libraries, 100 Riverview Center, Middletown CT 06457. *Choice*, like *Booklist*, is an influential guide to librarians selecting new titles. Write for a free sample copy.

Consumer Alert—The Vanity Press. Federal Trade Commission press release dated January 14, 1970 (FTC Bureau of Consumer Protection, Washington DC 20580). This should be required reading for anyone contemplating a publishing agreement with a subsidy press. A warning of the pitfalls.

The Design of Books. Adrian Wilson (Layton, Utah: Peregrine Smith, 1974). This richly illustrated book will serve as an introduction and guide to the many possibilities available to the designer of contemporary books.

Dustbooks, Box 1056, Paradise CA 95969. This publisher has issued a series of books useful to anyone involved with the operation of small presses. These range from directories to guides on the establishment and management of the small press. Write for a list of publications available.

Editing the Small Magazine. 2nd ed. Rowena Ferguson (New York: Columbia University Press, 1976). A sensible and thorough guide for anyone who plans to begin publishing a little magazine. Look before you leap.

Editor & Publisher International Year Book. See listings for Chapter 9.

Entertainment, Publishing and the Arts: Agreements and the Law. Alexander Lindey (New York: Clark Boardman Co., 1963). Examples of the forms of legal agreements used in publishing transactions, with commentary. Borrow this one from a law school library.

How to Publish Your Own Magazine. Don Rice (New York: David McKay Co., 1978). An experienced magazine producer tells you how to budget, publish, produce, sell your own magazine. Information on advertising, finding readers, graphics, costs, and making your own rejection slips.

International Directory of Little Magazines and Small Presses. 16th ed. Len Fulton and Ellen Ferber, eds. (Paradise, Calif.: Dustbooks, 1980).

Library Journal, 1180 Avenue of the Americas, New York NY 10036. Like *Booklist* and *Choice,* its book reviews influence librarians in charge of acquisitions.

The Little Magazine in America: A Modern, Documentary History. Elliott Anderson and Mary Kinzie, eds. (Yonkers, N.Y.: The Pushcart Press, 1979). A large compilation of facts, figures, essays, memoirs, and interviews discussing the history of the little magazine and various editors' efforts to keep the finest literature alive in spite of overwhelming odds.

Newsletter on Newsletters. See listings for Chapter 10.

The Practice of Printing. Rev. ed. Ralph W. Polk and Edwin Polk (Peoria: Charles A. Bennett Co., 1971). A first-rate primer for anyone launching into the art of printing. Excellent and numerous illustrations support the text.

Printing It: A Guide to Graphic Techniques for the Impecunious. See listings for Chapter 8.

The Publish-It-Yourself Handbook: Literary Tradition and How-to. Rev. ed. Bill Henderson, ed. (New York: Harper & Row, 1979). A new generation of writers has found this guide to self-publishing a gold mine of practical information and an inspiring commentary on the goals of literature in our time. Together with the Pushcart Press list of selected manufacturers, it will tell you where to get the work done and what to expect in the way of cost.

The Pushcart Prize: Best of the Small Presses. Bill Henderson, ed. (The Pushcart Press, PO Box 845, Yonkers NY 10701). From the host of small-press publications this excellent editor has chosen the most sparkling offerings. Annual.

A Writer's Guide to Book Publishing. Richard Balkin (New York: E.P. Dutton, 1977). However little you are involved with the actual processes of publishing, this book should interest you in how it is all done. Learn about contracts, advertising, and promotion.

For books about the mechanics of editing, see the listings for Chapter 10.

Other helps

Coordinating Council of Literary Magazines (CCLM), 80 Eighth Ave., New York NY 10011. This active and well-informed organization has been of service to many little magazines. It is a channel for funding as well as information and assistance in distributing periodicals struggling with a shoestring budget.

COSMEP (Committee of Small Magazine Editors and Publishers). See listings for Chapter 9.

Dial-a-Writer, American Society of Journalists and Authors, 1501 Broadway, Suite 1907, New York NY 10036. 212/586-7136. Editing and in need of a writing pro for your periodical or other project? She's as near as your telephone.

Library of Congress Card Division, Washington DC 20540. For applying for catalog numbers, information on copyrights, and searching for almost any reliable source, check with this government source.

Chapter 16

Every Woman's Guide to Time Management. See listings for Chapter 5.

"How to Win the Reader's Digest First Person Award." Jerome E. Kelley. *Writer's Digest*, June 1976.

"Titles That Talk." Mort Weisinger. *The Writer*, August 1975.

"The Working Trip and How to Survive It . . . Almost." Nancy Winters. *Travel & Leisure*, June 1980.

Writing and Selling Non-Fiction. See listings for Chapter 3.

"Writing for the Hidden Markets." Alan R. Blackburn. *Writer's Digest*, July 1977.

"Writing for Social Change." Ronald Gross. *Writer's Digest*, January 1976.

Index

■■

Other Writer's Digest Books

General Writing Books
Writer's Market, $17.95
Beginning Writer's Answer Book, edited by Polking, et al $9.95
How to Get Started in Writing, by Peggy Teeters $10.95
Law and the Writer, edited by Polking and Meranus (paper) $7.95
Make Every Word Count, by Gary Provost (paper) $6.95
Treasury of Tips for Writers, edited by Marvin Weisbord (paper) $6.95

Magazine/News Writing
Craft of Interviewing, by John Brady $9.95
Magazine Writing: The Inside Angle, by Art Spikol $12.95
Magazine Writing Today, by Jerome E. Kelley $10.95
Newsthinking: The Secret of Great Newswriting, by Bob Baker $11.95
Stalking the Feature Story, by William Ruehlman $9.95
Write On Target, by Connie Emerson $12.95
Writing and Selling Non-Fiction, by Hayes B. Jacobs $12.95

Fiction Writing
Fiction Writer's Market, edited by Fredette and Brady $16.95
Creating Short Fiction, by Damon Knight $11.95
Handbook of Short Story Writing, edited by Dickson and Smythe (paper) $6.95
How to Write Best-Selling Fiction, by Dean R. Koontz $13.95
How to Write Short Stories that Sell, by Louise Boggess $9.95
One Way to Write Your Novel, by Dick Perry (paper) $6.95
Secrets of Successful Fiction, by Robert Newton Peck $8.95
Writing the Novel: From Plot to Print, by Lawrence Block $10.95

Special Interest Writing Books
Children's Picture Book: How to Write It, How to Sell It, by Ellen E.M. Roberts $17.95
Complete Book of Scriptwriting, by J. Michael Straczynski $14.95
Guide to Greeting Card Writing, edited by Larry Sandman $10.95
How to Write and Sell Your Personal Experiences, by Lois Duncan $10.95
How to Write "How-To" Books and Articles, by Raymond Hull (paper) $8.95
Mystery Writer's Handbook, edited by Lawrence Treat (paper) $8.95
The Poet and the Poem, Revised edition by Judson Jerome $13.95
Poet's Handbook, by Judson Jerome $11.95
Successful Outdoor Writing, by Jack Samson $11.95
TV Scriptwriter's Handbook, by Alfred Brenner $12.95
Travel Writer's Handbook, by Louise Purwin Zobel $13.95
Writing and Selling Science Fiction, Compiled by The Science Fiction Writers of America (paper) $7.95
Writing for Children & Teenagers, by Lee Wyndham. Revised edition by Arnold Madison $10.95
Writing to Inspire, by Gentz, Roddy, et al $14.95

The Writing Business
Complete Handbook for Freelance Writers, by Kay Cassill $14.95
How to Be a Successful Housewife/Writer, by Elaine Fantle Shimberg $10.95
How You Can Make $20,000 a Year Writing, by Nancy Edmonds Hanson (paper) $6.95
Jobs For Writers, edited by Kirk Polking $11.95
Profitable Part-time/Full-time Freelancing, by Clair Rees $10.95
Writer's Survival Guide: How to Cope with Rejection, Success, and 99 Other Hang-Ups of the Writing Life, by Jean and Veryl Rosenbaum $12.95

To order directly from the publisher, include $1.50 postage and handling for 1 book and 50¢ for each additional book. Allow 30 days for delivery.

Writer's Digest Books, Department B
9933 Alliance Road, Cincinnati OH 45242
Prices subject to change without notice.